BOY'S OWN

The complete fanzines, 1986-92

DJhistory.com®

Credits

Editors Frank Broughton & Bill Brewster
Design Dave Barlow & Frank Broughton
Cover Dave Little
Printed in China by C&C Printing Factory
Distributed by Republic of Music and Bertrams Books

Published by DJhistory.com

51 Beverley Crescent
Bedford
MK40 4BX
tel +44 (0) 7958 595128
www.djhistory.com

ISBN 978-0-9561896-2-2

A CIP catalogue record for this book
is available from the British Library.

smiley not snidey

Boy's Own thanks

Fleur, Rocka, Norman Jay, Gary Haisman, Adam Porter,
Phil Thornton, Rob Leggatt, Dave Swindells, Rocky & Diesel, Paul
McKee, Chris Sullivan, Gary Crowley, Oakey, Danny Rampling,
Mick Mahoney, Kev Sampson, Peter Hooton, Dave Little,
Steve "Brenda" Lee, Louise Gray, Richard Norris, Jane Bussman,
Johnny Meehan, Brummie Chris, Nick Block-up, Big Keith
Mugsy, Fiona & Fran at Sign of the Times, Peteski Heller, Plug
& Chinny, Barry Mooncult (stay strong bruv), Jackie Buckner &
the girls, Micky Stacey, Ginger Steve, Wizz, Osman, Clive "In the
Pink" Henry, Billy & Chips, Fabi Paras, Charlie Chester, Phil Perry,
Sue Farley & the nippers, Digs & Terry & Liam, The Ladbroke
Grove New Jersey Appreciation Society, Dave Dorrell, Gilles
"Breakdown Bitch" Peterson, Trevor Fung, Ashley Beedle, German
Nick, Claire Heath, Ginger Mick, all the Faith crew: Jimmy, Dave,
Sarge and Stu; Leigh Marlin, Boylan, Starski, Danuta, Pete Wylie,
Simon Dawson, Big Al the Gooner, Dean O'Connor, Paul Wellings,
Philippa Grant, Camilla Deakin, Dave Hill, Pricey & Timna, Sparks,
the two Kevs, Rod & Wayne Shires, Max, Justin Robertson, Butler
& Gina, Nancy Noise, Rob & Chris the Bromley fashionistas,
Spencz Blainz, Sean & Steve, Roundshaw Crew, Lisa Burke;
the then-teen's Darren, Hayden, Mark C & Elliott; Jeff Barratt,
Pete Tong, Robin Turner, Lucy Farthing, Shirley, Scarlett,
Paul Byrne, Dropjaw, Ed & Tom Chemical, Coxy the Euroguvnor,
James Jewells, David Henley, Rick Smith, Nina Walsh, Karl Hyde,
Finnie and Dan, Michael Holden, Smithers, Rollsy, Simon Stussy,
Stripey, Tatty, Ben Turner, Darren Emerson, Phil Howells, Sarah
Hall, Jade McCarthy, The Sexpets, Frank Broughton, Bill Brewster,
Darren & Spencer, Little Hanna, Jon "Mates" Richardson, Helen
Riley & Sandra Jones, the Fluke boys, Chip & Gina, Digger &
the Woking crew, future torch-bearers Oscar, Cherry & Joseph;
Damian Harris, Mark Ashdown; Paul & everyone on the Boy's
Own Appreciation Society, Matt Wells, Simon and Simon and
the Defecteds, the lovely Harriet Seashell, and finally Lisa
Grayley, Adam & Breeze (RIP).

Introduction

Every now and then dog-eared copies of the original Boy's Own fanzines (and sadly some Jeckyl photocopied ones) appear on eBay, going for the sort of cash that makes me wish I'd kept all those boxes of mags that collected dust or became roach material at our old office over Ladbroke Grove. The fact that people have looked after them for all this time – and that others who weren't around then are willing to pay for them 20 years later – really does surprise and delight me, but then I suppose when you're right in the middle of an event such as acid house you really don't see its significance until later, as you're far too busy living the moment.

> *"Terry, Cymon, Andy & all the original Boy's Own gang, please forgive me*
> *for selling these. It is for a skint South London Knowledge boy, who will not*
> *be charging the fare if you ever get in my cab in the future."*
> **– seller's note on a recent eBay auction of Boy's Own fanzines.**

This book is a collection of all the fanzines in their original glory, untouched, full of typos, bad '80s terrace slang, strange political views, and pre lads' mag stories and articles that were robbed throughout the '90s. Of course robbing is something we at Boy's Own knew about, and once again I doff my rare groove cap to the lads at The End whose fantastic fanzine we drew "inspiration" from.

In these days of the internet and mass media, fanzine culture is long forgotten, but back in the day it was an important way to get across a view and culture that the music and fashion press ignored totally. I really hope the older heads buying or blagging this book will enjoy reading it today just as much as when they were skinny long-haired kids sitting outside of the Café del Mar hoping to blag the cash for a bocadillo and a cheeky half. And I hope the younger readers will feel its vibe and maybe get a little closer to understanding the original acid house culture of Britain that Boy's Own represented. It certainly has its flaws (don't we all) and has an arsey Cockney attitude that's maybe out of tune with today's clubbers, but it is what it is, and we are all proud of the fanzines, the book and the original readership who have kept the faith with us.

Terry Farley

Acid house scrapes & capers

Many of you will have bought this book because you played a part in the jolly escapade known to archaeologists as "The Acid House Revolution". In fact, there's a picture of you wearing espadrilles and hugging Charlie Chester on page 94. Others may be less certain of what it was all about. And even if you know that acid house was a brief golden moment in British history when it stopped raining for a couple of summers and everyone sallied forth dancing in hedgerows and hugging football villains, you may need some explanation of the role Boy's Own played in it all.

If you're under 35 you'll also need a good imagination. Imagine a time when only two magazines knew nightclubs existed, when no-one got through the door in central London unless they were booted and suited, or wearing at least one piece of Vivienne Westwood, when suburban kids had to bring a change of clothes if they wanted to watch Chelsea in the afternoon and stand a chance of getting into the Wag the same night. You'll also have to imagine a time when only about ten people had mobile phones (which were the size of bread), and look: when magazines were put together with felt-tip pens, a typewriter and Pritt-stick. (It's quite a moment when those **Apple Classic** fonts make an appearance.)

While house music and ecstasy were the fuels powering the dance revolution, Boy's Own was the siren on top of the speeding vehicle, a loud satirical *BLERRK* screaming out at bystanders, and with little mercy even for its own scenesters. Boy's Own grew into a record label (and spawned a son, Junior Boy's Own), releasing records – by Underworld, Farley and Heller, X-Press 2 – which helped define British dance music. It began life as the scurrilous fanzines collected in this tasty volume.

When you connect all the dots there are scores of supporting roles and guest appearances, but at the heart of Boy's Own were Terry Farley, Andy Weatherall, Steve Hall, Cymon Eckel, and Steve Mayes: a loose group of mates who met in the shadowlands of London around Slough and Windsor, part of that anti-magnetic ring a 20-minute train ride from the capital. In 1986, inspired by Liverpool football fanzine The End, ("If fuckin' scousers can do it then I'm sure we can!") Farley decided to give vent to their thoughts on funk, footie, politics and fashion. Boy's Own connected these topics in a way that would be a lads' mag staple a decade later, but which had hardly happened before. With Farley steering, Weatherall leading the writing (he's "The Outsider") and legions of suburban soulboys providing articles and enthusiasm, Boy's Own was quickly a voice to be reckoned with. Southern working-class "casual" culture – full of football's keen wordplay and tribal micro-fashions – was finally captured in print. "We are aiming at the boy (or girl) who one day stands on the terraces, the next day stands in a sweaty club, and the day after stays in reading Brendan Behan whilst listening to Run DMC," it declared.

Soulboy gas-fitter Farley and shop-assistant/record collector Weatherall were already DJing on the warehouse scene. As characters who could mobilise a sizeable suburban crowd, they'd long been recognised by the established London promoters, who called them, with acute condescension, "the footsoldiers." "It seemed like the whole club scene was run by a St. Martin's art school clique," says Farley. "We got the hump that we'd go along to these things and they'd let four of us in but not all of us. I knew as much as they did, I knew loads about records, but I could only come in if I got changed. We hated that scenario."

They had the music and the following, and now the magazine too, so when the barrier-breaking culture of acid house arrived it was all they needed to stage their

' BOYS OWN '
THE ONLY FANZINE
THAT GETS RIGHT
ON ONE MATEY !

coup. As some of the first to embrace the Balearic vibe, Farley and Weatherall were quickly drafted in as supporting DJs in the early acid clubs Shoom and Spectrum. Inevitably, Boy's Own drifted from dissecting the soulboy and rare groove scenes to documenting the nascent house culture.

For Steve Hall, then working at British Airways, acid house was the excuse he needed to avoid settling down "It was massive for me. It changed everything." Like many, as the energy of the scene became clear, he jacked in his job and, putting his weight behind their parties and setting up the label, started making Boy's Own a serious cultural force.

Embarking on their own Balearic adventures, Boy's Own sowed the seeds for the rave movement that would follow. The fanzine became, as Weatherall calls it "the village paper for the acid house scene," musing on the slang, the records and the styles of the moment. In the spring of '88 it proudly declared itself, "The only fanzine that gets right on one, matey." In August that year, in a barn near Guildford owned by a hippie mate of Eckel, they threw the first official Boy's Own party. As one of the era's first outdoor dance event, it was the prototype home counties rave, complete with the first "bouncy castle".

Though driven by disdain for the peacocks of the earlier '80s, Boy's Own eventually found themselves members of London's clubland elite. Like anyone on the vanguard, they grew protective, and some of the fanzines' best bits are the rants at the "teds" who got it all ever so slightly wrong and, while screaming "acieed," took the formula mainstream.

The lads found common cause with a handful of clubs across the country, the so-called "Balearic Network", and though Boy's Own remained decisively London-based, in later issues the spirit of national ecstasy unity is clearly evident. And in 1990, with a deal inked with London Records, they cemented their cultural influence and became a label too. Boy's Own and Junior Boy's Own forged a credible UK house sound, signed Underworld and the Chemical Brothers, and with consistently great music and Dave Little's powerful graphics, set the standard for the flood of independent dance labels that would follow.

So the mags gathered here are important. Boy's Own represents a turning point in British youth culture. Acid house, with its origins in the casual world of beach-loving, E-smuggling hooligans, was when the suburbs stole the reins of popular culture from the middle class art school grads who'd been hanging on to them since the late '60s. As Hall puts it "All those people who had spent years grooming their career at The Face were surplus to requirements, out on their ear in favour of some scally football-hooligan types that had good drugs and knew where to get cool records."

Some of it has dated, some is far too earnest, but most of Boy's Own remains wildly original and properly hilarious. It's been impossible to date the issues very precisely; indeed it took a big effort to even put them in the right order. There were only two or three thousand copies of each printed at most so if you've got any originals you might one day see them in Sotheby's next to a moth-eaten Beatles wig.

What you're about to read is as close to an acid house chronicle as you'll find. It would be an exaggeration to say that Boy's Own was always in the driving seat of acid house – in fact it was usually way over the limit – but it was definitely in the cockpit, observing from the front.

Frank Broughton & Bill Brewster

Boy's Own interviewed

Steve Hall: We were part of that suburban soulboy scene, that's where we all came from. And that went off into New Romantics and we were all part of that but based out in the suburbs. So we'd all meet at jazz-funk nights in Sutton, or the Belvedere in Ascot, which had Sunday jazz-funk sessions. We were just part of the south-west London suburban clubbing gang really.

Terry Farley: I was living in Slough and it was nicer over Windsor, a few posh birds there, so we used to go over there.

Steve: I'm originally from Egham. I was a local friend of Andy's. We used to go to the same Bowie Nights. I was a bit older than him and I became friends with him and Cymon. We used to go clubbing, and shared musical interests: Tom Waits, a bit of disco, punk etc. I met Terry through them. We were friends for years but I started working with them during acid house days when everyone jacked their jobs in.

> ## " Everyone went to the Project Club, and they all bought an E, and everyone did it at the same time. Very experimental! "

Cymon Eckel: *Growing up in Slough there was the soul scene, which I got into later than Terry and the others. There were all these all-nighters going on in Slough Community Centre. We went to this Funky Fox night with Alan Sullivan DJing, Heatwave were playing I think. People giving it the big 'un on the dancefloor. Loads of little firms. And some dancers who were incredible.*

Andrew Weatherall: *It was that classic suburban thing of people meeting at the one decent clothes shop – Cassidy's, this guy Johnny Rocca worked there. I met Terry there, and Gary Haisman, the guy who did the "Acieed" record. Pre-acid house we used to meet up every Friday at 9 o'clock and drop a tab of acid, which is where that post-punk compilation I did got its name from: 9 O'clock Drop. Then we'd head into town and go to the Beat Route or Mudd Club or something like that.*

Cymon: *No matter where you were or what you were doing you had to drop your tab at 9 o'clock. We would go out with £10: £5 for the tab of acid, £5 to get in. We'd put a quid each in for the petrol in the car, a blue Cortina 1600 LS; from Windsor to the Mudd Club and back again and the petrol needle would be back where it started.*

Terry: It was a weird time in London clubs. We all got the hump that we'd go along to these things and they'd let four of us in but not all of us. We couldn't go straight from football, we had to go home and get changed. It did piss us off. It seemed like the whole club scene was run by a St. Martin's School clique. Ollie who ran the door at the Beat Route was Welsh, Chris Sullivan was Welsh, Chris Marney from Demob was Welsh! I didn't mind the clothes they were wearing in these places, but it was the inconvenience of being told what to do in your city, by people who were... Welsh. I knew as much as they did, I knew loads about records, but I could only come in if I got changed. We hated that scenario.

Steve: Graham Ball used to describe us as the footsoldiers. "We used to love all you lot, we'd never have got anywhere without the footsoldiers." We were the guys who queued up outside Le Beat Route. Sometimes you wouldn't be allowed in and sometimes you were. Then things like Dirtbox started and that became more our type of thing than trying to get in with Robert Elms.

Terry: When house music came along it was slightly ignored by London, not because people didn't like it, but because the whole rare groove scene was so good at the time. The reason it took up north first was because they didn't have such a strong scene as we had down here. There were some brilliant clubs in London. Discotheque and The Wag were really good. London didn't need house music. It was bang in the middle of the early rap thing, when people were mixing rare groove with Eric B and the Beastie Boys.

Then the drug thing came back from Ibiza and that was what tipped the balance. Paul Oakenfold brought Alfredo over to a party at the Project Club in Streatham in '87, which got raided by the police. Everyone went there, and they all bought an E, and everyone did it at the same time. Very experimental!

London was terribly snobby. House music definitely broke down all kinds of barriers. Shoom was very sexually mixed: gays, straights, all sorts of gay palaver going on which some of the kids in there, who were football hooligans, would *never* have seen. Michael Clark and a Scottish guy called Sandy, who worked for Vivienne Westwood, they had these little urchin kids from south London who would follow them round like flies. It was like they were mesmerised by these Beautiful Creatures.

Cymon: *Shoom was a magnet for all the hedonists in London. It just pulled you in. We'd started going in February '88, myself and Andrew. We found out about it late January. It just turned into these frenetic conversations on a Monday, Terry talking for two hours on the phone about this club: "Fuckin' 'ell, I've just had the club experience of my life." Which was a report of them going to Shoom. Next week it was Paul McKee, same thing, two hour conversation. So we were into Shoom and away.*

Terry: Danny was all-important – because of the dance. The whole acid house dance is Danny Rampling. Waving his record while he's playing. Until then DJs used to just put records on. They didn't do anything. During the rare groove time you wouldn't acknowledge the crowd. They wouldn't even smile at the crowd. The crowd wouldn't smile at the DJ. There was no connection. Suddenly Danny's standing there and he's waving his record around, shouting, and people shouting at him and hugging. And it was like, "Fucking hell!" That was his dance. Then it became the Shoom dance, then the Shoom dance became the Spectrum dance, then the whole of the fuckin' country!

Steve: If there was one thing I could go back and relive it would be going to Shoom. It was what made me want to do what I'm doing. I've had a great time. And I work with loads of really creative people. But without those moments: walking down the steps at the Fitness Centre and seeing Danny DJ... It was a complete revelation. I'd been clubbing for years and I'd never seen a DJ who was so into what he was doing as Danny was. I'd never seen DJs make the atmosphere like he did.

Terry: For me that whole movement came pre-packaged. You had the dance, which was so different from everything else. The first night at Spectrum when there was just 100 people, there was a guy that I knew, a rare groove guy, really good dancer, top face. And he was standing there with his girlfriend watching all these kids doing the Shoom dance. I remember seeing him at the end of the night trying to do it and he couldn't. He was crap at it. I remember thinking, "He's such a good dancer yet he looks really crap, it isn't his thing." These other kids who weren't good dancers, had ripped jeans on and Converse, looked fuckin' brilliant. You had the drug. You had a series of records that were totally overlooked by everyone, and they'd already been hits in this club Amnesia, and you had to find them and buy them. Rough Trade? Where's that? I'd never been in Rough Trade records. It wasn't a soulboy shop, why would I have gone in there? First time I met Rocky I was in there trying to buy Nitzer Ebb and the Woodentops!

Andrew: *I'd started collecting records when I was 12 or 13 years old and whenever there was a get-together I would be asked, "Bring your records" when everyone else was more interested in copping off and drinking party sevens. The next step was, "Get that bloke with the weird record collection to play some music." That was a couple of years before Shoom, so that was '85-'86. And the same happened at the birth of acid house: "Call that bloke with the weird records to play at six in the morning." But then because my name started to get associated with Shoom and Spectrum, people would book me without really hearing what I did. They probably booked me so they could put Shoom in brackets. So I was getting booked to play main spots and going down like the proverbial turd in the salad because I'd been playing weird music at six in the morning. So I had to incorporate more and more house and disco tracks and learn how to mix.*

Terry: Weatherall and I had been playing at places like the Raid, and then it was just an obvious thing to put on our own parties. We did a few small ones before acid house, with him playing Gun Club and me playing soul records.

Cymon: *The Raid was a lot of go-go being played and some early house. Those parties were hedonistic, everyone drinking Crucial Brew. Everyone getting nutted. Great group of people. I started doing parties with Gary Haisman called Pandemonium. We did one for 3,000 people in Battersea Park in Gerry Cottle's big top in 1987 into New Year '88. I found this place, Café des Artistes on the King's Road where you could throw a party. The door price was only a fiver but you got some food as well. You could fill it up with 150 people.*

Terry: All our gang was going out. A lot of people had jobs down the King's Road in clothes shops or hairdressers or doing a bit of ducking and diving, and basically you had a ready-made crowd there.

Acid house grew out of casual culture. The football hooligan was dead and buried for the trendy hooligans. The casuals who were at the cutting edge of style, the ones who probably weren't the best fighters but who were the best dressed, had knocked it on the head, and were going to Shake'n'Fingerpop and puffing in the corner together. When acid house and E came along the creative forces on the casual scene became, by and large, the creative force on the acid house scene. The whole acid house thing grew out of that suburban soul scene. Whether it was Danny Rampling or Paul Oakenfold, they were just suburban soul boys.

Steve: Suburbia's our heartland really. We were quite West End snobby, but at a certain point we realised our support came from somewhere else. It was Slough, and it was Kingston and it was Romford and it was all of those places. We brought people into the West End. We were definitely suburban.

> **"Acid house grew out of casual culture. The football hooligan was dead and buried for the trendy hooligans."**

Terry: And the same people who started doing parties in places like Leeds and Edinburgh, they were all football casuals. I think it was very much an alternative gang culture, only without violence. You got the same high as being part of a firm and it was a way of making money. They put the party on, and they dealt the drugs and ran the door. It's no coincidence that the biggest radio station was Centreforce and that was the ICF. Even the name: CF! They decided they didn't want to fight any more and this was the new buzz.

I remember me and Andy Weatherall standing on the door at Raid in late '87. Guys who I knew from Millwall were coming up in really dusty old shoes, Chevignon jackets and fucked up trainers. Obviously, they'd all come back from a mad Ibiza summer and they had the start of pony tails, with little top knots. I remember a month or so later being taken to Shoom, and suddenly I realised that these people were the new faces at these clubs. They knew the records and they did the Amnesia dance. It wasn't people from the Face and i-D who knew about this, it was these kids.

Acid house gave casual culture a focus. Before, the only way that casual existed was through football. It had no other creative outlet. There were no magazines or anything. It brought that casual scene together for the first time ever. Before that, it had just been groups of kids in different towns trying to hurt each other. Suddenly you could go up to Leeds for a do. I remember a do that Charlie did at the Corn Exchange and about 500 people from London went up and suddenly we were talking to these kids who, a few years before, would've been trying to kill you.

Steve: The label came about because a close friend of ours, Paul McKee, was an A&R man at London. He used to take Boy's Own into work, and of course Terry and everyone had a relationship with Pete Tong. They'd DJed together for years. And in those days a label deal was nothing. It was more like, "Come in and tell us what records you like and we'll take them off you and exploit them for you." And that was fantastic for us. So in 1989 Pete said get your friends involved and Paul brokered a deal and that was in about 1990.

We were all Factory fans so that was a loose blueprint: the indie/punk ethos but taken into dance music. The idea was to sign what was representing London, band-wise, and DJ-wise as well. We were supposed to be signing Flowered Up, but we could never agree on which bands to sign up and eventually Heavenly signed them. Natural Life were friends of ours and they ended up signing to Warners. Terry wanted to sign one thing, Andy wanted to sign something else and Cymon wanted us to sign his band, Airstream, and he went off to One Little Indian. We couldn't really get a direction together. London used to look at us and think why do they do all their good work for other people? Like Pete and Terry remixing the Mondays, and Andy with Screamadelica. They couldn't understand why we couldn't do it for them.

But I'd been trying to sign the Chemicals and Underworld and they both said they'd stay with me. Terry was making his records with Pete, so we had them as well. I started managing One Dove instead of being their A&R man. It started coming together. The other thing was Rocky and Diesel had started making records, so there was a group of people forming around us who the majors weren't interested in and actually it seemed like we knew what we were doing. We'd had a record deal. We were attracting people towards us. We had a vibe going on.

There were no home studios then. And because of the parties, we could always stump up a bit of cash for people. So we were able to help people who didn't know how to make a record get in the studio. They needed someone who'd put £200 or £1,000 to book time in a studio so they could get stuff done. We were the most professional in a very unprofessional world.

Ed and Tom used to follow Andy wherever he was DJing. They were real fans of his. One time they gave him a white label of "Song To The Siren", which has being pressed up next door to our offices, CT Records. They said go in there and pick up a copy. Andy played it to us. I really liked it. So we said can we put it out for you properly? That's how it started.

And it all climaxed with the "Born Slippy" summer. Being number two in the charts for almost the whole summer. Selling millions of records and thinking it was going to go on forever. Working with Underworld is the thing I'm most proud of.

> **❝ There'd never been anything like it before. A prototype rave. We needed something for the garden, so Cymon suggested a bouncy castle.❞**

Andrew: *Boy's Own was a magazine first though.*

Cymon: *Terry came round one day and said, why don't we do it? And that was it. Around a cup of tea and a pack of biscuits. Let's get ridiculous. Nothing more than, "Let's have a laugh." My role was photographer; Andrew, Terry and Steve Mayes more on the editorial.*

Andrew: *Terry was enthralled with The End. His words at the time were, "If fuckin' scousers can do it then I'm sure we can!" or some such pep talk. And we did. It was Pritt sticks and cutting things out on my coffee table.*

Terry: I used to write silly letters to The End. And they'd print them, stuff about football fashion. I said I'd like to do a fanzine like the End but about London. Weatherall was up for creating this monster and he was very clever. My schooling and Steve Mayes' schooling was pretty non-existent, and Andrew, of the first half a dozen magazines, he did nearly everything.

Andrew: *Steve Mayes and Terry and all that lot, they'd get these things from football. I wasn't into football. but I totally got what they were saying. So it was like, let's give it a go. I just saw it as a chance for expression and I'd be able to write about music. It's a fanzine, so it doesn't have to be particularly current. You've got nobody's product to push so you can be quite abstract.*

I was "The Outsider" because I was a bolshie little bastard! I always want to be in a gang but then I don't want to be. I want the best of both of worlds. So I thought I'd be able to write a sarky piece deconstructing or taking the piss out of everything you're about to read in the magazine. I wanted to have my cake and eat it I suppose.

It was literally what anyone had listened to that week or read or what had happened. After acid house kicked in it became the village paper for the acid house scene. There was only two or three clubs! There were pictures of parties where only 2 or 300 people had been. It was very insular. After a couple of years, John Brown Publishing offered us national distribution and we were like, it's pointless, cos people'll just think, "Silly cockney cunts". It would have appeared too cliquey. Obviously people from up north did buy it but they were people that came to the parties.

Cymon: *And from going out together and doing this magazine we started forming this little band. It grew from that.*

Terry: Early on in '88 we said we wanted to do a party. We found a guy who owned a big house in Guildford. He had a small barn and a big garden.

Cymon: *We didn't even call it a Boy's Own party, we called it a Karma Collective! I met this guy through being in hospital. In May 1988 I'd had an accident and chopped my fingers off. Myself and Andrew were working on film sets, with him as my chippy's mate. I was building a set for a George Michael video, I cut them off on a machine called a cross cutter. Even in the hospital I was still espousing the benefits of acid house! So I was on to this couple in there who knew about this venue. He was friends with a bloke who'd got his fingers trapped in a credit card machine.*

Steve: There'd never been anything like it before. A prototype rave. We tried to get Danny Rampling to play but he wouldn't because he didn't want to shut Shoom for the night. It was a friend of Cymon who owned it. A hippy musician guy. Terry played, Andy, Steve Proctor. There were maybe 200 people, a few Shoomers, a few people from Future, Clink Street.

Cymon: *That was the first infamous party, a lot of West Enders there, people like Graham Ball, Boy George, Paul Rutherford, Pete Wylie, Josie Jones, Bananarama, all these people that had just got on the acid house buzz.*

Steve: It was the first time I'd ever been to anything outdoors. I'd never been to Ibiza at that stage and I think it was the same for most people. First time you'd ever seen a big sound system in a country setting and a full fuckin' rave going on!

Terry: We needed to do something with the garden so Cymon suggested a bouncy castle. *"What!?"* This is why bouncy castles took off! I remember the bloke who owned the place was sitting there at about six in the morning with Boy George singing Karma Chameleon or something like that and this bloke says, 'this is the greatest moment of my life!'

Cymon: *Boy George ended up on the sofa with Steve who owned the farmhouse and had a recording studio there. He played the saxophone brilliantly with Boy George singing. Fucking amazing.*

Terry: It got to about 8.30 in the morning and everyone was really going for it. There was not one complaint. The police turned up. I've got pictures of this, it's appalling: there's smiley shorts, bandanas. It's really bad. They said, "What's happening here then?" "Oh, we're from London, we're on these coaches here and we're having a party." They went, "Right, there's beer cans in the street, can you pick them up." So we walked over there, off our nuts, picked up the beer cans. They said, "What time are you finishing?" We said, "Er... eleven?" "Alright then. See you lads!" A year later they're using truncheons!

Cymon: *Boy's Own gave me some brilliant times. Photographing Mick Jones from B.A.D. or Martin Stephenson from the Daintees. Meeting Matt Dillon. If I hadn't have been Cymon from Boy's Own I'd never have met Matt Dillon.*

Andrew: *It's funny but I don't actually own a copy of the magazine. There was a certain point – on too many ecstasies – that I gave away most of my possessions. Most of my test pressings, acetates and everything. "Yeah, go on, I love you!" There are a bits of it that I find a bit embarrassing but other people might think are really funny. And throw the vernacular of acid house into the equation as well! It would be pretty essential in years to come for people researching the birth of acid house. It's a good, unpretentious document of those times.*

Cymon: *Acid house has been the longest backdrop to anything in my life. I think it changed the world around me more than anything. It freed up a lot of people's minds in the business world as to how to do business. I know I'll never forget it.*

Steve: It was massive for me. I was probably drifting away from everything up until acid house kicked off. I was 26, I'd met my girlfriend who became my wife. We were sort of settling down into that, "Oh shall we buy a place?" but acid house happened and she became a partner in crime and got involved with everything that we did. It stopped me from taking a real normal path through life. It changed everything.

Andrew: *We all shared a common love of going out and all that that entailed. The music, the clothes, what happened afterwards when you discussed things like books, art... It was the whole social scene that generations before us had had. I just wanted my scene. I was a bit too young for punk. So it was kind of my thing. Again it's that thing: I wanted to be part of a scene but for nobody to understand! It was that again.*

Terry: I've kept all those friends, those people have all stayed close, they've all gone on to be productive in one way or another. A lot of these people then were in fairly menial jobs or bumming around not doing anything. A lot of people, obviously, are in the music industry now, and a lot of photographers and writers. All my friends now are friends I made then. If we had a Boy's Own party now, nine out of ten people there would be the people who were there in early '88.

You have been watching

Rob Leggatt

In 1992, giddy from the success of being Boy's Own's building site correspondent, Rob Leggatt downed tools to write film and music related frippery for Mixmag, Select, Neon, and Q. In the new millennium he began directing pop videos for bands such as Baby Bird, The Avalanches, Dirty Vegas, Spiritualized and New Order. He then fell into advertising and is currently doing his bit to hasten the onset of global warming by directing TV commercials. Married with two lovely saucepans, he lives in leafy Brighton in a house designed as an exact replica of Tony Montana's mansion in Scarface. He still holds a huge fondness for acid house and is a minor DJ on the nu-wedding scene. Rob's favourite hip-house record is "Yo Yo Get Funky" by DJ Fast Eddie. Occasionally undertaking small carpentry projects, Rob recently made a wooden compost bin that looks a bit like a beehive. Like everyone else in Brighton, Rob Leggatt grows his own vegetables and is writing a screenplay.

Millwall the dog

After the Birmingham play-off riot, Millwall had to leave town rather sharpish, and got himself plotted up in a lovely pub with a huge garden in Kent that was owned by an ex-flying squad detective that was a "friend of the family". Despite his advanced years he squired many an offspring during his well earned retirement. Millwall the dog died in 2006; his ashes were thrown over the site of Jew's Hill, Bermondsey.

Terry Farley

Alas Terry isn't in a good place at the moment; his attempt at mixing a magic show with spinning '80s classic house fell on its arse after an unconvincing debut on a cruise ship tour that took him from Dover to Amsterdam and back... and back... The magic circle in fact revoked his license to "thrill" after allegations were printed in Mixmag that he once took ecstasy with Jade Goody's mum at a Rockley soul weekender (to be fair the picture looks only a bit like her). The whole of Farleys "minimal magic" collection can be found floundering on the bay as we speak.

Phil Thornton

Phil "Northern Correspondant" Thornton currently resides in a small industrial town halfway between Liverpool and Manchester where his identity crisis has deepened and he can now be spotted at AFC Liverpool games wearing an FC United away kit. Phil went on to write for numerous angling fanzines, international nu-fogey fashion titles and even wrote a book about knobheads in golfing sweaters attacking whoppers in tennis shorts at Scottish second division matches. A fanatical self-publicist and man of letters, his ma calls him "the Keith Flett of the internet", and he can be spotted in notorious Liverpool ale-houses playing Barry St John tunes to beaked-up brickies.

Steve Hall

"Boy's Own has been good to me," says Steve Hall. "Without meeting the chaps in a pub in Windsor sometime in the early '80s I'd probably still be... in a pub in Windsor." Steve has spent over 20 years in the acid house, in the VIP rooms of clubs around the world and dodgy East End warehouses, flying first class across the Atlantic and in the back of Transit vans. He has worked with multi-million selling artists and sold white labels for cash. Today Steve works with stadium techno act Underworld, watches Chelsea whenever possible and lives quietly with wife Sarah and daughter Harriet in leafy Surrey. He can occasionally be tempted to put on his dancing shoes and best shirt "If there's decent toilets and somewhere to sit down."

Steve Mayes

Retired to the London theatreland district of Drury Lane where he sells hand made walking sticks with ornate handles, hand-crafted by a bunch of Dickensian children who have squatted in his basement. Steve is a man about town and can be found bowling about most Sunday mornings with a cheery smile and a swagger to match. He is available to do guest "door" appearances at acid house reunions and 50th birthday parties and can be contacted through his agent Harvey Wiener of Weiner & Co, Whitechapel.

Tarquin posh facker

Gave up knocking out the garys to the posh set and went to work for David Cameron where he taught him everything he knew about youth culture, even lent him a pair of palladiums and some old Paul Smith linen trousers so the acid house generation could identify with the next Tory prime minister. Tarquin left the Conservative party after the Stanford bank scandal implicated him and several other ex rave promoters and record label kingpins in a massive swizz.

Adam Porter

Someone showed me Boy's Own's first issue and I was there. I remember talking to Andy on the phone and met Terry, Mayesy and Andy at the Trip in 1988. I was trying to become a journalist while working in a post-room, my dad's shop and Hammersmith dole office. I remember talking to Terry in Heaven about trying to make a living, from music in his case, and journalism in mine. I got lucky, I managed to write full time at the Evening Standard from 1989. Lucky in that I earned a living from journalism, but I don't share the paper's politics and ended up booted out five years later, arguing over racism. Lie with dogs, get up with fleas. But I've worked – to live I might say – all over. The Daily Mirror and Loaded probably the best known, I had a great 18-month gig in Brussels. But I've written for everyone. Journeyman scenes. I went with my missus to Tokyo on and off, we lived in France for three years. I had a heart attack in 2004. But at time of writing I'm alive they tell me. Now I cover oil companies, specialist, better cash, I like geo-politics, not celebrities. I still go out. Me and my missus love Quentin Harris, who I'm sure I must have first heard about through the unremittingly excellent musical taste of Mr Farley. Good old house.

Cymon Eckel

Cymon Eckel, aka Sir Les. In the early days of the fanzine Cymon took the role of intrepid photographic correspondent and became known for his "unusual techniques" which confounded his many critics. Cymon worked tirelessly behind the scenes creating and directing many of the parties where his methods were considered haphazard but generally effective. His experience in late-night activities led him to the world of corporate events where he took money from "the man" organising stuff for Sony Playstation, The Brits and Levis among many others. Cymon owns and runs The Griffin and The Britannia, two of East London's finest eating, drinking and debating venues, and regularly wears camouflage. There are currently no plans for an Airstream reunion.

Andrew Weatherall

...Wevvers... an enigma... a breeze that cools you on a summers day... a whisper in your ear that is barely audible... to be honest we asked him what he was up to but he couldn't be arsed to tell us... That's Andrew – a techno freedom fighter from the Windsor hood.

diggin' *YOUR SCENE.*

Don't read any further without the right soundtrack

No. 1
Summer 1986

boy's own. 40p

AMAZING VALUE

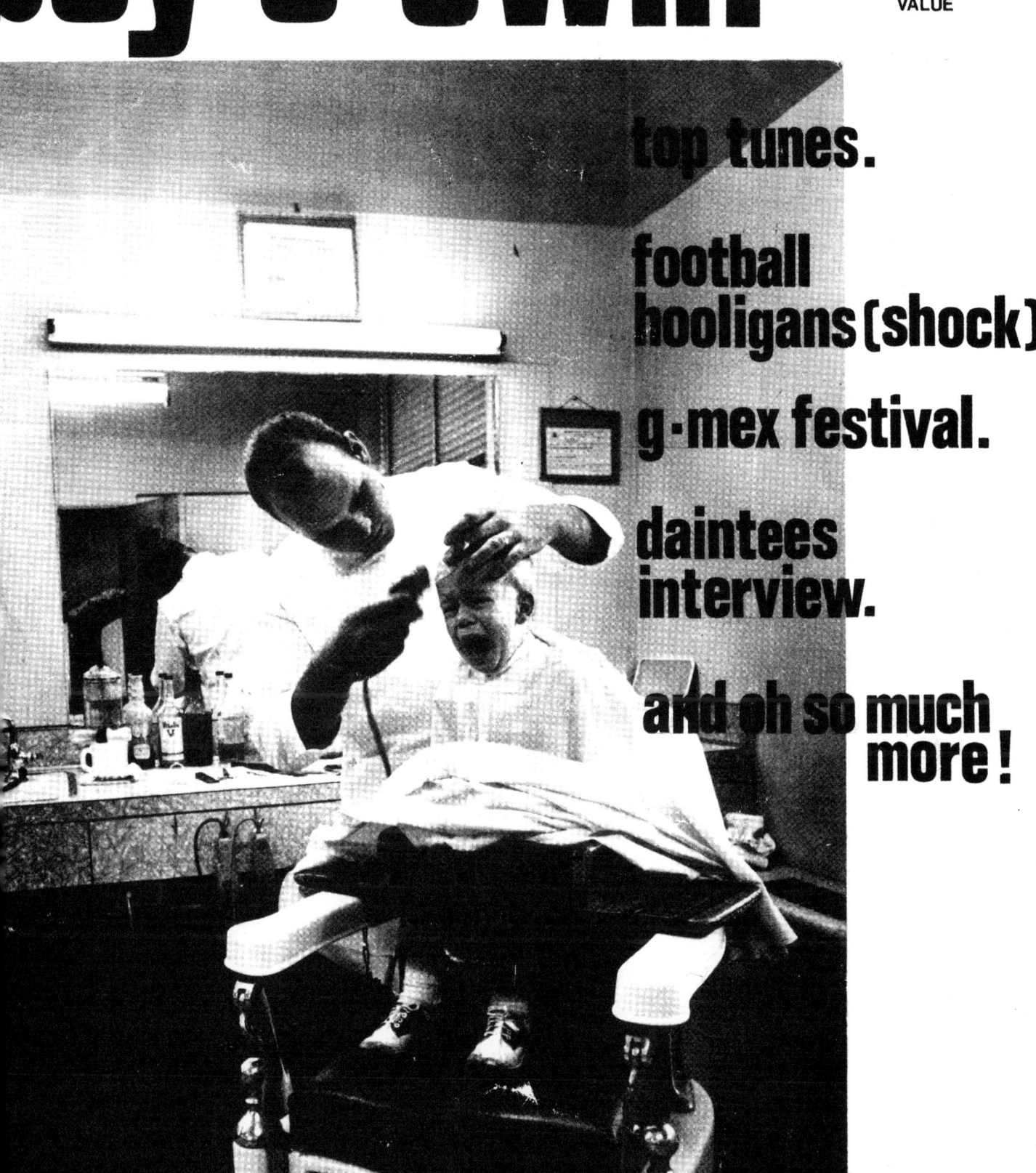

top tunes.

football hooligans (shock)

g-mex festival.

daintees interview.

and oh so much more !

issue one

Dear Sir or Madam,

Thank you for subscribing to issue one of "BOYS OWN", the periodical for the discerning reader. I hope between its covers you will find something to make you laugh, cry, gasp in wonder, throw it away in disgust.

As yet we have no plan for world domination, just to bring you, the punter, informed scribings every couple of weeks. We don't want to pigeonhole our readers, but are aiming at the boy (or girl) who one day stands on the terraces, the next day stands in a sweaty club, and the day after stays in and reads Brendan Behan whilst listening to Run D.M.C.

You won't find any £400 japanese clothing in this magazine (although we are giving away free Yamamoto shirts with ish. 3), or people wearing deflated footballs as hats cavorting around with Leigh Bowery. Positively no ray - bans were worn at any stage in production, all the plans were written in lion brand notebooks, not Paul Smith filofaxes.

Read on and enjoy

Lots of lurve

THE OUTSIDER

- x -

PLEASE SEND ANY COMMUNICATIONS TO :**BOYS OWN**

I3 ILMINSTER GARDENS, CLAPHAM JUNCTION, LONDON, S.W.II

DEATH OF THE SOULBOY

The summer of 1976 was long and hot, Just as hot was the style of the people
in the queue outside a run down west end disco. The queuing youths wore
mohair jumpers, pink 'n' red pegs, plastic sandals topped off with skinhead
style hair. The Oxford street public doing their lunch-time shopping stared
at the queue, the youths stared back with equal contempt.
The club was called CRACKERS, the queue was called soulboys, they named the
shoppers Joe public. The year 1976 was to be soulboys finest hour, Joe public
laughed at soulboy, he looked queer. Many were gay, in fact the hippest clubs
used by soulboy were definately gay, Chagaramas and Louises were the clubs
to be seen in, while Scamps (Hemel) and The 100 Club were places to dance in.
During the next year or so, soulboy had the crack, the funk was hard and the
clothes fast, A.C.M.E. to Browns, Sex to Stanley Adams, Joe public looked
out of the pub window and jeered.
The highlight of the summer was down at Margate, lunch-time sessions at the
Atlantis, all night parties and a never ending supply of blues. Little did
soulboy realise as he bumped away to "Inside America", that along the coast
something was about to happen that would ruin his life.
Bournemouth was used as an alternative to Margate by the out of town soulboys
whos attitude and dress were very much different. They went for wedge haircuts,
and loafers, Joe looked at these boys but never laughed. Joe started snopping
at Cassidys and clubs like Frenchies became popular with him.
With the arrival of Joe onto the scene, came a commercialisation, every disco
started soul nights and they was'nt cheap. At Crackers it was £1.00 entry
and free sausage and chips, soul now meant money and soulboy was'nt getting
anything free, chips included. Joe public loved all-dayers, baggy jeans,
jazzfunk T-shirts and 12" singles, it was soulboy who was laughing now. The
all-dayers and clubs were now full of Joe's, building pyramids and getting
drunk, in fact doing everything except for the two main things in soulboys
life, serious dancing and dressing up.
Joe also had no etiquette, at Crackers you only danced if you was good, if
you was'nt, you practised hard until you was. Joe did'nt give a fuck, he
swayed side to side, he even took hes pint onto the dance floor, soulboy
only ever took talcum powder to the floor. By 1978 Shags and A.C.M.E. had
gone punk, Contempo was shut and Crackers was full of soulboys younger
brothers. During the following years a few desent clubs kept him sain but
he had to wait until 1980 for London to get hot again. The "LE BEAT ROUTE"
was soulboys heaven, the clothes, the music and drugs, he zipped up hes hair
and ripped up hes levis it was like being 16 again and London was still hot.
Joe looked on again instead of laughing he went straight to the barbers.
Its now ten years since the lunch-time queues at Crackers, soulboy still
checks Londons hot clubs like The Wag, while Joe likes Caister and drinks
at the Belverdere. It's funny, Joe no longer laughs, but you can't help
thinking it was all better when the music was harder and Joe called you a
poof!! .

SOUL BOYS TOP TEN

1. Reuben Wilsons - got to get your own.
2. Pink Pegs from A.C.M.E. attractions
3. Fatback band at the California ballroom
4. Suede Sandals by Zapata
5. Kicking it off with skinheads at Margate
6. Sexy - M.F.S.B.
7. Rubber T-Shirts by Sex
8. Girls who did the hustle
9. Red Smith's
10. Dexy's & Blues 3 for a £1.00

SOMETHING A FOOT

As the sun beats down and people bask in the warm glow of summer there appears
to be something distinctly a foot, I refer to the "wearing of deckshoes" by an
increasing number of people. I don't know whose responsible for this epidemic
to hit our shores, but I feel it has something to do with those american tourists
Now summers in the past have spawned such items as ESPRADRILLS and CANVAS BEACH
SHOES the wearers of this footwear, probably going for that BRONZY BEACH LOOK
as many an ankle will testify. It seems these docksiders can be perchased in either
slip on or lace up variety, with bold bright colours the order of the day although
it seems two-tone suede ones appear to be gaining popularity. The epidemic is
being helped no end by all those hooligan types who have discovered docksiders
as an alternative to trainers no doubt. It appears that portmouths infamous
6.57 crew appear to be the proudest wearers of these sick shoes, I think the
fact that these bumpkins live by a harbour might have something to do with it
Those wags from Pompey have even been spotted buying deck shoes on their day
trips to Le Harve no doubt helping cement relations between France and England ha ha.
Mind you Pompey after years of adidas I think I would like a change. The
trouble with anything that becomes a so called fashion accessory it starts a
domino like reaction and this results in the lemmings picking up on it. All
fashion or fads have a very short duration 3 months at most before the trendies
move on, while the lemmings flog something to death till it becomes the butt
of pub jokes. Everywhere I tread my eyes catch sight of these bloody docksiders,
even the milkman who comes up my garden path every morning has been seen sporting
a pair of pink deck shoes I could not see no yacht, only his milk-float, I can
assure you that our milkman is definately not fashion conscious.
Being an avid reader I am quite often popping in and out of libaries so you can
imagine my dismay when I observed 2 libarians and the janitor wearing deckshoes!
I dropped my books and left rather swiftly the sight of those sick coloured
moccassins being to much for my sensitive eyes. I am thinking of staying indoors
till the winter comes hopefully everyone will have stopped wearing

DOCKSIDERS!!

"BUSINESS AS USUAL" Pompey's fashion crazy 6-57 crew....

BOYS OWN EDITORIAL STAFF TUNES (WHAT TASTE!!)

ANDY

1 King Chicago - Bible
2 Everything But the Girl - Little Hitler
3 Pogues - Haunted
4 Rolling Stones - Coming Down Again (Oldie)
5 R.E.M. - I Belive

_____

TERRY

1 Bobbys Boys - Bobby Can't Dance
2 Raze - Jack The Groove
3 Jazz Jeff - Girls Of The World Aint Nothing But Trouble
4 James Brown - In A Jungle Groove (LP)
5 Johny Rocka - Jack Your Bird In

_____

1 Duncan Edwards and Munich 58 - 14 Cockneys On A Ferry
MAIZE 2 Camper Van Beethoven - Take The Skinheads Bowling
3 Ted Hawkins - Watch Your Step (LP)
4 Elvis Costello - Tokiyo Storm Warning
5 Talking Heads - Wild Wild Life

_____

TRENDY NITECLUB NEWS (REALLY!!)

RIGHT GET YOUR SPLIFFS AT JANTY ANGLES AND LEAVE YOUR
ECSTASY TABLETS WITH "SPEEDY DUCK" ON THE DOOR. THE
HOT NEWS IS THAT THE MURDER RAID CLUB HAS MOVED OUT
TO FULHAM, THE RIVERSIDE STUDIOS TO BE EXACT. THE NEXT
BASH IS ON SATURDAY 4TH OCTOBER AND WITH WICKED MIXES
BY PETE TONG PLUS A RATHER DODGY WARM UP BY OUR OWN
FARLEY - IT'S NOW LONDONS FINEST SATURDAY BASH.

Martin Stephenson first came to the attention of Keith Armstrong of "Kitchenware" records while busking. He was quickly recording for Armstrong and released "Roll On Summertime". The Daintees spent time supporting various bands, including Aztec Camera and Prefab Sprout, and it was touring with the latter of these two bands with led to the recording of a single "Trouble Town". However whilst all this was occuring, there were numerous internal changes within the band, culminating in a disappearance to europe with singer, songwriter Roy Buchanan. Returning to blighty Martin joined Virginia Astley for some low - key acoustic shows before going into the studio to record the (In my humble opinion) classic L.P. "Boat To Bolivia".
Critically acclaimed almost everywhere "Boat To Bolivia" is a refreshing record of, at times, very personal story songs. Delivered with Martin Stephenson's superb voice, and backed with an amazingly tight band. Nothing particularly new, but rather a "rock" album with an edge, likely to be picked up by compact disc owning "serious" music fans and humble radio-gram users alike, as long as it makes Mr Stephenson some money it hardly matters, the album deserves all the success possible, and I hope this little article will boost sales by 2 or 3!
We contacted the Daintees one sunny afternoon and were slotted into their busy schedule to meet them the following morning, the venue a hotel in Bayswater by the name of the Columbia. The dining room was very rock and roll, littered here and there with young chaps wearing tight black jeans topped off with various tour sweat shirts, feather cuts and bunches of keys from the belt. Rock'n'Roll! it was in this atmosphere and over an orange juice or two I spoke to an apparantly hung over Martin Stephenson. I don't know who was more nervous him or me?
YOU DON'T MIND IF WE CONCENTRATE ON "BOAT TO BOLIVIA" ?
"No..."
WELL, WHY "BOAT TO BOLIVIA", WHY NOT "BOAT TO ROKER PARK" OR SOMETHING ?
"It dosen't sound as good, and the photograph for the cover came across really South American, and I just juggled about with names".
WAS IT A COMMERCIAL VENTURE OR AN ARTISTIC VENTURE, AS A GREAT DEAL OF EFFORT SEEMS TO HAVE BEEN PUT ON PROMOTING IT.
"Keith (Armstrong) told me we could have a double spread advert and left it to me, it took two years of conflict to get to the situation we're in now"
A slight pause as the breakfast order is taken, Martin politely declining the offer of a cooked breakfast.
SO WHAT DO YOU RECKON YOU'VE DONE RIGHT THIS TIME ROUND, TO WARRANT DOUBLE PAGE ADS ETC ?
I probably just waited and developed"
DO YOU THINK YOUR SONGWRITINGS DEVELOPED, AND IS THAT WHY ITS NOW "MARTIN STEPHENSON AND THE DAINTEES" ?
"No -it's just something that happened last year, I did a few things on me own and no-one came to me gigs, so I thought I'd put both things on a level par because sometimes I feel strangled by a group".
EVERYONE SEEMS TO LIKE THE ALBUM HAVE YOU HAD ANY UN-FAVORABLE REACTIONS ?
"No ! theres one or two things on it I don't like".
YOU'VE JUST ANSWERED MY NEXT QUESTION...
"There's one or two songs, like 'Caroline', should of been done on just a piano".
ITS A VERY PERSONAL ALBUM, SONGS SUCH AS 'CAROLINE' ETC., ARE YOU MORE INTERESTED IN PERSONAL POLITICS THAN PARTY POLITICS ?
"Well... it comes across more on the album"

WOULD YOU PLAY FOR A RED-WEDGE TYPE ORGANIZATION ?
"I was gonna' do one but I had to pull out because I had something at the
same time which was really important".
WERE YOU NOT INSPIRED TO WRITE A SONG, SAY, BASED ON THE MINERS STRIKE ?
"I think there's too many people doing that who do it better, ya know,Billy
Bragg. I just don't like doing them".
DO YOU WRITE BETTER WHEN PISSED OR PISSED OFF ?
"I write better when something traumatics happened, like me girlfriend's left us".
IS 'RAIN' (FROM'BOAT TO BOLIVIA') TRAUMA INSPIRED ?
"No, that was just done by being alone, when I left home last year".
More ordering of tea and a move to another table...
WERE YOU A TEENAGE PUNK-ROCKER ?
"No, I was a teenage on-looker".
WHY PARENTAL PRESSURE ?
"No, I did'nt like the clothes or anything, but I really got off on the music.
I've always been a strong individual, I do'nt like being involved with movements
or anything like that, I like to on-look".
WITH THAT IN MIND, WHEN YOU WERE FORMING THE BAND DID YOU LISTEN TO ANYONE IN
PARTICULAR AND THINK ' I WANNA MAKE RECORDS LIKE THAT' ?
"Peter Perret (lead singer of the Only Ones, one of Britain's most underated
groups, who sadly no longer exist), I used to be obsessed with him. In my
opinion he modelled himself on Syd Barret. Julian Cope does that now"
I'M NOT WITH YOU ON THE JULIAN COPE, TOO SELF INDULGANT.
"I think he's striving to make an L.P. like 'The Madcap Laughs' (Barret solo
album).
WHAT'S THE NEXT FOR YOU RECORD AND LIVE WISE ?
"We've just brought out 'Crocodile Cryer', and maybe one more single from the
L.P., but I don't like the idea of bringing out every single track".
WHY RELEASE 'CROCODILE CRYER', RECORD COMPANY PRESSURE ?
"No, everything we've done has been by ourselves "
HOW ABOUT LIVE SHOWS
"We're doing a tour in August of little clubs, we busked outside a load of
H.M.V. shops as well".
ONE LAST QUESTION, DO YOU THROW STONES AT GREYHOUNDS ? (YOU'LL HAVE TO BUY
'CROCODILE CRYER' AND PLAY THE B-SIDE TO APPRECIATE THIS)
"Erm....no!"
A bit more jovial banter occured over yet another glass of orange juice, including
me poncing a freebie tne then forthcoming gig at Dingwalls,(which by the way was
an excellent evening, although I was'nt put down on the guest list, mind you
Anthony Dunn (bass) swears blind I was put down. I don't know, never trust a
popstar) and Martin posing gracefully outside for a few snaps, then we pulled
away into the Bayswater Rd. A knock on the roof, what could it be ? it was
Mr Stephenson out of breath clutching the Boy's Own cigarette supply.
"Ya left these on the table!"
"Cheers mate, see you on Tuesday"
We turned to each other and smiled,
"Fuck me, what a good bloke..."

**MARTIN
STEPHENSON
and
a
member
of
the
BOY'S
OWN
editorial
staff**

As the new football season is rapidly approaching Boys Own thought it would
be nice to throw some light on a character(s) who thrive within the hooligan
scene that exists within the football fraternity. There are a small number
of chaps or faces as they are know who for one reason or another are
considered to be the cream then there are an even bigger number who think
they are!
These are the ones we would like to concentrate on, the paper chaps who
bowl around giving it the large one playing their foolish game of bravado.
Anyone who goes to football will know what I mean?
Our would be heroes sport the latest trainers pretending to be rock hard!
when it comes to an off these pretenders seem to be lacking in the old dutch
courage or as they say NO BOTTLE. They seem to like talking about rucking,
but the idea of actually indulging in it is quite alien to them indeed. Our
great pretenders are often seen in pub & clubs of London describing incidents
with a series of animated gestures, reminiscent of a method actor! But as we
know method acting has its flaws does'nt it? i.e. when a real chap appears
on the scene our great pretenders become distinctly quiet i.e."giving it the
low one" which puts pay to the pretenders ace line they are "in sweet with the
chaps".
The thing that kills us is when you put these pretenders in a northern town
on a match day then suddenly they have got all the front in the world, acting
out their fantasies no doubt. Still its easy to give it the large one up
north theres no come backs is there lads! Everyone knows who these pretenders
are but they do'nt mention it to them, its when you get London derbies that
the pretenders "get coated" by rival faces often flapping when it "kicks off"
Our would be heroes have been known to utter one liners as "theres to many
of them" or "look out its the gavvers" this being the reason for them flapping!
Fibbing is high on the list of the pretenders attributes i.e. when the fighting
is finished our budding krays will swear blind that they was there "really
having it" when you know they were'nt, probably worried they might dirty their
clothes. Still our foolish pretenders will bluff their way out of it. We can
only say be yourself lads either you got it or you have'nt! have a good season.

P.S. STAY TUNED FOR PRETENDERS ON HOLIDAY.

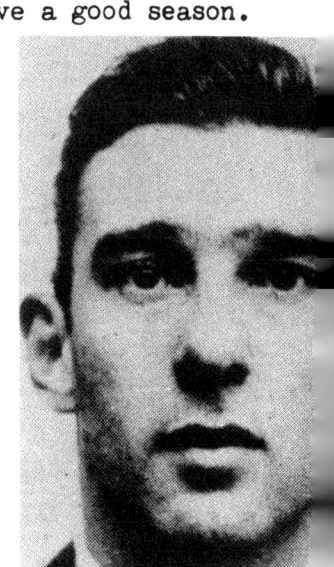

"MY PENIS IS SHAPED LIKE A CARROT"

Welcome everybody to the Sunday social injustice programme. A double edged
(but extremely blunt) sword, giving the viewer on the one hand "What a big
one" type smut, and on the other well rehearsed, badly acted out, concern
for the little man against injustice, the blockhead vs. bureaucracy. (Well
they've got to be blockheads to get strapped up like they do) I'm talking
of course about that great defender of the general public and all round
'News of the world' with moving pictures, "That's Life".

The latest series of non-stop banal twaddle is proving to be a real winner
with the punters, with an average of over IO million concerned citizens
tuning in each Sunday. It's approach has been similar for years, with only
the so called 'celebrities' changing. Apart of course from good old Esther
In charge of the smut department is now Mollie Sugden giving us 'Jokes'
bordering on the cretinous 'Are you being served' never ending 'pussy' type
humour. To my credit I don't even know the names of the other presenters, but
good old Esther watches over them like a dependable nanny.

In swans Esther at the beginning of the programme, swathed in yards of third
rate tacky material to thunderous applause from an adoring audience. And
there she perches, presiding over her parlour as the young go-ahead
presenters are once again introduced to us (not me thank fuck), like old
friends we can always rely on to right wrongs and blow raspberries at those
silly councils and cowboy builders.

Firstly we get the weekly dose of silliness and behind the hand schoolboy
giggling material. A swift run through of vegetables shaped vagely like
genitalia, suggestive mis-prunts, silly holiday snaps of shops abroad whose
names mean something extremely smutty over here. For all we know the Tibetan
version of 'That's Life' probably find the words Mobil Garage equally as
amusing, with viewers sending in photographs with monotonous regularity
because Mobil Garage means "My yak has a throbbing ..." anyway Esther back
to you.

"And now viewers our roving report"... and it's out on the street to make
un-suspecting passers by devour food which the audience find side-splittingly
funny, but in reality is a standard overseas dish. But as we all know, those
foreigners do have strange eating habits, and don't we know it as the thirty
second celebs grimace and squeal when told just what it was they had just
eaten.

Another roving report (so I am told) was a member of the 'Thats Twaddle'
team trying out make-up for men on the streets of Brighton, dishing out
false eyelashes, rouge etc.. to male passers by. All this accompanied by
nudge, nudge homosexual innuendo. Because as we all know gays are mincing
make-up wearing fagots. Mind you it's kinda strange that they pick Brighton
with one of the biggest gay communities in the country to do their report.
Did they think they could capture one alive to add to the so called humerous
impact ?.

Now after the good natured piss-take of various minorities we find Esther
and her siblings stern faced behind the 'serious' desk. I'ts now petty
bureaucracy time with Esther once more taking a member of her public under
the protective corporation wing (out of the frying pan, or what ?). The
whole ethos of "That's Twaddle" is contained in this selection of this
tedious programme. The struggle of Joe Soap against heartless, chinless
wonders. The audience softened with heart rending family snaps involving

cont'....

small children and family pets, up against faceless (no snapshots involved) council officials. And what a coup if the camera can get faces behind curtains and cameramans feet trapped in slammed car doors (fast, flash foreign cars of course).

But so what I hear you cry, if they help one family it's worth it. Yes I agree, but where Thats Life is dangerous is because it deals only in over-sentimentalised individual cases and never deals with overall problems often caused by central government stupidity. Mind you we can't have the loveable team rocking the boat too much can we now ?

The very title "Thats Life" can be questioned as it very evidently is not "Life", because for every one mediocre case of hardship portrayed on this programme there are thousands more harrowing cases struggling with day to day existence without the protective probing of nanny Esther.

The only major problem Esther has turned her matronly gaze to is drugs. But that's not in the 'That's Twaddle' context but rather on the almost as appallingly false "Drug Watch", and how can you take her concern seriously when only the night before you've seen her cheerily introduce a dog that can whistle through it's arsehole.
Still good readers "Thats Life".

UNTIL NEXT TIME VIEWERS - BE ON THE LOOK OUT FOR

1. 28" TRUNCHEONS AROUND YOUR EARS (THE NEW POLICE BILL).
2. PEOPLE ON SULPHATE INSISTING THEY'RE HAVING A GOOD TIME.
3. PEOPLE SPENDING YOUR MONEY ON ROYAL WEDDINGS.
4. THE 'RAID CLUB' WHO BY THE TIME YOU READ THIS WILL BE CARRYING THE SWING.
5. ORANGE FLAVOURED CHOCOLATE CHIP COOKIES.
6. AN IMMINENT 'BEASTIE BOYS' TOUR.
7. FLIMSY TORY EXCUSES.
8. THE PATSY CLINE REVIVAL.
9. TEARING THE ASS OUT OF A JOKE.
10. ISSUE TWO OF 'BOYS OWN' (SUBJECT TO AVAILABILITY).

TORIES TELL LIES

THE CONVERSATION

Being some what of a film buff, in a very minor way of course, I'm quite
often popping in and out of those growth industry shops, you know the kind
I mean, Video Palace, Video City, Video Today, to name but a few. Now I'm
not going to start criticising these places as they serve a purpose as this
eager writer can more than testify.

I'm more concerned with the characters they seem to attract, although I'm
being rather nice calling them characters.

Still more to the point, here I am in a video shop feasting my eyes on row
after row of films. Perhaps I should pick "Kiss of the spiderwoman" as this
looks rather interesting, "Ah, whats this ?" as I pick up another film 'Copvin,
My mind is turning over trying to decide which film I should take, when my
ever receptive ears locked onto a conversation going on behind me. I shifted
sideways to catch a glimpse of this double act, I could not help but smile
as these two wallys were engaging in a distorted discussion of ifs and buts
i.e-

Ist Man - Here get this one, it looks good

2nd Man - What one is that ?

Ist Man - You know what one this is, it's the one thingybob told you about
          in work the other day

2nd Man - (looking rather perplexed at this point) Oh yeah that geezer whose
          in all the films

Ist Man - Whats the name of that other film we saw him in, where they freed
          hostages and killed everyone else in sight

It's interesting to note at this point that at least one of this charming
double act could vagely remember the plot "if there was one" if not the title
at least.

2nd Man - (by now looking decidely uneasy with the conversation) I know who
          you mean he says scratching his head

Well the first man has totally confused his sidekick by picking up another
film

Ist Man - How about this one it looks great

2nd Man - Whats this then ? (he says without takin the trouble to read
          the back for information)

Ist Man - It's about some geezer who goes on a orgy of violence as revenge
          for his mate being killed by some gang. As you can see one of
          them reads the back for information anyway- back to the other
          half of the dynamic duo

2nd Man - Sounds great that, lets get it the birds will like it

At which point our two loveable rascals proceed to pay for the film

cont'...

and swagger out of the door full of foolish bravado, to jump into the obligatory Capri 2.0 litre and upwards to roar off, like one of the characters in one of the many silly films they have seen before in the past.

I think the readers would like to know what films our dynamic duo were discussing the first one was Invasion U.S.A. the second Delta Force and lastly The Exterminator. Well what can I say - surely the titles say enough

I could write all 'nite long about the comings and goings in a viddy shop the interesting people you bump into and such like. Before I end this article I would like to mention that if ever Videodrome became a reality then heaven help us if our cretinous double act saw such a film - so beware.

KNOBHEAD VIDEO CHART (KNOBHEAD TOP TEN)

NOT TO BE HIRED UNDER ANY CIRCUMSTANCES-EVEN WHEN PISSED OR A WET SUNDAY AFTERNOON.

EXTERMINATOR 2

MISSING IN ACTION

DELTA FORCE

RAMBO

BRONX WARRIORS

RED DAWN

THE EXTERMINATOR

UNCOMMON VALOUR

ROCKY III

MISSING IN ACTION 2

Last month over I00,000 people demonstrated in London against the pretoria
regime and for the introduction of full sanctions. These sentiments were
echoed by every decent person in Britian, however the demonstration and the
wishes of millions were again totally ignored by our goverment.

"I hate to see the blood flowing, but it's good to see resistance growing"
- Gil Scott Heron.

Without doubt the struggle against South Africa is the major political
and moral issue of the eighties. The ANC and the freedom fighters in Namibia
S.W.A.P.O. will be victorious with or without sanctions but a long drawn out
death for apartheid will benefit no-one, including the white minority. The
argument that withdrawn British investment would'nt return is crap, all the
multi-nationals would be falling over each other to get thier sticky and
bloodstained fingers back into the pie.

"Agitate, educate and organise"-Brother Dee.

Meanwhile down the good old British rub-a-dub you can still hear the flower
of English manhood speaking between pints, "It's got nothing to do with me"
as another school-kid is shot in the back by a sixteen stone afrikaner nazi
on the pub T.V. The only medical help for these people is to replace their
tacky gold chains for a burning neckless of the Soweto variety.

Britians support of the Botha goverment is done in yours and my name, and
it's our lack of direct action that lets Thatcher get away with it, and in
turn allows Botha to get away with more MURDER.

"SO WEAR FLARES"

As the years roll by me I find myself becoming less and less interested in "Fashion" and more interested in style. The dividing line is very thin but in time becomes more and more evident.

What is the difference I hear you cry with a rousing chorus of apathy. It's easy, if you don't know the answer then you have no style, and if you know or don't give a shit you're almost there.

The very word "Style" must be rapidly becoming the most over-used word of the nineteen-eighties, whilst also being the most mis-understood. Most of the images we are being bombarded with seem to tell us there is no difference i.e- fashion equals style, without fashion there is no style and visa versa. This dear reader is a complete un-truth. It is quite easy to be stylish but unfashionable without having a clue about style.

For two paragraphs the word "Style" has been bandied about without any sort of an explanation, far be it for me to give the difinitive answer in a one page essay, I would however like to give some very large clues. To put it simply, fashion is what is currently toted by a strange un-known elite to which anybody who is interested in fashion wants to belong, a strange self perpetuating circle of fads and fancies, ins and outs. The right label in the shirt, the correct colour, the proper soundtrack all have to be currently in Vogue. That is fashion.

Style on the other hand utilises these aspects of life, but in far more of an outsiders manner. They are important but at the same time totally un-important. Being stylish has much more to do with naturality than fashion has. It is getting on with your life collecting clothes, sounds, experiencies etc... because it comes naturally and not out of a magazine which tells you why and where you can get these elusive articles and dictates the colours you wear, the books you read.

Style is getting on with it, fuck the rest, it is living relatively free from constraint, unlike the fashion followers held back by worry of wearing, saying or doing the wrong thing or going to the wrong place.

However it is important to remember that style cannot be brought over the counter, it is what you read, what you listen to, what your politics are, all of which must to the largest extent be self dictated with as little thought as is humanly possible. It is all about contradiction and adaptation, dressing up, down and sideways. An ability to turn heads or fit in totally, depending on the mood.

Fashions adaptability however is dictated, style's self induced. Fashion knows little of mood, and experience, it just worries about being correct. It's only adaptability being that it might change next week because a magazine says so. Don't get me wrong though boys and girls, fashion does have it's uses. It's magazines can give inspiration, even if it is inspiration to reject the looks they portray. It can also be a stepping stone to one's own style, but be prepared for liberal doses of embarassment on the way. Basically thats what style is, not getting embarassed, in other words being classic, being able to look back at old photos and say "Fucking hell what a chap".

Reading this little tome it would be quite easy to think that I thought style equalled correct dressing...not true. Style is also what you have seen, what you have read, who you have talked to in you short life. Shit...style is not trying to write articles defining it, it's just getting on with it, because it comes naturally. Tread that thin line, but tread it without watching it, and take little notice of writings like this.

Fashion is a manufactured product.

Style is a naturally occuring element.

Now there can't be many people out there who have'nt at one time or another listened to Londons favorite radio show. I'm talking of course about Tony Blackburn, the man who de-throned James Brown. The new godfather of soul is loved by millions but there are some of us who prefered the original Tony.
Tony was the leader of the original brat pack, who can forget zany Ed Stewpot or wacky Dave Lee Travis, these funky three were the dude's who gave us FUNK in the early seventies. Alas tones show now is a mixture of inane sexist chat and sanitised pop music

disguised as soul. Have you heard the divvy birds and frustrated housewifes who ring radio London for their daily fix of innuendo these surburban sex kittens giggle madly at the mention of twelve inchers or hard nipples.
Meanwhile in Hounslow, Kev parks his XR3 and rushes inside, Level 42 is being played on the stereo and Kev likes Level 42 Kev is typical of the male knobheads who ring up radio London, it's strange as soon as Kev gets on the air his voice changes into a heavy East-End accent he tells the listeners, "everythings sweet tony, went out to Stringfellows with the

geezers blagged a malt, know what I mean", our leader does. The only redeaming factor in Blackburns life is the fact that he gets paid untold money to be a prick Sad Kev does it for free. Of course everyone knows a Kev, although you would'nt admit to being friends with one. Black-burns fans deserve plenty of stick without them we would'nt have him. Come on everyone switch to LBC and he'll be gone before Arnold can go woof T.B. stands for everything Boys Own hates including S.O.S. band records, twelve inch remix or not.

TROUBLE FUNK 'LIVE

TROUBLE FUNK - PAINTING THE WHITE HOUSE BLACK

Black American Bands have of late gained a reputation simular to the one given to British Heavyweight Boxers, soft and flat. Trouble Funk and Frank Bruno are the exceptions to this dodgy rule, while sadly Frank failed, Washingtons finest bashed the opposition into surrender.

All the people who had slagged Go Go off as a media hype should have witnessed their London Shows and the crowds reaction. The Town and Country Club was packed with a mixture of hardened Funksters and Pop Stars and was it A Party! Big Tony Fisher and a stage full of D.C. Homeboys Kicked Ass in a severe way, "Pump Me Up", "Say What" and "Express" all wrapped up into a 45 minuete. Go Go Jam sent the crowd wild. A massive version of "The Show" complete with human beatbox mixing into Whoudini's "Big Mouth" played homage to New Yorks influence on the D.C. sound.

The new single "Good to Go" went down a storm, while "Still Smoking" and "Drop The Bomb" raised the roof. The Band looked like a bunch of Black Guys from Slough High St. None of that Las Vegas style glitter from these boys. Over two nights in London Trouble Funk proved that Go Go's best heard live and that it aint no hype.

The tune saved until last proved the best of a brilliant bunch "In The Mix". Go Go won't be beaten as they say the "Beat is Bad."

"MANCHESTER SO MUCH TO ANSWER FOR"

A short story based on the festival of the IOth summer.
The friday night before had been somewhat hectic. Bedtime 4.a.m., rise time
saturday 8.30a.m.clothes in a bag, black and white in the hair. The crew was
four strong, and we would end up four weak. The small cassette player perched
on my knee blasted out anything from Level 42 to Los Lobos as the compact
black vehicle sped steadily along the M.I. The crew swapped anecdotes of past
northern adventures, "Do you remember that night in Leeds, a foot of snow
and just as much speed...", these boys were hardened.
The ASDA superstore just outside Leicester (yes, your four heroes had missed
the M.6. turn off) beckoned as hunger and the need for a road map increased
One atlas and several scotch eggs later the M.6. was ours for the taking.
Birmingham looked dead from our position atop an ever winding elevated section,
an occasional gasp of smoke from a dying factory being the only clue. More
motorway, more stories "What about north Wales, the ice rink and the acid..."
drugs to have a good time?, not these boys, New Order was nearly enough!.
Three hours from the off we swept happily into Manchester, the nearest we
could get to a Manchester soundtrack was the Bunnymen, (what no Smiths!) This
could be nowhere else but north, a strange un-explainable atmosphere that
could only be Moss-side. We were just tourists, not for us the real Manchester
just driving blindly through. Park up, pile out, pub bound. The nearest one
was decided upon, it could mean death, it could mean life, it did mean a
much needed drink. Quite pleasant really, I.R.A. propaganda on the toilet
wall, Easterhouse on the jukebox.
Now the Arndale centre beckoned, strangers in a strange town. Its funny I
thought, we're actually playing up the southern accent, still its good to
feel differant, isn't - isn't it?. The girls were pretty, the boys were
scruffy, but the thing is they didn't seem to care. Neither did the two old
Jamaicans playing banjo in the plaza, neither did the neat young man selling
communist newspapers in the square outside MacDonalds (the small man against
the multi-national?).
"Your fighting a losing battle mate", I said in the best southern accent I
could muster.
"Still good on ya", as I handed over my 30p for a brief read - preaching to
the converted or what!.
There it was at last, The Greater Manchester Exhibition Centre, an old
railway station, a new coat of paint -   very industrial, purpose built
IOO years ago, just for today. T-Shirts and posters, piss-heads and touts
all milling around outside. We strode through the whole lot, we looked good,
and were on a mission. The four of us stood in a line and looked down the
length of the hall,a miniture Wembley Arena type affair with two banners
hanging from the ceiling and plain black curtain across the stage. First the
essentials, drinks and souvenirs. Bollocks!, the bar was shut, but at least
we could buy a decent T-Shirt, a nice white job with a so modern small collar
an baggy short sleeves, discreet IOth summer logo. Ten quid - bargain,"We'll
have three please, oh and that very fetching plan of the Hacienda , great in
a clip frame in the front room". No I'm not taking the piss, the items were
purchased, worn and framed.
To our heroes it was heaven, the hall abound with short haired, smartly attired
young girls, all with lilting accents - all too, too much. So why was it that

cont'..

the only girl who spoke to me was a pissed, boot-faced skin-head who staggered
over and asked the question we were dying to be asked by the more delicate
manc maidens...
"Are you a cockney" she slurred
"What do you mean do what John, leave it out on me manor, 'ave a whelk!"
"Aye, thats it"
"No never heard of 'em", and made a quick and discreet exit as this buxom
wench fathomed it all out. But what of the music?.
Well, from what I can remember the first band we witnessed was Orchestral
Manouvers In The Dark. Just the two chaps playing versions af their annoyingly
catchy top twenty tunes. However we were more interested in the young lady
standing on the mixing desk platform, Joseph leather jacket, blonde hair,
winsome looks, any age between 15 and 25. Sod the tunes who is she?.
More wandering aimlessly about eyeing the punters until another pop group
took the stage. Next up a group of evidently popular young beat musicians
The Fall. A nicely painted back-drop, and everybody seemed to know the words,
getting their tongues easily around Mark E Smith's verbal meanderings   as
deftly as the man himself. To adapt a cliche, you either love The Fall or
couldn't really give a shit. I turned to one of my equally bemused fellow
travellers.
"What do you reckon then?"
"I don't really understand the appeaal"
"Nah' a couple of singles I've got are alright,"Totally Wired","Oh Brother",
but most of it leaves me cold".
Are we philistines?...probably.
So it was to be, a cup of vending machine coffee had more to offer, maybe
one day I'll learn.
Coffee on the balcony, surrounded by the other revellers, looking across
the rooftops. The yellow and blue flag fluttered in the breeze, FAC 51 it
read...later.
The sound in the hall was pretty terrible, even The Smiths got boring - and
those bods down the front throwing flowers around, there was me thinking that
sort of behaviour had gone right out of the window. Manchester so much to
answer for still it was worth it just to hear "Panic".(see top tunes section)
Hang the blessed D.J.? no, he was quite good tonight.
Mr Hatton hobbled on with the aid of crutches (N.H.S. and not private I hope),
to an extremely mixed reception...
"Fuck off you scouse wanker"
It was bellowed in my ear, but directed, amongst other racial insults, toward
Mr Hatton. This I think and hope, was the main reason for the slagging - a
mancunian dislike of scouse celebs, not socialists.
Our heroes retired to the bar area, paid for a baked potato and stole a
cheese sandwich - there was only one thing to do with it, flick it at passing
security men.
"When are they on then"
"Dunno, I think its Pete Shelley next"
It wasn't it was Howard Devoto. I just couldn't get into it, reading from Proust
indeed! its the same with all these sort of events, I get restless. Maybe if I
had a seated ticket, a bag full of sandwiches, and a flask of tea, I could have
been more constructive and actually listened to a few bands.
"When are they on then"
"Dunno I think its Pete Shelley next"
It was, I still didn't listen, well only to 'Homo-Sapien' and 'Telephone Operater'
"Boredom, boredom...be - dum"
"When are they on then"
"Got to be next"
"No look its John Cale"
A short set, accompanied only by the electric piano...what a philistine, I
still wasn't really listening. The two lines at tea time were making me very
impatient. We began to gather and snake toward the front. Hang the D.J.?
                                                      cont'...

definately   not, some nice funk and electro sounds thumped from the P.A.,
the best sound quality yet.
"Whos the best pop group in the world" yelled Mr Morley at the crowd.
"Frankie Goes To Hollywood" shouted back one wag.
"New Order" shouted the masses.
An azteca stadium wave went through the seated section and on they came.
"Eligia"wafted over the swaying standing section. Even this mellow ditty
began to bring out the naughtiness in the assembled order - ites.
Me, I was shirtless, jostling, and a mite disappointed. They seemed to be
holding back. Even "Shell - Shock" was low key. Still Hookies hair was
beginning to look good again!
"It's the State Of The Nation"
"Wooh! our salvation"
Fucking marvelous, need I say more, other than release it as a single as
soon as possible.
The opening chords of "Ceremony" hit the crowd and on sauntered Ian McCulloch
with what appeared to be the words on a sheet of paper, he still got them
wrong. Still for novelty value alòne it was quite interesting. The punters
punched, kicked, and threw each other around with the typical good natured
violence that occurs amongst the chaps gathered in front of Peter Hook, only
this time he didn't say a word.
New Order left the stage and the sweaty masses after a short, held - back
set, and returned two minutes later.
"This is a bit of a cliched song to do as an encore...but it's such a nice,
nice song..."
"Oh you've got grey eyes..."
"Temptation", one of the finest pop tunes ever written, almost saved the day.
As we sauntered out of the hall to the strains of "The Vikings" (any regular
New Order gig - goer will know this rousing tune), the general concensus of
the day was"average".
Maybe we'd exspected to much, or built it up into something it wasn't, but the
festival of the tenth summer didn't quite cut it. This was supposed (I think)
to be about punk rock, but I have the sneaking suspicion that the events at
Wembley over this week-end (i.e. The "U.K. Fresh" Festival) had a lot more to
do with the spirit of punk (whatever that is). A change of clothes, and the
Hacienda beckoned, but that my lovelies is another story, for another day.

THANKS FOR THE INSPIRATION TO THOSE
LOVABLE SCOUSERS AT THE END. RESPECTS
ALSO TO GARY & STARSKI (THE RAID BOYS)
GRANT, CYMON, CLAIRE, PAUL AT LONDON
RECORDS, JOHNY ROCKA, THE CHELSEA
NORTH STAND BOYS AND EVERYONE WHO
ACTUALLY PAID FOR THIS FANZINE.

TILL THE NEXT EDITION - TARA

No. 2
Late 1986

BOY'S OWN.
ten shillings (50p)

" Boy's Own...
— The magazine not read by
people whose cigarettes are smoked at a
jaunty angle.... "

Good Morning Chums,

Welcome to issue two of the
Periodical you've all been waiting for.
First of all the excuses for why there's been no
dramatic follow up to number one as quick as it could
have been. Production was somewhat held up by a
visit to Hackney hospital by two of our editorial staff.
The chaps saturday night was ended by flying backwards
from an automobile and lying in a road in a state close
to death... we have spent the last few weeks
investigating to find those responsible for this
shocking crime. Several suspects immediately
spring to mind. (1) A mini-van load of irate Belvedere d.j.'s
(2) Leigh Bowery (not in a car, just wearing his
crash-helmet)
(3) A man even more arseholed than our chaps.

" We'd like the public's help on this one as it's a
particularly nasty crime and we want to stop
these maniacs striking again " (Inspector Snidely, Hackney C.I.D
Were not sure whether he was talking about our
magazine and those responsible or our car crash and
those responsible ....

Until next time
keep 'em peeled !
The Outsider

INDEX

pages 1 to 93

"OH NO, NOT BOYS
OWN AGAIN!"
a punter reacts

· Sansom & Jesset ·
· haircutters ·

· Powell & Co ·

GENTS OUTFITTERS

11, ARCHER ST, SOHO
01~734 5051

UNDER MY SKIN....

From Cretinous 'Mum and Dad' bulldogs and roses to beautifully mastered designs, the tattoo remains with us (some more than others). Although now tattooing goes across all class barriers and some are more ready to show their private artwork than others, they were sported at the outset by two extremes of the social ladder. Royalty and Outlaws. Into the first category falls King George V, The Duke of Clarence, Czar Nickolas II. Into the latter falls any group from the japanese yacuza (centuries old) to the Hell's Angels (a relatively new band of brigands). The reason for this, without I hope reading too much into the art, is that tattoos to some are a statement of uniqueness (if done tastefully) and self-determination, sometimes in the face of anti-tattoo legislation. It's therefore not unusual that bikers and empire builders everywhere have adopted tattooing as their means of expression.

Japanese tattoo art is known as 'Horimono' and developed during the 1700's and has remained almost unchanged ever since. The distinctive style revolves naturally enough around the samurai, dragons, giant carp etc. i.e. 90% of what we see in british studios today. 'Horimono' means, literally, 'digging in the skin' and is done without the aid of electrically powered tools, favouring a series of triangular edged gouges to force pigment under the skin.

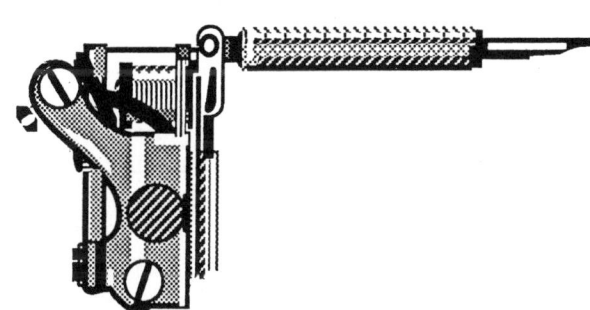

Meanwhile, in the rest of the world, we were a little more squeamish. America gave the world the 'electric tattoo machine' in the last decade of the 19th century, invented by one Samuel O'Reilly.

The first non-indian (red variety) tattooing practiced in America was brought over by European immigrants and was done by hand. A certain Will Sturgeon (an Englishman) discovered electromagnetism in 1823, this was the basis for Edison's stencil pen of 1875. O'Reilly saw that Edison's design (slightly modified) could be used for tattooing and off he went, greatly standardising the art of tattooing.

O'Reilly's invention heralded the change from personalized designs favoured by various American underworld figures (including Billy the Kid who had dots and crosses on his hands), to more common flash (the name given to an artists standard range of designs). O'Reilly's machine made tattooing faster and more profitable. Since those early machines, various technical changes have taken place including a great improvement in the quality of inks.

What has also changed is the quality of work. Although the dick-heads can
still have 'Love and Hate' scrawled across their knuckles, the more discerning
punter can have beautiful fine line personalised designs or the increasingly
popular black-work (which, as its name implies, uses only black ink, sometimes
lightened by water-shading). This style in many studios is a new addition but
in reality it is a continuation of pre-Christian Tattooing tradition. This
up-surge in interest toward blackwork represents, to the humble writer, what
good tattooing is all about, stunning design and subtle detail coupled with
individuality, not some prat wandering about in a cap-sleeve t-shirt showing
garish, badly executed, pictures of mongoloid bulldogs.

It is this latter image which represents the one thing which has never changed,
or I fear is ever likely to, and that is general public attitude to tattooing.
In the pre-Christian societies of cultures as diverse as the Egyptians and
Vikings, Tattoos were sported only by the upper echelons. In fact, the
earliest evidence of body art is of Egyptian origin, consisting of dots and
lines on a mummified female. Sadly, since then attitudes have changed. Over
the last century or so people have thought (and I speak from personal experience)
that one's I.Q. drops in direct proportion to the number of bodily illustrations.
The sad thing is that in 75% of cases, this can be true but these people would
be divs anyway, regardless of flesh adornment. There are, however, many people
out there with some very beautiful torso doodlings. People you have known for
years without realising, they will, if they have any sense, not brazenly display
but rather give you a glimpse as they stretch an arm across the dinner table
or remove that last item of clothing before bedtime. Believe it or not,
tattooing can be about great subtlety and beauty.

And remember boys and girls, take heed of the warning in many a Studio ....

"Tattoos last longer than romances"

LOVE, KISSES, AND ROSES ON YOUR BOTTOM ...

                                        THE OUTSIDER.

UNCLE STEVEN'S POETRY CORNER.

(it's grate!) —

STEVE WRIGHT

Your banal show is a fucking joke
Your stupid sayings appeal to all folk
Radio one bosses are as bad
Mike Reid, Jonathan King, they are very sad
But you Steve Wright, you're such a twit
Why don't you shut up, you four-eyed git.

Soaraway Sun

A right wing paper, it gives all the news,
like another blonde Rod Stewart screws
George Best is back on the booze
It's really quite a joke.
Dirty Den is a smashing bloke
it appeals to lots of working folk
Page 3 girls give "me such a thrill"
Silly stories from Phil Neal
Woodrow Wyatt and his fascist quill
I don't want to read about what's really going on
the dialogue between Mikhail and Ron
or the latest City con
I read about reds like Ken Livingstone and Peter Haine
as I'm going home on the train
you must have guessed, to read the Sun you need no brain.

TEBBITS TITLE

You're Chairman of the Conservative Party to help boost your party rating
a gimmick that's for sure, you go on and on with your militant hating.
Your policies are working you say but we know Norman, you're full of bull,
in seven years of this government, you have done fuck all.
I hate you for all your evil ways, you sit and gloat full of your Party's lies,
but don't worry Norman, people are learning, they are getting wise,
When your party's lost the election, political obscruity will be your prize.

CILLA BLACK

The yesteryear of the Sixties is your place
but you're come back to haunt our face
with such gems as Surprise, Surprise and Blind Date
television must be in a sorry state.
We must be thankful at least you're not singing
or do I speak to soon, your agents phone is ringing
No it's only ITV with another show for you
you will have to wait, it's a Surprise Surprise get it.

THE GOALHANGER WITH A SMALL KNOB.

Lurking somewhere in my relatively small (but perfectly formed) tape collection, is a coverless C-90 scrawled on with biro. It bears the following legend, "GARY CROWLY'S LAST TUESDAY CLUB". The tape represents just one of the feathers in Mr Crowly's cap, that of capital radio D.J. His show was greatly varied, a bit like John Peel without the Einsturzende Neubauten or art for arts sake. We were given the Bluebells to Barry White, Orange Juice to O'Jays, sound pop music and toptunes for the urban soulboy to the suburban student.

Gary recently (temporarily I hope) curtailed his radio career to move onto bigger and better things. Boy's Own cornered him one night in the Wag Club on one of his successful "Whiskey-a-go-go" events. We would like to point out that Mr Crowly bought the beers thus putting him high up in the 'Martin Stephenson Good Blokes Challenge Cup'. Now Read On ....

BOYS OWN: Before we get into some serious questioning, how about a brief personal history?

G.C. I used to go to school off the Edgware Road, Steve Walsh used to go there, so did Phil Daniels, even then he used to go to the Anna Sher theatre and enjoyed bossing people about in school plays. I was gonna go there .... but couldn't be bothered to go all the way to Islington. So I missed being in Quadraphenia.

BOYS OWN: Are there any embarrassing pictures of you in a parka?

G.C. Ooh ... Slightly! There's too many to mention.

photo:shameless o'tallboy

would you buy a used scooter from this man?

After this not too surprising revelation, we took a slight refreshment break.
Several lagers and some idle chatter about a recent holiday (dodgy boxer
shorts and camp holiday snaps) we continued.

G.C. Anyway, back to the life story. Me and some mates (including Dave
Dorrell) took over the school magazine, a bit mod and two-tone dominated
and because I was the biggest Jam fan walking the streets, I called it
"The Modern World". (If anybody out there has a copy, we here at Boy's
Own would definitely like to peruse!)

BOYS OWN: Are there any copies surviving?

G.C.: I hope not ... I'm a bit embarrassed about it actually, it was well
dodgy.

BOYS OWN: O.K. back to current affairs, what's the situation with Capital,
why did you leave?

G.C.: I'd been there five years ya know, and just thought it was time I
did something different. But I do want to get back on the radio, I really
miss it.

BOYS OWN: What else have you got lined up?

G.C.: Bits and pieces really, a bit of writing. Actually, I've just signed
a contract with H.M.V. I'm the 'Nipper' of the eighties ... without the
black eye.

BOYS OWN: What's your favourite band of the moment?

G.C.: Big Audio Dynamite, Martin Stephenson and the Daintees, I really like
INXS, the Style Council, Beastie Boys, Run D.M.C.

BOYS OWN: What's your favourite biscuit?

G.C.: I think Chocolate Digestives really, I lick the chocolate off and dunk
the digestive.

BOYS OWN: Do you have anything to do with Red Wedge?

G.C.: No, nothing at all, I do get stick for that, mainly from Weller.
I've got no interest in politics what-so-ever, never have done.

BOYS OWN: But you play a lot of black records, how about Artists Against
Apartheid?

G.C. Oh Yeah! I've done things for that.

BOYS OWN: Alright ... not Red Wedge, but something with a socialist base.

G.C.: I can see what you're saying, Wellers given me loads of grief about it,
but I just think I'd be cheating myself and others. I hate politics,
politicians and wankers. I don't trust any of them. I'd rather enjoy myself
than get tied up with all that bull-shit, which is what ultimately I think it
is. They're all two faced.

BOYS OWN: Some consider yourself, a certain Mister Vaughan Toulouse and others
as a new-age 'brat-pack', do you agree?

G.C.: I suppose there is a bit of a gang. Me and Vaughan used to be dodgy
mods. I first met him at a Specials gig, or was it a Merton Parkas gig with
Madness supporting? He'd just come off tour with Stiff Little Fingers.

Gary now begins to reminisce on those halcyon days that were the mod revival
(I think they were a Tuesday and Wednesday a few years back).

G.C.: The mod thing was brilliant, those early gigs, going to the Wellington and the Kings Head in Deptford. Oh well, the real die-hard mods think I'm a cunt anyway.

BOYS OWN: Have you ever been seen standing on the terraces?

G.C.: A long long time ago, when I used to live in White City I went to Q.P.R. I once waited outside Rangers ground for four hours just to get Gordon Jago's autograph. That really is blackmail stuff! It was so exciting then, like the way pop music effected me. Rodney Marsh, Stan Bowles. I used to go to school round there, every other day I was round Q.P.R's ground. That pop star thing surrounding footballers in those days, Peter Marinello, Charlie George, they were real chaps weren't they. I mean, Gary Lineaker? Fuck Off! I don't go anymore. I just play now and then, as a goalhanger.

BOYS OWN: What do you think 1986 will be remembered for on a personal and also a countrywide level.

G.C.: Good Question. Very good question. I passed my driving test. Never buy an old car. On a countrywide level, the way Bobby Robson cheated us all and managed to keep his job.

BOYS OWN: Have you ever been influenced by a book?

G.C.: Yes, one book "Generation X", 1964 interviews with youth of the day. One of the best books ever. 20p from a local bookshop.

BOYS OWN: Who are your favourite drinking partners?

G.C.: Julian Palmer, the Raid boys, and Mark Reilly (of Matt Bianco).

BOYS OWN: Last Question. How big is your knob?

G.C.: Actually, it's very very small. Two peas and a chipolata Crowly they used to call me.

Ask Paul McKee.

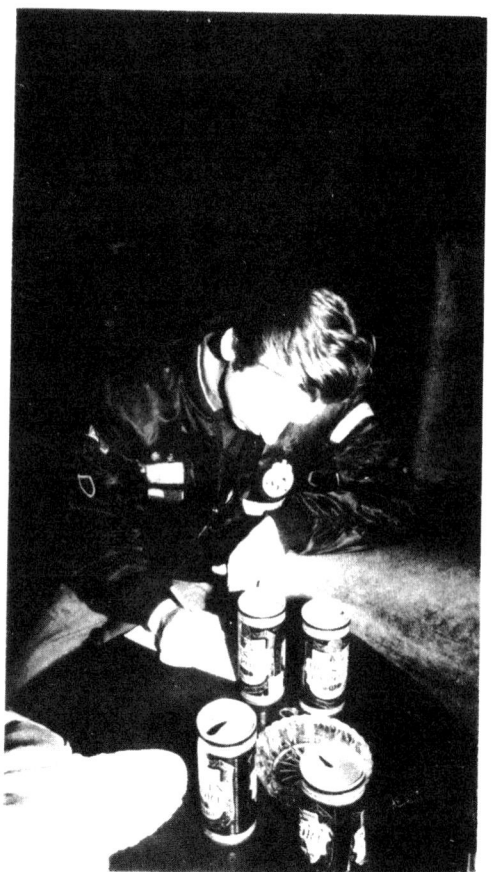

"It's not for ME honest ... just put
all the best Gary-x-"
G.C. signs copies of his best selling
auto-biography "I WAS GORDON JAGO'S
SECRET LOVE-CHILD"

THAT WAS
THE YEAR THAT WAS.
(CUT OUT AND THROW AWAY SUPPLEMENT)

Come on, own up, you're not really interested in yet another review of 86, now are you? It doesn't matter in the grand scheme of things what we or any other rag think about soap operas or the length of hemlines. However, it does fill up a few pages and gives us a chance to spout off twaddle and try to inflict our dubious taste on you. So here it is ... 'Another tedious review of 86.' (Sorry that should read 'in depth analysis of Art, Literature, Music and the Socio-political events of 1986' (Fuck Off. Ed.)

CINEMA

Lashings of crap, mediocre amount of mediocreness. Very little goodness. Everything to be said about '$9\frac{1}{2}$ weeks' has been said, an ice-breaker for chaps taking out a new girl, a turn on for chapettes savouring the rourke grin. However, the film of films 86, 'Aliens'. Absolute cringe-making politics and plot, blinding effects and gadgets. Worst film of the year? Anybody remember 'Flesh and Blood'. Ruteen Haver's Mad Max meets Noggin the Nog? Disappointment of the year? Could Bob Hoskins really emerge from Nick such a naive tit?

VIDEO RELEASES

Death, blood, mayhem, tits, death, part four, horror, bottoms, no-good commies, 'Sweet Dreams', 'Defence of the Realm', space-ships, low budgets, scream, girgle, slurp,

Greatness amidst shit.

MUSIC

Depending on yer bag maan, there was plenty about. Flavours of the month became flavours of the day, the hip-hop did stop, and Joe Public sank to even deeper depths of stupidity (hands up who bought 'The Final Countdown' or 'Every Loser Wins'). 5 years too late and even 5 years ago it was fifteen years too late, Knobhead Party, c'mon 'Shout' everybody, re-release of the year? Reet Petite.

Record that deserved more. Bambaata's Theme featuring one of the best movie themes for many a year ('Assault on Precinct 13'). People who might have made it if they had an ounce of personality and a stock of snappy replies to hecklers, of the year. Sigue Sigue Sputnik.

On the live front, there was plenty, pogues at the palais on St Patrick's night, trouble funk anytime anywhere, the Triffids at the Town and Country Club (rousing version of 'Sympathy for the Devil'), B.A.D. Porchester Hall (I lived up to my name and had to stay outside, while the rest of the editorial team got down inside), Beastie Boys at the Hammersmith Odeon absolutely breathtaking! Piss-up gig of the year? New Order at Brighton Centre.

POLITICS

Lies, lies, huge porkies, lies, deciet, cover-ups, fibs, lies, un-truths, dogma, anti-left wing hysteria, frightening and dangerous cretins in control, more lies, old men playing spy games, whores with brown envelopes, lies, lies. Public couldn't give a toss, Good Night.

FASHION

   BOLLOCKS...

WANKERS OF THE YEAR   (OR IN FACT ANY YEAR)

Mike Smith, Noel 'Dead Whirley Wheeler' Edmonds, Robert 'Traitor', sorry, Kilroy-Silk, Bobby Robson, Woodrow Wyatt, Leigh Bowery and the Egg-Box Crew (awarded the long service medal for services to being a total cunt), Junkies in general, Wogan, Nick Kamen (Nashville Indeed!), Sun Journalists.

EVENTS OF THE YEAR

Anti-Apartheid March (with a big fuck-off to anyone who didn't go on the march and then moaned when the marchers turned up and spoiled their view).

Van-Burn's imitation J.P.G. steel toe cap boots coming adrift from the steel caps at the Café de Paris. (Peep-toe D.M.'s anybody?)

THE SOCIAL AWARENESS PAGE.

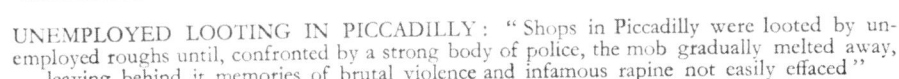

UNEMPLOYED LOOTING IN PICCADILLY: "Shops in Piccadilly were looted by unemployed roughs until, confronted by a strong body of police, the mob gradually melted away, leaving behind it memories of brutal violence and infamous rapine not easily effaced"

"I HAVE GOT A LARGE HOUSE IN BUCKINGHAMSHIRE. MOST PEOPLE IN KNOWSLEY NORTH DO NOT. NOW HURRY UP CAMERA 3, GET MY BEST PROFILE."

THE ANTI~SOCIAL BEHAVIOUR PAGE.

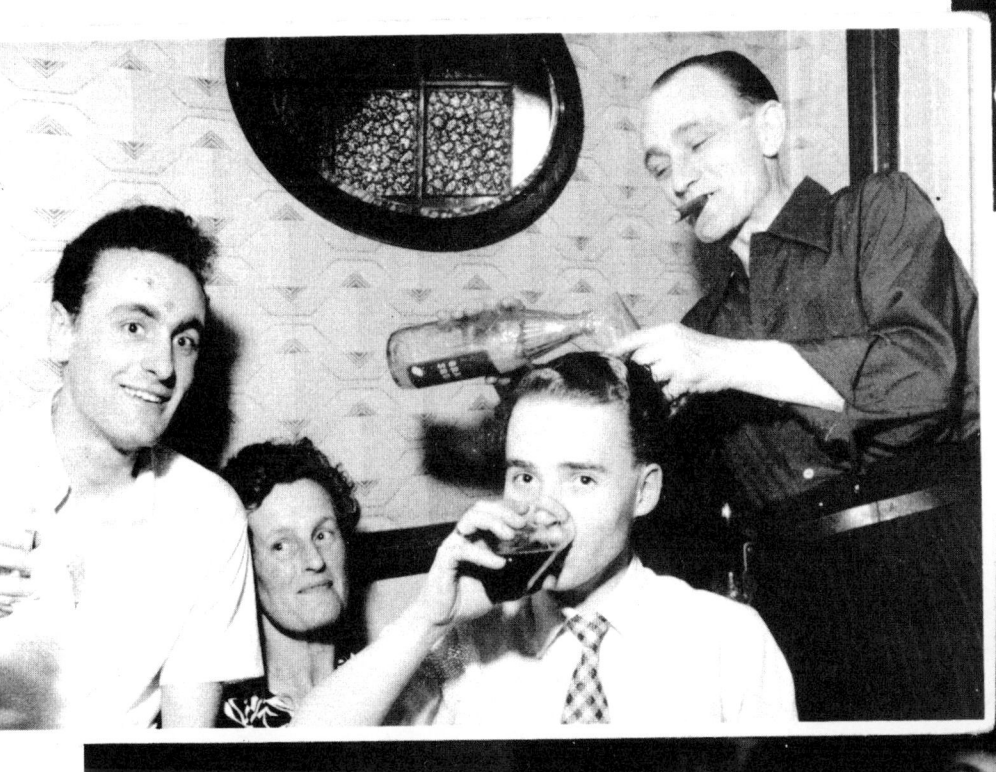

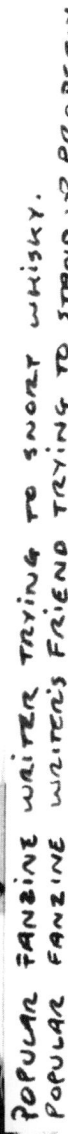

POPULAR FANZINE WRITER TRYING TO SNORT WHISKY.
POPULAR FANZINE WRITER'S FRIEND TRYING TO STAND UP PROPERLY...

J. ROCKA HEAD COACH FOR THE ALL ENGLAND SYNCHRONIZED TAKING AND DRINKING TEAM LIMBERS UP FOR HIS IMMORTAL ON RECORDS PARTY APPEARANCE...

P NIGHT-SPOT GRAMAPHONE RECORD PLAYER VENTS AMYL-NITRATE IMPREGNATED SPECS...

BOY'S OWN TOP TUNES TOP 20

1. $E = MC^2$ – Big Audio Dynamite
2. LOVE CAN'T TURN AROUND – Jackmaster Farley Funk.
3. GODSTAR – Psychic T.V.
4. HAUNTED – The Pogues
5. WAITING FOR THE GHOST TRAIN – Madness
6. CROCODILE CRYER – Martin Stephenson and the Daintees
7. HOLD IT, NOW HIT IT – The Beastie Boys
8. MEDICINE SHOW – Big Audio Dynamite
9. SHELL-SHOCK – New Order
10. MY ADIDAS/PETER PIPER – Run D.M.C.
11. PANIC – The Smiths
12. ROCK THE BELLS – L.L. Cool J
13. ALL AND ALL – Joyce Sims
14. SINFUL – Pete Wylie
15. CAN YOU FEEL IT – Original Concept
16. SLOW LOVIN' – Martin Stephenson and the Daintees
17. LEVI STUBB'S TEARS – Billy Bragg
18. FUNKAHDAFI – Front 242
19. DIGGING YOUR SCENE – The Blow Monkeys
20. BABY I LOVE YOU SO – Colour Box

'We'd like to thank everyone who voted for us'

The above top tunes represent some of the best of 86, compiled from votes cast by Steven, Terry, The Outsider, Gary Crowly, Cymon, Vaughan Toulouse and various chaps and chapettes.

Bye!

SOUNDS
LIKE THE NEW THANG.

1986 has seen an explosion of new musical departures and influences, ranging
from heavy metal inspired funk to folk flavoured rock. Thrown out into the
world have come some blinding bands and records, from Schooly-D to Shane
McGowan, Weather Prophets to Beastie Boys. There have also however been
some tunes that have been far from top. Here is a review of just some of
them.

THE SURFING PILLOCKS - "BILLY DON'T BE A BILLY" ('PISSED UP IN THE CLARENDON'
RECORDS)
"ere Steve, the Pillocks are playin' Saturday. If I can borrow dad's car
do you fancy it?"
"Not many!"
"I'll get me mum to iron me new Guana Batz t-shirt"
"Eard the new single?"
"Dunno, still it don't matter, they all sound the same anyway."

THE MEN THEY COULDN'T SEND TO THE DENTISTS -
"A FRIEND OF MY SISTER IS IRISH, HONESTLY"
('Listen to Dubliner's originals' records)
Spirit of punk ... Evan McColl ... back to basics ... Christy Moore ...
professional drunkards ... straight up I bought Wolfe Tones records years ago.

THE ANORAK TOGGLES - "WE'VE GOT FEEDBACK AND WE'RE GONNA USE IT"
(' MY OLDER BROTHER'S GOT ALL THE OLD VELVET UNDERGROUND RECORDS' RECORDS)

Spirit of punk ... silly band names ... back to basics ... old 'Nuggets'
L.P.'s ... professional tea totallers ... straight up I bought the Buzzcock's
albums when they first came out.

WORKING WEAK FEATURING COURTENAY PINE-KITCHEN
"SUBURBAN WINE BAR SOUNDTRACK"
('CHRISTOS TOLERA HAD THE RIGHT IDEA' RECORDS)
Blue Rondo looked good, had a laugh, drank heavily, took the money and ran.
Working Weak look bad, don't laugh, although they drink heavily took the
money and fell over.

A MAN IN A DODGY SUIT AND GOLD CHAINS TRYING TO LOOK FLASH.
"BENG TENG A LENG BENG, MURDER, RIPPIT, A LENG BENG TENG ... OINK"
('WHY AM I TALKING LIKE THIS, I'VE LIVED ALL MY LIFE IN ACTON' RECORDS)
Nearly all the reggae do's I've been to feature guilt ridden whiteys who
can't dance, 'freaking out' to crap reggae. Well it has to be good, it's
reggae isn't it. A word in your ear. There is good reggae and shit.
Don't be afraid to say so.

RUCKING HABITS

Well it has to be doesn't it ... that legendary fracas afloat, of course
First Prize goes to West Ham Vs Munich 58 on the Ferry. All involved get
a gold plated fire extinguisher to hurl down any ships staircase of their
choice.

TELEVISION

Worth staying in for :

King of the Ghetto, Bilko, Brookside, The Singing Detective, The Way They
Were, The Tube, Dead-Head, Blankety Blank, The Trap Door, Fawlty Towers,
South Bank Show, London's Burning, South of Watford, and a few more I'll
no doubt remember tomorrow.

Worth going out for :

Eastenders, Late Late Breakfast Show, Top of the Pops, North and South,
Duty Free, The Documentary about Michael Clarke, Wogan, Girls on Top,
No Limits, Drug Alert, The Price is Right, Dallas, etc, etc. Sadly, the
shit out-numbers the stuff worth watching.

If I paid my T.V. Licence, I'd be gutted!

Also sad is the number of people who watch soap-operas for some sort of
Kitsch satisfaction, thinking it's dead wacky to be into Dynasty or East-
Enders.
'Oh yes, they're so bad they're brilliant...'
Fuck off; they're so bad they're dreadful.
However, stay tuned for further T.V. analysis in forthcoming editions.

LITERATURE

THE FACE : Turning into a very sad self parody, whereas in early issues they
reported new trends in music, fashion etc. They now add their view as self-
proclaimed trend setters and comment on the news they are reporting. This
could see a demise in popularity. Face review of 86 was very sad indeed,
I suggest you lay down in a darkened room with a copy of Boy's Own.

i-D : Once upon a time there was a great little fanzine type mag full of
grainy photos of people going about their business in their chosen mode of
dress. 5 years or more on the mag's still full of grainy photos, but now they
are of the latest in Azzadine Alaia strapless leggings and Club 'celebrities'.
Like The Face becoming very much a self parody. However, amidst the pretentious
crap lurks a very sound writer, take a bow William Leith.

NIGHT OUT OF THE YEAR

Various cavorting and falling over occurred most regularly or with most
enjoyment at the wag, The Raid, with one off night award taken easily by
lots road in the summer.

DOORMAN OF THE YEAR

Belgium can we have your votes please?
'Erm, yes .... crackle ... speedy duck ... dix points'

'doorman
of the year'
MR S.DUCK
RELAXING
WITH
"BUSINESS
FRIENDS"

DRUGS

A very good year for Her Majesty's Police Force, as they seem to have most
of them at the moment, they must be planning one fuckin' cracker of a
warehouse party. Will Doorman of the Year be Kenneth Newman this time
next year? Let's do some ecstacy and rap about it, Yah!

DRINKING HABITS

Right about now I like to relax with a beer, so when it's been a hectic day
at the office, relax with a red stripe crucial brew. All your troubles will
melt away ..... Trouble is, so will half your brain.

Another six pack please!

<u>VIZ COMIX</u> : Fuckin' marvellous, snap up any copies you can, your life will
never be the same again.
Signed, Victor Pratt the Stupid Twat.

<u>BOYS OWN</u>

A newcomer onto the news-stands, its earthy no nonsense, happy-go-lucky
attitude could take it to great heights.

<u>PRACTICAL BOAT-BUILDING</u>

A newcomer onto the news-stands, its earthy no nonsense, happy-go-lucky
attitude could take it to great heights.

<u>BLAH, BLAH, BLAH</u>

Sorry chaps, but we lost your letter. We think your mags rather super too.
Write again.

Lastly, but not leastly, chaps and chapettes of the year, proving that girls
as well as boys can have bollocks. Come to the awards ceremony please,
Johnny Rocka, Paul Rutherford, Chris Sullivan, David Blunkett, Alexi Sayle,
Alexandra Pigg, Beastie Boys, Muriel Grey, Shane McGowan.
Joanne Whalley, Stanley Unwin, Martin Stephenson, G.C. The Busy Bee,
Ivor Cutler, Mary Coughlan, any National Health Nurse, Mathew Ashman,
Kevin Rowlands, Josie Jones .... etc, etc...

"TERRACE RUMBLINGS"

FOOTBALL THUGS KILL FAN

The death of young men due to football hooliganism used to get front page headlines with the words, "INNOCENT FAN", "ALWAYS DRESSED SMART", followed by the boys distraught mum telling the press how he "NEVER GOT IN TROUBLE AND WAS A GOOD BOY".

Things have now changed, there have been too many dead youths for the papers to get much mileage out of dead soccer fans. The reward to these people for donating their lives is now a half column next to a dodgy bird on Page 3.

Those of you who "HAVE IT" at football will know that most of the victims of soccer violence are not 100% innocent anyway, just unlucky to be the one who got caught when it came "on top".

Another thing is that these "victims" tend not to be the "Hard Core" firm members anyway but geezers who are out for the crack and don't really know the score. The real chaps of the London firm's know each other, if not personally, at least by sight and there is always the chance of a squeeze from mates in the opposing mob.

The victim also doesn't really understand the rules of the game, like when to "stand" and when to "have it on your toes". The victims don't usually realise what's happening, till some scousers are drawing a map of the London underground on his back with a Stanley.

One thing is certain. If you go with your teams firm just for a laugh, the chances of you becoming a victim are high. So either go shopping with your girlfriend on Saturdays or let your mum know you aint that innocent - at least it will stop those embarrassing "innocent fan" headlines.

FIRM FAVOURITES.

Now most of you will be saying "no-one sings at the match anymore" ... true ... all the boys have smoked so much gear that to get a coherent sentence out would be impossible anyway. Over in the seats though the barmies are still at it. Here is the "Boys Own" worst 10 chants (soon to be released on K-Tel's "20 Rucking Greats".

1. "ONE MAN WENT TO MOW" - CHELSEA.   probably the divviest song of
                                            all time, c'mon boys the jokes
                                            over ...

2. 'SHE WORE A YELLOW RIBBON" - ARSENAL. CLOCK END.
                                            John Wayne and the 7th Cavalry
                                            meets the Gooners. Awful ...

3. "SHANKLY 81" - MANCHESTER UNITED. PADDOCK.
                                            A sad song from a sad mob about
                                            a great man ...

4. "FUCK THE QUEEN AND THE U.D.A." - CELTIC.
                                            More Scottish dickheads.

5. "ONE SLIPPERY RUNWAY" - WEST HAM.   A pre-season classic.

6. "YOU'RE GOING HOME IN A FUCKING AMBULANCE" ... MAD GEORDIES ...

7. "E FOR B AND CLYDE BEST" - WEST HAM.   A chicken-run vintage classic ...

8. "CHELSEA AND RANGERS ARE MAGIC" - CHELSEA (NOT AGAIN)
                                            Londoners praising a sweaty sock
                                            team with a complete bastard
                                            manager and fans who wear scarves
                                            and jean jackets. ... DOUBLE SAD ...

9. "YORKSHIRE BOYS, YORKSHIRE BOYS, LACED UP BOOTS AND CORDEROYS" -
                                            LEEDS SOUTH STAND.
                                            Jimmy Pursey turns in his grave.

10. "OO, TO BE A GOONER" - ARSENAL NORTH BANK.
                                            The Gooners cringe ...

ALL TOGETHER NOW !

GOING TO THE DOGS.

Today it seems you can't move in South London without bumping into a Staffordshire bull terrier or for that matter, an English bull terrier. Now Boy's Own can sit and wonder the reason for the sudden popularity of these so called fighting breeds, but no doubt their gladiatorial past will give a good clue to this. Since the Romans first invaded our shores many years ago with dogs, there has existed many sports involving our canine friends. These so called 'sports' became most famous during the Edwardian era of our history. Now these bloody contests went under various guises, included were bull baiting, bear baiting, rat killing and dog fighting, in which many dogs gave their life for a small fee or wager.

These brutal contests were popularised by the richer gentry of the day (Royalty included), although it does seem that towards the end of the 1700's, dog fighting became strictly a working class past-time. Owners of these dogs wanted a beast that was strong and courageous but also quick and agile, and so began the genetic construction of fighting dogs. Bulldogs, various terriers, dalmations, and even pointers were used in this genetic cocktail, although these experiments were more pragmatic than scientific. Thus we got English bull terriers, Staffordshire bull terriers. However, today's versions are probably not like the originals at all.

In 1835, Parliament introduced legislation out-lawing all blood sports (the fighting kind that is), although many sports disappeared overnight, one at least went underground and continue to flourish. I refer, of course, to dog fighting. Once more (after several revivals) this illegal sport has once again become popular in certain circles (South London take note). Anyway, onto a slightly more pleasant note; dogs as fashion accessories, which is what a lot of these dogs are now becoming. In the late 1800's early 1900's, English bull terriers became very popular with the English gentlemen of the day, known as "London Swells". It seems that these chaps, intent on looking dapper in their top hats and canes, considered the terrier a final accessory for their social attire. The Staffordshire bull terrier appealed more to the miners, chain-makers and blacksmiths of the black country, hence "Staffordshire bull terrier".

After about 1930 however, the fighting breeds suffered a decline in popularity, but lately it seems everyone owns one. Given the history of these dogs, I can see the appeal but really, in most cases, a dog is a domestic pet not a pair of trousers to be discarded, considered to be 'out' or unfashionable.

Think about that one lads.

SPiriT Of 76

The sound system is blasting out Led Zeppelin guitar Riffs, the vocals screamed out by three white punks from N.Y.C. the dead Kennedys on tour? no just another soul alldayer. The venue is Thorpe Park a sort of poor mans Disneyland, in attendance are about 500 of what used to be called "Jazzfunkers" plus the south's top mainstream soul djs, that punk records?, the Beastie Boys of course.

" Let me clear my throat, kick it over here baby pop and let all the Fly Skimmies feel the beat."

Rap has totally conquerd Londons dancefloors, eighteen months ago the majority of the Thorpe Park crowd would'nt have entertained a hardcore Rap record except as a novelty item, the "Soulboys" have now caught up with London's B Boy possies and Mud Clubbers, raps gone clear, Original Concept, Eric B, Kool Mo Dee a new set of stars on 45 leave the racks of the import shops every week. The current "Geezer" of the moment though is Schooly D, a philly street gang member and Gunman or so the press releases (and the NME) would have us believe. Schooly's erie combination of echoed slurred vocals and stark beats make a sinister sound of dance and violence, twothings that always go down well with the discerning punter.

While Schooly D is this weeks number one Yo-boy (URGH) and Run DMC are the guvnors as far as sales are concerned the peoples champions are the BEASTIES BOYS.

BEASTIE GROOVE

Ten years on from punk the true spirit of 76 is captured by three white middle class Jewish rappers, King AD-Rock, Mike D and MCA started out in "79" as a four piece hardcore punk band, the female drummer Katie Schellenbach was later sacked for being a awful rapper, something that didn't stop the other three becoming totally awesome (as they say in N.Y.C.)

In 81 they released "Polly Wog Stew" a mini 7" EP containing such classics as "Egg raid on Mojo", totally awesome. The Beasties live act was by "83" at least 50% rap and the release of "Cookie Puss" Heralded the birth of the Beasties as we know them now. The big break cam when Double Dee the Beasties scratch Dj left the band and set up his own record label. Rick Rubin, Def Jam recordings, the Beasties were an obvious signing, their first (and best) Def Jam single was "Rock Hard" followed by the Run DMC track "Slow and Low", a string of underground hits followed, the boys were on it.

London went totall Beastie apeshit in 86, with our heroe's playing at Delirium and on the Raising hell tour. The chaps did their reputation no harm either with beer swilling performances at the Cafe de Paris and skateboarding shows around town.

BEASTIE BOYS

e Beasties have just released their first LP, "Licensed to Ill"
riginally called "Kill All Faggotts") on Def Jam records and
th 13 tracks it makes a great value Xmas pressie for the whole
mily.

e Beasties are simply the best punk band in the world in the
ue sense of the word punk this is, if the Pistols were starting
t today Rick Rubin would have them on his label, LI Cool Jay
Rap, Run DMC are Rap, the Beasties are punk. Providing the
cord company aint wack, expect to see the boys on top of the
os singing "GIRLS" sometime in the new year, whats the time, "its
ne to get **ILL**".

STOP PRESS

News has just reached Boy's Own headquarters concerning 'The Ringpiece
Brothers' who we can only describe as an English Beastie Boys with an
attitude to match. Check out their debut single "Lager, Drugs and a
Hearty Snog" on ANAL INC. Records.
Produced by Johnny Rocka ... the sound is hard!
Stay tuned for more news and an interview if we can get it.

ROBOT

37 FLORAL ST,
COVENT GARDEN W.C.2
TEL 836-6156

323 KINGS RD, SW3
TEL 352-6549

"A big thank you from the Boy's Own staff to the following people ... without whom we could still get the mag out ! ''

VAL THE DEMON TYPIST, BOYLAN, GRANT, CLIVE the YID, ALL THE LONDON FOOTBALL BOYS (PAST AND PRESENT) ANYBODY WHO PURCHASED ish 1, RockA, SIMON HOLBROOK (the TORY TART WITH A HEART), MUM, dad, aunty Freda AND All at the corner shop ...

we can be slagged off or praised to the heavans at: 13 ILMINSTER GARDENS, clapham junction, LONDON S.W. 11.

DEDICATED TO ARTHUR SPIRES.
(a hero to rough haired youth R.I.P.)

No. 3
Summer 1987

boys own

it's bullseye.

50

— 'Boy's own,
the only fanzine not written
by anorak wearers...

Good evening viewers,
Welcome to number 3, of the magazine everybody loves but no bastard buys...

Luckily success hasn't changed us here at Boy's Own mansions and we haven't altered our lifestyle a bit. To prove this point I shall describe in fine Evening Standard style a typical week in the crazy life of a Boy's Own contributor.

Monday: Roehampton Cribbage Circle — crazy guys, playing a crazy game, living life on the edge; bring your own dominoes. Then onto a practice session with the Boy's Own formation ligging team — crazy guys etc etc.

TUESDAY: 'Really Potty Nobby's' — loads of young Sloanes going crazy apeshit to the latest discotheque punk-funk faves. We don't go there, just meet round my house and discuss blowing the place up.

WEDNESDAY: Go to the shops.

THURSDAY: Go back to the shops. I forgot Wednesday was half day closing — crazy!

FRIDAY: The weekend starts here cats and kittens, so its pull on your lurex balaclavas and do the mashed potato like a crazy mutha. Or stay in; whatever you like really.

SATURDAY: 'Club Crowded'. No door policy, no bar staff, no atmosphere, no you cant come in without an M.A.1 on. known to a small elite as the 'Asteria'

SUNDAY: Invite my crazy media and entertainment chums round. They're so crazy they don't bother turning up... or replying to the invitations.

So there it is, a totally fab and crazy insight into the world of the fanzine writer. I bet it makes you wonder how we jolly well get to write anything at all.

Oh well until the next crazy, protein packed, crispy coated edition,

Its goodbye and a hearty Bollox to you all!
The Outsider
—x—

(osher, sounded a bit like bollocks... ed)

GIVE US A LINE

"HOWDY!!!" AFTER CHANNEL 4'S EXCELLENT A-Z OF COUNTRY & WESTERN (DIG THAT CRAZY HANK WILLIAMS SUIT, PARTNERS) HOW ABOUT C4 DOING A SIMILIAR VERSION FOR SOUL. THE PRESENTER??... HANK WANGFORD LOOK-ALIKE CHRIS HILL OF COURSE ... IF IT MOVES LASSOO IT!!!

WELL SLAP MY THIGH (AND OTHER BITS) IF OLD HARVEY HASN'T BEEN UP TO IT AGAIN. STILL IT'S GOOD CLEAN FUN ISN'T IT? NO NOT IF IT HAD BEEN A LABOUR MP. I CAN'T BEGIN TO IMAGINE THE WANKY SUN HEADLINES "LOONY LEFTIE GAY SPANK SCANDAL"

ASHION CARES - IT CERTAINLY DOES.
ESPECIALLY WHEN MORE FASHIONABLE
MILEAGE CAN BE SQUEEZED
ROM SOMETHING. OUTFIT IN 'BAZAAR'
ABOUT £250 UPWARDS.
HS NURSE TREATING AIDS PATIENT
ABOUT £125 DOWNWARDS.

Professional Man seeks friend (young) for housework. starting at the bottom, but things will soon look up. contact 'Harvey' Westminster.

fuck off....

ON THE LITERARY FRONT ... CHECK OUR "THE LAST ELECTION" BY PETE DAVIES. NOT SO MUCH PREDICTIONS OF THE FUTURE, BUT OBSERVATIONS BASED ON CONTEMPORARY BRITAIN. ENGLAND TOMORROW THROUGH THE EYES OF TODAY OR ENGLAND TODAY THROUGH THE EYES OF TOMORROW? READ IT AND MAKE UP YOUR OWN MIND. (NOW AVAILABLE IN PAPERBACK THROUGH PENGUIN)

WHAT WAS MAN ABOUT TOWN AND PUBLIC SOCIALIST ROBERT ELMS DOING WRITING FOR 'ELLE' THE WELL KNOWN RUPERT MURDOCH FASHION ORGAN. ANSWERS ON A POSTCARD PLEASE. "SPANISH MORTGAGES DON'T COME CHEAP" WILL NOT DO.

WHILST ON THE SUBJECT OF 'ELLE'.
ARE YOU SURE?
BOY'S OWN FASHION TIP FOR SUMMER -
ELLE FASHION WRITERS ON LEADS.

BOW WOW! The vital accessory for men in fashion is a dog. Led, perhaps, by Azzedine Alaia's neurotic Yorkie, Patapouffe, Jasper Conran is trailed by a whimsical white shih-tzu, Louis.

'ELLE' april 87
"owned by a cunt written by wankers"

IF YOU ONLY DO ONE HONEST THING IN '87 MAKE SURE YOU VOTE. WEARING RUSSIAN BADGES WON'T PUT LABOUR BACK IN POWER BUT A BIC PEN WILL.

X VOTE!

what the paper's say.... on

Boy's Own

Issue One. Surprising to find a wideboyzine at a New Order gig, but there it was in all its soul-like glory. Subjects are covered that rarely see light, such as a sketch in a video shop, the demise of the soul boy and a blistering attack on the pretenders who flap when it kicks off.

With more pictures, this would be rather good. Trouble Funk - Flares and Style - Manoy bands - South Africa. 40p + SAE, 13 Ilminster Gardens, Clapham Junction, London SW11.

blah blah blah

Jacket in.
(an eighties addiction saga)

THERE HAVE BEEN MANY DANGERS TO THE YOUTH OF LONDON RECENTLY HIGHLIGHTED IN OUR POPULAR PRESS, CRACK (NEVER SEEN IT), COCAINE (CAN'T AFFORD IT), AND ECSTACY (ANYONE GOT ANY?). BUT NO-ONE HAS YET EXPOSED THE GREATEST DANGER. YOUR SOAR-AWAY BOY'S OWN IS LEADING THE WAY IN THE FIGHT AGAINST THE VILEST CORRUPTOR OF YOUTH, THE BLACK SHINEY MA1 FLYING JACKET.

THIS SAD JACKET FIRST APPEARED MANY YEARS AGO, BUT A REVIVAL ABOUT 2-3 SUMMERS AGO HAS RE-LABELLED IT THE "BUFFALLO". IT CAUSES PERSONALITY CHANGES VERY QUICKLY, ONE WEEK OF USE WILL MAKE THE USER START SHOUTING "YO" AND "TIME TO GET ILL", A CRAVING FOR RUSSIAN BADGES SOMETIMES OCCURS IN MORE EXTREME CASES. WE TALKED TO ONE SUCH ADDICT, BEN X (HE PREFERRED TO REMAIN ANONYMOUS FOR HIS FAMILY'S SAKE). BEN IS 28 YEARS OLD AND WORKS AS AN A AND R MAN FOR A TRENDY RECORD COMPANY.

ALTHOUGH IN HIS LATE TWENTIES THE CONTINUAL WEARING OF THE MA1 HAS GIVEN BEN THE FACIAL APPEARANCE OF A 15 YEAR OLD FEMALE SLOANEY.

"AT FIRST IT WAS JUST A GOOD BUZZ, I THOUGHT I COULD HANDLE IT, BUT IT CONSUMES YOU TOTALLY MAN"

BEN SLIPPED INTO A BEASTIE BROOKLYN ACCENT, ANOTHER SYMPTOM OF THE MA1 USE. "I ONLY GOT ONE TO KEEP THE COLD OUT, HONESTLY, THEN ONE DAY I WENT OUT FOR A PINT OF MILK, LOOKED AT MYSELF IN A SHOP WINDOW, AND SAW TO MY HORROR THAT I HAD MY CAP ON BACK TO FRONT"

BEN NOW REALISED HE WAS AN ADDICT.   HE LOOKED UPSET BUT THE BOY'S OWN
INVESTIGATOR TOLD HIM IN A SINCERE AND SYMPATHETIC VOICE THAT TALKING
ABOUT IT WOULD HELP.

WE LEFT BEN X AND CAUGHT A BUS TO CARNABY STREET, DEN OF THE MR BIG OF
THE MA1 TRADE. THE SIGN SAID 'GUPTA FASHION UNISEX BOUTIQUE'. POSING
AS PUNTERS WE ENTERED THE PREMISES AND WERE SHOWN BY MR BIG (AKA GUPTA
PATEL), A PILE OF BROWN PAPER PACKAGES, WHICH HE SAID CONTAINED MA1'S,
WE DECLINED HIS OFFER OF A SAMPLE AND LEFT BY THE FIRE EXIT.

WE KNOW IT AINT EASY GOING COLD TURKEY AND GETTING RID OF YOUR FLYING
JACKET, BUT BEING LAUGHED AT BY THE REST OF THE WORLD IS SURELY
INCENTIVE ENOUGH... ISN'T IT?   YOUR CARING, SHARING BOY'S OWN HAVE
SET UP A HOT LINE WHERE MA1 WEARERS CAN RING WHEN THEY FEEL THE NEED
FOR A FIX APPROACHING. THE PHONE LINES WILL BE MANNED BY EX-WEARERS,
SO EXPECT SYMPATHY RATHER THAN RIDICULE, WELL YOU MIGHT GET A BIT OF
SNIGGERING. SPEAKING TO A FRIEND, WHO HAPPENS TO BE A WEARER, AT THE
SPECIAL BRANCH WEEKENDER HE TOLD ME BOY'S OWN HAD NO RIGHT TO TELL
PEOPLE WHAT TO WEAR, WELL THIS AINT DRUGWATCH AND WE AINT ESTHER
RANTZEN BUT IT'S THE FASHION REPUTATION OF YOUNG LONDON THAT WE ARE
DEFENDING. HELP US
FOOTNOTE;
          WE RECENTLY SAW BEN X, HE WAS SPORTING A JEAN-PAUL GAULTIER
          BASEBALL CAP WITH DETACHABLE SUNGLASSES. HE HADN'T WORN AN MA1
          FOR A WEEK, AND HE FELT AND LOOKED BETTER ALREADY. PROOF THAT
          THERE IS LIFE BEYOND THE "BUFFALLO" JACKET.

terry

IF YOU NEED HELP

RING THE VICTIMS SUPPORT LINE ON

01∘∘430 0871

PAUL OAKENFOLD. AND GUESTS

project club :
LONDON.

EXCLUSIVE PRESENTATION EVERY FRIDAY

NOW SHOWING ZIGIS , 225 STREATHAM HIGH ROAD , LONDON SW16 – 01 769 3300

Licensed Bar. Prog 9·00pm » 2·00am   Doors Close 12·00am

£3·00

T SEEMED A GOOD IDEA AT THE TIME...

BUNDESWEHR VESTS

STEEL TOE CAPS

DROPPING ACID ON YOUR
OWN IN THE LEEDS AWAY END

CARRYING C.S. GAS FOR THE CRACK

TRYING TO BODY- POP

OUTRAGEOUS CLAIMS...

1. "I WAS A BEAT-ROUTE REGULAR"

2. "I WENT TO MILLWALL IN 76,

    IT WAS A STROLL"

3. "BOY's OWN 3 ? IT's AT THE PRINTERS"

4. "I'd NEVER PAY TO GET IN THE WAG,
    I'M SWEET WTIH WINSTON"

5. "I'VE PLAYED HIP-HOP FROM THE START"
    (VARIOUS SOUL-MAFIA D.J's)

EXCUSES EXCUSES...

"NOT NOW I'M OFF ME EAD"

"IREALLY WANTED TO HAVE IT,
        BUT IM ON A SUSPENDED"

"I WOULD GIVE YOU A NOSE,
        BUT I'VE DONE IT ALL"

"BOY's OWN 3,

NO IT's <u>STILL</u> AT THE PRINTERS"

"I WOULD PAY YOU BACK

UT ME GIRO GOT LOST IN THE POST"

FIRM FAVES 2 (top mobs from history)

1. "GENGHIS KHAN AND HIS MONGOL MARAUDERS"
    (TOOK ON THE WORLD AND ALMOST WON)

2. "SHAKA'S ZULU WARRIORS"
    (CANED THE BRITS SEVERELY
    WHEN IT KICKED OFF AT ROURKE'S DRIFT)

3   "SITTING BULL'S CAMP-FIRE CASUALS"
    (SMOKED SOME DRAW AND KICKED IT OFF MENTAL
    WIPING OUT CUSTER'S ENTIRE MOB.
    SERVES HIM RIGHT
    FOR BEING A LONG HAIRED BEAUT.)

4. "SOUTH YORKSHIRE CONSTABULARY"
    (STOUT UP-HOLDERS OF THE LAW
                - CRUEL BUT FAIR!)

5. "DERBY LUNATIC FRINGE"
    (THE NAME OF A VERY SILLY HAIRCUT, OR
    A VERY SILLY MOB OF NORTHERNERS
    FEATURING 14 YEAR OLD's WITH MOUSTACHES)

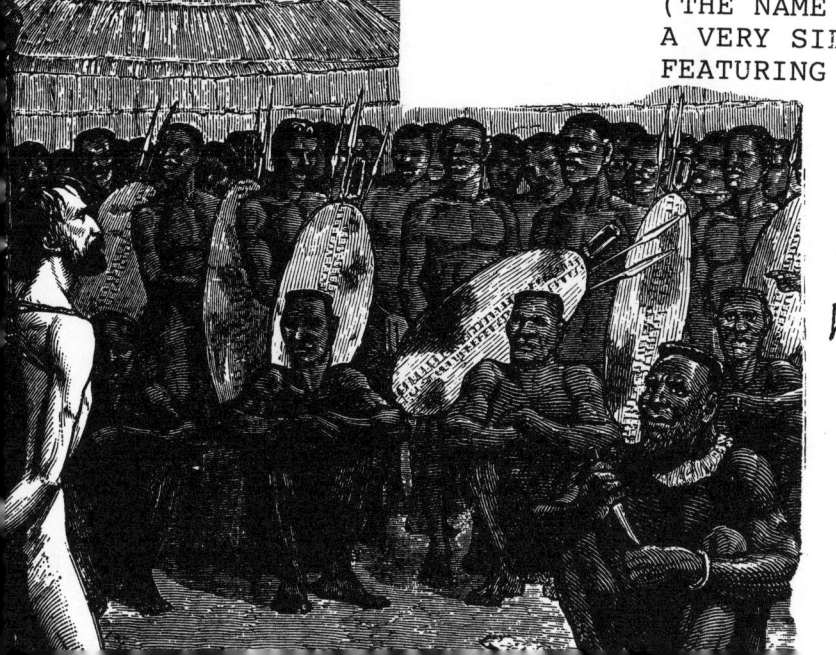

D.I. Snidely of Fulham C.I.D.
flushed with success at
tracking down Chelsea's Headhunters
had less luck when dealing with
the Birmingham Zulus (top mob –
                    sad plod!)

· Sansom & Jesset ·
· haircutters ·

· Powell & Co ·

GENTS OUTFITTERS

11, ARCHER ST, SOHO
01~734 5051

diggin'
YOUR SCENE.

CLUB
PROFILES : Nº1 Norman Jay.

Maybe not one of the most fashionable or most publicised DJ's in London, Norman Jay is without doubt one of the best. The 28 year old West Londoner has gone from the dancefloors of Crackers, the Blackpool Mecca and the Lacey Lady to the forefront of the Rare Groove scene. The current hype surronding 'Rare groove' somewhat amuses Norman: "People think they've discovered a new scene, they haven't, they've just discovered us." He is also aware that Rare Groove is the current big thing. "The bubble will burst, but we'll still be there, we always have been, we don't follow anyone's idea of fashion."

Rare Groove is basically early to late Seventies tracks that either weren't considered good enough, or tracks that got missed in the real golden years of funk, plus music like Maceo and the Macks that are newies to the under 25's. Norman Jay has gone from small warehouse parties to pulling in 1500 Rare Groovers at a recent bash in Kentish Town. It is also the first time that bootleggers have really raided the funk vaults. The Jackson Sisters, Jeanie Reynolds etc are all now available on moody white labels, fine if the record companies aint sussed enough, but £15 for Maceo and the Macks is a bit of a liberty eh chaps?

Norman, who also plays under the name "Shake 'n' Finger Pop", hosts an excellent show on London's pirate Kiss FM radio, and along with a proposed trip to New York for a London style warehouse party it seems it will be a long, hot and rare summer for fans of the Groove.

As an ex-Spurs boy, and someone who has faced the equal dangers of Feyenord away and upstairs at Global village, he seemed like an obvious candidate for the 'Boy's Own' team and he'll be writing columns in future editions. When the Rare Groove bubble bursts, (remember the hype that threatened to kill Go—Go) a guy like Norman will still be dropping his own kind of bombs. Catch the boy soon.

ONCE UPON A TIME... IN THE WEST END.

One of the strongest images I possess of Mick Jones is buried deep in the vaults of my childhood memories. At the tender age of 15 I first saw The Clash play a rock against racism do in Brockwell Park. There he stood, shoulder length hair, large guitar, leather, and white jeans. This was the future of Rock 'n Roll, even though we were all rather unsure about the length of the locks.

A hundred years on Mr Jones still carries the swing, summing up, even more I feel than The Clash, a spirit or feeling that is London (with a liberal dash of US of A). I won't bore you anymore with my sycophantic waffling, but just to tell you that the feeling one gets after an audience with B.A.D is better than any artificial stimulants (well almost).
[SING MICHAEL SING - SING ON THE ROUTE OF THE 19 BUS!]

ARE YOU IN A DILEMMA BETWEEN FASCINATION WITH AMERICA AND AMERICANA AND DISGUST WITH AMERICAN ATTITUDES AND POLITICS?

"NO... I'M NOT IN A DILEMMA ABOUT IT. BUT YES IT'S THERE, BUT I DON'T THINK THE RUSSIAN SIDE IS ANY BETTER."

BUT YOU'RE MORE INTO AMERICAN IMAGERY THAN RUSSIAN. I WOULD HAVE ASKED THE QUESTION WITH A RUSSIAN SLANT IF YOU WEREN'T.

"I DON'T TRUST THE RUSSIANS EITHER, THAT'S ALL I'M SAYING."

"WE TRY AND USE THE IMAGERY ON OUR SIDE. WE TAKE STRONG IMAGERY AND USE IT TO OUR OWN ENDS. AS THAT STUFF'S THERE ANYWAY WE JUST TAKE WHAT WE CAN, SO THAT WE'VE GOT SOME OF THAT STRONG IMAGERY ON OUR SIDE. THAT IS MY EXCUSE."

DO YOU CONSIDER YOURSELF A REFLECTION OF ENGLAND IN 1987 AS THE CLASH WERE IN 1977?

"YES, DEFINATELY. THE MUSIC AND THE WAY WE LIVE REFLECTS OUR ENVIRONMENT. I WANTED TO BE LIKE GEORGE MICHAEL THIS TIME ROUND, BUT IT DIDN'T WORK OUT."

ARE THERE ANY OTHER BANDS WORTH LISTENING TO IN ENGLAND TODAY?

"I LIKE A LOT OF STUFF, SHIT I EVEN LIKE THE SMITHS"

THEY REFLECT ENGLAND AS MUCH AS YOU DO, BUT THEY REFLECT MANCHESTER ON A WET WEDNESDAY WHEREAS YOU REFLECT NOTTING HILL ON A WET THURSDAY.

"I WISH WE COULD REFLECT IT ON A SUNNY SUNDAY IN SUMMER!"

I PERSONALLY THINK B.A.D = LONDON, BUT I GET THE FEELING YOU THINK B.A.D = USA?

"NO, NO THIS IS A MISCONCEPTION ABOUT ME. IT'S ALWAYS BEEN LEVELLED AGAINST ME. EVEN WHEN I WAS IN THE CLASH THEY USED TO SAY 'OH, HE'S IN AMERICA', I WAS ALWAYS HERE, I JUST DIDN'T MAKE A BIG DEAL OF IT. SURE I USED TO GO OVER THERE AND CHECK OUT THE SCENE, BUT I USED TO COME BACK AND USE IT AS INPUT. I LIVE HERE, AND WAS ALWAYS HERE WHEN YOU HAD TO VOTE. THEY ALWAYS SAY 'HE WASN'T HERE WHEN IT COUNTED' BUT I WAS, I JUST DIDN'T GO AROUND BLOWING MY OWN TRUMPET.

WHAT IS YOUR FAVOURITE EALING COMEDY?

"PASSPORT TO PIMLICO"

HAVE YOU EVER BEEN SENT A FILM SCRIPT?

"NO I SORT OF GET THEM UNDERHAND"

WHAT ABOUT 'STRAIGHT TO HELL

DID THEY ASK YOU TO BE IN THAT?

"NO"

WERE YOU DISAPPOINTED ABOUT THAT?

"NO...I'VE SEEN IT"

"IT'S ALRIGHT ACTUALLY, THOUGH I'M A BIT BIAS 'COS I KNOW A LOT OF PEOPLE IN IT."

DO YOU STILL POSSESS ANY OF THE MYTHICAL SPIRIT OF '76?   "YES, I THINK SO"

ALL TIME TOP FIVE B.A.D FEATURE FILM FAVOURITES?

"NO 1 'ZULU' NO 2 'SCARFACE' NO 3 'MY FAIR LADY' I'M TRYING NOT TO BE TOO OBVIOUS HERE NO 4 'HEAVENS GATE' AND NO 5 'ONCE UPON A TIME IN THE WEST'"

'CARRY ON' FILMS — CHEAP SEXUAL EXPLOTATION OR IMPORTANT SOCIAL DOCUMENTS?

"CARRY ON B.A.D IS THE SORT OF FILM I'D LIKE TO MAKE. AN OLD FILM, BUT AS I CAN'T I'D HAVE TO MAKE A TACKY FILM INSTEAD."

CARRY ON CONSTABLE WAS ON THIS AFTERNOON...

"YEAH 'CARRY ON PLOD' I LIKE IT!

KENNETH WILLIAMS IS AN IMPORTANT FIGURE ON THE SCENE"

DO YOU SEE YOURSELVES AS WORLD COMMENTATORS OR WORLD CHANGERS?

"NEITHER. I'M TRYING TO SIMPLIFY IT SO EVERYONE CAN UNDERSTAND. IT ALL STARTS AT HOME, AND THEN YOU TRY AND GET IT ALL IN PERSPECTIVE. YOU HAVE TO THINK OF THIS COUNTRY'S PROBLEMS FIRST AND THEN IN RELATION TO THE REST OF THE WORLD, BUT I DON'T SIT AT HOME THINKING'OH MY GOD WHAT ARE WE GONNA DO NOW' ABOUT THE CURRENT SITUATION IN SWAHILILAND, YOU'D EXPLODE. YOUR HEAD EXPLODES IF YOU THINK TOO MUCH."

"I DIDN'T LIKE EITHER OF THOSE. 'COMMENTATOR' SOUNDS LIKE DAVID COLEMAN AND AS FOR 'WORLD CHANGER' YOU MUST NEVER SAY YOU'RE ONE OF THOSE"

"I JUST WANT TO MAKE A BIT OF A SCENE! THERE'S A BIT OF CHANGE GOING ON, I JUST WANT TO BRING IT TOGETHER. YOU CAN ONLY CHANGE THE INDIVIDUAL NOT THE WAY THINGS ARE. BUT WE'LL ALWAYS GET LIP SERVICE FROM THE GOVERNMENT."

BUT IN A WAY YOU'RE GIVING LIP SERVICE TO PEOPLE WHO DON'T WANT IT FROM THE GOVERNMENT. YOU'RE A POLITICIAN IN A WAY.

"NO, I DON'T LOOK AT MYSELF LIKE THAT. I LOOK AT MYSELF AS A SONGWRITER IN A GROUP AND TRY TO KEEP IT LIKE THAT. I DON'T WANT THAT RESPONSIBILTY THRUST UPON ME. WHAT WE SHOULD DO IS TRY AND INSPIRE OTHER PEOPLE BY TALKING ABOUT IT. ALL WE CAN BE IS AN EXAMPLE, I'M JUST AN EXAMPLE, I PLAY MY GUITAR AND SING MY SONGS, AND THAT'S WHERE I CAN DO MOST GOOD. IF IT'S AN INSPIRATION TO OTHERS, GETS PEOPLE MOTIVATED, THAT'S A START AT LEAST."

IT'S ALSO A MISCONCEPTION ABOUT THE AMERICANA IDEA OF B.A.D, A LOT OF STUFF LIKE HANK WILLIAMS, FARREN YOUNG, PATSY CLINE REALLY STRIKES ME AS GENUINE, HEARTFELT STUFF, AND THAT'S WHAT I'M TRYING TO DO."

"I DISCRIMINATE BETWEEN WHAT'S GOOD, AND WHAT'S BULLSHIT, MACDONALD'S IS BULLSHIT, MIAMI VICE IS BULLSHIT, EVEN THOUGH I QUITE LIKE IT."

YOU SAID THIS TIME LAST YEAR 'I FEEL INCREDIBLEY LUCKY TO HAVE HAD A SECOND CHANCE'. HAVE YOU USED THAT CHANCE THE BEST YOU COULD, OR ARE THERE THINGS YOU MAY HAVE DONE DIFFERENTLY?

"I STILL FEEL LUCKY, WE'VE BUILT UP A GREAT FOLLOWING.

SOMETHING'S
HAPPENING BEYOND B.A.D. WE'VE SET UP A CLUB. WHEN WE FIND ANOTHER GOOD VENUE WE'LL DO IT AGAIN. THAT'S PART OF THE IDEA OF THE SCENE"

"LONDON'S BEEN GOOD TO US, WHEREAS USUALLY THEY DON'T WANT TO SEE YOU DO THAT WELL. OVER THE YEAR IT'S JUST GROWN, WE CAN GO UP NORTH AND THERE'S A CREW UP THERE. THEY SEE US AS AN ALTERNATIVE TO ALL THE STRAIGHT STUFF. THE STUFF YOU GET IN THE 'SUN', WHICH IS BASICALLY FOR YOUNG DICK-HEADS AND AIRHEADS."

THAT PAPER IS DANGEROUS, NOT JUST DICKHEADS AND AIRHEADS BUY IT. PEOPLE BUY IT 'COS IT'S A LAUGH', AND THAT'S EVEN MORE DANGEROUS BECAUSE THEY'RE TAKING IN THE MESSAGE ON A SUB-CONSIOUS LEVEL.

"YEAH, AND THEY START TALKING LIKE IT, AND PRETTY SOON WE'RE ALL LOONY LEFTIES."

WHAT ABOUT THE NEW ADVERTS, IT'S ALL HAMBURGERS AND AMERICAN FOOTBALL?

"I HAVE NOTICED ON THE LAST TWO TOURS UP AND DOWN THE COUNTRY, IT'S GETTING MORE LIKE AMERICA OUT THERE IN A HORRIBLE WAY. BIG SIGNS FOR HAMBURGERS CREEPING UP. IT'S NOT A CONSPIRACY BUT ALL THINGS FIT TOGETHER; THE GOVERNMENT'S A CERTAIN WAY, SO IN ORDER TO FIT INTO THAT THEY'VE GOT TO HAVE CERTAIN TELEVISION PRESENTERS WITH THE SAME OPINIONS, AND PAPERS THAT WRITE THAT LINE, AND EVERYTIME YOU MENTION A 'LEFTIE' NOW IT'S A 'LOONY LEFTIE', YOU KNOW 'LOONY, LEFTIE, LOFTY' WHICH IS REALLY SAD, AND ANYONE TRYING TO DO SOMETHING IS TORN DOWN BY THIS WHOLE SYSTEM, WHERE 'WOGAN' FITS IN, THATCHER'S THERE, AND FUCKING MURDOCH. I DON'T BUY THE 'SUN' AND I WISH NO-ONE ELSE WOULD AND THEY'D BE FUCKED RIGHT OFF."

BUT CAN'T YOU USE YOUR POSITION TO CHANGE PEOPLE'S MINDS?

"I'M NOT THERE TO COMMENTATE, BUT IN A WAY WHAT THEY'RE DOING AT WAPPING IS A WASTE OF TIME. YOU CAN'T FIGHT THAT SORT OF TECHNOLOGY, YOU HAVE TO NOW THINK IN TERMS, AND THIS IS SOMETHING THE GOVERNMENT NEVER MAKES ANY ALLOTMENT FOR, AND THAT'S WHAT ARE PEOPLE GOING TO DO WITH THEIR LEISURE TIME. NOT THE STIGMA OF NOT HAVING A JOB. FUCK ALL THAT, I DON'T WANNA WORK IN FUCKING PRINT WORK OR A COALMINE ALL MY LIFE, AND I DON'T WANT TO FIGHT TO HAVE MY CHILDREN IN THAT SHITTY LIFE. I WANT TO DO SOMETHING WITH ALL THIS SPARE TIME I'M GETTING."

SO DO YOU THINK UNEMPLOYMENT CAN HAVE A GOOD SIDE IN THAT IT BRINGS COMMUNITIES TOGETHER?
"NO, IT DOES NO GOOD. PEOPLE JUST THINK 'IT'S NO GOOD, I AINT GOT A JOB, I'VE GOT NO MONEY'. IF IT'S A QUESTION OF SURVIVAL YOU DON'T THINK 'OH WELL MAYBE THE GOVERNMENT BLAH BLAH AND THE SYSTEM' YOU JUST THINK 'WHERE AM I GOING TO GET THE NEXT MEAL FROM, WHAT AM I GOING TO DO,' ON THE POINT OF DESPERATION... I'VE GOT ALL AIREY IDEAS, I'M NOT QUALIFIED TO COMMENT. I'M IN A PRIVILIGED POSITION."

P.T.O.

BUT YOU COULD USE THAT PRIVILIGED POSITION TO TRY AND CHANGE THINGS.

"IN A WAY THOSE YOUNG PEOPLE ARE A LOST GENERATION.   THE GENERATION AFTER MY LOT ARE LOST AND ARE GOING TO SUFFER FOR IT, AND I DON'T KNOW WHAT TO DO ABOUT IT.   THE NEXT LOT OF KIDS ARE GOING TO HAVE IT A BIT SUSSED OUT.   I'M BECOMING PART OF THE LOST GENERATION AS WELL.   IF I'D JUST DONE MY PUNK BIT I'D BE PART OF HISTORY, BUT I'M COMING OUT INTO THE LIMBO-ZONE WITH YOU LOT."

WHEN WAS THE LAST TIME YOU WENT TO THE PICTURES AND PAID, AND WHAT DID YOU SEE?

"I ALWAYS PAY, I ALWAYS PAY FOR MY RECORDS AS WELL, EVEN IF I B' SOMETHING AND IT'S A RIP-OFF I CAN FEEL RIGHTFULLY INDIGNANT ABOU IT!   THE LAST FILM I SAW WAS 'SALVADOR' A GREAT FILM."

DID YOU GET INVOLVED IN ROCK AND ROLL TO CHANGE THE WORLD OR FOR T' DIRTY BIRDS AND DRUGS?

"... TO IMPROVE MY SOCIAL STANDING..."

credits; organization: Starski and T-ic
photos : cymon' I know why that didn't come out 'Eck
cartoons; Monsieur DAVID 'geordie Bastard' Li

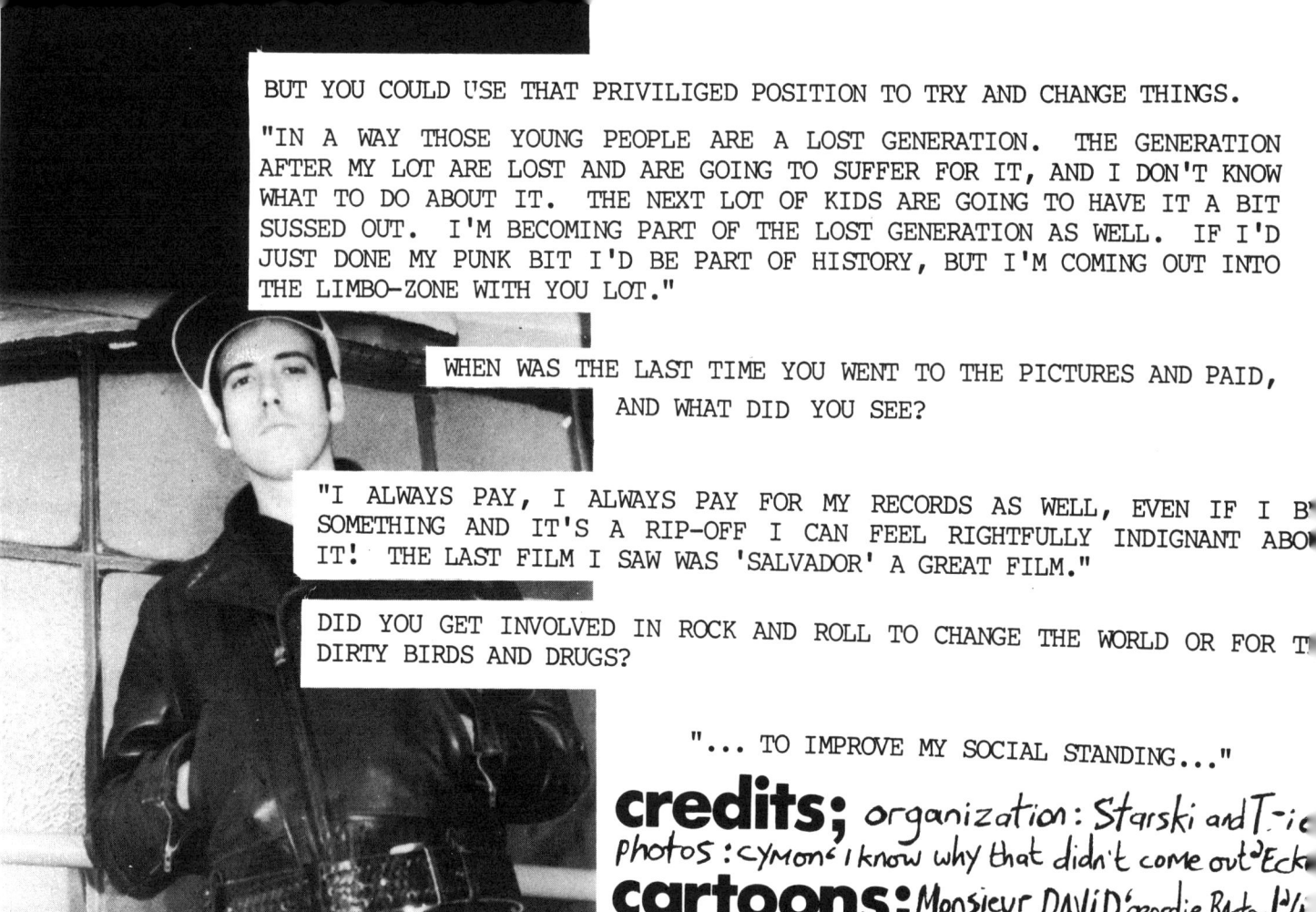

ROCKLEY style & sand.

Despite driving around Poole for ages and getting a different direction from every yokel asked, we finally arrived at Rockley Sands, a Soul Weekend away not to be confused with a Soul Weekender, confused?

We were greeted by Jay Strongman still playing Lyn Collins' "Think" and a lack of drugs. The dancers were a mix of soul boys and the Raw club (circa '84) look of the urban slurgans, a long way from Caister perhaps but also just as far away from any new scene that had been hinted at. What Rockley lacked (no not drugs) was the something that made Caister brilliant (for some) and that something that makes the real West End lowlife so hard (also for some). What we ended up with was a large group of people wearing MA1 jackets desperately trying to hide their Caister past.

Highlights of the weekend were the excellent "Bouncers" drama, Tongy playing the Fly Boys, Holloway dropping Carly Simon and the two fashion victims who danced all nite with just a bottle of poppers and black tights, black adder 3. Good serious music was played by the respected Bob Jones and Giles peterson, new DJ additions, the Bagel Boys, "Sovvy" the Boilerhouse Boys Ben and Andy were stuck on at a moody mid-morning spot, so their time will have to come or at least that's what their PR company tells us.

Credit must go to Nicky Holloway for sticking his neck out and doing something a little way different. Come October Rockley Sands, I believe, will find its feet and own identity. Check it, it may surprise you.

FARLEY.

SAYING OF THE MONTH 2 "PINT OF, DOWN THE LAMB AND"
(ANYBODY IN A CERTAIN JAMES ST. BOOZER OVER THE WEEKEND)

THE ANTI≈SOCIAL BEHAVIOUR PAGE.

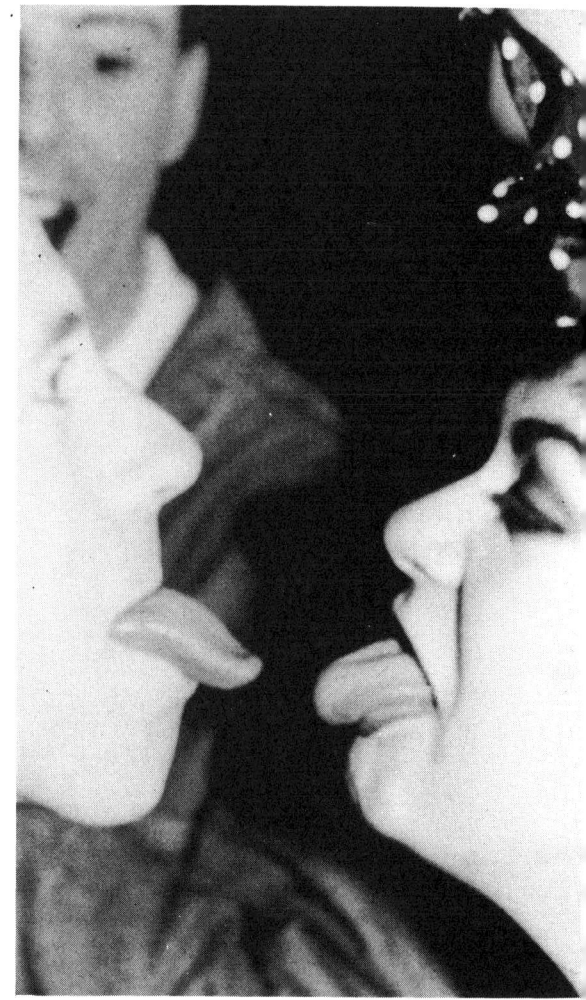

•REMEMBER kidS •AlwAys WeAr
A SURGiCAL

Mad LEEds Utd. SupporterS Hire A Van
to get To WembLEy • N.b. THis picture
Taken BeForE the Coventry Result WAS' HEA
" Fuck it, were COMiNG. ANyWAY YOU NO (
SOUTHErN NANCY BOyS" — Leeds SUppOrterS

"On tonight's
Packed show we
have the first Y.T.S.
doorwoman, MR. S. Duck
Popular entrepeneUr,
And A veRy LARGE
ColoURED GENtleman.
Special guest: A member of
the Boy's Own editoriAl
staff FormAtion liggiNG
teAM "

SiMoN DEE's secret
LoveChild trys to get
down to SOME Serious' REAduiG.

THE SOCIAL ≈ AWARENESS PAGE...

SUNDAY EVENING AT THE ANARCHISTS' CLUB IN BERNERS STREET, E.:
" ' Awake, ye men who toil !—Up, proletarians ! '—followed by groans for the Capitalists and heers for Karl Marx, the German Socialist writer who is now a refugee living in London"

private enterprise goes apeshit crazy£

"POLITICS DON'T AFFECT ME"

I'M GOING OVERGROUND
(how the soul was sold....)

While mainstream London 'Solid Souled' and surburban soulboy 'foamed' at yet another weekender, something unexpected happened at the hub of London's clubland. The 'Warehouse' party was now with us. This was a breakaway faction of young, bored clubbers doing their own thing. Here we had a rave that was fresh, fashionable, daring... A rave that was safe from the wedgeheaded wallies and East End, high heeled dolly birds who frequented the capital's tack holes at weekends.

be the Wag's Heavy Duty DJs Paul Guntrip, Dave Henley and Justin Langland, the Rivertown band Giant, the outrageous You You You and further surprises. What more could you need to know? Trains: half-hourly from Victoria; B&B: Call Angie at the Zap Club (0273-727880) for the local low-down; Beer and Booze: all-day license on Saturday...It's so easy... **Jivers** do it in the city. Another all-dayer (also featuring an all-day bar) comes on Monday courtesy of the energetic **Tom Ingram**. Hot on the heels of the successful all-dayer at the Clarendon recently comes this bank holiday special concentrating on the talents of some of the country's best Real Rock 'n' Roll DJs...

At the time of going to press **Stallions** (437 0047) and the **Fifty Club** (437 8973) are closed pending their licenses being renewed. You are strongly advised to phone the clubs in advance if you're planning a visit as Jacko doesn't know whether they'll be back in action yet...
Jacko Clubs

★ — a one-off or occasional event.
NEW! — A one-nighter during it's first month of operation.

WEDNESDAY 15

★**The Elle Party** at the Limelight. £7, 9.30pm-3am. This night has not been confirmed — Phone 434 1761 for further details.

Cafe de Paris 3 Coventry St, WC1 (437 ░░░6) Piccadilly Circus/Leicester Sq tubes. Me░░ £5. 9.30am-3am. A beautiful ░ ░r 80's style-merchants ░ DJ Albert ░░░

THURSDAY

★**The Raid** at the Wag. £4, 10.30pm-3.░ Gary and Paul storm back to the Wag, loa░ down with extra hi-fi hardware for a real u░. House party with Pete Tong, Terry Farley and Paul Oakenfold spinning a mix of solid hip-hop, go-go and hard funk rhythms to a trendy B-Boy/Girl crowd.

NEW! **Across the Tracks** at Dingwalls. £3 mems, £4 guests. 9pm-2.30am. DJ Simon Goffe aims to go 'across the tracks' of musical conservatism, bringing together soul, jazz, hou░ R&B, hip-hop, rap and rare grooves: diverse ░ rhythms for the musically radical. There's a raffle and prizes and tonight he's joined by ░ Nite FM 'Mad on Jazz' DJ Gilles Peterson.

Ascension at Maximus. £4. 10.30am-3am. ░ host Tony Gordon returns to Maximus wit░ similar trash/funk/disco faves and high-fashio░ mix with DJs Mark Lawrence and guests.

NEW! **Big Willies Soul Situation** at Roxannes. £4. 10pm-2.30am. Real Soul boys Max and Chris spin Tamla, Philly, Stax and other classic soul trax from the '60s to the '80s.

Blitz Ball at Crazy Larry's. £4. 9pm-2am. Comfortable, trendy Sloaney disco-bar-restaurant with DJs Ken Hume and Steve James mixing soul and funk faves, '60s and pop rock on the decks. No jeans, trainers etc.

★**Big Bad Thursday** at the Limelight. £7, ░.░░ ░ ░░░ Following their successful ░░ ░imelight ░░

For those in the know, the warehouse party was now a place where you could jig around like a nutter all night, blag a Sloane if you wanted to, and generally get smashed on good gear. (Oh bliss!) The revellers would come from all social circles. Mad Punks; Sloanes, lazy college liggers and clued up yardies could all be found raving together in some rundown, empty factory or warehouse in areas such as Kings X, Docklands, Southwark or even below Paddington Station. They would all be getting down to solid Funk; Tamla, James Brown, hard reggae (not the commercial shit) and Hip-Hop. Fucking brilliant! These parties proved to be the salvation of London trendies and 'lost' soulboys who'd given up West End clubs as a bad joke, for they now had somewhere to rave all night long in wild and sometimes dangerous surroundings (often with no bogs) cheap booze (or you brought your own). Great sound systems, good visuals and above all, hard core sounds played in an unpretentious way by young, virtually unknown DJ's. All this for a couple of quid. Fucking safe!

For the last couple of years, these parties had gone on virtually undetected by Joe Public (thank fuck!), mainly because news of them was spread by word of mouth and safe selective ticketing. Crews such as 'Shake 'n' Finger Pop' and 'Soul to Soul' rose to prominence with the emergence of these great but illegal parties. But now, what with the Old Bill heavily on the case (armed with info on the whereabouts of such parties happily supplied by fucked up club owners) and joe became increaingly aware of what was happening by tuning in to pirate stations such as Kiss FM, they were forced to keep a low one for a while.

Depending on location and promotion, top crews could pull as many as 2,000 punters to their jams on a Saturday night. Moody 'jams' became more frequent (many were bollocks) and the inevitable happened, a lot were raided and some were shut down even before they fucking started (what a piss off). This action resulted in crews looking to more legitimate venues to stage their parties.

During this period 'safe' crews such as the 'RAID' boys (who did legal venues) and 'Shake 'n' Finger Pop' to name a few were among the few teams who successfully managed to recreate the original warehouse atmosphere (remember the 'RAID' party at Riverside Studios and 'Shake 'n' Finger Pop/Family Function' at the Town and Country Club) at club level. The raves were again catering for London's style and fashion concious, flat top trendy, and clued up clubber.(Thank fuck!)

★Bournemouth Easter All-Dayer at Co-Cos, Hinton Rd, Bournemouth. £6, 12 noon-1am. More soul, jazz and funk from local and London DJs Chris Dinnis, Nick Power, Bob Povey and guests. Call DJ Graham T ... details

NIGHTLIFE PLACES
Africa Centre 38 King St, Covent Garden tube.
Empire Douglas ... ross tube/BR/L ... Marte

★ — a one-off or occasional event.
NEW! — A one-nighter during it's first month of operation.

The danger is that now the whole underground/warehouse scene is no l nger underground. Why? Because moody crews, snide DJ's looking for instant cred, lack of good suitable venues and the invasion of nonses (Arrghh!) has helped fuck up (yet again) a once safe scene (shame). Meanwhile Joe's now bought himself the 'uniform'. You know; those bloody black flight jackets, Doc Martens (oh no) ripped his FU's (well they wouldn't be 501's would they?) and boogies on down in the raves convinced he's a trendy (silly cunt!). Oh for the days of Dockland and Bear Wharf!! So the next time you go to a warehouse party in Harlesden, Leyton or anywhere else think twice, you could be stuck in a rave full of posse and whistles, being mugged off on your draw and deafened by an ex yardie sound with distorted mid range playing the latest white label bootlegs.

NORMAN JAY

SPECIAL BRANCH

ROCKLEY SANDS, POOLE, DORSET.
OCT - 16, 17, 18. - '87

AT THIS STAGE IN THE SHOW I WOULD LIKE TO INTRODUCE A NEW MEMBER OF THE BAND. IN ISSUE 2 AS YOU ALL NO DOUBT REMEMBER WE TOOK YOU TO THE HEADY LITERARY HEIGHTS WITH "UNCLE STEVEN'S POETRY CORNER", AND CONTINUING IN THAT GREAT MIND EXPANDING TRADITION WE BRING YOU WHAT IS HOPEFULLY THE FIRST OF MANY CRITIQUES WRITTEN BY A MAN WHOSE HOSPITALITY YOU HAVE ALL NO DOUBT ENJOYED OVER THE PAST X YEARS. I REFER, OF COURSE, TO MR CHRIS SULLIVAN, POPULAR CHANTEUSE AND YOUNG PEOPLE'S DISCOTHEQUE ORGANISER. SO IT'S A LARGE BOY'S OWN WELCOME TO...

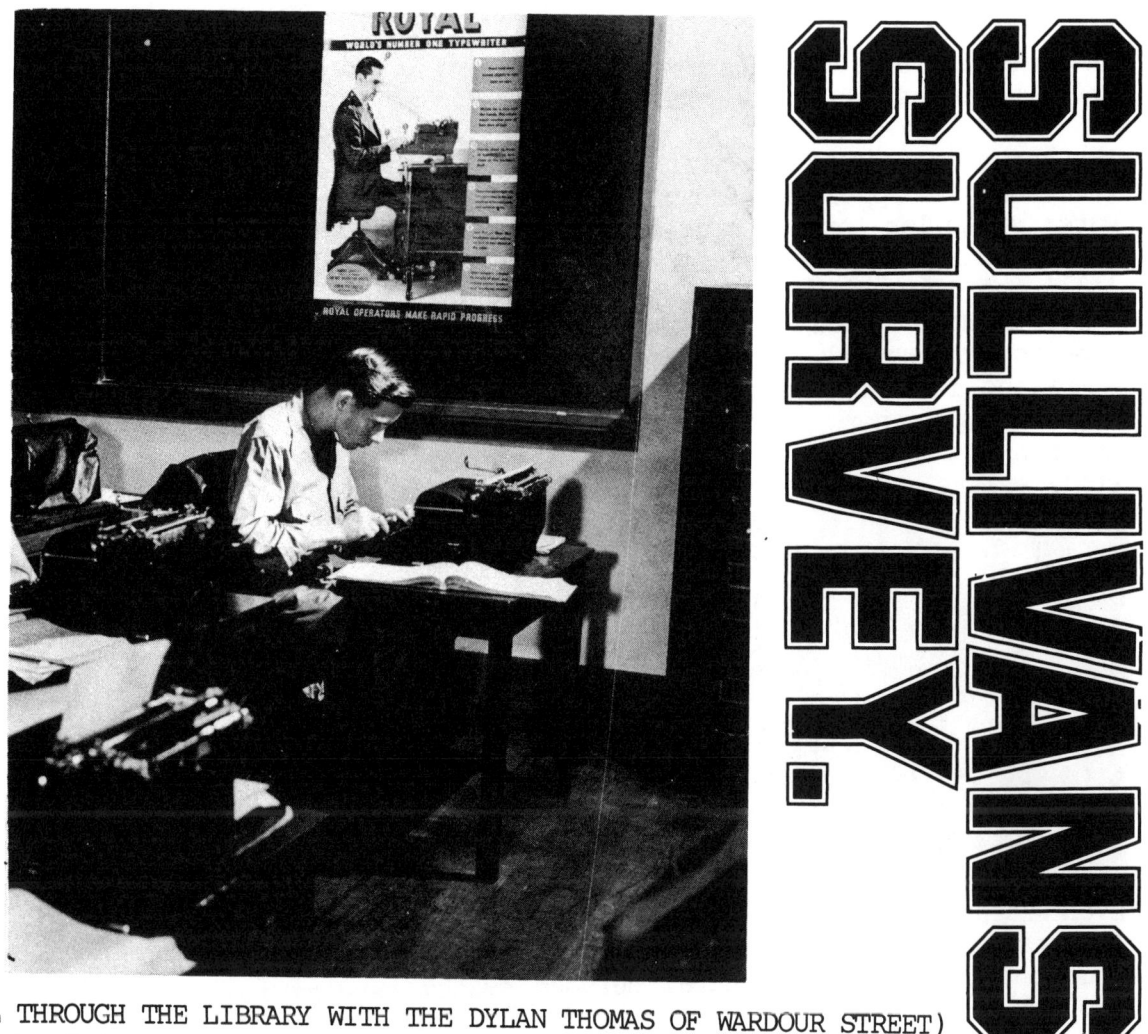

SULLIVANS SURVEY.

(A STROLL THROUGH THE LIBRARY WITH THE DYLAN THOMAS OF WARDOUR STREET)

№1, IN THE BELLY OF THE BEAST.

On reading this most worthy of periodicals I was struck by the notion that what was needed was a brisk, informative, but carefully selected and recommended book review section. After all a book unlike a record does not take forty minutes to complete, and it is a bit late after four hundred pages to decide you don't like it. So for all you people who like a good read (which must be all of you otherwise you wouldn't be reading this) here's the first of hopefully many recommended book critiques.

When faced with this task I could either pick my most recent read or my favourite, but I'll pick neither and go for what I think would kindle a spark in your intellect whether it be malignant or otherwise. The first therefore is "In the Belly of The Beast" (Letters from prison) by Jack Henry Abbott, who at the age of twelve was committed to the Utah State Industrial School for Boys for "failure to adjust to foster homes" and was released five years later Abbott was charged with murdering one inmate and wounding another in a fight behind bars and tried receiving an "indeterminate term" of three to twenty years, good behaviour determining the length of his sentence – the assumption being that no-one serves the full sentence. A wrong assumption in Abbott's case, who at the age of twenty six escaped to commit his one serious crime against free society – a bank robbery.

In short Mr Abbott went on to serve light years of porridge, fourteen or fifteen years in solitary and enjoyed only nine months of freedom between the age of twelve and thirty seven. Therefore Mr Abbott suffered two-fold, once at the hands of the penal system and secondly at the hands of a curious dichotomy. Having spent all of his formative years under the scrutiny of the state penal system and living under the rules set by both prison and prisoners where to back down is to die and not to is also to die in yet another more horrible sense. The punishment meted out by the penal system and described in the book are horrible even to the most phobia-free individual but even more horrendous for the claustrophobic Abbott, spending months at a time in a room designed to supply complete darkness where a mechanism has been installed so that the feeding of the incarcerated denies him the smallest chink of light.

Another instrument of denial is the 'strip cell' where the prisoner receives the opposite of total darkness in a concrete room with no water or toilet (except a hole in the middle of the floor stained with urine and fecal matter of former detainees). The bare lightbulb is on 'all' the time, there is no bed, no bunk and the inmate has to request water from the guard (you may gather that the inmate is reduced to begging for water). All there is is the stench of shit and piss emanating from the open hole without the flush. What, you may ask, might a prisoner do to receive such treatment. The answer is anything, a contraband book, a stolen sandwich, and the strip cell still exists today.

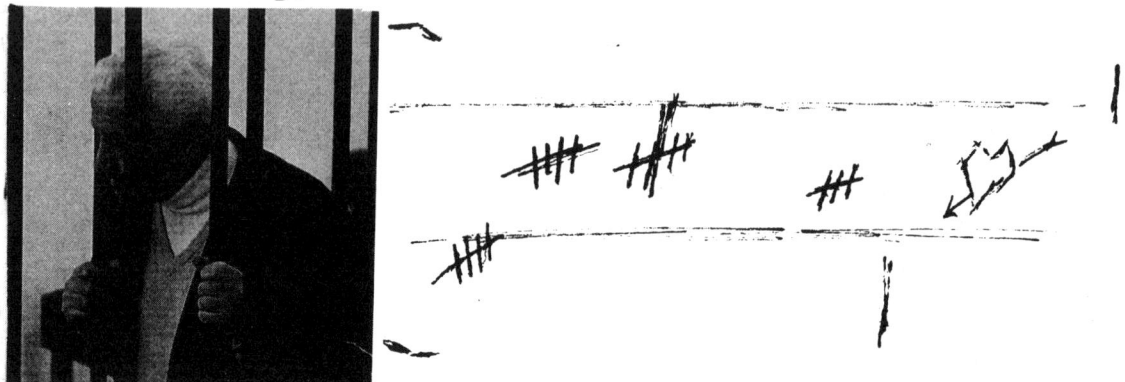

Even after such punishment Abbott still could not conform to the rigours of prison life and was promptly injected with Thorazine, a drug that attacks the central nervous system sending its victim into violent spasms, wracking the body from within. Even after this and ten times the prescribed time in starvation cells Abbott survived and what's more created. After years of solitary, depravation of light and food Abbott gourged himself on page after page of literature, Marx, Engels, Schopenhauer, Nietsche etc etc. Like any full vessel he overflowed and Abbott's flow took the form of letters to Henry Mailer who at the time was writing the "Executioners Song". Explaining and retelling the story of punishments, physically and mentally, that are doled out to him, his impartial view is all the more remarkable as he is the subject. His rhetoric though is impeachable. In his suffering he is obviously stunned by the prolonged cruelty of the system and even as a double murderer appears as a novice in the sadist sweepstakes.

His crimes both the result of aggresion toward him appear tiny to the prolonged and continued sickness of the 'Beast' and he articulates while we doubt even the literacy of the screws. Above all the book carefully illustrates the strength of the human mind over the system. An intellectual Papillion without the romance or exotic location.

"In the Belly of the Beast" dallies with the once complex world of philosophy and propounds a watertight political and penal theory. I read it in a day and so will you.

Chris Sullivan

HOLIDAYS
IN
THE
SUN.

Time is fast approaching when the eager Sun Seeker can start licking their lips in anticipation of his or her forthcoming Summer holiday, those dark nights of last Winter shifting endlessly through holiday brochures trying to decide whether to go to those tourist traps of Greece or Spain for two weeks of sun filled, fun filled frolics (starting to sound like a tour rep).

It doesn't matter whether you sell insurance, stack bricks or fill shelves, these boring menial jobs are easily forgotton as our Sun Seeker packs their bags and heads for the departure lounge. In the departure lounge we get a good indication of the type of Sun Seeker that is jetting off to meet our European friends and spend, spend, spend. The normally quiet atmosphere of the destination lounge is throbbing to the beat of disco music. Yes the holidaymakers have arrived with their portable cassette players, not forgetting the Level 42 tapes. We meet many groups of young people adorned in Hawaiian shirts and those awful dark glasses (phoney Ray-Bans).

Then there are the girls normally in packs of 10 or more talking in loud South London tones and then giggling quite deliriously at the thought of the old currant bun. We mustn't forget those long haired beaut types - baggy trousers, espadrilles and cut off T shirts. It looks like the solarium courses paid off lads!

The worst of this sorry bunch is the professional beer man, fat stomach and Union Jack shorts with the obligatory Hitler World Tour T shirts. It's hard to miss these cretins as they are normally pissed up and singing 'here we go, here we go' or 'we're all off to sunny Spain'. They seem to think they are the epitome of British masculinity (whatever that is).

Let's now have a look at the resorts themselves as the Boy's Own staff have wandered amongst the best and worst Spain has to offer a friendly tourist. One must disregard certain parts of Spanish life ie the gun toting Guardia Circl, dirty streets, noisy motorbikes and cars and any frosty stares from the locals.

Anyway let's get back to the main reason for this article. The boys have settled in to the same boring routine, pushing fully clothed people into the pool, showing the white spotty bum to howls of laughter - very funny I must say. Night time is when the fun really starts in this den of iniquity. Drinks are consumed and all sorts of strange things happen, ie the blokes in particular (Londoners) seem to talk in exaggerated tones - 'alright babes' or 'yeah sweet luv'. The funniest thing with these Cockneys half of them come from Basingstoke or Braintree (very London indeed!)

Mind you it's when the blokes get together the next day and start conversing about the previous nights encounter - 'Course I blagged a sweet richard last night' or the classic 'I pulled a sweet malt'. It seems one has to be bi-lingual these days.

pto

We mustn't forget those loveable Northerners who keep up the fine tradition of pissed up holiday makers abroad, shouting the usual sexist and racist banter. Some people never learn!

I am afraid the girls must come in for a bit of stick as they only seem to come to life at night in the bars and clubs playing with their curly perms, twiddling with their chewing gum and drinking cocktails they can't pronounce and trying to talk like Lorraine Chase (whoever that is!)

When surveying the scene one can see that 'Chelsea Girl' and 'Next' have done a roaring trade in their Summer line - very sad indeed. All these resorts are the same, the names might change but the places don't. What the attraction is I don't know. One could write all day about the pitfalls of a doomsville holiday resort but magazine space is short, so I leave you with a short message. "BE CAREFUL OUT THERE PEOPLE"
"DICKHEADS ARE MORE DANGEROUS THAN AIDS"

A TEN POINT GUIDE TO A DOOMSVILLE RESORT

1.   PHONY RAY-BANS (AND THE REAL ONES)
2.   DRUNKEN SCOTS WITH THE SCOTTISH TEAM JERSEY ON
3.   MEETING MORE THAN THREE GIRLS CALLED DEBS OR TRACEY
4.   UNION JACKS HUNG OVER BALCONIES
5.   MORE THAN FIVE IN A HIRE JEEP

UNCLE ANDREW'S - 5 GEETAR GREATS

Jesus & The Mary Chain - Kill Surf City
Gaye Bikers On Acid - Nosedive (E.P.)
Dwight Yokam - Little Ways
Led Zeppelin - Dazed And Confused
Die Young (E.P.) - Metro-Trinity

SHAKE 'N' FINGER POP'S RECOMMENDED GROOVES.

1. TOMMY STEWART   - BUMP AND HUSTLE MUSIC- ABRAXIS.
2. MARVA WHITNEY   - ANSWER TO MOTHER POPCORN- PEOPLE.
3. BARBARA RANDOLPH-CAN'T I GET A WITNESS- TAMALA.
4. MELBA MOORE   - PROMISED LAND- BUDDHA.
5. LORETTA HOLLOWAY- RUNAWAY- SALSOUL.

KEEP YOUR EARS AND FEET READY FOR A VERY YOUNG AND VERY HOT
FUNK POSSEE SENDING SCALPING PARTIES INTO THE WEST-END FROM THE
WILDS OF NEW CROSS GATE, CALLED 'THE FUNK COMITTEE'. THEY
CROP UP ANYWHERE FROM THE HARP CLUB TO THE AFRICA CENTER.
THANKS FOR THE TAPE BILLY- SHIT HOT!

stephen

WHOMP THAT SUCKER

THURZDAYs

War.

DJ, ROKA, & BOBBY.

AFTER THE MEGA SUCCESS OF WESTWORLD 3, THE BEST NIGHT OUT
MONTH LOOKS LIKE BEING THE BEASTIE BOYS AFTER GIG-LIG, THE
VENUES A BADLY KEPT SECRET, ALL WE KNOW IS THAT THE RAID B(
HAVE THEIR STICKY FINGERS IN THE PIE. SPEAKING OF THE RAID
CLUB, THE BIG BASH IN JUNE LOOKS LIKE BEING THE RAID ALL-
NIGHTER AT THE SCALA PICTURE HOUSE, KINGS CROSS.
CHECK IT OUT, MAAN!!!

"I WAS A TEENAGE ANORAKSIC"
or 'HOW I WAS HYPNOTIZED BY THE VOICE OF THE BEEHIVE'

Parked the motor. Me and the lens-man surveyed the scene. It was
anorak heaven alright. Earnest young men and women milled around the
front door trying their hardest to show that they were having no truck
with the vagaries of fashion. I, however, knew better, especially
when I spied the Rolls-Royce of anoraks, the Demob red needle-cord
with yellow and black checks. Me and lens-man finally fought our way
past the overgrown Enid Blyton characters and into the dressing
room... There it was, Rock n' Roll carnage. Several tins of lager
and ... ham sandwiches.

The band sat around the small room and eyed us quickly before we began
our interrogation. There was Mr Bedford, the classically attired
bass-man, drafted in from top beat combo 'Madness'. Missing was his
rythmn twin Daniel 'Woody' Woodgate. The two of them were Camdens Sly
& Robbie, with considerably less hair. The mean, moody, and extremely
silent guitar picker Mr Carr stayed mean, moody and silent. Tracey
and Melissa Beehive sat resplendant in charity shop psychedelia. It
was their show alright ...

So, how did you meet your rythmn section?

  "Boring!"

Sorry, but we'd like to know who the mutual

friend was.

"OK, it was Dave Balfe" (Food Records supremo

Do you agree with the description

'Madness, Rezillos, B52's?

"Yeah, sounds good to us"

Are you worried about becoming a 'novelty' act?

"No. We're too intelligent for that,
    we wouldn't let anyone turn us
    into a novelty act"

What if you were offered thousands of pounds to appear on Top of the
Pops singing an old Shangri-La's number?

"For a start I like the Shangri-La's, I'd also like to be on Top of
the Pops, I'd also like several thousands of pounds! I would however
draw the line at going on Top of the Pops wearing leather gear,
singing a Madonna song."

What are your plans for world domination?

"Shit ... Well we've got a gig tomorrow. That's about as far as we've
planned really"

Are you worried by the fact that some people will react to you by saying 'let's go and see that band with the two blokes from Madness in it'?

Mr Bedford:
"No. It doesn't really bother me, as long as they come and see us for whatever reason they'll soon realise it's a good band whoever's in it. Anyway I'm leaving after the next two gigs."

To do what?

"Dunno"

Fair enough ... Does politics enter your life or work?

"Of course. Just getting up in the morning and entering the world invovles you in politics. Living in London is all about politics, it effects everything you do. We just don't particularly write political songs though."

Does acid enter your life or work?

"Acid? Just because I'm wearing these trousers... No!"

If you had a choice of record producer and video director who would you work with?

"David Byrne, for a record and video. Oh and Hugh Jones."

How about Lee Thompson, Mr Bedford? "Not particularly. He was just the chap in Madnes most interested in video."

Finally a flippant question. Do you sew all your own sequins on?
"Oh yes"

Mr Bedford? "Nah, I wear a tiara instead"

And then he departed, leaving me and lens-man talking to the real voices of the beehive. Two extremely likable, Californian girls with a lot of suss. Mr Woodgate missed the interview but joined us later and sat in the top half of a wardrobe. Oh the wacky world of wock and woll. Hope to meet you again one day ladies and then you can give me the dirt on Zodiac Mindwarp. By the time you read this, the voice of the Beehive's first single 'Just a City' would have bubbled in and out of the indie charts. Buy the next one. You won't be disappointed.

' an ex-member of top north London psycho-Bill combo 'Madness', comes out of the closet '

(ooh er, sounded a bit like 'clo ed.

FOOTBALL ∘∘THE FINAL SOLUTION?

Much fuss has been made over Lutons banning of away Supporters from their ground, they have since been barred from the leagues own Challenge Cup Competition, the "Littlewoods Cup".

Odd that the single most effective move to eradicate football violence has been met with such hostility. Segregation, blanket policing and video cameras are all very well, if the thugs are naive enough to fight inside the ground which most of these are not. The Police apparently were relieved when the Leeds fans away ban was lifted, saying it was easier to control the Supporters once they are enclosed in one group inside the ground. This is undoubtedly true, as the vast majority of soccer orientated violence in London occurs away from the ground. These incidents are rarely chance encounters, rather pre-arranged rendezvous often hours before or after the match miles from the ground.

If the Police were to arrest the outlawed away fans as soon as they arrived at their destination, it would not take long for the thugs to get the message. The Police may wish to know what exactly to charge these people with? Causing a disturbance is good enough. Who wants to travel half the length of the country only to be arrested on arrival, locked up for several hours, sent home and then forced back to appear in Court, not even Leeds fans are stupid enough to go through that rigmarole too often.

LONDON football thugs are long past being restricted to feuding at the match alone, ARSENAL and WEST HAM carried out a year long battle along Hackney Road every Friday night. Millwall have a habit of picking off their opponents weeks or months before the match is to take place, tactics which are obviously easier to employ against other London Clubs, as they know where they drink on a Friday or Saturday night. An old custom which has been readopted is going "Up West" following the recent tragic death of a young West Ham Supporter, Millwall Supporters, or rather the bushwackers were reputed to have stabbed six Everton fans the next week, all taking place around Charing Cross.

MILLWALL F.C. may well not exist this time next year, as the League has, oh so subtly, arranged for the team to play five potentially explosive home games in succession, which is bound to trigger some sort of riotous behaviour and give the Powers that be the excuse to close the Den forever. Having read this far, you may think this is the best move all round, you could be right but it might give the disgruntled youth of a massively dilapidated area reason to become even more hostile towards society. Banning Millwall won't stop the problem, South East London will still exist, its large criminal element won't disappear with the football club. If all away support was banned from Millwall, there would be no need to deprive the local people of there trips to Cold Blow Lane. It is likely that the Club would not lose out on revenue, as not many people turn up anyway except for big games, and even then the money is swallowed up by policing the event.

Away supporters travelling, standing in large groups and singing was originated by Celtic and Rangers (Pre-Season and European games). This quickly became adopted by the Lancashire Clubs in the sixties. Later came the Soccer Specials, making it cheaper and jollier for the young thug going to London in the secure knowledge that there are plenty of other lads going with him. After the Special trains came the Police escort from the Station to the ground, over the last ten years the Police have become progressively better at this and have made it near on impossible for supporters to get in to any sort of trouble. The problem is the thugs don't travel on the Special trains or Supporters Coaches. For years now, they've been hiring their own coaches. The joy of this is that after a game up north, you can terrorise small towns on the way back down. Arsenal made the inside pages of one of the tabloids last year when the Northamptonshire Police had to call in Officers from neighbouring Shires to deal with Arsenal thugs running amok in Northampton town centre. A month or so later, the "herd" went back and this time the Police ran out of cells to put them in, after sticking road blocks on all the exit roads. This is nothing new, Chelsea have been doing it for years and only last year were out again terrorising Blackpool after they had played at Everton.

Banning drink from grounds may seem a sound idea, yet it does not effect
the thug contingent, as most of them don't drink at the game in any case.
The theory that all get drunk and lose control is naive, to say the least.
The point is, banning away supporters from all but finals is the only sure
way to stop soccer violence. The introduction of identity cards for all
male football fans over fifteen years of age and making each Club responsible
for its supporters would possibly make grounds a lot safer, therefore bringing
back those so called missing millions. A total ban on away supporters would
also convice U.E.F.A. that we are serious in our endeavours to eradicate the
problem, and they certainly need convincing. In the possibility of future
Cup ties between West Ham and Real Madrid, it would be up to the Club who they
let in from the Card Carrying Public. The most obvious drawback with the
identity card system is when it is most needed, it becomes useless i.e.
London Derby matches. What is to stop a Chelsea thug getting himself an
entry card for all the other London Clubs? One suspects that the process
could be made so tedious that application to more then one Club would deter
even the most determined thug, it may also have the same effect on Joe Public.
As it also comes down to a massive infringement of his rights as a citizen in
a democratic country, so what else is new. BAN away Supporters, Stop soccer
related violence and transfer it to the High Street.

mick mahoney.

Having spent all my adolescent years in South London, a time when
impressions are made on you and a pride begins to develop within you,
"South London La La La" being the cry as you kick it with divvy out of
London clubs.

I now find myself writing to ask where all the chaps in the area are
going with their ideas. I speak, of course, of how Danny the Boy, who
stands on the halfway line week in week out in his Fiorucci jeans and
Inter Squash trainers, has stopped trying to develop style within
himself but has an extension of himself on the end of a three foot
chain, the staff. He no longer needs to kick it, the dog does it
instead. There is also no need to chat to a 'malt' in Drovers because
he's got an american Pit Bull called Millwall. The dog attracts the
comments of 'isn't he lovely'.

As if this wasn't enough there is also a new development on the
scene. I speak of course about Suzuki Jeeps. Driving past pubs in
the area you can see half a dozen of the Old Kent Road Safari Wagons
parked as close to the pub entrance as possible. Has style gone from
the area completely? I'm glad to say I don't think so, as the girls
seem to be as clued up as ever. People will read this and chuckle,
maybe because they recognise someone they know, or perhaps even
themselves.

I know things won't change yet, but I can still look for something
different. I'm just off to the pet shop to buy a poodle in my Morris
Traveller. By the way I was born an East-Ender, but I don't put it
about... Grant -x-

a letter over from the SOUTH. a London view point.

FOUND THAT SSENCE......

RARE

NUMBER one... RARE

LOCATION,

SOUND, 3 tracks with a sound ranging from a pocket A.B.C. to Prefab Sprout meets Solid Soul. Un-cluttered, but crying out for a hard-edge both lyrically and musically. Soul boy sensibility meets the pop ethic, hardly gonna change the world but might provide it with some pleasant tunes.

Next to the current crop of tasty metal edged sounds available for the discerning punter this may seem a touch insipid. However in the right situation when the last thing you want to hear is the latest Gaye Bikers on Acid 12", and want well structured soul tinted pop, you could do a lot worse than listen to Rare....

FREE GIFT

REMEMBER IN DAYS GONE BY THE SHAME AND HUMILIATION OF BEING TURNED AWAY FROM A CLUB OR RESTAURANT WITH THE WORDS "SORRY SIR, NOT WITHOUT A TIE", RESOUNDING IN YOUR EARS. WELL NOW THE AVID SOCIALITE FACES EMBARASSMENT OF EVEN MORE TROUSER FLARING ENORMITY. IMAGINE THE SHAME WHEN YOU FINALLY REACH THE DOOR OF THE SLOUCHO CLUB OR DROSSKOS AND HEAR THOSE DREAD WORDS "SORRY SIR, NOT WITHOUT SIDEBURNS."

WELL NOW YOU CAN AVOID ALL THAT WITH A PAIR OF 'BOY'S OWN' SOCIAL LIFE ENHANCING SUPER STICK ON SIDIES.

AVAILABLE IN THREE COLOURS THEY ARE A MUST FOR THE SERIOUS TRENDOID. WE PRESENT FOR YOU THE STANDARD '70'S SUPERS' AS A FREE GIFT. BUT WHY STOP AT JUST ONE PAIR, THE CATALOGUE INCLUDES 'JASON WYNGARDE', 'THE RUSTIC', 'THE NORTHERNER', 'THE RHODES BOYSON (WITH FREE MOUSTACHE), AND FOR THE MORE ADVENTUROUS 'THE LEONARD NIMMOY'.

READ WHAT SOME PEOPLE HAVE SAID ABOUT BOY'S OWN STICK ON SIDIES:
"MY CAREER WAS ON THE DOWN SIDE UNTIL I DISCOVERED BOY'S OWN STICK ON SIDIES"
...MIDGE URE   "ABSOLUTELY OVER THE MOON WITH MY BOY'S OWN STICK ON SIDIES"
                ...GEORGE BEST
"BOY'S OWN STICK ON SIDIES ABSOLUTELY CHANGED MY LIFE ...GUV..."
...THAT LOVEABLE COCKNEY GARY KEMP (PLUCKER WITH TOP COMBO THE SPLENDID WALLETS

"FUCK OFF AND DIE"
...CHRISTOS TOLERA

STUD1O
FIFTY THREE.
haircutters.

53A WELLS STREET W.

a hearty goodbye From all the EDITORIAL STAFF....

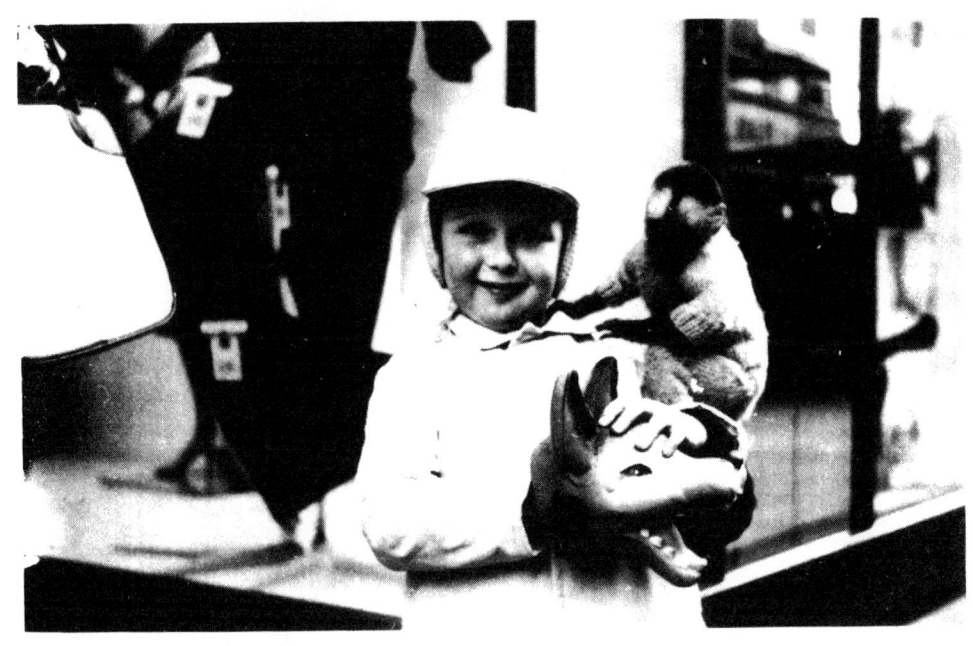

Terry.

terry models the latest collection from one of the newest designer labels, "Alexi Sayle Menswear."

STEVE...
Hat by Demob.
Glasses by N.H.S.
Car by Austin.

Andrew x
plastic spade by Paul Smith.
trunks by Janet Reger.
plastic sandals by Ladybird.

EDITORIAL STAFF : Terry, Steve, Andrew

CONTRIBUTORS : Norman Jay, Grant, The Outsider, Chris Sullivan, Mick Mahoney.

Boys Own welcomes with open arms any contributions. Get involved by sending any photographs, articles, demo tapes, record company promotional gimmicks (especially) to Boys Own, 13 Ilminster Gardens, Clapham Junction, London S.W.11.

Advertising is a frackin' bargain to sell your wares, contact Cymon on

0753 864664.

IF ONLY I'D GONE TO SASSOON'S

WOMEN / MEN: 44 SLOANE ST. 11 FLORAL ST. WOMEN: 130 SLOANE ST. 60 SOUTH MOLTON ST. MEN: 56 BROOK ST.

VIDAL SASSOON

No. 4
Spring 1987

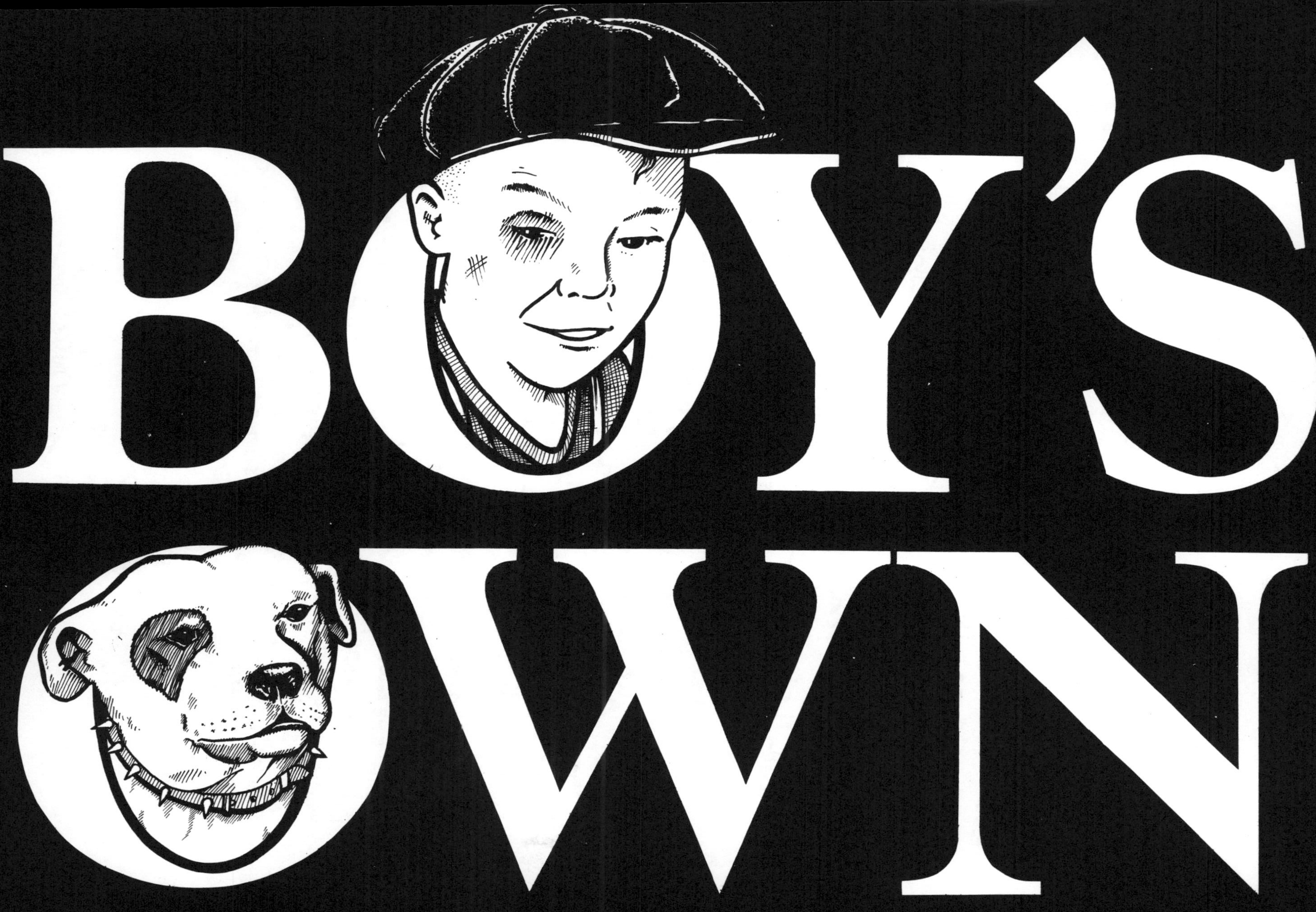
BOY'S
OWN

BOYS OWN ★ ★ ★

'Boy's own, the only fanzine not written by anorak wearers ...

HELLO THERE FLARES WEARERS,

Long time no see, but when you read this bumper fun packed ish I think you'll agree it's been worth the wait.

Since we last spoke we've had our very own discotheque which I believe is very popular with you young people although I found the gramaphone player a touch on the loud side.

Many of our showbiz chums were there and it was quite a, and I think this is the right word, lig. However many people we invited didn't turn up so here is a list of shame, you won't be getting a mention on the guest list at the next do thats for sure!

TERRY WAITE, CHARLIE COTTON, GLORIA HUNNIFORD, JOE PEARCE (WHO INVITED THAT SLAG -ED), BERNIE GRANT, KIETH CHEGWIN, SINBAD FROM BROOKIE, LEIGH BOWERY (OUT BUYING A NEW CRASH HELMET), MAZE'S GIRO, GRIPPER STEBSON ALAN TITCHMARSH, BOB TODD, GRANT (I COULDN'T MAKE IT) GOODGE ANDY SWALLOW, TARBY (PLUS GUEST), CHRIS QUINTEN, MONICA ROSE (MORE 70's CRED -ED), PATSY CLINE, SEARGEANT Br STEVE STWANGE, THE KEMP SISTERS, HARRY THE DOG, THE FOX FAMILY, CHARLIE ENDELL, AND A STAFF BULL TERRIER CALLED TREVOR.

TIL THE NEXT TIME PALS
LOADS OF LERVE

The Outsider
—X—

P.S. LIG OF THE YEAR AWARD · DAMON GRANT'S FUNERAL ·

GIVE US A LINE

FILM OF THE YEAR 1988 AS VOTED BY SCOTLAND YARD'S TACTICAL
FIREARMS UNIT ..... "LETHAL WEAPON" .....
THE SUN SAYS THAT PUBLIC EXECUTIONS OF COCKNEY VILLAINS
IS GREAT. WELL WHAT HAPPENS WHEN SOME SCHOOLKID GETS A
STRAY BULLET IN THE BACK? OF COURSE THE FAMILY WILL BE
ENTITLED TO COMPENSATION. MEANWHILE WHILE THE ACTION'S
LOW THE T.F.V. ARE WATCHING COBRA ON VIDEO, AGAIN!!!

AFTER LAST ISSUES SLAGGING OF
MONSIEUR ROBERTO ELMS WE FEEL
THAT WE SHOULD RE-DRESS THE
BALANCE AND PRAISE THE MAN
FOR NOT ACCEPTING A LARGE
PILE OF CASH FROM A WELL KNOWN
AUSTRALIAN PAPER VENDOR FOR
HIS STORY CONCERNING A CERTAIN
HALF-CASTE CHANTEUSE. ALSO FOR TURNING
DOWN A JOB ON THE TIMES AS A FOOTBALL
REPORTER DURING THE WAPPING ESCAPADE.

TOP OF THE CRIMBO
PRESSIE LIST HERE
AT B.O. MANSIONS
IS THE RANGE OF
'VIZ COMIX' T-SHIRTS
(AN EXAMPLE OF THESE
BLINDING SARTORIAL
ITEMS ABOVE)

WHILE THE WILD CHILD'S ARE TUCKED UP IN BED BY MATRON, THE RECORD BIZ ARE
LOOKING FOR SOMEWHAT MORE MATURE TALENT. ENTER "GO BANG", FRONTED EX 400
BLOWS SINGER LEAH THIS IS POWER POP WITHOUT THE TANTRUMS ....
RECOMMENDED.

The fact that the Birmingham City
Zulus got the big capture from
The Forces of Darkness (A.K.A.
The Police Soccer Squad) soon
after Boys Own's little wheeze
about the Zulus and Fulham Old
Bill's favourite plod P.C. Snidely,
does not point to a "Bertie Small's"
on our behalf, just stupidity by the
Zulus, "Photo Albums" and "Diarys",
don't some people ever learn?

So Thatcher wants the Communist A.N.C.
Freedom Fighters to give up their
struggle against the Facist Botha
Regime, its funny I don't remember her
mentor Winston Churchill asking the
90% Communist French Resistance to
stop fighting Hitler, then again they
were white.

what the papers say....

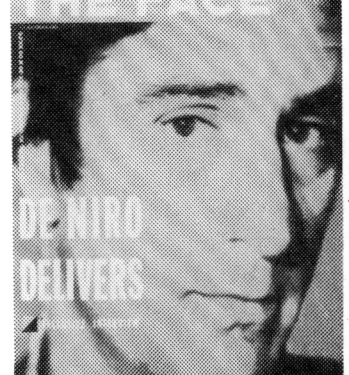

Boy's Own (1)

It seemed rather sick that in the issue
you chose to highlight the constructive work done by the alternative
soccer media (FACE 91), you printed a
letter from *Boy's Own*, a fanzine with a
large terrace-thug readership that is
also dangerously trendy. Please assure
us it was an oversight on your part and
not a sick joke that belongs in *Boy's
Own* rather than a responsible magazine.

AS FEATURED IN THE FACE!

THIRD KEMP -SHOCK (no wonder

Anyone out there old enough to remember Spandau Ballet ? Well
Boys Own can exclusively reveal the exsistance of a third Kemp
Twin!!! A reliable Boys Own source stumbled upon Gary and
"The Other One" Kemps secretbrother "Eric" locked in a toilet
at the Beat Route Club London.

Eric Kemp had been cruelly locked in the cubicle by his evil
brothers six years ago when the Splendid Walletts were making
a video for "Chant No 1" at the then trendy Soho watering hole.

Apparently Eric Kemp was (still is-Ed) so fucking ugly that the
Kemps knew that there future would go up in smoke, if Eric's
ugly boat ever got public attention. Eric also sadly could'nt
grow sideburns and to be frank looked two-bob in a Zoot suit.
Eric was lured to the club on the pretence that the young
Turkish boy who run the cloakroom fancied him, once the trap
was sprung, Eric was locked into the carzi with just a half
empty can of warm Pil's and a cheery cry of "see ya ugly" from
the Kemps.

Over the past six years the punters of the Beat Route thought
that behind the locked door lurked nothing more mysterious than
a Yuppie/Sloaney having the large-nose up.

Club regulars Debbie and Sharon said "if only we had known about
poor Eric we could have lobbed the odd Donner Kebab over the top
every now and then". A source close to the Kemps and even closer
to the bar upstairs at the Wag, claimed that the real reason for
Eric's detention was his accent. Eric's suburban brogue would
have ruined the "Cockney" Kemps chances of ever playing Ronnie
and Reggie, whether in a film or the much malined Spands musical
"Tartan Kilts Down The Blind Begger."

Recently though rumours have reached Boys Own mansions of
clandestine meetings outside Tubby Issacs cockle stall between
one Steve Dagger and certain very shady customers in Gabicci
Jumpers, in other words move over Al Capone/Bobby De'Niro, the
real chaps are about to hit the screens. Now seriously if the
Spands could by whatever means get this project off the ground
we would all applaude the kilted ones, but who will play the
twins. The Kemps could turn a piece of sinister London culture
into a sort of "Carry On Jack The Hat," now if Bruce Paines got
a twin brother !!!

Eric was rebuilding his life but the real turning point
came when he walked into Robot in the Kings Road, and purchased a
copy of "Boys Own 3" complete with stick on sidies, (A Free
Gift Folks!) with his new found style and confidence he ligged
around town, a teaming up with similar looking bod's, resulted
in Eric fronting what has now become last month's big thing,
check them out, at a toilet near you soon, oh sorry! The Band's
Name "Boys Wonder."

stop press:1

STOP PRESS....THE WHOLE STORY IS A PACK OF LIES.
WE ARE NOW CERTAIN OF THE TRUTH, THE BOYS WONDER TWINS AND THE KEMPS
ARE ALL THE BASTARD SONS OF CHARLIE COTTON. THE SIDE BURNS, THE STYLE OF
DRESS, WE SHOULD HAVE GUESSED EH!. NOW THIS LEAVES THE REAL THIRD KEMP
TWIN AS .....NICK(LEAVE IT OUT NA)COTTON.

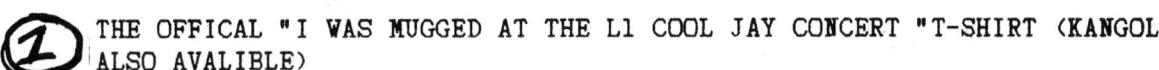

UNDER FIVES—5 WORST CRIMBO PRESSIES

(1) THE OFFICAL "I WAS MUGGED AT THE L1 COOL JAY CONCERT "T-SHIRT (KANGOL
ALSO AVALIBLE)

(2))STREETSOUNDS "ANTHEMS" LPs
ALL THOSE CAISTER MEMORIES FLOOD BACK LIKE A
BAD ACID-FLASHBACK,PYRAMIDS,CLONE DANCING,MOODY COCKNEYS FROM ESSEX ,
CHRIS HILL SINGING "SHOUT",PLUS THE OBLIGATORY DODGY BIRDS FROM ILFORD
(SEE THE TRULY AWFUL COVER FOR PROOF).HOW WAS WE FOOLED FOR SO LONG ???
GIVE IT TO SOMEONE YOU TRULY LOATHE,,,

(3) KERRY DIXON BEING TRANSFERD TO YOUR CLUB,
"HE GETS THE BALL AND DOES FUCK ALL".

(4) BUYING ECSTASY CAPSUALS FOR XMAS EVE ONLY TO DISCOVER THAT YOU HAVE
FINALLY STOPPED THAT RUNNY NOSE,,,,,CONTACT 2000,,,,

(5) PRESSIES FROM YOU GRANNIE ,,,,DEF JAM BASEBALL CAP,FILA TRACKSUIT TOP,
STAFF BULL TERRIER ,K-TEL'S 20 RARE GROOVE GREATS,,,,,,

• Powell & Co •   GENTS OUTFITTERS

70's cred quiz

THE SUBJECT OF QUESTION ONE.

NOW BEFORE YOU CAN RUSH DOWN TO THE DUFFER OF ST,GEORGE FOR YOUR FLARES AND DONNY CAPS,TAKE 5 MINS OF YOUR TIME TO COMPLETE OUR SEVENTIES QUIZ. "YOU GOTTA FIGHT FOR YOUR RIGHT TO WEAR FLARES,,,

NAME THE FOLLOWING,ONE POINT FOR EACH CORRECT ANSWER.

1. RICHARDS ALLENS PLAISTOW SKINHEAD,EARLY 70'S ESSENTIAL COMPREHENSIVE SCHOOL READING.

2. CHILD STAR OF H.R.PUFF'N'STUFF AND THE ELEPHANT AND CASTLE SCHOOLBOY CAPER "MELODY",(A BOY'S OWN FAVE).

3. NAME 3 ARTIST'S FROM TROJAN'S TIGHTEN UP VOLUME 2, THE CULT LP OF THE 4TH FORM.

4 THE SMOOTH'S FAVE FOOTWEAR,CREPE SOLES AND BUBBLE NOSED, SOLD FOR 12 SOV'S IN CARNABY STREET.

5 THECAFE ADJOINING THE WIGAN CASINO, CHEWING GUM THE SPECIALITY FOR THE TEENAGE SPEED FREAKS (NORTHERN BASTARD READERS ONLY)

6 THE GANG NAME OF WEST HAM'S MID SEVENTIES (PRE-I.C.F.) DRESSERS THAT TERRORISED THE SOUTH BANK, BUDGIE JACKETS, POLO NECKS, OXFORD BAGS AND PENNY COLLARS.....WICKED!!!!

7 MEETING POINT FOR ALEX AND THE DROOGES WHERE MANY A PINT OF MILK-PLUS WAS SUNK.

8 NAME THE SINGERS OF THESE YOUTH CLUB CLASSICS..."ROCK YOUR BABY," "HEY THERE LONLEY GIRL," "HEY GIRL DON'T BOTHER ME."

9 NAME THE THREE FIRMS IN PANORAMAS DOCUMENTARY OF MILLWALL F.C. PLUS THE
NAME OF A CANINE-LIKE TERRACE CHARACTER OF MID-SEVENTIE'S SOUTH LONDON.

10 TRENDY TEENAGE DISCO DOWN THE KINGS ROAD (NOW KNOWN AS HENRY J. BEAN'S), GO-GO DANCERS, WATNEYS RED BARREL, GEORGE BEST, AND ALWAYS A RUCK BY 12 O'CLOCK....

FREE ANGELA DAVIS

RIGHT ON · LONDON 88 ·

ANSWERS AND RESULTS AT THE BACK OF BOYS OWN...

MILLWALL the DOG

I recently managed to get my paws on a two bob fanzine called Boys Own, now writing does'nt come easy to me, not like your muggy staffs or poodles but I've got to tell you <u>Boys Own</u> connaughts my feelings on that dodgy eastenders letter. What do you lamps know about my manor or me, eh! I was born and bred one of a litter of six so I've never had it easy but I cut my teeth on inter squash trainers and there is no alternative.

Make no mistake though, I'm the guvnor I lead where I wanna lead and that dont mean the old Kent road does it mugs, and I wouldn't wanna mix with you boys own plums in your dodgy black clothes anyway. I mean how could I spot my owner Danny over Southwark Park at night, I've got him well clued up in a loud best company sweatshirt, ("South London's Finest") Your mag is just not "appening", only mugs like your readers could get addicted to a M.A.1. jacket, all I need is my studded collar and my <u>half Millwall half Rangers</u> bobble hat. I go dahn to cold blow lane now and then, I've got me own Dog Possie we were bushwacking away fans while the bushwackers were in the junior Supporters Club. We ambushed Birmingham coaches the other week I got a capture by the rozzers after chucking a half eaten bone through one of them Northern low life slags windows, so I suppose its 3 months bird at Battersea for me. Me and Danny get about <u>South London</u> in he's Suzuki jeep its ideal transport for a top dog like me I've got a well crucial view and no moodys touc the cassette while I'm about. Anyway you boys own logs could'nt cut it on my manor so no mor snide remarks about South London dog owners or we'll have to pay you a visit, know what I mea Anyway I'm off now to drop 2 ecstasy capsules my winalot as I've pulled some sloaney's pup from Clapham and I'll give her some south Lond pork swording doggy style, so from me and Dann and the halfway line its "nitto you sighs".

MILLWALL, THE DOG
JAMAICA ROAD

BITES BACK

nineteen 88: THE BEDTIME STORY.

The milk bottle full of petrol sailed through the air, toppling on cold winter
air currents, met the window pane with a resounding and satisfying crash and
exploded into a huge hot orange mass. The large blue and white plastic sign
that once read 'District Conservative Association' began to melt and drip down
onto the paving slabs below. The large crowd that had gathered cheered loud
and long, punching the air and any Tory foolish enough to have turned up for
the night's 'End of Health Service' party.

This scene was by no means an isolated incident. Throughout the country
happenings such as the above had been go9ng on sporadically as the year got
older. The running down of the Health Service had been the last straw.
November 87 had seen Mr. Lawson. (the then Chancellor) promising several billion
pounds to the N.H.S., a promise he certainly kept. 2 Billion pounds was the
amount spent on large demolition projects around the country, beginning with
Guy's Hospital and culminating in several sheltered homes for O.A.P.'s biting
the dust.

The bell sounded with a deafening clatter, as far removed from a ring as humanly
possible. Drew sat up, greeted the day with a heart-felt "Oh fuckin Hell"
and scratched every available, unwashed orifice within easy reach.
"That bloody dream again, he thought.
That bloody superb, idealistic, never going to happen, dream".
For the third night running the baddies had been run out of town in a hail of
abuse and large projectiles. For the third morning running Drew had woken up
feeling dead pissed off with dreams that didn't look like coming true.

It was shortly after several morning rituals (farting, washing, and tea-making),
that the second bell of the day intruded into Drew's life, this time it was the
door. The peep-hole gave him a strange large nosed gargoyle view of the face on
the other side. Even with the head looking like a mixture of Rowan Atkinson and
the Ex-Housemartin's drummer with a stocking covering his handsome features, Drew
easily recognised his early morning caller.

"Morning Jack"

"Alright Drew, how's life?"

Jack was a few years younger and a lot less world weary than Drew, together they
made a good mixture of cynicism and youthful high spirits.

As Drew made the tea the stereo blared out F.M. Radio One.

"Wow, that was, yeah wow, really something, another great example of the current
crop of records using what we in the Biz call sampling. It features excerpts from
Spagna, Roger Whittaker, Bon Jovi, the Goombay Dance Band and Rick Astley".
Once again the great British public had caught on several years too late, watered
it down and fucked it up. What next thought Drew, 'Shakey Meets The Jams'?
Turning from 'Tuner' to 'Phono' he put on the Morissey Memorial single and listened
to the last record the maudlin Manchester master committed to vinyl before being
killed by his ex-partner Johnny Marr in an argument over leather trousers and
vegetarian kebabs.

Having just risen from the pit Drew was dressed in bed-wear; Jack, however, was
dressed to kill (or if not kill severely injure). Early in 88 Next Inc. became
the State clothes store grabbing even more of the market than they once had.
It was fiendishly clever, at the first hint of any new youth style their highly
trained observers would pinpoint it, rip it off, water it down, and knock it out
to an eager style hungry public.   The idea was simple, the Government highly
subsidising the Stores, their reward being that any youth cult (in their eyes a

terrible threat since the Grebo-uprising in early 88) would be nipped in the bud and its instigators forced to expend energy looking for something new to wear instead of trying to smash the system. Jack once fell foul to the State stylists, but was now beginning to see the light, and wore nothing but his own designs made up by ageing tailors that only he knew. AT the first hint of High St. copying the garments would be ritually burned, a large effigy of Terence Conran placed squarely on the top.

THE FIRST ANNUAL
LEMMY MEMORIAL MEETING
WHICH ENDED IN THE
GREBO UPRISING...

AFTER GOVERNMENT
RE-EDUCATION THE RINGLEADER.
'SHIT KEV' IS NOW A
MORTGAGE BROKER IN ESSEX.

"Is that the new copy of 'FLACID'" Jack asked,

"Yeah mate, have a look if you want, its full of nonsense, but I always buy it, you know read it on the bog, there might be something in it".

There never was.

The magazine was a merging of two magazines which summed up the fashion frenzied eighties, 'The Face' and 'I.D.'. After the successful satirical magazine 'Boys Own' had exposed the fact that both magazines were written by several chimpanzees and an old Olivetti and produced on a large corporate computer by the same firm of Accountants, they decided "What the hell....we'll put out the one magazine and wow, great idea, we'll mix the two names and incorporate them into One World which summed up the whole whacky world of fashion in 1988...."

"What a load of crap!"

Jack's judgement was short, sharp and totally correct.
"Pass me the 'Time Out', I'll check out a venue for tonight".

The fashion mags weren't the only ones to ring the changes. 'Time Out' was now a xeroxed hand out after going bankrupt thanks to a costly libel trial involving an American Evangelical Organisation called 'Rich Bastards for Jesus'. The influence of such organisations was getting more widespread, but still not as outrageously influential as in the States. What little faith Drew had in the great un-washed masses was that they wouldn't fall under the spell of the T.V. evangalists. In the good old U.S. of A. the situation on this front was worsening, censorship was becoming rampant and arbitrary and the 'blue rinse wives against all things nasty and un-American' now even had representatives in the Senate.

"I see the Wag's still closed down then"

Jack was indeed right, it had happened that Summer when forensic scientists discovered that Crucial Brew was in fact, if administered in the correct way (i.e. in large quantities through a straw), a powerful halucogenic drug. PLOD were not amused. They shut the club in July and Crucial Brew was changing hands at ten pounds per can. Ecstacy on the other hand was finally revealed as an elaborate placebo type hoax involving paracetamol and experiments in mind control by a small group of Oxford chemistry undergraduates.

The bell sounded with a deafening clatter, as far removed from a ring as humanly possible. Drew sat up, greeted the day with a heartfelt "Oh fuckin hell"

And scratched every available, un-washed orifice within easy reach.

"That bloody dream again" he thought.

He looked at the calendar, December 24th 1988.
"Thank God for that, things aren't all that bad".

Drew had gone out the day before and bought the beers in for that night's Christmas 'Boys Own' bash. He knew the chaps well and was happy for them now that they'd signed the deal for the television series and had agreed to hold the party in his flat.

The second bell of the day intruded into Drew's life, this time it was the door. The **gargoyle through** the peep-hole was dressed in dark blue with matching hat and silver accessories.

"Good morning sir, this is a search warrant, we believe you have some Crucial Brew on the premises".

END

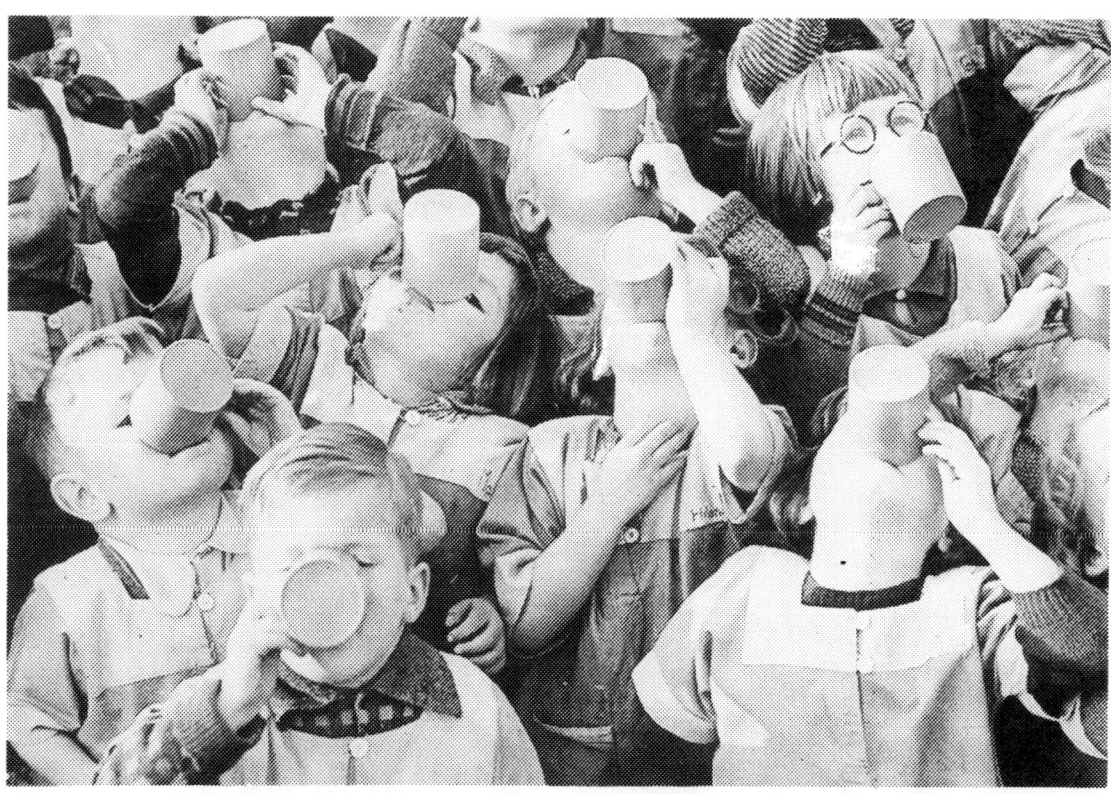

BOYS OWN
fizzy pop+disco party.
23 DECEMBER 10 til 3am
GAZEBOS argyll st w.l.

10/- NIGHT OUT

Tuesday 15th December At the **Jolly Boatman** Hampton Court 8 . 3 0 - 1 . 0 0 am. Chris and Wayne's Christmas Party, Ten shillings admission

ROADBLOCK

Sunday 20th December at the **Jolly Boatman** Hampton Court Lunchtime 11 - 4 bar No admission after 2.15 £2.00 or £2.50 including food.

BOXING NIGHT BASH

26th December At the **Jolly Boatman** Hampton Court 9 - 2 am £3.50 with invite £4.50 without D.J.'s **Bob Jones, Wayne M Dave** (Grand Groove) and Guests

SOLE

SOLE Christmas Party Saturday 19th December **Sole at the Metropolitan** Farringdon Road £3.00 members £4.00 guests

~1988~
the band

THE LATEST WHITE HOPES TO HIT THE MUSICAL TRAIL FOR FAME, CASHMONEY,
GROUPIES, THE COVER OF SMASH HIT'S, SEX'N'DRUGS PARTIES, AND A
APPEARENCE ON WOGAN ARE PERFECT DAY

NOW APART FROM HAVING A HUNKY LEAD SINGER THAT MOVES LIKE YOUNG TOM
JONES AND HAS A LUNCH PACK TO MATCH, WHAT IS IT THAT PERFECT DAY HAVE TO
OFFER THE POP PICKERS OF TODAY. "SONGS", " THE SEVEN INCH IS BACK, WE
WANT TO RETURN TO THE SONG," THESE CONFIDENT WORDS ARE SPOKEN BY MARK
JONES THE SAID SINGER OF HAYES FINEST BAND. "DON'T LOOK FOR ANYTHING TOO
DEEP WE ARE A POP BAND WHO AIM TO BECOME A CLASSIC POP BAND,"WITH SONGS
OF CLASSIC QUALITY."

PERFECT DAY HAVE A QUITE UNIQUE STYLE THAT COMES ACROSS AS DANNY WILSON
MEET'S ABBA AND ONE LISTEN TO THE NEW SINGLE "JANE" WILL CONFIRM THIS
EVEN TO THE MOST COMMITTED ANORACKED JANGLEY GUITAR FAN....PERFECT DAY'S
FIRST SINGLE JANE IS RELEASED EARLY IN 1988 ON LONDON RECORDS...YOU HAVE
BEEN WARNED.......

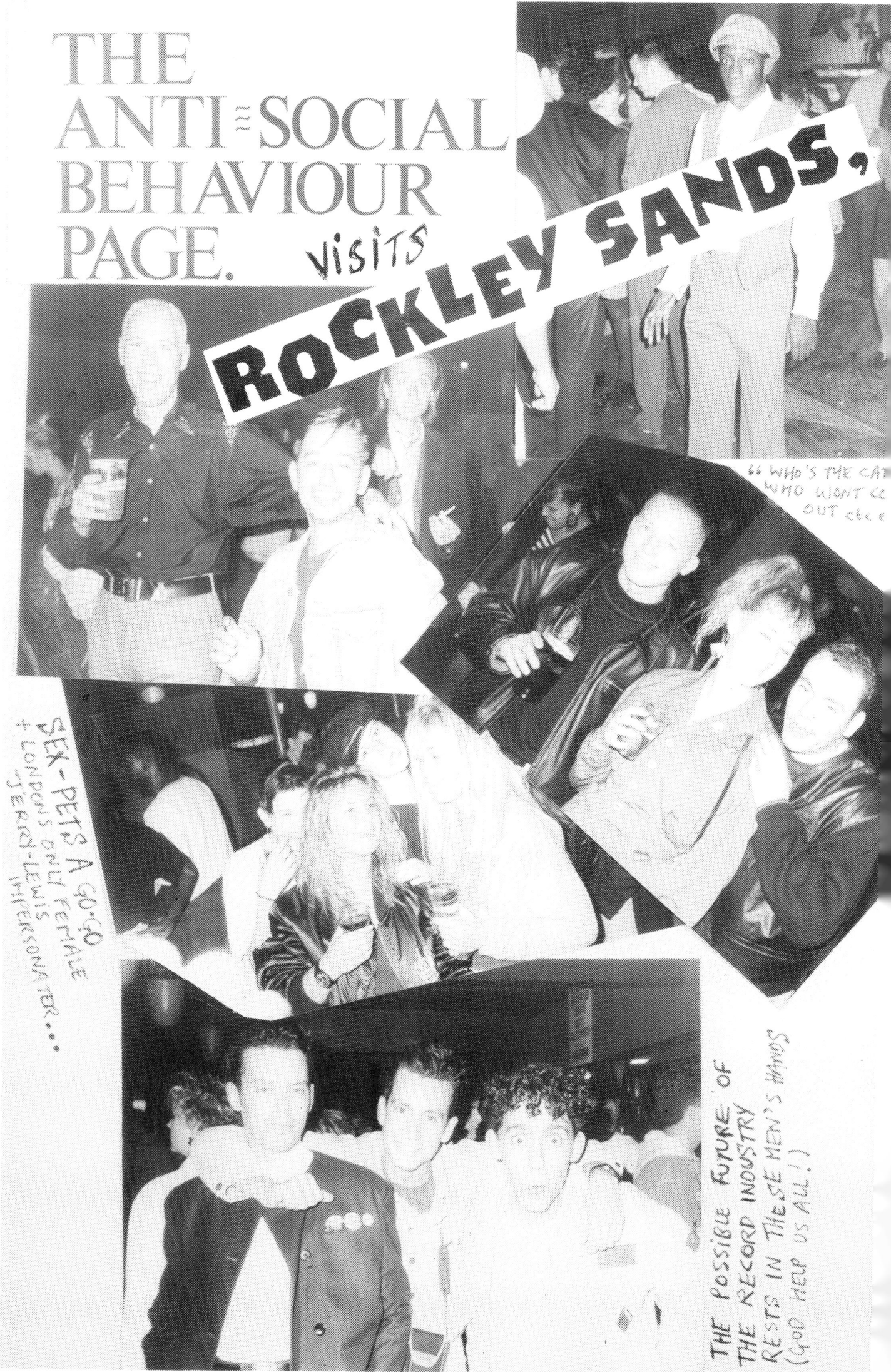

THE ANTI-SOCIAL BEHAVIOUR PAGE.

VISITS

ROCKLEY SANDS,

"WHO'S THE CAT WHO WONT CC OUT CC"

SEK-PETS A GO-GO
+ LONDONS ONLY FEMALE
JERRY-LEWIS
IMPERSONATER...

THE POSSIBLE FUTURE OF THE RECORD INDUSTRY RESTS IN THESE MEN'S HANDS (GOD HELP US ALL!)

THE SOCIAL ≈ AWARENESS PAGE...

In an historic act of collective stupidity (not to mention greed and self-interest), the British public elected Thatcher and her cronies for a third consecutive term in June. Labour, however, also managed to earn a place in the history books with the election of Bernie Grant as the first black M.P., followed quickly by Diane Abbott and Keith Vaz. Despite the election setback, there were other political highlights: the hilarity of seeing the Government making complete twats of themselves scurrying half way across the globe to prevent publication of a book by an old man in a dodgy hat and, in the process, caught lying, being "economical with the truth" just will not do, my Son.

On the domestic front, randy old Cecil returned to the Cabinet, having served his time in the political wilderness and proving that the old adage "absence makes the heart grow fonder" can be completely wrong. However, despite Cecil's "rehabilitation" the Tories didn't let us down and obliged us with yet another scandal in the form of poor Keith Best (formerly of Yvesmon and Brixton Prison, harassed M.P. and barrister caught with his signature on one too many B.T. share application forms.

Meanwhile, the drama continued in another court as a jury retired to decide whether Monica Coughlan was telling the truth and Jeffrey Archer did in fact have a spotty back. Half a million quid later and Jeffrey was vindicated. No doubt the money can go towards a few bottles of Clearasil and we'll hear no more of acne-ridden politicians, thank you!

The teachers continued their disruptive, albeit justified, action in schools nationwide, whilst Education Secretary, Kenneth Baker - most loathed ex-grammar schoolboy amongst the teaching professions - in a typical display of Tory democracy removed their negotiating rights and proceeded to lay plans for the decimation of the State school system and the re-introduction of latter-day grammar schools. Not so much Tory radiculism as Tory retrogression. In the City, meanwhile, a modern-day 1929 Wall St. occurred and Yuppies were seen crying into their vodaphones as the repo-men towed away their Porsches en masse. The Yuppie became the Pumpie (Previously Upwardly Mobile Prat) and no sensible person shed a tear for them. The Government's flogging of B.P. went ahead anyway but everyone knew that their privatisation of everything possible including Aunti Maude, had backfired and left the Government disappearing up their own arseholes.

On Your Knees To Madame M

SUDDENLY, YOU BELONG TO THE PRIVILEGED FEW

TAKE THAT YOU DAMNED TROT

project club

NOW SHOWING ZIGIS . 225 STREATHAM HIGH ROAD . LONDON SW16 – 01 769 3300

EXCLUSIVE PRESENTATION EVERY FRIDAY

THE PERFECT TEN

87 78

SINGLES

THE TUNES OF 87 THAT MADE US GET UP AND DANCE OR SIT DOWN AND LISTEN,,,BOYS OWNS FAVES,,,

1,ERIC.B AND RAKIM—I KNOW YOU GOT SOUL.
2,BARBRA AITKEN—AM I THE SAME GIRL.
3,PETROL THAT EMOTION—BIG DECISON.
4,HEAD—I AM THE KING.
5,PUBLIC ENEMY—REBEL WITHOUT A PAUSE,
6,COLDCUTS—SAY KIDS,
7,METRO TRINITY—DIE YOUNG.E.P.
8.MACEO AND THE MACKS—ACROSS THE TRACKS.
9,NANCY GRIFFITH—LONE STAR STATE OF MIND.
10,SPOONIE GEE—THE GODFATHER.
11,THE SMITHS—GIRLFREIND IN A COMA.
12,L1 COOL JAY—IM BAD,
13,TRIFFIDS—BURY ME DEEP IN YOUR LOVE.
14,DEREK B—GET DOWN.
15,THE JAMMS—ALL YOU NEED IS LOVE.

GREAT RECORD SHAME ABOUT THE MR. BYRITE SCHMUTTER...

P PRESS • YEAH YEAH WE KNOW IT'S NOT ΠOL THAT EMOTION • BUT FARLEY'S ONLY JUST SSED OUT HOW THE WORD PROCESSOR WORKS • IT SHOULD OF COURSE READ 'EMOTION THAT, PETROL •'

OUT ON THE FLOOR

<u>1987</u> was a weird year as far as the Club scene was concerned, a big influx of new punters and new clubs actually diminished the quality of the scene in many ways, not least musically, "<u>Oi</u> <u>Mate</u> <u>you</u> <u>gonna</u> <u>play</u> <u>any</u> <u>records</u> <u>by</u> <u>that</u> <u>James</u> <u>Brown</u> <u>Geezer</u>, <u>or</u> <u>wot</u>!!!" The whole of London went Rave groove crazy, suddenly every DJ became an overnight authority on 70's Funk and every club played the same stale floor fillers and the sound of the West End began to merge into one big compilation album of boredom.

" YEAH ... I'M BACK , I'M BACK, I'M BACK " ...OH FUCK OFF (Ed)

The big break through for RAP was due to many things, fashion, rare grooves popularity, hype, but it owed most to a silly little dance called The Whop, (See letters page-ed). The Whop made people realise you didn't need 12 ft. of lino to appreciate Rap, the whole thing exploded in our faces as every <u>Darren</u> and <u>Sharon</u> from Ilford to Southend "whopped" around their handbags and we knew another groove was lost to the moneymen. "<u>Rebel</u> <u>without</u> <u>a</u> <u>Pause</u>" was now the soundtrack for the "<u>Next</u> <u>for</u> <u>Men</u>" and "<u>Miss</u> <u>Selfridge</u>" generation.

While the New York Rappers hid behind James Brown's Republican Seventies groove, it was left to London, Leeds and Glasgow to push the fresh beats forward. The brilliant <u>Coldcut</u> Team of <u>Matt</u> <u>Black</u> and <u>Jonathon</u> <u>Moore</u> went where Double Dee and Steinski feared to tread, with the Boss "<u>That</u> <u>Greedy</u> <u>Beat</u>" being my favourite of the pack, (Was that Augustus Pablo I heard in the mix). Respects due to London's <u>Dereck</u> <u>B</u>, <u>Diana</u> <u>Brown</u> and <u>the</u> <u>Brothers</u>, from Leeds the massive beats of the <u>Age</u> <u>of</u> <u>Chance</u> and the totally awsome and neglected <u>Justified</u> <u>Ancients</u> <u>of</u> <u>Mu</u> <u>Mu</u>, (Glasgow's finest) too acid for many closed ears, but give it time ....

The Boss waxing as far as LP's went was <u>Public</u> <u>Enemys</u> "<u>Yo</u> <u>Bum</u> <u>Rush</u> <u>the</u> <u>Show</u>", carrying on where the last poets left off, at last we had a <u>RAP</u> Group whose lyrics actually matched the toughness of the music. Speaking of militant black lyrics, the band to watch for in 1988 will be "<u>The</u> <u>Voices</u> <u>of</u> <u>East</u> <u>Harlem</u>" an early seventies Gospel Band with massive rare groove potential.

Top Clubs as voted by the Boys Own "<u>Lagging</u> <u>and</u> <u>Ligging</u>" team were Brightons – <u>Escape</u> <u>Club</u>, Manc's – <u>Haciender</u> and London's <u>City</u> <u>of</u> <u>Angels</u> with a durability award going to <u>Rooster</u> <u>Fish</u>. The North's DJ's kept on moaning about London's rare groove scene, a chip on the shoulder plus large inferiority complexes are things they aint short of, its the music they lack. <u>House</u> ruled the North and while <u>Deep</u> <u>House</u> may break the music down South, I'm still not convinced. For the moment I'll let London's empty dance floors have the final word (so far) on House. 1988 should be the year of <u>Disco</u> with the fashions to match; let's hope that doesn't mean tackyness (taboo style) but the style and sound of the early seventies Black Cinema Genre, "Cleopatra Jones", "The Mack", "<u>Slaughters</u> <u>Big</u> <u>Rip</u> <u>Off</u>", etc. 1987 was the year of M.A.1. jackets, the Whop, and higher door prices, things must get better in 88. Lets just hope though that when some divvy starts a Disco-Revival night at the WAG he won't call it <u>Studio</u> <u>54</u> or even worse <u>2001</u> .... "Do the Bump".

LONDON'S MOST SUCCESFUL D.J.S TOGETHER UNDER ONE ROOF

From THE SPECIAL BRANCH:
Pete Tong,
Nicky Holloway
From THE WAG CLUB:
Gilles Peterson,
Derek B.
From SHAKE'N'FINGERPOP:
Norman Jay
From RAW:
Dave Dorrell
From THE MUD CLUB:
Jay Strongman
From THE BOILERHOUSE:
Ben+Andy

BRING THE NOISE!

Special Branch presents

ALL DAY DOO

*December 28th
Bank Holiday Monday 3–12pm
Le Palais, Hammersmith, London.

☆ ☆ ☆

All day bar, food available

Visuals, slide shows & gadgets

Record stalls & accesories
Comedians and Alternative Cabaret

Advance Tickets only – £10

From:
Starship Enterprises Ltd.
Premier House, 77 Oxford Street,
London W1R 1RB
01-439 2628
01-439 2687
Coaches available
VISA AND ACCESS ACCEPTED
PARTY NOW PAY LATER!

ABSOLUTELY NO PENGUINS

norman jay's

NEW YORK SPECIAL

A fascinating array of Doc martens, 501's and James Brown tapes, sported by a crazy collection of some of London's style and street elite, amazed the pathetic looking Mr. & Mrs. Nondescripts who queued patiently for ages to check into a dodgy Asian airline in the vain hope of blagging the few ramaining stand-by seats for a flight to New York. Who were these loafer clad, would be jetsetters? who couldn't be bothered to fly the world's second worst airline, (Air India being the living worst) 'British Scareways' Intrigued? read on.......

With London clubland locked in a 'rare groove' stranglehold and the once underground dance scene exposed to ever increasing interest from the ....POSSE! For those in the know and those who could afford it, it was decided that the time had now come for the hipper of London's clubbers to explore the possibility of the ultimate rave thousands of miles from home (some people will go to any lengths to get away from nonses eh!) A small, but intrepid band of dead trendy revellers were about to write a new chapter in clubland folklore. The party consisted of a good cross section of London fun seekers (and some low life) ranging from the "Its simply ages since I went abroad" types, to the "Jesus, I barely managed to scrape me bloody air fare" DHSS ligger who tried unsuccessfully to cash his giro in exchange for US dollars. This was no moody club 18-30 bash or a weekender for 'Miss Top Shops' and 'fashion blunders'. This was a holiday for the cashed, the trendy and the true raver... the 'real deal'. Perfect strangers coming together in their quest for musical adventure, who by the end of the trip would be united in their mutual love of a good rave, a decent smoke and an underlying fear that it could 'come on top' at any time 3,000 miles from home. At last, New York was about to be invaded by the new ambassadors of London's funky underground, SHAKE AND FINGERPOP & FAMILY FUNKTION. After a seemingly endless flight (7 poxy hours) and unnecessary agg from fucked up customs officials, our heroes emerged from JFK prepared for anything the unpredictable City had in store for them....a week's raving in Ronald Reagan's equivalent to Millwall's 'half way line'. Would the 'Big Apple' (what a totally meaningless nickname for a city God!) be just as they'd pictured it? read on ....

While the style conscious found favour with the cheap 'Bass Wee Jans' and 'Converse', the vinyl junkies got the fix of their lives with the abundance of 'rare groove' that was easily available in the endless record shops. Others tried in vain to convince their mates (sorry, buddies) that the 'Rolex' they'd just bought or scammed wasn't a snide fake (fat chance). The rest were straining at the leash to fire into legendary clubs such as the 'GARAGE', the 'TUNNEL', 'NELL'S' and the crazy but 'iffy', 'SAVE THE ROBOT', a mad English run club.

The London hipsters staged their 'party' in the 'WAG's NY' extension, 'BLACK MARKET' club. The music was a funky mixture of upfront 'House' (which drove some of our lot half out of their sculls with boredom) and classic NY disco (circa Studio 54) along with a liberal sprinkling of safe 'Salsoul' which went down a storm with 'Brit' and 'Yank' alike, a wild and wicked time was had by all. What with limo's half a mile (or hour) long, buildings straight out of a 'king kong' movie, clubs which went on till noon and endless 'Dallas' types screaming 'have a nice day! (arrgh!!), New York was just as I'd pictured it. This was 'Americana' at its best, most blatant....It had every type of vice our converse clad crew could ever want (brilliant). We'll be back next year to sample more dangerous delights (on the dodgy subway where your arsehole drops at night) in the 'city that never sleepzzzz'....... Have a nice day!!

NORMAN JAY

WHEN YOUR BOTTLE'S GONE... ...IN SE.1

BY
MICK MAHONEY

This play was written in 1981 and first performed at the Soho Poly

in 1982. The play is set in Reggie's living room on the Aylesbury

estate and tells the story of his efforts to get off it.

Reggie is a young postman who goes to Millwall. He believes some

local youths are out to get him. He has always hung around with thugs,

yet has never been one himself. He believes that these unemployed

teenages have sussed him out and are determined to make him pay for

his sins.

The interesting thing about this production is that the characters

originaly white are played by black actors, with no script changes,

Lets get it on.

Address: Dalby Street, off Prince of Wales Road, London NW5.

THE FIRST CUT IS THE DEEPEST......

When I was younger, having a relative, neighbour or even worse, my father cut my hair was like a Boys Own horror story....from 'egg-head' to 'basin bonce', to 'patch' the play-ground names came as thick and as fast as the hair on my head lay thin and grew slow.....

Sitting in this cushioned cosy high-chair at Cuts, it occurs to me that the average man goes to the barbers or hairdressers or, as they're euthamistically called, unisex salon in search of three things; first consideration of course is cash - he wants a head of hair that doesn't cost him an arm and a leg, but he also wants a hair cut that doesn't make him the butt of endless jokes about butchers, lawnmowers and law-suits, and thirdly, he wants to have a hair cut without having to experience pre-hair cut tension - the sense of pending disaster that he knew so well as a child......furtunately I think I've found just the place; an overcrowded box with three walls, four barbers' chairs, one large shop window and lots of steam in the heart of Soho....Cuts.

Number two on top and number one 'round the sides and back, isn't it?, Dan asks, as he peddle pushes my chair higher off the ground. I nod a 'yes', and feel even more cosy, since he remembers, simple as it is, the kind of hair cut I have.

'No, sorry', I remember saying to my last barber when he'd finished my hair and also proved that he had a good eye for right-angles, 'no, I'm sorry, that's not what I wanted', I said, later wondering why I'd done all the apologising and even left a tip.

There's a jazz track playing on the cassette in front of me, but before I get the chance to ask who it is, a large silk white bib falls and rests lightly on my shoulders, tied 'round my kneck, it covers the whole upper span of my body down to my lap, I slouch into relaxation and listen to the upful tune coming out of the cassette as the hot buzz of the clippers gets closer and closer......

Cuts is to say the least, a very peculiar establishment, although it's one of the best and most traditional barbers in London, the workforce don't altogether confine their creative talent to the cutting of hair.

CUTS company

Ever scheming fun boys, most of these barbers are in their twenties, except for Georgie, who seems more like a disinterested godfather figure, they all seem to know their trade in every which way and have such a wickedly blase confidence with the blade and clippers that is sometimes quite worrying; often sent on sessions for magazines, they can find themselves cutting hair anywhere between the Lake District to Lagos.....

...The clients vary from Georgio's slick backs to I-D kit buffallo boys and girls who come for a new crop to those young Soho socialites who want to put up posters, make phone calls, catch up on the gossip, leave dodgy messages or find out what parties are on,last time I was here someone came in to buy a bike and got one.

From where I'm sitting I can see Georgio, who invariably speaks in Italian and whose chair is always nearest the shop window. On his wall mirror there's a sign that says 'Georgio is here only on Mondays, Wednesdays and Thursdays,...his grey, groomed and gelled main make Georgio look so mafioso it's untrue...at least I think it's untrue.

A wild eyed wanderer comes in off the street and parks in a waiting-chair.
'Have you got an appointment?' Dan asks him, as he changes the length of the blade.

'Yeah, with Mark'.

'Oh, he's gone to get some coffee, he'll be back in a minuete'.

Coffee means next door means Bar Italia, an authentic Italian style coffee bar with stools instead of chairs and tables, this little place has a high screen that shows Italian t.v. programmes all day and Italian football matches on Sundays, they say it was in absolute beginners, but I must have slept through that part. (Didn't we all Ed?)

'You don't want the back of your neck shaved do you?'

'No, just shaped with the clippers'.

As Dan goes over by the sinks to fetch the small clippers, I look up at the ceiling cluttered up with posters and leaflets for this party or that club; they're all at such funny angles, I can hardly make them out.

Just then, Lenny the leaflet walks in - a shifty character if ever there was.

'Alright if I put some of these down? Could you stick up this poster for us as well?8

Seeing little Lenny, with his demob duffle bag full of leaflets, it's hard to imagine his significant role in the scheme of things....like street fashion, leafleting is a people's form of expression; t.v., radio, bill posters can all go by the board because this is the age of the leaflet; if you've got a gig to publicise, a party to advertise, even the opening of a new shop - leaflets is the best and cheapest way to make sure that the right people (and wrong people) find out first - as Lenny will testify. Arch handout merchant, Lenny's been known to work Kensington High Street, the King's Road, Soho, Covent Garden and Portabello Road all in the same afternoon.....P.T.O.

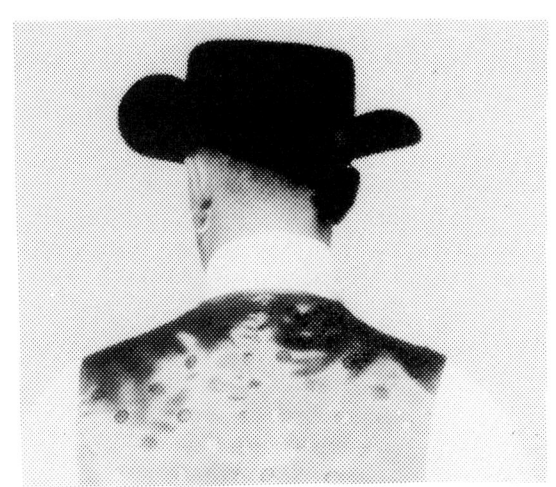

**DJ ROCKA IS BACK.
YOU KNOW WHERE.
YOU KNOW WHEN.**

Mark comes back with a box full of cappacinos; after a few visits, you soon realise that Cuts is an endless stream of cappacinos, teas and crazies.

Lenny hands each of us a leaflet, except Georgio, whose air of indifference is more than a match for our hand-out hero.

While Mark has his coffee, the wild eyed cat digs for the phone which is on the floor under a mess of magazines and appointment books....the argument with his girl friend is pretty quick, and so's his exit.

'That's the third client I've lost today' Mark says, not too bothered.

'Here are some free tickets', Lenny says, again gesturing but not getting very far with Georgio; as Lenny the leaflet leaves, I pocket a handful of tickets.

'Here, you may as well hold on to one of these too', Dan says, handing me a flexi disc. 'Its got the address to a warehouse party on this weekend'.

'Oh, I gave up going to those years ago, they're too unreliable', I say, sticking the record in my pocket. It's at this point that I'm beginning to feel a chill around my head - the back and sides are now just a soft mat of bristle.

Now, three years ago, on the other hand warehouse parties were a very rare commodity indeed; back then in their real hay-day, a warehouse party would cost three quid, have a live band, boast a handful of excellent d.j.s., go on till six in the morning and suffer virtually no police worries at all, but after a while these irregular, low key, low budget gathering became bigger and bigger and far more regular; and the bigger they became, the more illegal they became. The police, in the early days, would quite often turn a blind eye to the question of licensing, but later it became

a question of break-ins   Which were altogether a different matter....now they've become big money making schemes, void of their original private-party-for-everyone atmosphere....but this one, of course, could be different... 'We went to a couple last weekend' Dan returned, 'when we got to the first one, it turned out to be someone's house, people were sitting on the pavement outside, hanging out the windows, looking well rawdy, so we went to the other one, but by the time we got to that one it's been raided by the police'.

'You going to this one?' I ask, coughing on a cloud of white talcum powder.

'Yeah, we'll give it a go, if it's naff we'll go to the wag, haven't been there in a while. Finished, hold on while I get the hand mirror'.

'No, don't bother, I'll trust you', I say. 'See you later'..........

The wind whistles past, biting at the side of my near shaven head;as I walk down Old Compton Street I remember my real reason for going to Cuts this morning. I stop immediately, check to see if I've enough cash left and head back there....to see a man about a bike.

JASON LUCAS JULES. . .THE SIMPLE SOUL BOY.

letters to ED.

Dear Boys Own

I've got Issues 1 and 2 of your mag
and I can't understand the digs at
the Portsmouth 6.57 Crewe. Years ago
I used to get the 3 mins. to seven
train to Away Games, in recent times
something called the 6.57 has emerged
even though the train now leaves at
6.59. Mind you, one of the best
laughs I had last year was when
"Docker Hughes" stood for the 6.57
Party in the General Election in
Portsmouth South.

                    All the Best
                    Ray Gillen
                    North End, Portsmouth.

Why the digs at the 6.57? Everyone
in London laughs at the Pompey logs
and we did spot one trendy soul
wearing trimm trabbs at the QPR/PFC
Match; speaking of which why didn't
the 6.57 turn up at Ladbroke Grove
for the arranged "Off"; obviously
the 6.57 rushed home to watch Blind
Date.

        - Boys Own.

Boy's Own, in your worst soccer
chants you failed (wonder why?) to
mention that current fave of the
highly articulate, intelligent and
charismatic Chelsea barmies.
"Rudolf Hess he aint dead he's the
leader of the shed"....Dickheads....
                              Jon W.10.

If we started criticising the songs
Chelsea sing our magazine would be
a book. ED.

Dump the Pump

Now while Boys Own should be supported
in its crusade against all things
moody, such as the infamous M.A.1
Bomber Jacket illness, Leeds soccer
casuals and the possie wankers, you
have failed sadly in not exposing a
sickness of equal moodyness to those
already mentioned...."The Pump up the
Volume Dance".

This awful Soho mating ritual has now
spread nationwide, even the Young
Tories were seen performing it recently, (dancing as only Young Tories know
how) after their Facist Conference the
other month. Now many of you will
already be aware of this obscenity (the
dance and the Tories -ED) by way of
visits to the birthplaces of "The Pump",
The Wag, Raw, and Special Branch have
all helped this disease to spread without
remorse.

The fact that to perform this dance
properly you have to be under five
feet tall, wear bandana's, DM's and
hooped earings has also caused problems. Girls are deliberately stunting
their growth in order to gain acceptance
on the London dance floors. Look at what
one visit to the Wag did for poor old
Lena Zavaroni.

Now my main problem with this dance is
the fact that every time I hear a fresh
beat, my head starts flickering, then my
wrists and heels twist in a totally unco-
ordinated mess and suddenly its "Pump up
the Volume" time.

So its back to the bar for me and I'll
wait for London to get back on the good
foot, "Barman mines a tequilla slammer",
as J. Walter Negro once said, "Shoot the
Pump".

                    Johny Favourite
                    Bishopsgate, London.

LETTERS

Boy's Own,

We've just received your fanzine and
its got the Double Def rating.
You need not have worried about us
not liking it, because its "very
London", we're not all "woolyback
twats" in Wales ya'know.(Yes you
are - ED). Your coverage of soul
and football is well appreciated,
cos apart from fanzines the two
biggest youth lifestyles receive
little attention from a largely
off the ball media. Swansea City
does have quite a large thug element
for a 4th Division Club and we can't
wait to batter the shit out of
Cardiff and the other Clubs in the
4th this season.

The only problems we envisage this
season are up at Molineaux. I won't
pretend us "Jacks" are top dressers
but some of us are wearing Timberlands,
Chevignon and Chipie.

P.S. Do the "Orient Murder Squad"
exist? c/o A toilet wall in Hereford.

        CIAO for now
        "King Jack D and Bowley B"
        Swansea City Jacks 87.

(The Murder Squad are no doubt as real
as that other fantasy firm the Pompey
6.57. - ED.).

                    Terry Shields
                    Toxteth
                    Liverpool.

Dear Boy's Own

Hello Steve

How's it going, its Terry the scouser who
was down for Chelsea v EFC. Nice to meet
you. Thanks for the Mag. I was surprised
at the reaction it got from the lads at
Everton. A few said it was a rip off of
The End which was my first reaction but
quite a lot of the lads loved it.
Terrace rumbling was all right, so was
the bit about Dogs. I had a meeting with
a dog as you know in the Worlds End after
the game, which wasn't very pleasant, but
I enjoyed my weekend especially beating
Chelsea. I was well pleased. Pity after
a few grogs a few Chelsea lads had a go
at me but I can handle things like that.
I hope you are carrying on with the mag
cos I enjoyed reading it. I heard Mick
Mahoney was doing a bit for the mag.
That should be good cos he's a good writer
Mick is. He did quite a few good ones
for The End which is quite popular in
these parts. The End is out next week so
I'll send you one up when it comes out.
Jonty was in Liverpool on Saturday for
the Derby game and he's coming down again
next week so if your mag is out John will
bring me one down. Anyway Steve, not
much more to say except keep up the good
work and be lucky.

        TXS EFC

        THE END

What can I say, London's a lawless place.

70's EXAM RESULTS

1.JOE HAWKINS 2.JACK WILD.

3.PIONEERS,CLANCY ECCLES,
  DANDY, RUDY MILLS, SOULMATES,
4.TOPPERS. 5. JOKER CAFE.
6. MILE END 7. COROVA MILK BAR
8. GEORGE McCRAE, EDDIE HOLMAN
THE TAMM'S
9. HALFWAY LINE, TREATMENT, F-TROOP,
HARRY THE DOG.
10. THE KINGS RD BIRD'S NEST.

1.TO 3. POINTS - FALIURE, YOUR EITHER TO YOUNG OR
YOU WENT TO A GRAMMAR SCHOOL, WENT TRAIN SPOTTING AND
STOOD IN THE BOYS PEN AT Q.P.R.

4. TO 7. POINTS - YOU PROBABLY KNOCKED AROUND WITH
THE LADS AT SCHOOL BUT I BET YOU NEVER WENT ON STRIKE DU
PUPIL POWER (1975).

8.TO 10. POINTS - I WISH YOU WAS MY MATE AT SCHOOL THEN
WE COULD HAVE PULLED THE CHICKS WITH THE FEATHER CUTS AND L
LEATHER COATS (DROOL, DROOL.)

A HEARTY THANX TO ALL THE FOLLOWING...

ROCKA, GARY HAISEMAN, SIR LES OF BOND, DAVID (GEORDIE BASTARD) LITTLE, THE ECSTATIC NICKY HOLLOWAY, NORMAN JAY, GRANT, CLIVE THE YID, DANOUTA, LISA FOR THE BADGES, PAUL McGOO AT LONDON RECORDS, LITTLE MARK AT ROBOT AND ALL THE OTHER CHAPS INCLUDING THE FAT NORTHERN BASTARD WHO BREEDS PIGEONS AND PUTS WHIPPETS DOWN HIS TROUSERS. WAYNE.M, PAUL OAKENFOLD, CHRIS SULLIVAN, JULES AT THE LIMELIGHT, MICK MAHONEY, ALL THE BOYS AT CLASSICS, CROWLEY AND ANYONE WHO BUYS THE MAG (ANYONE ELSE CAN FUCK OFF).

CONTACT US (FOR ANY REASON) 216 GOULDEN HOUSE, BULLEN ST, BATTERSEA, LONDON S.W.11. OR BELL CYMON ON 0753-864664.

THE END OF ISSUE 4 : DANGEROUSLY TRENDY AND READ BY THUGS!

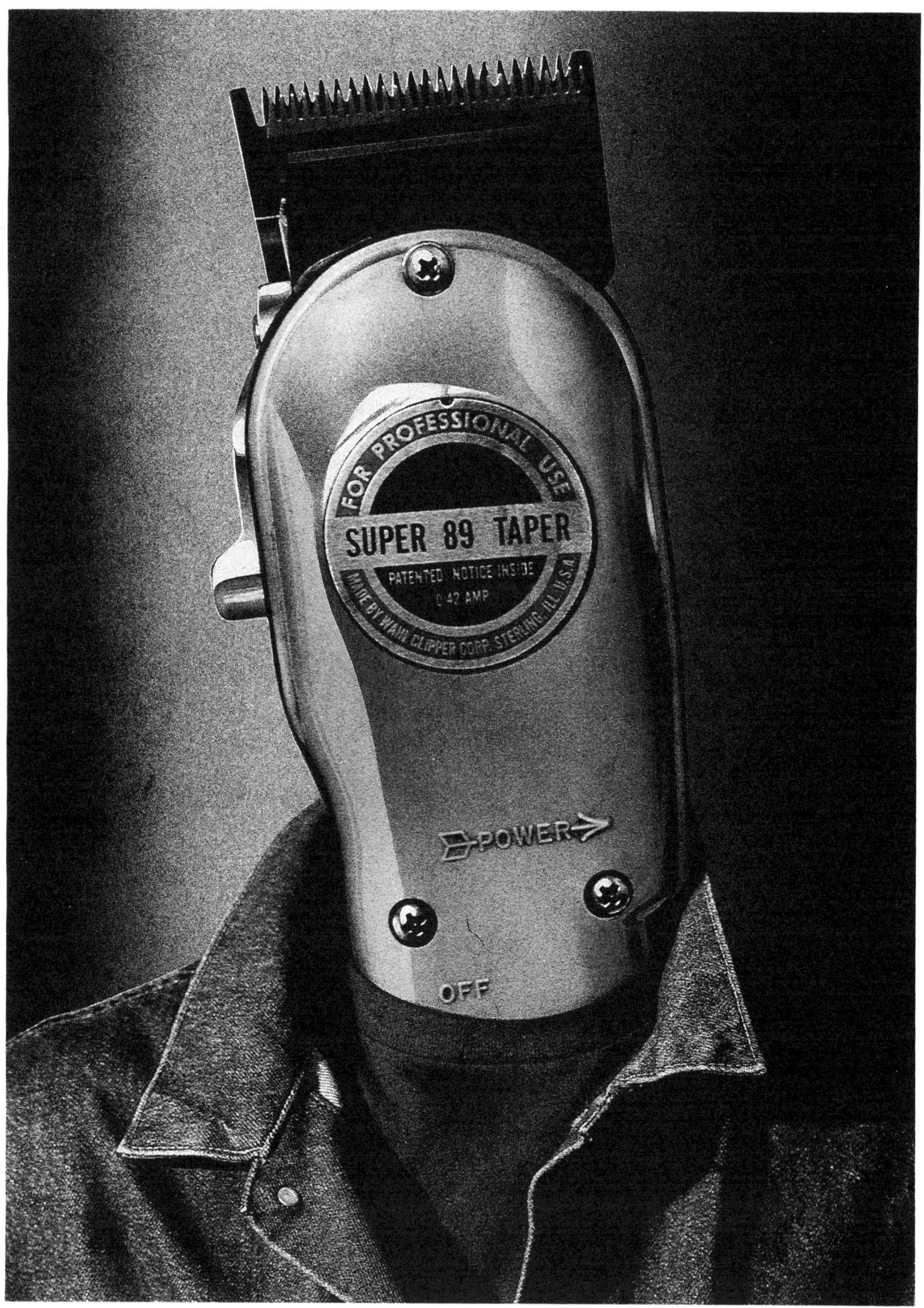

B A R B E R   S H O P S

LONDON: 56 BROOK ST, W1. TEL: 01-493 5428. 44 SLOANE ST, SW1. TEL: 01-235 1957. 11 FLORAL ST, WC2. TEL: 01-240 6635.

MANCHESTER: 19/21 KING ST. TEL: 061-833 0681. LEEDS: WEST RIDING HOUSE, ALBION ST. TEL: 0532 448636.

VIDAL SASSOON

No. 5
Spring 1988

60p

BOY'S OWN

Good MORROW MATEYS...

NOT much time to stop and chat, just a few words (after several issues) on the THINKING behind BOYS OWN, Prompted by certain accusations from people who are possibly a little Hard of Thinking.

Accusation ONE: <u>Racism</u>: Bollocks! THE BOYS OWN Writing team is a <u>multi-racial</u> experience.

Accusation TWO: <u>Homosexuality</u>: None of the Boys OWN team are dinner MASHERS, however I once slept with a geezer who was. THIS was After a business meeting at "FREDS" and was purely a career move... " Well at least we got an ad out of it "

Accusation Three: <u>sexism</u>: o.k. It's a fair cop guvnor, The mag's written by chaps (despite trying to recruit female type writers). It is at this point I can suggest a top periodical penned by Ladies, The one, The very ONLY '<u>FRESH AIR</u>'. A top Fanzine put together by people who look Better in a bra than we do!

Accusation Four: BOY'S OWN is <u>WRITTEN</u> BY <u>FOOTBALL</u> <u>HOOLIGANS</u>. This is nonsense, TWO are Confirmed Cowards, whilst the other two were recently Seen handing out Flowers at the NORTH STAND gate...

A Final note Mateys... BOYS OWN is all about Peace love and having Fun.

LURVE The OUTSIDER
— X —

GIVE US A LINE

QUOTE OF THE YEAR

" Never trust a teddy boy."
The venue,the Metro cinema
70's nite,the accusers;two
young flares wearers moaning
about the music,the victim...
Jay Strongman. The spirit of
'76 lives on.

Once more, the 'Boy's Own
says Oppurtunity Knocks' team
bring you a bango trio
extraordinaire;the zany,
jingly,yet spikey,rough-edged
but fluffy....Mexico 70.
I'll let the band describe
themselves in their own words:
" Cactuses;cigarettes;lager;
   Hillman super minx;Brighton;
   Fish;Love;Summer;Memorabilia;
   Tattoos;Seventies discos."
Does that make it all clear?
No?-Well check 'em out for
yourself at a pop music venue
in your town.

QUOTE OF THE YEAR 2.

Poncho-wearing clubber outside Theatre of Madness club,
central London,Monday night,
4a.m. " I don't mind telling
you,matey,I'm right on one
and I feel like I'm on holiday."

" MEXICO 70 "·1 TARBY AND FRIENDS·O "

Although this month sees the
opening of Boy's Own hero,
Mickey Rourkes' " A Prayer
For The Dying," most gossip
around town is not about the
movie but a 'method' tattoo
that Mickey apparently had
done in honour of the Provi-
sional I.R.A. Several unkind
sources close to Boy's Own
claim to have spotted Mickeys
artwork at Discoteque recently
and claim it to be the dodgy
work of a pissed Kilburn tatt-
ooist,with a dreadful taste
in red hands and the letters,
1690. Well,Mickey is American!

,the lady is not for turning...
less there's votes at stake,if
e recent concessions to the Social
curity Bill are anything to go by:
e stench of hypocrisy is overpowering.

One wonders how long Jesse Jackson
would have lasted had he secured the
Democratic presidential nomination.
Maybe we should ask Martin Luther King,
Malcolm X, John F.Kennedy, Bobby Kennedy etc.
God Bless America.

From the same banal 'Groucho Club
School of Journalism' that gave us
" Freddie Starr ate my Converse tra-
iners," now comes...ACID CASUALS...(Yuk!)

BERMONDSEY GOES BALERIC.

When talking about the state of London's clubland,the one thing everyone (except the promoters) is agreed on is the fact that the scene is too big and much too samey. The one real exception is the House Hippy scene of clubs like the Shoom and Future. This scene is unique in its music policy,dress sense and attitude and blatantly sneers at the West End trendys.

When you walk into the Shoom,maybe it's the 18 year old girls with their heads stuck down the bass speakers that tells you it's different,or maybe that Eric B has been fucked off by the Woodentops. The dress code of Ponchos,Converse and pony-tails is certainly one that would get you a 'not your night,boys' at most W.1. clubs;here,your attitude and the ultimate dance trance is all important.

With the Shoom and Future,you will either love them or hate 'em; either way,it's better than being bored to death,surrounded by mincers in the West End. D.J. Paul Oakenfold traces the roots of the scene,not from Chicago but the Amnesia club in Ibiza to Londons S.E.1. in cold February.

Just as a coin has two sides,so does Ibiza.

On the head side is the Club 18/30,booze,sun,exotic leeches,romantic moonlight and a nightlife of endless,old-style all-dayers. These beer-swilling lobsters fill up at clubs such as STAR,PLAYBOY,IDEA and ESPARA-DISE with loud music,cheap booze and single women. Their days are spent roasting red hot on the beach and rolling up the hours in a numerous amount of beach bars and cafes. For most,their nights end at 2-3a.m.

You flip the coin over and show the other side and watch how the nights come alive. Their day starts at about 2.00p.m.,when most of them get up and go down to the Cafe Del Mar in San Antoine,where they try and blag some hash and sip tall glasses of coffee. Later in the season though, they don't seem to get up until about 7.30p.m.,when they might go down to the Cafe Del Mar to watch the sun set.

Early in the season,people would go into Ibiza town and meet up at Lolas or Marisol. Lolas was the bar where the more fashion-conscious people would go. They buy their clothes from shops like END,TRIP,MAGIC and VICTOR. These shops sold mainly Spanish designer clothes from Barcelona and also some Italian. The trendy side was very Spanish orientated last season. There were a number of fashion shows at Lolas and clubs like KU, but these were more for the English fashion ideas like BOY etc.

Because Ibiza hasn't a great phone system in their shops,there is alot of credit card theft and fraud by workers. This isn't a new thing, it has happened every summer for years now;it pays for the gear,yes?

As the season goes on,the people sleep longer and stop going out for meals and survive on small snacks etc.,just enough so they can survive the night.

The evening starts at Lolas at around 12-1.00a.m. where people would meet up. Then it's off to PASHA,which was probably the most trendy club in Ibiza last season,full of native Ibizans,Spanish and other Europeans,who come over to Ibiza in droves to experience the music and atmosphere of Ibiza clubs. A unique style all of its own. The clientele is overridingly gay,with a splattering of transvestites. It's for the more dressed up people,very much like the Cafe de Paris in London(stand and pose).

The D.J.'s name is Caesar,who has played in Ibiza for years,previously DJing at KU in the late 70's and early 80's. The music has a full range of dance sounds,from House and Euro-beat(though not Hi-Energy)with a splattering of London dance tunes. PASHA is a half-open,half-enclosed club.

Around 4a.m.,the hard core moves over to Amnesia,half-way between Ibiza town and San Antoine. Alfredo dee-jays,as he's been doing for a few years now,establishing a great reputation for himself. Amnesia is more of a street club,in the sense that people don't dress up;they dress down and come to dance the night through to 6a.m. The club is completely open-air, with music in the style of House,Euro-beat and rock. It's at Amnesia that you start to see a unique fashion style of baggy clothes and dungarees worn for comfort and ease of movement,when dancing for hours non-stop. On their feet are Converse-style boots of various colours.

At 6a.m.,the crowd moves down to Glorys,which is just opening;the music is a heavier mixture of House and indie rock,probably the most alternative club you will ever experience. The music is now harder than ever because,by now,you need it. The music at both Amnesia and Glorys is purely for dancing and people come from all over the world to experience this scene.

1987 was probably the best year to date for Ecstasy. It's been around for a long time but this year it happened in a big way in Ibiza. There was,also,Mescalin-a drug produced from the cactus plant-but the main drug was Ecstasy. Bigger than James Brown playing the KU and bigger than Freddie Mercurys party,where you couldn't imagine the things that happen. It takes you up and gives you a feeling of freedom. You know what you're doing,you just feel more confident of love. People tend to take the drug and dance the night away.(You hippie,Oakenfold-Ed.)

THE "DANCE TRANCE"... SPECTRUM.88....

"LUCY"...SHOOM'S MARGATE TRIP...88. ☺

As dawn appears,people start to mellow out and head home. It's now you can flip the coin again and as some are going to bed,the 18/30's are getting up and going down to the beach with their flip-flops and towels.

This made people almost live for the night-life,especially Amnesia because Alfredo played the music that best suited the mood you were in and seemed to follow your moods all night.

These people are now back in the U.K. and looking for the right club atmosphere again. For those of you looking for this,there is a club in London with the atmosphere of Amnesia but if you really want it,it's down to you to find it.

BUT THE POLICY IS " NO TRENDYS PLEASE."

"OAKEY" AND FUTURE DJ..."NANCY NOISE".. LONDON '88

Since this article was finished, the 'Shoom' club has shut due to
outsiders,with a ruffian attitude,who felt threatened by a club full
of people who just wanted to 'get on one' and dance.
    The following chart was compiled by the 'Shooms' Danny'Happy'Rampling,
who,by the time you read this,will be kicking up the dance-floor at
'Shoom 2'(Joy?) and if you've got a happy head on,you'll be there too.

" The Get On One Matey Chart. "

1. Thrashing Doves- Jesus On The Payroll.
2. Bang The Party- Release Your Body.
3. Phuture- Acid Trax.
4. John Lennon- Give Peace A Chance.
5. Jack Frost- Shout.
6. Adonis- Poke.
7. U.2.- With or Without You.
8. Todd Terry Project- Bango.
9. C.C.Rodgers- Someday.
10. Cyndi Lauper- What's Going On.

    There is a real prejudice against this scene by the establishment of
the West End. Sure,fashion isn't important and maybe the dancers do look
straight in style but in attitude,no fucking way. Anyway,if you 'aint hip
enough to enjoy the City of Angels on a Friday and then just to stick on
your jeans and T-shirt the next night for a real rave,then bollocks,why
are you reading Boy's Own....

UPPERS & DOWNERS

The following inane piece is, firstly, in 'Boy's Own' to take up invaluable space and, secondly, to show what really was the good,the SAD and the ugly (Steve Walsh) of the Seventies....

UPPERS

Travelling to disco's on your sister's space hopper

Fish fingers and spaghetti on a Friday night

Laurie Cunningham's jinking runs

The Jackson 5 cartoon series

Making your hand go dead before wanking

Singing " Bobby nicked the bracelet " to " Mooro ".

Sniffing Glue(the fanzine)

T.V.ads for K-Tels superbad records(5,4,3,2,1,-get your whistle and blow!)

Skindles soul club

The Johnny Seven Gun revival

Your first wet dream

Crowd violence at Subbuetteo matches(remember the Brazil vs. Leeds riot at Farley's house...no Old Bill at all...wicked!)

Contempo record shop

The California Ballroom

Disco Tex and the Sex-o-lettes

Jaws disco(East London)

Chelsea taking the Holte end

The little girl who worked in A.C.M.E. Attractions

The Q.P.R. No.10 shirt.Stanley and Rodney (God)

Banana Splits ('Dear Drooper...')

Al Green on T.O.T.P.

Being young....

DOWNERS

West Ham away(no escort,no segregation,no away fans,although most had sick notes from their Mums)

Snogging reanies with hair lips

The donkey-jacket fashion at Spurs (Norman Jay and Sammy Skye's specials)

Puppy Love(Donny)and puppy fat(Boy's Own staff-Do you mean Farley?-Ed.)

The National Front(who?-Ed.)

The super-glue on the bog seat craze at school(ouch!)

Van Der Valk(the record and the T.V. programme)

Centre partings

Steve Walsh's food bill(fat bastard with no manners)

The chaps who stood outside the match in Gabiccis,Crocs and Farahs pretending to be touts!!

Pan's People getting nobbed off T.O.T.P.

Your Mum throwing away your World Cup coins(well sad!)

Having a spotty back in Benidorm(speak for yourself,Farley!)

Getting caught wanking by your Mum

Don Revie's England kit and his dossiers

Thatcher the school-milk snatcher

Leeds United woolly-backs who wore Alice Cooper make-up(Don't forget the star jumpers-Ed.)
P.S. Shame about Paris '74(Hee,Hee,Hee!)

Turning up late for a riot(Do you mean Sir Les of Stork?!-Ed.)

Being too young...

Ron, KRAY

ALL THE BEST

FOR SELF MEASUREMENT

Please observe these simple points

1. Please describe garment fully, with full style details.
2. Check measurements.
3. List measurements in correct order as given.

DRESSED..... MESuRMenTS

GO TO............
11, ARCHER ST, SOHO
01-734 5051

FIGURE 1 - JACKET

1 - 2	NAPE TO WAIST	18
1 - 3	JACKET LENGTH	29½
4	WIDTH OF BACK	9
5	ON TO ELBOW	20
6	ON TO CUFF	31½

FIGURE 2 - VEST

7	CHEST	41½
8	WAIST	36
1 - 10	VEST OPENING	13½
1 - 11	FULL LENGTH	26

FIGURE 3 - TROUSERS

9	SEAT	41½
12	TROUSERS SIDE LENGTH	41
13	INSIDE LEG LENGTH	30½
14	WAIST	36

OTHER SIZES

CAP	
SHIRT COLLAR	

FIGURATION ✳

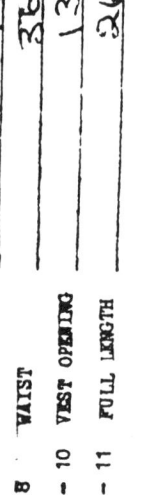
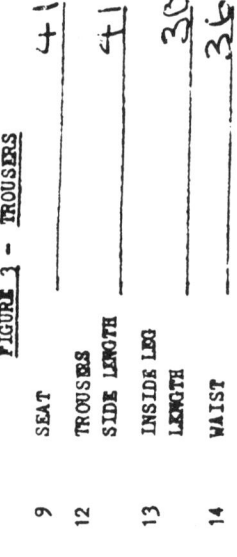

NORMAL STOUT CORPULENT ROUND BACK VERY ERECT
HEAD FORWARD NARROW BACK
FLAT CHEST PROMINENT CHEST

PLEASE INDICATE FIGURE NEAREST YOURS

SQUARE SHOULDERS SLOPING SHOULDERS

NORMAL

Please mark the line showing the height of your shoulders

GENTS OUTFITTERS

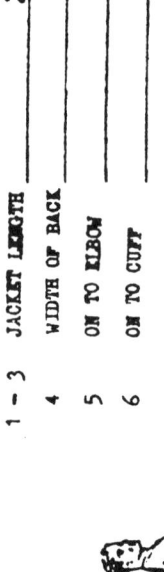

FIGURE 2

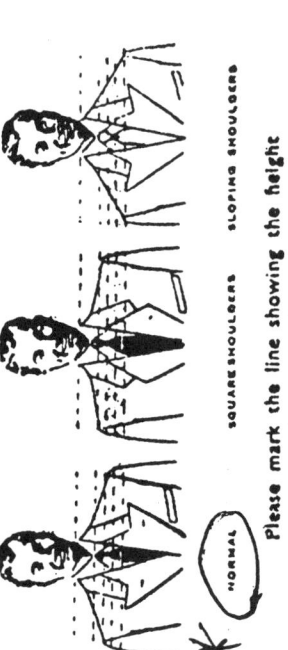

MILLWALL

I'm back, I'm back, I'm back,alright logs, this
is Millwall the Dog back on the case again,(with
a double sad James Brown impression-Ed.) Those
lefty dinner mashers at Boy's Own Mansions have
had a flood of fan-mail for yours truly,so dawn
raids or not,I'm back.

    Well,what's new in the smoke? The poor old
Gooners alarm clock went off early one morning
and it wasn't the milkman knocking,while the
Chelsea boys are still getting grief from the
Brady Bunch. Now footie is no value at the moment,so I'll turn my roving eye to other matters.
Did anyone see that 'Fear' bollocks? What nonsense! Who honestly ever heard of North London
gangsters anyway? The only thing to'fear'that's
ever come out of Islington was the Kemp Bros.
dress sense. Who was that dodgy actor type who
played 'Carl'. His accent was a cross between
Michael Caine in 'Alfie' and Harry H. Corbett
in 'Steptoe and Son'. Carl obviously attended
the Dick Van Dyke school of learn yourself 'Cockney',Danny Baker previously being a Head Boy. Does
anyone read the letters page in Boy's Own,full of
letters from smack-head Northerners about silly
named footie firms. Listen chaps,give it up,you
will only end up in the Scrubs,banged up with
some moody England N.F. type.

    Is that " Loads of Money-logg " a right divvy, a typical Tottenham fan(Hee,Hee,
Hee-Ed.) " Bugger all money's " much better, though all Viz readers will spot one
of their favourites straight away. Plenty of travelling up North for the chaps
next season, especially the ones who remember Everton in the Cup in the mid-Seven-
ties; it's been a long wait, Mickeys. Anyway, I've been up North already but it's
always been shut.

                  Till the next time logs,fuck off and die,
                       ...Getting busy...
                     Millwall the Dog,
                      Jamaica Road,
                      South London.

               P.S. To Perky 'the Gooner' cat,in the immortal
                words of Public Enemy..."You're Gonna Get Yours..."

MILLWALL the DOG
BITES
BACK

i heard
a rumour......

"'Ere,guess what I've just heard...."
How many times have you been standing at the bar,on the dancefloor,in
the urinal (standing in the urinal? Rather unhygenic-Ed.) and heard
those immortal words,followed by a piece of info concerning somebody's
narcotic,business or romantic antics so trivial that you feel that at
least ninety-seven other close friends,or people walking past must know
about it. Now I'm not here to go into the sociological importance of
gossip and rumour-you know,the bush telegraph and all that gear-but just
to have a look at the type of rumour that abounds,how they start and
where they lead.
NUMBER ONE: THE SEX RUMOUR.
Todays ligger,lagger and clubber cut his (or her) teeth with this sort
of gossip,when in the playground,they spied one of their chums playing
'I'll show you mine' in a quiet corner,during a break from British Bulldog,or a chorus of that immortal song, "Join on for war". A few years
later playing on the dancefloor with the big boys and girls still pro-
mpts a very similar response....
"Hey! I've just seen (insert name here) snogging with (insert name here)"
or,
"Leave it out. (insert name here) hasn't been blagging (insert name here)
 for weeks now."
The logical conclusion to this line of rumour is the 'she only gave him
a dose' punchline,followed by barely audible stifled laughter and gasps
of "Your kidding!" If you hear this in a crowded gentlemans powder room,
take a look at the chaps examining their tackle for a longer than usual
amount of time,during an apre urination shakedown. This one's a long runner,folks!
Another form of rumour-mongering learned early in life is,
NUMBER TWO: THE PARTY RUMOUR.
This was the logical step in growing up from the raunchy loveromp rumour and involved gangs of small boys,wandering the streets,(until Mums
called them in) clutching half-drunk bottles of Woodpecker and knocking
on the door of any house which had the slightest sound of pop music
eminating from within.

"OI, GUESS
WHAT I'VE
JUST HEARD ?
"....
WHATS THAT TH
....
"THEY RECKON
THAT READING
BOY'S OWN
GIVES YOU
PARKINSON'S
DISEASE !

The progression of this is piling into a taxi,with a luke-warm
4-pack,knocking on the front door and asking, " Is Debbie here? She said
it'd be alright to bring a few mates. " This rumour is usually heard in
pubs or clubs,a few milli-seconds before chairs are put on tables or
shutters come down on bars. Beware! It is sometimes started by the pro-
prieters themselves,as it ensures swift off-sales and take-outs of the
crap,cheap lager they've been trying to shift for the past fortnight,
it being the only thing the hapless punter can now afford in any 'respectable for blagging into a party' amount....
(see also chapter entitled " That Dirtbox Phil geezers having a warehouse party ")
A type of rumour definately not learned in the playground,unless you
went to a very progressive primary school,or count the line," Watsons
got twenty No.6 in his satchel " is,
NUMBER THREE: THE DRUGS RUMOUR.
This is one of hundreds of rumours which usually starts with the immortal opening gambit," You see that geezer over there..." A word of warning my children,following up on the info can end in tears or,at the very
least,embarassment,when you stroll over and ask a bod,who you only know
from seeing him prop up bars in various drinkers, " I'm a mate of Dave's,
he said you might have some gear. " The replies are numerous but can be
simplified....
1." Fuck off."
2." Leave me alone."
3." Twelve pounds a gram."
4." You're nicked."
5." Who's Dave? "

"'ERE DID YOU SEE THAT?"

So there you have it;a small insight into rumour-mongering. But
really,my siblings,the best way to experience what I have described
is to try starting a few rumours yourselves,so here they are then,a
few lines(if you'll pardon the right-on drugs reference)to try out
yourselves. So here,for the hard of thinking,is a list of rumours to
start yourselves. See just how far you can take them before people
(a.) start questioning your sanity,(b.)start sending you soliciters
letters or (c.)start kicking your head in.
1. Boy's Own is out tomorrow.
2. Jean Paul Gaultier is a lathe operator from Hemel Hempstead.
3. Masturbation makes you wear flares (what other reason could there
   be apart from being a wanker.)
4. The Wag doorman's got an Open University degree in Humanitarian
   Studies.
5. Ecstacy gives you Parkinsons Disease.
6. All of the letters in Boy's Own from Northern football fans are
   written in joined-up writing (see No.10.)
7. Paul Oakenfold is not a hippy.
8. Jay Strongman is not a teddy boy.
9. Ronnie and Reggie (a.k.a. the Kemps) are not New Romantics.
10. None of the letters in Boy's Own from Northern football fans are
    written in crayon.

OUT ON THE FLOOR

"o STROBES"
"o ACID"
"o FUN"
"OUR IDEA!!!"

"I'M NOT ONE
ONE MATEY!!"

The last Westworld was kicking it in more ways than one. Upstairs was brilliant but we can't all get up there can we chaps. A change of venue is well in order.

SHAKE AND FINGERPOPS AMSTERDAM JAM was well tough we hear but why did Norman and Majors sleep in the tram depots. Answers in Norman Jays next column, we don't think.

The top new clubs in town are, without doubt, Mondays at Heaven...SPECTRUM, serious Baleric and Acid played to a wild crowd of regulars.

When the ROOSTERFISH shut, London lost a major part of its scene. 'Afters' has now filled that gap; no address to be printed but find it, it's well worth the cab fare.

It now seems that the real underground has gone Baleric Beat mad and respects are due to D.J's Oakey, Rampling, Steve Procter and Johnnie Walker (wot about Nancy Noise?!). All others are bandwagon jumpers...Fuck off. Top Baleric sound at the moment is the tough Scouse sound of Wylies " Sinful " while Steve Procters attempts at breaking " Black Betty " is applauded at Boy's Own mansions.

Anyone who is brave enough to want a mention in 'Boy's Own', send the details to us and we'll oblige....Bye,bye ravers...

© THE FARLEY FOUNDATION

'Knobhead-of-the-year and it's
only May' department
brings you,take a bow;
Yo!Bum rush the show and other
hippety-hoppety phrases:give a
big hand to Tim Westwood,
king of the Ipswich yo-boys.
Is this man serious? Sad to
say,I think that he reckons he is.
Let's hope N-Sign Radio springs a
leak very soon and Mr.Westwood
returns to graffiti art on
the walls of Midlands shopping
centres-' Tune in,chill out and
knob off'.

" YEAH I'VE BEEN A SOULBOY SINCE, ER, AT LEAST 1985. I'VE GOT LOADS OF RECORDS, ALL THE UPFRONT STUFF LIKE, ER.---- 20 MOTOWN GOLDEN GREATS AND THE VERY BEST OF LEVEL 42. YEAH AND OUR POSSE, THE SURBITON UZI CREW, GO TO ALL THE TOP GIGS. WE WERE AT THE L.L. SHOW AND DID A BIT OF STEAMIN'! WELL WE ROBBED 3 VW SIGNS AND SHOUTED "YO" ALOT. DOES THAT COUNT? ANYWAY I'VE THREW AWAY ALL THAT LLOYD COLE AND SPEAR OF DESTINY SHIT THAT I USED TO BE INTO AND NOW I PLAY "REBEL WITHOUT A PAUSE" AND WHAT'S IT CALLED ? THAT'S IT 'COMBINE HARVESTER FOR THE WORLD,' YEAH BY THE EYELIDS OR SOMETHING LIKE THAT. YO! WORD! DEF! "

" Norman, get yourself a bloody answering machine or something or else, you lazy yid! "

That was the rather terse message scrawled on filthy note-paper unceremoniously shoved through my letter-box this week,reminding me,in no uncertain terms,that the 'chaps' down at the "Foundation" had been trying unsuccessfully to get in touch with me. I think that somebody was trying to tell me that my regular article for a mag,considered by some to be " dangerously trendy and read by thugs ",was long overdue! So,being someone who can take a hint,here it is....

Well,we're well into 1988 and the underground/alternative dance scene, as I see it,is now a whole lot healthier (due to the fact that Joe has now tired of that 'rare groove' 'cause the trendy ol' sod now has all the tracks he wants on his Streetsound compilation L.P.'s) and far more diverse than a year ago. Warehouse parties made a brief and welcome return to the raving calendar over the New Year period,with several successful jams happening around the capital,including our own Shake and Fingerpop bash at Hammersmith,attracting a crowd of over 800 red-eyed and drink-sodden festive ravers on a mild winter night,right under the noses of plod....wild!

But,clubwise,only two gigs of any significance have successfully managed to generate that necessary spark of excitement,which,previously, could only be felt in a 'happening' rave,one of which is sadly now closed again due to the fucked up attitude of moody club management. The other, happily,is firing every week,defiantly flying the flag of the 'new' underground and attracting the unwanted interest of music know-alls,who then pretend to their mates (or in the case of certain style or music rags such as the N.M.E.) they were into it all the time and adopt the " I said this would be big,didn't I? " or " this is the scene everyone will be into in '88 " approach. What a lot of shit! They're the same know-all wankers who wrote off 'House' music as a legitimate music scene even before they'd understood it or,in alot of cases,heard it! They're the same bunch who, in their divine wisdom,proclaimed that rare groove was now officially dead;disco would be the sound of '88 and that 'acid' would never work on a London dance-floor. Try telling that to a " Shooomer! " Not surprisingly,nothing they've predicted has come about.

The first club,which is sadly now closed,was a tongue-in-cheek 'brotherhood' bash called PERFORMANCE. Situated in the bowels of Earls Court,this seedy little haven of 70's retro,run by the 'Persuaders',had been discreetly kicking shit since November last year. Undetected,unde- terred and unashamedly hoards of young 'throwbacks' would dress up in hot pants,flares,donny caps and platform shoes and get on down,every Sunday night,to authentic 70's Blacksploitation film sound-tracks and R'n'B. A fun scene of fashion and music unpretentious in its blatant exhibitionism and vibrant in its refreshing approach to having a good time. A scene which evolved from the,sadly,now commercial rare groove scene,went 'public' with the hugely successful 'Carwash' party (which was actually held in a real carwash) of a few months ago. An event which attracted the media like flies to shit,even though the plebs had previously been quietly knocking 70's black music because they'd heard one James Brown record too many,and,on the other hand,publicly proclaiming,with massive articles (yes,the Face,N.M.E.) the resur- gence of 70's fashions and how everyone used to wear clothes just like some high-flying,two-timing,son-of-a-gun Harlem pimp! How could any- one be taken in by such bollocks ? If those articles were actually written by somebody who WAS around then,they would then know that some of us WERE going to funk clubs in London in the early 70's and that some of us DID model a trendy style (40's gear;round-rimmed specs a la Glen Miller). We DIDN'T all wear 'The Harder They Come' hats

and that it was no fun running out of candles on a cold,dark,winters night during a power cut or not being able to earn a full weeks read- ies because you were only allowed to work a three-day-week under a bloody Tory government! You'd only know that if you were old enough to suffer it! So,in future,my advice to those who willingly write mis- leading crap about 70's black music and fashions,write about what you know to be true and not about how a journalist in their mid-twenties (who probably wasn't old enough to see Saturday Night Fever first time round) imagined it to be. Till the next ish slems.....

NORMAN JAY

THE ANTI- SOCIAL BEHAVIOUR PAGE

"VIVIENNE WESTWOOD A WITCH"
WELL DARLING, RUSSELL HARTY
WILL NEVER DISS HER AJAIN !!!

MAN CALLED "VANBURN"
CHANGES THE GAS METER
AT SOHO'S MANYANAS !!!

PANDAMONIUM CLUB..LONDON
AL AND FRIEND AND CONSTANTINE...

THE SOCIAL ≈ AWARENESS PAGE...

ACISM, FASCISM & RESISTANCE

OURTESY.."SEARCHLIGHT.."
ANTI FACIST
MAGAZINE...

COURTESY... THE
WHOLE NATION
THATCHER... BEWARE!!

Saying no to the Poll Tax 1381

COURTESY... THE "AFRICAN NATIONAL CONGRESS"

TRIP

FIVE WEEK RUN FROM JUNE 4TH AT THE ASTORIA
HOUSE ∘ FUNK ∘ BALERIC BEATS

SINGLES

Big Mal,ex-Crystal Palace supremo and part-time Afro-American Islamic leader zooms into the 'Boy's Own' chart at No.4. An exclusive interview hopefully,next issue...

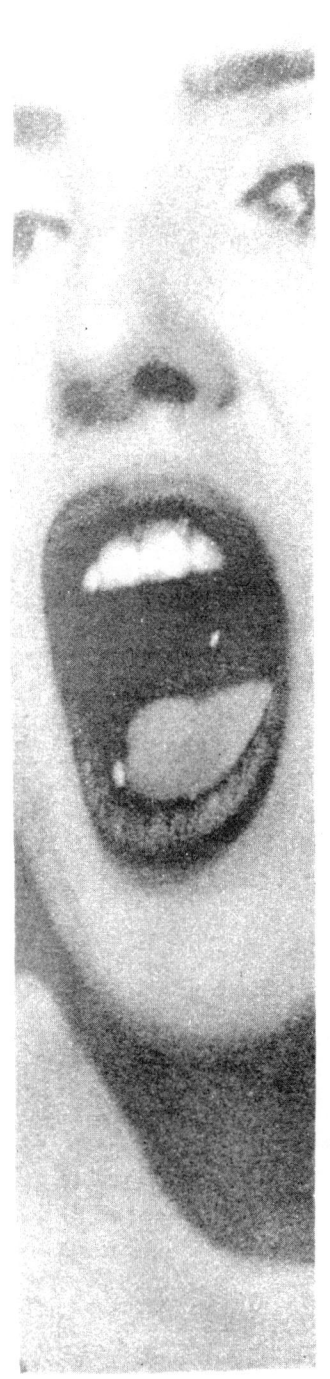

1. MANDY SMITH—I JUST CANT WAIT.

2. REVOLUTIONARY TACTITS—DONT PANIC.

3. BEATS WORKING—BEATS WORKING.

4. MALCOM X—BIRMINGHAM SUNDAY SCHOOL BOMBINGS.

5. KRS ONE—STOP THE VIOLENCE.

6. WILLIAM PITT—CITY LIGHTS.

7. JACKSON FIVE—GREAT TO BE HERE.

8. E.U.—DA BUTT.

9. TYREE—ACID OVER (REMIX).

10. GEORGE KRANZ—DIN DA DA.

11. BLACK RIOT—WARLOCK.

12. M—D—EMM—GET BUSY.

13. GENE AND JIM—SHAKES.

14. MARVA WHITNEY—HES THE ONE.

15. COCO,STEEL,LOVEBOMB—MIRACLES.

The 'Boy's Own Lagging and Ligging Team' have tried and tested the following tunes on the London dancefloors and all have passed our strictest quality control.
Go out and buy,steal or mug your local D.J. for them and any complaints shouldn't come to us as we were all well out of it at the time and even James Brown sounds brilliant when you're 'Rushing'...

THE FUTURE

前程

**EVERY THURSDAY
DJ's
PAUL OAKENFOLD & NANCY
AT

THE SANCTUARY
HUNGERFORD LANE
(behind heaven)
10-3·30am**

LAST EXIT TO BROOKLYN

BY HUBERT SELBY JR

Dear Reader,

     In my second review for this unheralded journal, I have decided, after much deliberation, to concentrate ye olde biro on the work of a certain Hubert Selby Junior, entitled "Last Exit To Brooklyn".

     The work in question in my mind stands not only as a literary beacon but a judicial one, as well as it was the subject of a long and much publicised legal wrangle. It's publishers were first prosecuted under Section One of the Obscene Publications Act, whereupon they had to suffer the seizure and destruction of three copies of the said book. 'Big Deal', you might say, but not satisfied with that, they were again prosecuted under Section Two of the very same Act. This time, however, they were fined a moronic ten grand, which in those days was no mean sum. The publishers of course appealed and after much lengthy diatribe, the case went back to the court of 'criminal' appeal, where defended by the now eminent playwright, John Mortimer, Q.C., the chap responsible for Rumpole of the Bailey etc., the previous verdict was overturned, the word 'obscene' redefined and the book unleashed on an unsuspecting public; a veritable literary cudgel thwacking large lumps out of competitors and critics alike.

     The relevance of all this legal bunny is that today this kind of legislation is flying all over t'shop, fuelled by those erstwhile buffoons, the Conservative government led by Margaret "Mussolini", Norman "Goering" and urged on by the sylph-like Mary 'de Torquemada' Whitehouse. They object to material that, let's be fair, is about as exciting as Good Friday Mass (three hours of Deist dribble which even had once the audacity to be delivered in a foreign tongue) and as controversial as a boil on a choir boys rump; I mean, did you read 'Spycatcher' (yawn), or see 'Brimstone and Treacle' (snore), do me a lemon Mary. My point being that if Shakespeare were around today, he'd have a hard job getting his plays performed and that if we don't keep our eyes and ears well and truly open, we could quite easily see such latter-day classics as 'Last Exit' fall prey to the Mets bonfire; in fact, I think this is more likely today than in 1964 (the trial year of L.E.B.). The subjugation of news items, for example, in the Falklands was immense; no, 'our boys' didn't leave their intestines, legs and grey matter in some obscure South Atlantic island, no, not them, they didn't even get dirty. We were and are told what they (the Tories) want us to be told: the newspapers and T.V. (especially the B.B.C.) are but Margarets puppets; so much for freedom of speech in the U.K., democracy in action, what a load of shite, shite, shite, but people believe it, as they did in Germany in 1934, the only difference is Thatch does not sport a black moustache and is uglier than her political soul-mate Adolf. I digress, but it's a point well worth a ponder; where will it end ?

POST-TRIAL EDITION
COMPLETE AND UNEXPURGATED
INTRODUCED BY ANTHONY BURGESS

PUBLISHED BY CALDER & BOYARS LTD   DISTRIBUTED BY CORGI BOOKS

Back to the book in question. 'Last Exit to Brooklyn'is, to coin a phrase,'Large',and is a must for anyone with a taste for the street,avenue or boulevard(that doesn't mean you eat bits of road,although some probably do)and is a must for anyone who knows what'IT'is all about;'IT' being without definition,a concept that can intrigue and destroy the individual.In other words,there's a vast difference between being streetwise and sleeping on it.

From the off,Hubert concentrates his typewriter employing all of its manifold variations of type to describe life(or something resembling it)in one grubby corner of a vast,sprawling urban conurbation known affectionately as Brooklyn.Absolutely no punches are pulled

'Mr. Selby's dream of reality, an urgent ticker-tape from hell, works stunningly.'   Kenneth Allsop SPECTATOR

in describing his fellow "humans" as predator,at once violent,lustful, vicious and,at times,completely loathesome (all good gear) and in a series of separate stories,all based on characters who,in the same book, are at once stars in one story and members of the supporting cast in another. By intermingling these folk,he builds up the book like a composer builds a symphony,in separate but inseparable sections,all housed under one overriding theme,the seamy side of life in Brooklyn,New York, New York.

The author uses every oppurtunity to break every rule ever taught in high school English class;in fact,he doesn't just break the rules, he kicks the proverbial faeces out of them:whole pages devoid of punctuation,capital letters and every literary device known to man. For example, in one of the chapters, 'Strike',a turgid tale of the tragic demise of a trades union official from picket line to poppers,from two up-two down, a wife and kids to common or garden fellatio,as administered by various transvestites,a typical literary demolition job is employed in this chapter, "FUCK YOU YA FLATFOOTSUNUFABITCH GOFUCKYASELF".

Ahem! In other parts,he uses no capitals and equally lacking in literary tackle,steams through page after page,devoid of commas,fullstops,parenthesis or any such pap.

Added to the subject matter (rape,alcoholism,transvesticism, drug abuse,G.B.H. and other such mundane comings and comings) this rapacious style does tend to punch a few holes in your tube journey; very much the Embankment when you wanted Leicester Square. One can feel Mr.Selby wincing as he refers to the story of Tralala gangbanged and left unconscious,she falls prey to the even younger neighbourhood produce who,

"took out their disappointment on Tralala and tore her clothes to small scraps put out a few cigarettes on her nipples jerked off on her jammed a broomstick up her snatch and left her lying among the broken bottles,rusty cans and rubble of the lot."

WINCE! WINCE!! WINCE!! WINCE!!

Last Exit to Brooklyn was found obscene at the Old Bailey November, 1967, a decision which was reversed by a historic Appeal Court judgement in July, 1968. Now, 'this honest and terrible book', as Anthony Burgess describes it in his Introduction to this edition, can take its rightful place as one of the major books of our time.

'It is a beautiful book, the kind of book you feel strongly about, and it is very, very moral.'   LONDON LIFE

In some respects,I can see why a few vicars,Tory M.P.'s,men who had the misfortune to be called Sir and frigid spinsters who never sucked dick (although probably all the rest did and do) but in my opinion,it is showing the degradation of this completely vile act in a disgusting fashion. Obscenity,in my opinion,is the glorification of the base (today that could have further connotations,so perhaps I should say glorification of the obscene) but Selby does not describe any of the somewhat unwholesome acts available to the reader in glowing terms;he describes them in graphic detail:a prick is a prick,not a penis;a shit is a shit,not a bowel movement. Last Exit to Brooklyn.

Most of the book is written in the vernacular and is,what I'd call,literary G.B.H. It shocks and stuns in a way that most cinematic efforts have difficulty in attaining,it's radical street and type setting throws the reader right into the world of schmucks,mooks and scumbags;it is a classic. As I am supposed to be writing a review,I think I should point out some of the books misgivings. Perhaps it's a bit over the top but on reading my copy of the Daily Planet ('Hong Kong Woman Cuts Off Husbands Penis') all I can say is "Heck as like." It may be larger than life but,on second thoughts,aren't most people. It may be slightly harrowing but who wants to read Mills and Boon? In my opinion,Selbys view of New York,albeit tawdry,is a realistic view,one that any individual may see just by getting off at the wrong subway, stop and walking North,only today it's probably worse. He never moralises,he never preaches,he just reports the incidents and does it in classic New York bridge and tunnel speak one hears from many a New York cabbie.

Q. "Hey,scumbag,whassatime?"

A. "Fourdthirty or some shidt like dthadt."

(The type of dialogue one hears in films but never believes until one visits New York.)

As I said in my last review,I only bother with the type of book you,the reader,would enjoy or get something from;in this case,it is definately the latter. What you would get is a blistering good read, with emphasis on the word 'blister'. I don't want to make the book sound too heavy,although the forced blow-job sequence,complete with human excrement still resplendant atop the perpetrators Peter was a might strong. There are paragraphs where no B,C,F,P or Y words are mentioned;some of the passages are amazingly succinct and,at times quite touching. At times,he even employs a liberal dashing of fullstops and even squeezes in a few semi-colons:in fact,I fancy a few myself,;;;;;;

The book,however riddled with controversy,is excellent in every respect and is completely essential reading. Today,the chapter 'Strike' for example,is perhaps even more topical now than ever,considering industrial action of the past few years;it is this timelessness that makes 'Last Exit' a literary milestone. I won't let to much out of the bag story-wise,as I want you to enjoy it as I did. It was given to me about twelve years ago by my father before I visited America and I opened it like any other book,only to find it's very unlike any other book I've ever read. I was,at times,shocked and taken aback. The title sounds completely mundane,not even slightly indicative of the book within.

Anyway guys and gals,y'all should check it. It is now available after a long absence (I still don't think it has a British publisher) in a completely tasteless jacket from Compendium Books,Camden Town. Don't let that put you off though,as this perhaps epitomises the adage "You can't tell a book,etc." Just read the blighter and have a good old cringe,as a bit of a cringe never harmed anyone. I loved it.

Gregariously Yours,
C.J.P.Sullivan.

'One of the most meaningful landmarks in the literature of this generation.'   THE SCOTSMAN

A FAIR COP?

P.C. NOSEY PARKER COME ON DOWN

A simple story of a policeman whose duties include policing football matches. Now read on...

Once upon a time there was a policeman called Anthony Darby, who, by no stretch of the imagination, could be called intelligent, but what he did not have in brains, he made up for in enthusiasm and hard work. When Anthony joined the force, he was an idealistic young man, eager for promotion but, sadly for Anthony as the years rolled by, promotion seemed to evade him. Consequently, Anthony was very pissed off. As he was out pounding the streets, he would wonder," What is it that I am doing wrong? I always go out with my fellow officers when it's one of their stag nights, even though it usually ends up in a brawl. I always do loads of overtime, etc. Anthony even went to extremes and joined the Freemasons, as the chance to mingle and be sychophantic with high-ranking officers was too good an opportunity to miss. But, alas, all to no effect.

All these things churned inside Anthonys mind, and, as a result, a strange metamorphosis began to take place. Gone was the caring, honest and upstanding man (that we had known and loved) to be replaced by a cruel, small-minded, vindictive little shit, willing to intimidate and harrass anyone who attended a footba match, on the pretext of maintaining law and order, ad nauseum...

It was at about this time that hooligans became the scourge of the footbal authorities and, for that matter, the Government. After the events of Luton and Heysel, the Conservatives decided that hooligans were a serious threat to our democracy(what democracy?-Ed.) Subsequently, very oppressive legislation, under the guise of the 'Public Order Act' was introduced. No-one really cared about the abuse of civil liberties that went with it, as the Act was needed to save our 'national game' from the disease that was killing it, as the Tory tabloids so succinctly put it.

This was just what Anthony Darby needed; an excuse to go totally over the top. Thus, armed with the Act and a steely determination (some call it paranoia) Anthony began his one-man crusade against Chelseas' hooligans. You see, years of being laughed at, outside Chelseas North Stand, by hooligans had turned Anthony into a hard and bitter man. Anthony took part in 'Operation Own Goal' a little undercover number-the first of its kind-whereby police in plainclothes infiltrated Chelseas gangs of hooligans and managed to bring them to task and have them convicted. This turned out to be a precedent, as many other clubs suffered the same fate. After all the praise he received from police cheifs, football directoi and so on, Anthony was finally promoted to Sargeant. Anthony was, of course, wel pleased at this and saw it as his first step up the slippery, slimy ladder of promotion.

Anthony had many tools at his disposal for his conquest of hooligans: police vans with visual surveillance, known as 'hoolivans'; cameras placed at strategic positions outside the ground; video equipment inside the ground to pinpoint 'potential flashpoints' as they were known. For Anthony it was just like Christmas with all these new toys to play with. There were even dossiers kept on known hooligans, their phones tapped and their houses watched but, unfortunately, the 'Big Brother' aspect of all this was missed by most people. Despite all this, however, Anthony still wasn't satisfied and so, every Saturday, he was sent to potential trouble-spots in London and even sometimes up North to Chelseas away games, with a view to helping his colleagues there to apprehend the hooligans. If they could not actually arrest them, then they resorted to that well-worn and time-honoured practise of verbally harrassing and intimidating them.

As a result of all this, Anthony became known as " hooligan-buster extraordinaire," a sort of primitive Bulldog Drummond on a one-man crusade. He knew no bounds as he plodded up and down the Fulham Road with his camera crew, often standing outside the Shed and being thoroughly obnoxious (not hard for him) to known hooligans, even if they had only come to watch the game. For Anthony, catching hooligans became an obsession but, as he continued his policy of harrassment, unknown to him, a group of ex-hooligans were plotting his downfall....

To be continued....

FASHION WAKE

Whilst I know that 'Boy's Own' is read by the odd square,most of our punters are extremely interested in dressing in the modern style,so it is for this reason that we have enlisted our very own frocks and slacks reporter,Steve Marney, a man who has waltzed his way into all our hearts throughout the years,to tell us all about Fashion Week.

10a.m. Friday British Fashion Week. Sitting next to me is a grey-haired woman with a real quilted Chanel bag. She is stuffing biscuits,twiglets and any freebies into her mouth or bag. Her assistant arrives. Natural hair. No make-up. Daughter to someone or other. Their conversation is enough to anesthetize any insomniac. " Exciting,eh! " These are fashion press!

The first show I see is not British,but the Belgium 6. Very well-staged and interesting clothes,plus male stripper,to the surprise of women and interest of men. (This is the fashion crowd). Clothes are expensive.

Next Rifat Ozbek or BLANCHE to his friends. Sorry,this show lacked any excitement. No over-the-top camp jobs for those dear old,Jewish American mums. " Sad,eh! "

Bruce Oldfield. What can I say!

Mictchiko Koshimo. Fun for only the young. Fake leather everywhere. Influenced by late 60's,early 70's. Models were half of London clubland. Everybody enjoying themselves.

Tony Gordon of Amen & Assention asked me, " Was this show for real? " " Did it sell? " Only time can answer that question,Tony.

SATURDAY.

10a.m. Today seemed forever.

Every show appeared to be geared towards department stores. So much so, that during Katherines show,I wasn't sure if Austin Reed's riding department had been given space on the show. If not,go to Austin Reed before buying anything from this horse-shoe collection.

Jasper Conran's show was nice!

SUNDAY.

Vivienne Westwood's show proved to be the most exciting. Her choice of tartan in bright colours was brilliant. Yet it lost strength in her boring men's and women's suits.
Her jackets influenced by armour,using tartans,were the best. Viv told the girls to be sexy. One tried,with a bottle in one hand,her dress pulled up over her belly. This was disappointing. Though the show was long,it was not boring.

John Galliano. Is he really JOHN? Came up with what was called a collection. Please John,answer this question. Who is Balenciagas Aunty? Reply to Freds,4, Carlisle Street.

MONDAY.

Finally,Hyper Hyper show was a tame affair,except for Pam Hogg's finale which was like a breath of fresh air. Wild with a flair.

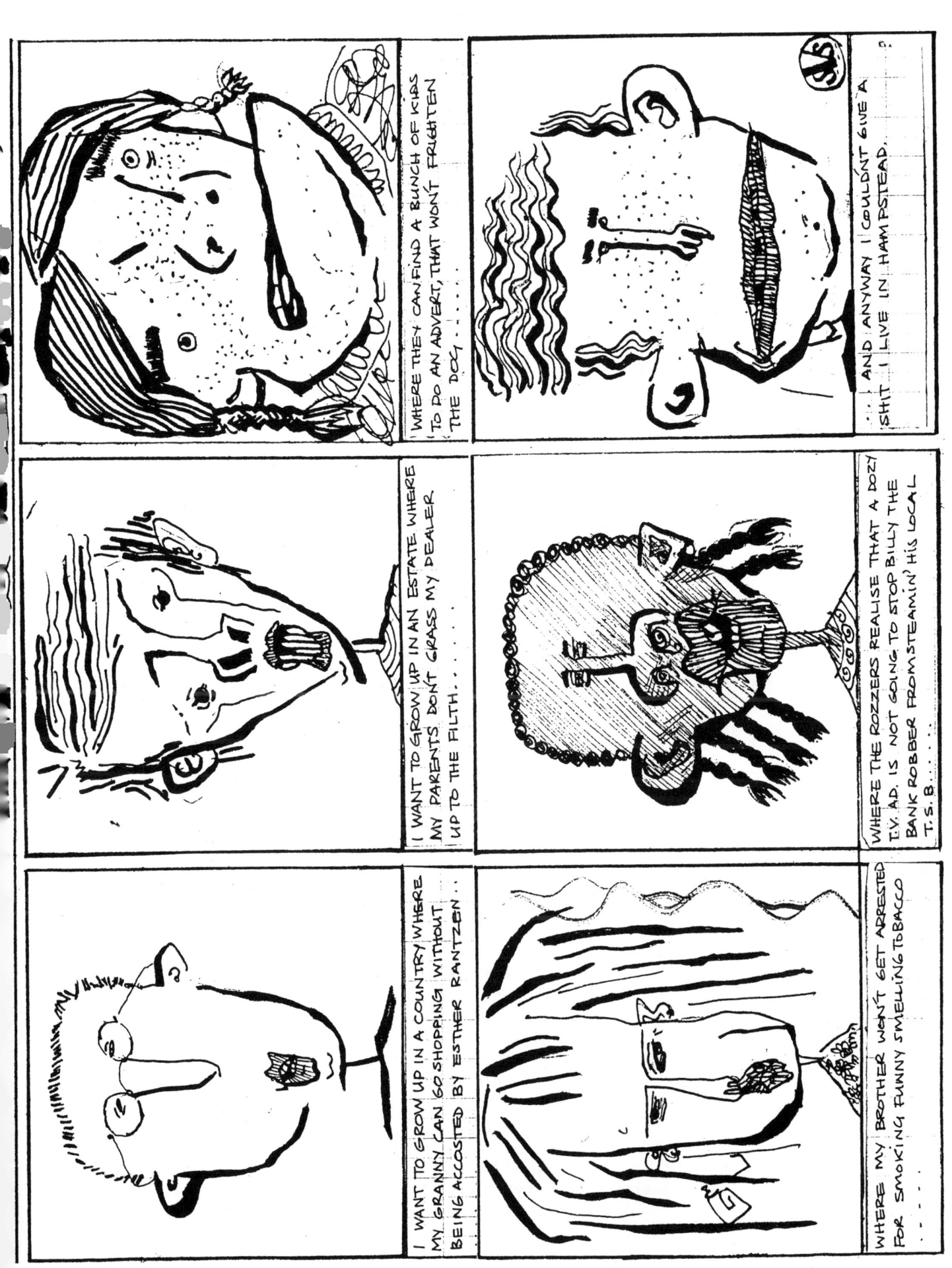

letters to ED.

Dear Boy's Own,

Here's a new target...
South London postmen. Being'on the
post'is now on a par with being a
black cab driver in the Cockney cred-
ibility league. Posties around Southwark wear Timberlands and positively
bowl around the streets. Also,forget
Paul Smith or Chevignon,as the'in'
thing to wear to the match is the
posties badge. It's the ream pleaser
for the geezers. "Postman Pat,Post-
man Pat,Postman Pat,with his black
and white staff".

Casper the milkman,M.F.C.

Ed.-You're probably the sort of per-
    son who moans about the people
    who stand on 'Yids Hill'and watch
    the game for nothing.

Dear Boy's Own,

Enjoyed your publication.
Much bigger and better than expected,
thought it would be a wee pissy leaflet;
a very good read. Best laugh was Millwall
the Dog. No,the best laugh was that Welsh
Swansea City sheep-shagger:Jacks? More
like jack-ass. Talking of sheep-shaggers,
Aberdeen are the only boys worth bother-
ing about up here but they are soon sorted. As for Rangers,just schoolkids and
tramps.
P.S. If you're ever up Scotland haggis-
hunting,check the Shake and Kangeroo Club.
Edinburgh.
" We always come home with a result. "

Steven Watson,Gilmerton,Edinburgh.
Hibernian Capital City Service.

Ed.-We don't go near Scotland,Steve,not
    since Hadrian's Wall fell down.

Dear Boy's Own,

I am one of your many
thousands of fanatical readers,altho-
ugh I haven't actually paid for one
yet. However,I've enclosed money for
all back issues and you can keep the
change(God knows,you need it). I wou-
be grateful if you would send them t-
me or I'll have to take drastic acti-
and bring a rhinestone herd from my
manor down to your Battersea H.Q. an-
ask for my money back. If this don't
work,then we'll...go home!!! I have
just one word to describe the firm,
fashion and accent of Swansea...Shit
(Boy's Own,4,letters). Also,the 6.57
definately do not exist. As for that
character,'Millwall the Dog',my cat
'Perky'says you're a mug and he will
have it with you any day.
Yours,in anticipation,
A.Gooner,Ealing.

P.S. If you print this pile of shit,
     please leave out my address,as
     my cat,Perky,can't really have
     it.

Ed.- Who said we don't print letters
     from Gooners? Be careful of tho-
     early morning calls from plod!

FACK OFF 'E'S LYIN' JADGE

NO M'LUD, I DID NOT STAMP ON THE DEFENDANT'S
TESTICLES AND JUMP UP AND DOWN ON HIS THROAT.
NATURALLY I JOINED IN WITH THE ATTACK ON THE
ARSENAL FANS,SO AS NOT TO BLOW MY COVER.
I WAS VERY CAREFUL NOT TO DESTROY THE TRUST
THAT I HAD GRADUALLY BUILT UP DURING THIS
UNDER-COVER OPERATION. THAT MAN IS A THUG,
A MINDLESS YOBBO AND I'M PROUD TO HAVE USED
ANY METHODS NECESSARY TO RESTRAIN THIS IDIOT.
I'M ANTI-VIOLENCE, M'LUD, BUT PRO-DISCIPLINE
THE BEST REMEDY FOR HIS SORT IS A SWIFT HEAD-BUTT.

letters

Hello Boysie,

          BILLY SOLLOX, Roving
Reporter here. Sitting here, out in the
midday sun on a hot Italian afternoon,
rocking the sunburns away to none other
than a splendid Boy's Own cassette. Missing the London night-life badly...We had
a visit from the (not so) Fat Tony-'that
famous Rare Growe' D.J. They even did the
club out with banners of platforms,flares
and Bjorn Borg. Everyone was disappointed
when they found out Fat Tony was skinny
and white. F.T. kicked off the evening
with the 'I give my right arm for' Rare
Growe classic, " We Are Family."

      However, an enjoyable night was had
playing up the 'lovable, cor blimey cockney'
and being a chummy hillman to the girl who
runs the Club 'Donut'. I haven't paid a
penny since. Anyway, it's 20 degrees in the
sun, I got wine, music and a topless
Italian beauty next to me. So I'm off to
roger the spa now, so catch you on the rebound,

             Ciao, " ha, ha,"
             Philip Goss
         Senigallia Italia.

      THE BANANA STRIKES BACK.

Everton,Everton,suckers once more,
Mighty Liverpool have shown you the door.
You played lots of replays and gave it some clout,
But was it all worth it,now that you're out?

You beat the Middlesborough and Sheffield so sound,
But then you met Liverpool on your own ground.
You laughed at our winger with the shaven head,
" Look at that monkey all in red."

You then threw bananas and held up your arms,
Until little Quasi played a 1-2 with Barnes.
He stuck it so firm with his magic left foot,
And bent it superb just like all that fruit.

All you Blues kept on shouting but who popped up,
Why,little Ray Houghton to put you out of the cup.
Off his head and into the net,
The Reds for the Double,I'll give you a bet.

Old man Reidy was knackered and bent,
His bottle of Grecian probably spent.

I hope you enjoyed this little verse,
The Number 9 shirt is still in your curse.
I'm glad I'm a Red and walk so tall,
It must be heartbreaking winning F... ALL.
           ....AGAIN.

From one good skin to another.

boys own six.... soon come.. ha

A LARGE HEARTY THANX TO THE FOLLOWING...

FIRSTLY AND MOST IMPORTANTLY TO CYMON ECKELS A TRUE BOYS OWNER ... JOSEPH HASEMAN A TRUE NEW FACE ON THE LONDON CLUB SCENE .... ROGER AND MAGGIE THE PROUD OWNERS OF THE BIG FUCK OFF HIPPY BUS ... TO SAUCEPANMAN AND BOG-MAN (AKA NKK) FOR MANY A HEARTY CHUCKLE... CLIVE, GRANT AND ALL THE THAMESMEAD CHAPS ... DAVE LITTLE, BOND, KEITH 'THE YOB' ALLEN, PETE 'ONE PUNCH' WYLIE, PAUL McKEE AND JOHNNY WALKER (TRUE LONDON RECORDS SHOOMERS), PLUG AND ALL THE KINGSTON BOYS, THE SEX PETS (FOR THE TEDDINGTON PARTY), THE FRESH AIR GIRLIES ... EDDIE at the DUFFER of ST GEORGE, ALL THE BOYS AT AMERICAN CLASSICS, 'ROCKA and REDD', ALL THE NORTHERN BASTARDS AT ROBOT, RAY FROM BATTERSEA AND ALL THE LOYAL SUPPORTERS WHO REALLY UNDERSTAND WHAT 'BOY'S OWN' IS ALL ABOUT.
TARA !

Boy's Own, Issue 5
was brought to you by
Terry Farley, Andy Weatherall,
Steven Mayes and Simon Eckel.

Contributers...Norman Jay
            Chris Sullivan
            Mick Mahoney
            Steve Marney
            Paul Oakenfold

Front cover
   By Danuta. Thanks also
to the Archway youth for the
tuff 'method' pose...

Any contributions to 'Boy's Own'
should be sent with a £50 note to..
      216, Gordon House,
         Bullen Street,
            Battersea,
               S.W.11.

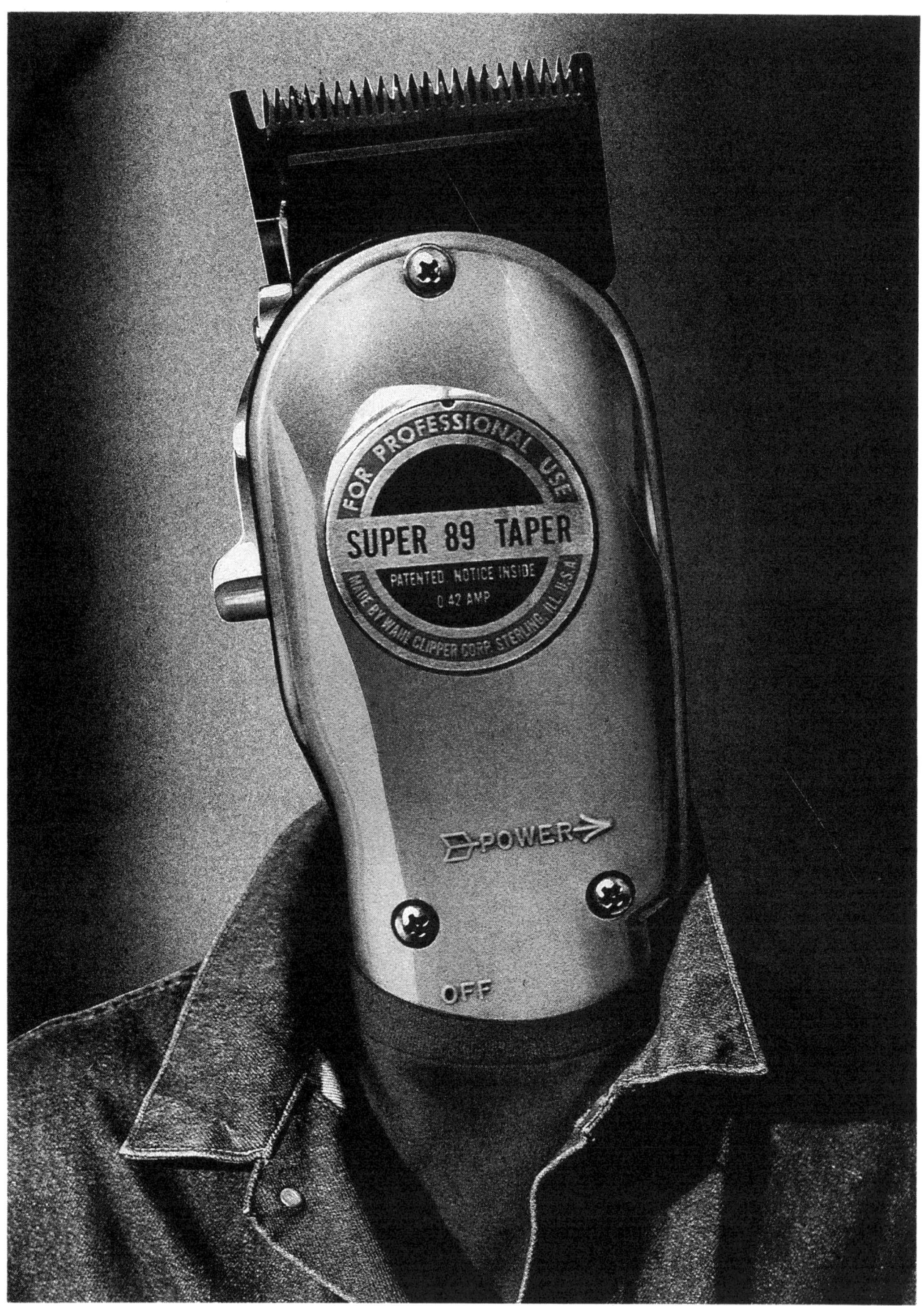

B A R B E R   S H O P S

LONDON: 56 BROOK ST, W1. TEL: 01-493 5428. 44 SLOANE ST, SW1. TEL: 01-235 1957. 11 FLORAL ST, WC2. TEL: 01-240 6635.
MANCHESTER: 19/21 KING ST. TEL: 061-833 0681. LEEDS: WEST RIDING HOUSE, ALBION ST. TEL: 0532 448636.

VIDAL SASSOON

No. 6
Autumn 1988

" BOYS OWN.
The ONLY FANZINE
that wishes it Hadn't
claimed to Be 'THE ONLY FANZINE that gets Right on ONE'
A Few months back — OOH ER Madam "

Good MORROW my YOUNG Siblings,
and WELCOME to Yet MORE Ramblings from the
Leaky Biros of Boys Own MANSIONS. Tis MANY MOONS
since LAST We spoke, so pull up a slice of cake
AND POUR YOURSELF A MUG of HERBAL tEA as We
take Another trip with those wacky Funsters,
the Loveable mop-tops themselves, the Boys OWN
EditORIAL Team. "So where have theY BEEN"; hear You
MURMER into Your PIPING HOT MUGS of LAPSONG SUCHONG,
Well when they PHONED ME to comission My usual FrontPiece
these are The stories theY Gave me.

FARLEY. To be truthful He didn't call me I called Him.
His MUM Said, and I quote " Terry's not very well at
The moment and won't be iN to work tomorrow... "
when she realised who it was she changed This to
" Terry not very well at the moment and the magazine
will be out in two weeks "

MAISEY. currently giving guided walks ARound
    KILBURN's MARXist LANDMAnks.

CYMON. BUSY at the typewriter DOING the first
draft of His LONG Awaited Novel a semi-fictional
work " LES, SoN of LES ".

ANDREW. Last seen working For Wandsworth
Borough street cleansing department, and moonlighting
as a Youth culture correspondant for the CHIPPING NORTON
PARISH MAGAZINE.

        All that's LEFT FOR Me to SAY is
" don't give UP YOUR DAY JOBS and call me in another
    6 months. "

        THANK You and GOODNight ...
            The Outsider _ x _

SHOCK HORROR PROBE DEPT.

At least once a week we are subjected to another expose in the media about the current club/drug scene...well, I suppose the headline **EIGHT HUNDRED ENJOY THEMSELVES** wouldn't sell many copies.

You must have seen those pieces of journalistic excrement written about lame-brains (they couldn't be any thing else could they? Having their photos taken whilst pretending to be out to lunch) for lame-brains ("Oi, Vera, go and see if our Jason's got one o'them Smiley shirts in his wardrobe...I always thought he was on drugs.")

But now comes the real club expose. Your soaraway **BOY'S OWN** exclusively reveals the evil world of the......**LAGER CLUBS.** Places where pushers with names such as Carlsberg and Watney's peddle their mind-bending drugs. They sell openly, without fear of prosecution, and even have special promotion nights where scantily clad pushers **MOLLS** hand out t-shirts bearing slogans such as:

        "I HAVEN'T GOT A DRINK PROBLEM -
        I DRINK, I FALL OVER, NO PROBLEM!"

                    and

            I'M A FAT BASTARD
            WITH THE I.Q. OF
            A RUBBER PLANT -
            GET ME A FOSTERS!

On a more serious note, these lager-crazed youngsters (and oldsters) then start beating up either eachother or the bouncers, terrorize taxi queues and abuse anything faintly female unfortunate enough to be in the vicinity. And, if these dregs manage to reach their motors, there's a very good chance that they'll kill themselves or somebody else on the way home.

These things happen on any day in any town with the violence largely unreported. And the curious thing is I haven't seen the likes of Richard Branson, flanked by heavies, confiscating pints. But then again that's the wacky world of double standards...................

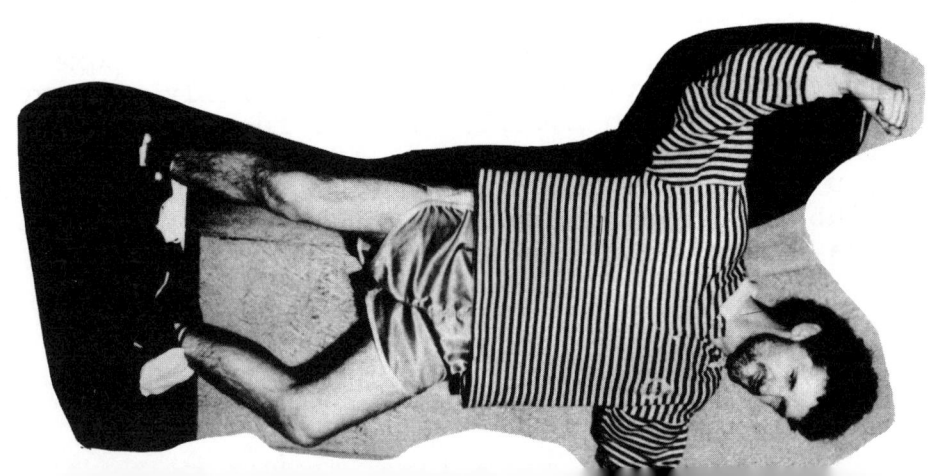

CLOAKROOM CAPERS

Now, those of you who are regular readers of this irregular periodical will know that last month our very own Andrew Weatherall (aka Jack
Hatchback) looked at the rumours that abound around town. Continuing this
flimsy theme, we now look at the main location where these rumours start,
described by some as the poormans 'Freds', offices to a thousand duckers
and divers..." The toilets of Londons clubland..."

For those of you innocent of the dangers these 'clubs within clubs
hold, here are a few of the characters to avoid when you simply just have
to go...

CHARACTER ONE...RALPH MOUTH, SULPHATE FIEND.

Now, before we start, most of us have a Ralph inside us, although
some of us let him out once too often...Well, you've been avoiding him
all night and you was only on nodding terms with the geezer anyway but
you're the only one left in the club who he hasn't talked the bollocks
off yet. True to form, you're captured in the Gents khasi and pinned to
the wall by Ralphs manic and totally interesting thesis on who exactly
is the most boring centre-forward ever to put on an England shirt, Francis
Lee or Gary (Interesting) Lineker.
Solution: Either get nosed up severely and enjoy this 3hr. debate or
          avoid the Gents when Ralphs about.

CHARACTER TWO...THE PRACTICAL JOKER.

The only good thing about the jokers is that Ralph Mouth always
falls for the same old trick. Yes, you know it, an enticing line of white
substance laying forgotten (apparently) on a urinal top. Do you, don't
you? Then the sniggering outside gives it away. Just one dab and you
would have been the butt of every joke for weeks. The only problem is
50% of the people who fall for it swear blind to getting a "right good
buzz".

CHARACTER THREE...PRINCESSES AND QUEENS.

At just about every one-nighter, the mens toilet is full of 16yr old
long-legged nubile temptresses always accompanied by some old queen. Now
the 'raving' is no problem, he's only there for the rumour spreading.
It's the willie-spotting females that are disconcerting, especially if
you're part of the Inter-City Small Dick Firm (also see Ralph Mouths
shrivelled willie section). Now this worry brought on by the presence
of these luscious ladies has caused many a hurried, embarressed shake
and led to those awful damp spots that us chaps know so well, eh!

Other characters to avoid are the drugs pests who follow everyone
into the toilet, followed by those immortal words, "Got any personal?"
Also, try to give a wide berth to the D.I.Y. chemist who usually bangs
on the door, while you're having a good dump, shouting, "Can't you find
somewhere else to go to shit?! People want to use this toilet." These
budding scientists can usually be identified by their white moustaches
and Hamleys under-fives chemistry sets.
Finally, it's the good old bouncer. Sometimes his attempts at playing Popeye Doyle are useful, especially when you're cornered by Ralph
Mouth, although usually all the fuckers want is a 50% share out...and
they say socialism is dead. If, unlike 95% of the Boy's Own readership
you don't fall into any of these categories, we have the perfect night
club accessory for you, keeping you safe from the dangers mentioned...
The Boy's Own Incontinence Bag.

CHARACTER FOUR...TOILET TEDS - THE ACID DICKHEADS
     These new additions to the toilets of clubland are usually to be
found cooling down their stir-fried brains underneath the cold water tap,
only briefly emerging to groan those immortal words, "Top buzz, geezer!"
Another strange ritual of the Acid teds is the Ecstasy handshake. It's
sweaty, long and vice-like, it should be avoided at all costs, especially
when you're having a 'night off'. Anyway, back to toilet ted, he's in
trouble...some joker told him mixing E with windowpane and a jaffa is the
supremo buzz. The only problem is that Ted swallowed the story..literally!
I'm afraid that one day the old Boy's Own saying 'Better dead than an Acid
Ted' may not be so funny for some!!!

The Earliest known photoGRAphic Evidence of ANTON le PiRate.

                    JIHAD

     The wacky, photocopied world of fanzines used to be the domain
of middle-class students with 'O' levels on the suicide of Ian Curtis
and his final note to the duffle-coated world. Now another breed of
trainspotters have put pen to paper: the soccer fanzines.
     Brought up on a diet of Peter Osgoods sideburns and wacky terrace
tales, these well-meaning lads yearn back to the days of Charlton, Law
and Fitzpatrick (Madman-Ed.). These fanzines are aimed though at the type
of punter who travels away to Newcastle armed only with a rolled up copy
of 'When Saturday Comes' and a thermos of minestrone, hardly the sort of
hardware to deter a pack of savage gremlins who have been mainlining Newcastle Brown all morning, while waiting for the Cockney special.
     Now onto the scene comes JIHAD, a soccer fanzine written by not
only genuine fans of the game but also boys who seem to know the score
and so maybe Jihads message of anti-racism just may get through to one
or two of the barmies who make monkey noises at gifts of God like John
Barnes. Quoted in Soul Underground as a more intelligent Boy's Own, Jihad
is nothing like Boy's Own. Frankly, those teds who write Soul Underground
have probably never read Boy's Own but my loathing of souls version of
the Sun is getting my thoughts off of Jihad, so I'll stop being bitchy.
     Selling around town for only 20p it's quite a bargain and with
writers that include Robert Elms, Adam Porter and Nick Ball you know a
sensible left-wing look at soccer is assured. The major plus of Jihad
though is the cartoons, especially 'Larry the lamb, He's an England fan'
who comes across brilliantly like a barmy Millwall the Dog.
     So, at last a fanzine for soccer fans who don't collect programmes
and listen to Half Man Half Biscuit records.

JIHAD - 40p inc. post.
     c/o 29, Heath Street, London, N.W.3 6TR

FIRST FLOOR KENSINGTON MARKET LONDON W8 PHONE 01 937 4431

UPPERS & DOWNERS

potty freddie boswell haircuts

kicker boot revival

tv pirates (Brookie's Sinbad)

ade's moped

potty korean boxing judges
pretending to be leeds fans

michael clark dancing in
celtic footie tops

paranoid persons who insist
that the hot dog man outside
future is plainclothes plod.

casey jones tv show

perfect day t-shirts

shakespeares potty harmonica

barry spectrum's designer
black eye

bandana clad banana heads

converse (acid stereotype)

tv pirates (the godfather
of acid house, hahaha.)

teds calling teds, teds.

everton boys pretending to
be korean boxing judges

network seven yuppies

plainclothes plod in
dayglo barbour.

boy's own t-shirts (well
sad)

people sticking amyl up
your nose when you're
catching forty winks.

total nonces who let
tv crews film in clubs
and raves.

the so-called experts who
slagged off ben johnstone.

kerry dixon

going up to people and
saying "what are you like?"

The No. 1 downer goes
this edition to Gary
(oi, oi, The Scab) Bushell
and Wick Sky for their
righteous campaign against
that home of homosexuality,
Black Yardies, Child
Molesters, El Tel, Loony
Lefties, 15 Stone Lesbians,
etc.... The Acid House Party!

A CLOCKWORK REMIX

THERE I WAS, OH MY BROTHERS, trying to make up my rassodock what to do with the evening with my faithful but fagged and fashed four-legged droog, Millwall the dog. He'd just come in after using up a large amount of energy expenditure performing a bit of the old in-out in-out on a weepy young poodle.

When, out of the blue, oh my brothers, I get a call from, you guessed it, Boy's Own mansions asking your hero to write a ditty for their nuking little fanzine without so much as a promise of some pretty polly for my efforts, but me being a brother and all that cal, I decided to have a bash.

The raskazz (story) begins back in '71 when a certain film director known as Stanley Kubrick, who's made such films as 2001, THE SHINING, FULL METAL JACKET, asks your humble narrator to star in a viddy he was making, A CLOCKWORK ORANGE, with a promise of FREE rucks with fat stinking Billy goat Billy boys and the old in-out in-out and driving around playing hogs of the road in a real horrorshow auto. I couldn't say no.

But, oh my brothers, this is where the weepy part of your humble narrators story begins. Little was I to know this piece of celluloid would make a nation tremble in their shoes. Daily gazzettas (newspapers) started accussations that it provoked a bit of the old ultra-violence, filthy stinking rotten drunkies were getting the odd tolchoking from bratneys (yobs) with no manners. Worst of all, art school chellovecks (boys) without ever tasting the joys of the old MILK-PLUS (bolshy great yarblockos to ECSTASY) started forming pitiful picnic-hamper bands named after the film; HEAVEN 17, ECHO AND THE BUNNYMEN, LABEL KOROVA RECORDS, their song " THE CUTTER." The odd droogie-inspired viddy also popped up: Frankies " Pleasure Dome " (driving scene) but worst of all was those globy bottles of cheap stinking chip oil, SIGUE SIGUE SPUTNIK, using your humble narrators fave subway and artwork to promote their wares. They recieved a swift boot to their guttiwuts (stomach) spewing out eggweg and lomticks (toast soldiers) of toast they had for breakfast for their efforts.

As you can imagine, oh my brothers, fellow droog Stanley pulled the plugs on the horrorshow movie, causing all you young malchicks and devochkas frustration, as alot of you didn't even get a chance to feed your glazzies (eyes) on the masterpiece. Anyway, more was to come. Stanley has now seized the rights of this movie in this country, stopping the release of it on viddy while he is in residence in this country, not as some people thought, because of Government suppression. Anthony Burgess, who'd written the novel back in 1962, changed the ending to the story by adding a final and extra chapter.

A small play of the film appeared in the early eighties, got into a lot of cal (shit) when Burgess found out, but being a horrorshow chelloveck, he eventually allowed it to continue, millicrates and all.

Underground viewing of the film has been shown in the capital under the pseudonym of Futuristic Holidays 2000 but they are few and far between. A film club based in OXFORD recently advertised that they would be showing the film for one week every night for free but Kubrick found out and slapped an injunction on them, a court case to follow. If you happen to be on vacation in France or New York, there are plentiful showings of it, also it's legally available on viddy throughout Europe.

But with a little bit of luck you should be able to obtain the odd bootleg copy out there. But beware my brothers, as your narrator found out, after hiring what was supposed to be the viddy of your dreams, I sat down with the old pee and em (Mum and Dad) flicked the old play button on the viddy machine, when, with a shock to my system, appeared in all his glory was this filthy rotten malchick with plentiful panhandle and yarbles dipping his love-stick into a devochka he had there. But, without so much as a scream, your hero ejected viddy (to eyeball at a later date) to save the day

the day, leaving pee and ems mouths jangling.

Well there we have a story of a young droog in a horrorshow movie cut off in his prime. Do not tell me Warriors or Wanderers ever came near it. Stanley, despite all his faults, made a movie never to be forgotten.

Anyway, I'm now going down to the Korova Milk Bar for some synthemese or drencom which will sharpen me up for the evening, making all the hairs on my plot and the old pan-handle stand end-wise.
REAL HORROR SHOW.

Paul McKee.

ROBOT

**323 kings rd. 37 floral st. hyper~hyper.
LONDON**

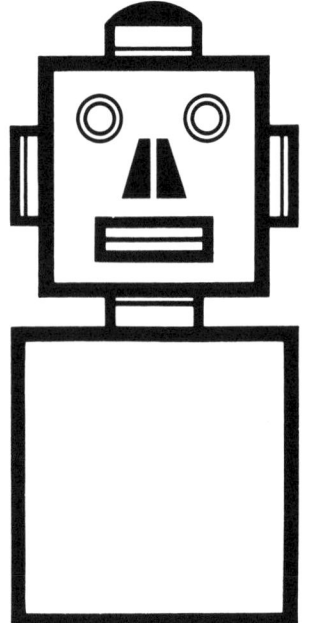

MILLWALL THE DOG

"...all right teds, Millwall The Dog is back and I've swopped me studded collar for a flower garland and I'm on the top buzz......anyway before I gib off down Clink, I'd better scribble this dribble for those sad cases at Boys Own and let my legions of fans know what's happening in town....
On the footie front it's all gone kybosh!!! Evertons' boys came ranting and raving out of Surrey Docks looking like a right herd of Harry Blurtmans, frothing behind the gaffers and all that caper. C'mon Scousers, you've obviously watched one too many re-runs of Hooligan......Speaking of logmans, anyone see that Network 7 Acid House milarkey?!!..."Anyone for Lucozade?" No thanks, yuppie, I'll have another bottle of amyl....yuppie wankers......We even had some geezer telling us he invented the word 'matey'. What is he? A bottle of bubble bath or wot?...Also them Chelsea boys looked well iffy - nice one chaps - although I'm not quite sure who you were taking the piss out of......Lastly go see that Jesus film. Well good. To be straight though they should have had an happier ending, with the geezer riding off into the sunset with that Mary-Doris...'til the next time my children......See ya Loggs!!!..............."

MILLWALL THE DOG.

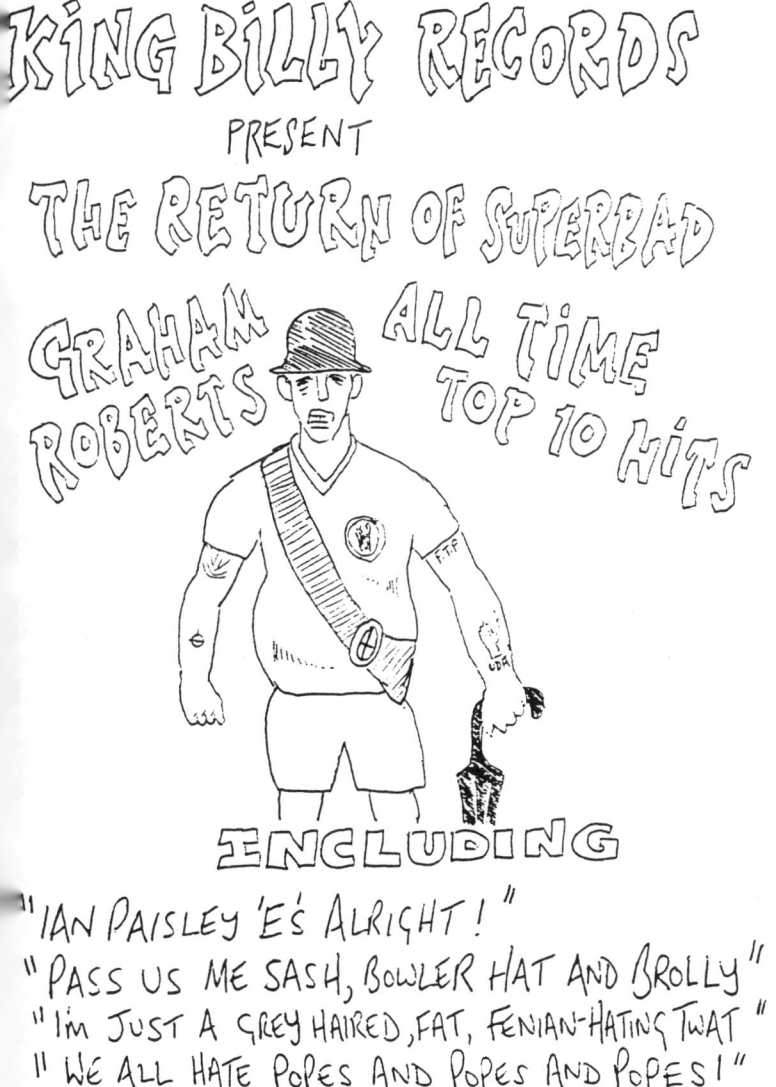

KING BILLY RECORDS
PRESENT
THE RETURN OF SUPERBAD
GRAHAM ROBERTS ALL TIME TOP 10 HITS

INCLUDING

"IAN PAISLEY 'E'S ALRIGHT!"
"PASS US ME SASH, BOWLER HAT AND BROLLY"
"I'M JUST A GREY HAIRED, FAT, FENIAN-HATING TWAT"
"WE ALL HATE POPES AND POPES AND POPES!"
AVAILABLE ON ORANGE VINYL

THE TONY BENN FUNK FORCE
LEFT SWINGING

1 9 7 6

Well, '76 was a pretty good year, wasn't it? Long, hot and funky. The Americans (the Black Americans that is) finally fused all of the early dance music influences together and very nearly got it perfect. Those were the days when the neighbourly folks of the good old US of A elected Presidents who could actually do their three times table and when the thought of the U.K. as a nuclear base was just a glimmer in Ronnies eye. Land of the free and home of the K.K.K!

It was only when some idiot thought up Saturday Night Fever, a couple of years later, did that spirit decline. I blame Mr.Travolta and Co. for our winter of discontent in '79! Yes, it was about as welcome as someone sticking a Garfield with sucker feet on your car windscreen!

Still, '76's influence still lingers. The clubs have changed, though many of the faces have remained the same. Global Village is now Heaven. The Lacy Lady begat the Beat Route. The Beat Route begat the Wag and now Shoom rises up. We've gone from "Young hearts run free" to "Slightly older hearts race quite alot!"

Jeans are still ripped but have lost their street cred. From Johnny Rotten to Bros. How the mighty have fallen. Indeed, we now have lost our rebelling punk influence in favour of a younger Y.T.S.-conscripted generation who don't remember what life under a Labour Government is like. Yes, TINA's taken over (There is no alternative).Our Gob-smacking, poll-taxing, war-mongering, bring-back-hanging, send-'em-back-where-they-came-from-ing Government of the Eighties. I tell you, if that woman told us to cut off our heads, 7 out of 10 people interviewed would do it!

Governments sadly remain (Not for long, I hope!) but the soul artists can stay as long as they like. Evergreens like the O Jays, the Whispers, Brass Construction, Johnnie Taylor et al.

Is todays music up to the mark though? I think it is. Of course, it is more pasteurised/homogenised but quality will always shine through and it is there in all forms of Black music from House to Jazz Fusion. In fact, '76 still has a big impact on todays music. Look at Wally Jump Jnr. or the Pasadenas. Also I think, Will Downings 'A Love Supreme' will be a fondly remembered track in years to come.

The spirit of '76 lives on!

Toby Walker.

THE KEMP TWINS

MART

GAZ

PHIL-T

WE BOTH FEEL THAT WE CAN ACCURATELY PORTRAY THE KRAYS BECAUSE WE HAVE SO MUCH IN COMMON WITH THEM. LIKE THEY WERE FROM BETHNAL GREEN AND WE'RE FROM ISLINGTON, BOTH NORTH OF THE THAMES Y'SEE AND THEY MURDERED A FEW PEOPLE WHILST WE MURDERED A FEW SONGS. THEY LOVED THEIR MUM AND SO DO WE...AND...ER...THEY'RE BOTH BROTHERS LIKE US. ANYWAY THE FILM'S CALLED "JACK McVITIE WORE A KILT."

OUT ON THE FLOOR

THE KARMA COLLECTIVE BARN DANCE.....THE REAL

SUMMER OF LOVE STARTED AND ENDED HERE.

BOY'S OWN MOAN

About seven years ago a geezer called Phil opened a club called
The Dirtbox. This heralded a whole new era for London's
clubland subculture. In the following years the warehouse
style of rave has been perfected by many - from Westworld to
the Raid club, Family Function to Dave Mahoney's shindigs.
Sadly the rise of acid House and its 'up all night' philosophy
has spawned cowboy promoters and a new low in warehouse
standards...Enter the Shithole.

What we now get for our fiver is damp, smelly firetraps full of
arsonists, ruffians, mugs and teds going apeshit to second-rate
DJ's playing "Can You Feel It?" The few girls who do dare
venture into these khazis face purse dippers or groping E-heads
who don't know how to handle drugs properly.

Anyway, Winter is coming and the dayglo shorts brigade will
soon be tucked up in bed or back down the pub. By then though
terminal damage may well have been done. Who will be left then
for the greedy promoters to charge a pound for a can of coke?
......Think about it chaps!!!

BOY'S OWN recommended clublist: LOUD NOISE (Tuesdays) THE RAID
(a welcome return), DREAMLAND, THE SHOOM (Members only, back
in November), KLUB TRICK, GOD'S DISCO, DESTINATION MOON.

OUT ON THE FLOOR

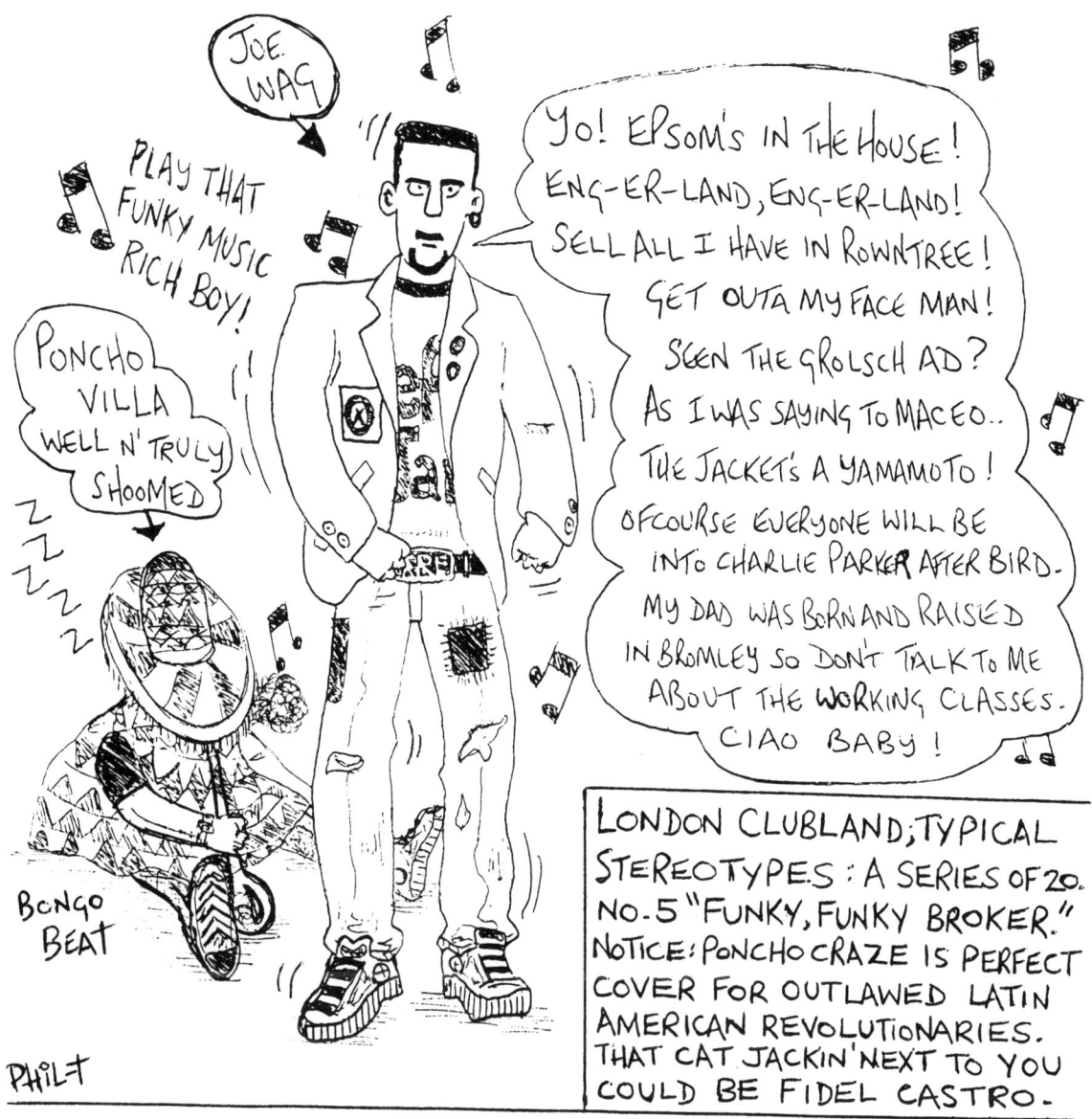

BALEARIC SMOKESCREEN

At the moment clubland is full of smoke; some real, some imaginary. Sometimes the smoke is so thick that you can't see the plain clothes gaffers until they've stuck their fingers up your jacksy. Already the scared DJ establishment are throwing up smoke over the real Balearic scene. Curious how the knockers seem to be white middle class DJs who tell you they come from 'the Grove' (Surbiton not Ladbroke - Ed). They simply don't understand what Balearic Beats are. To be honest Balearic isn't a style of music but an attitude and an awareness of diverse dance tunes that few dj's actually have. What's wrong with a club where you can hear A Split Second, Ten City, Front 242, Ce Ce Rogers and the Thrashing Doves all in the same night? Sure beats sexist, homophobic, big dick rap. At least we think so. The Top Buzz will not be beaten........

OUT ON THE FLOOR

AMSTERDAM TED-FREE ZONE

"Play the hardcore akid," was the demand from one over excited
Dutch clubber who was immediately ejected from the DJ booth in
the direction of his shocked pals. Meanwhile five hundred
punters raved enthusiastically to the happy, happy mix of
Balearic and House being spun by our own Danny Rampling.

The Amsterdam event, organised by London's Trance and the local
Soho Connection, provided a ted-free, plod-free rave and gave
London clubbers a chance to show Europe that not every British
kid wears an Invasion Of Germany t-shirt with an attitude to
match.   In fact after only an hour or so the flare-groove
attired Dutch and the Shoom/Spectrum kids blended into one big
Common Market Jacking Zone. With the rave ending at 5 a.m. to
the strains of "Big Fun", the only damper on the night appeared
in the form of a British camera crew who pestered Danny & Jenny
for the obligatory wild'n'wacky acid/drugs interview which
needless to say was declined:

"C'mon Danny, just say the acid house is very good in
Amsterdam."
"What is Acid House anyway?' replied our Dan. "The press
should know as the phrase is their invention."

Amsterdam itself is well relaxed, full of friendly people,
pushbikes and fucky fucky theatres frequented by British Marks
& Spencers clones...

"Well, it's something to tell them about at the Surbiton
Conservative club, dear. But tell me was that snake real?!!!"

Back to the gigs and midnight was upon us. The warehouse bash
was brilliant. Situated in the docks and as big as two
football pitches, it contained three separate dance rooms - a
reggae room, Norman Jay's room and a Shoom area in which Danny
and Colin Faver played happy classics to a top buzz crowd. The
t.v. crews were back, uninvited of course, they fell arse over
tit through a hole in the wall, causing half the wall to fall
on top of them. Why t.v. crews have to shlep over to Holland
for acid house horror stories, when the other half of London
wants to get their bandana clad heads on Network 7 amazes me.
All was kicking well until 5.30 a.m. when the sound man pulled
the plug, reason being the blown bass speakers.

The ending was all too abrupt for Shoomer Sandy (the 8.15 from
Aberdeen!) and his attempts to persuade everyone to tie the
sound guy up and turn the power back on failed, mainly due to
the fact that the geezer looked as if he had been a Viking
Warrior in a previous incarnation! All in all though three
thousand happy bods raved at Europe's biggest and best.

Sunday's smaller rave was well brilliant and Norman Jay's
euphoric blend of Garage, House and Philly had the crowd
screaming for more. One drunk invaded the stage demanding
'Agid House'. What's Agid House we ask? (Memories of
Broadstairs, eh! - Ed).

Overall then, a top weekend, with thanks to Kevin and Tunji of
Trance, Soho Connection, Norman, Danny & Jenni, Colin Faver and
the six-hundred strong London contingent. See you in December
when Amsterdam will be really hot!

TOP BUZZ ~ THE CHARTS

IF YOU SHOULD NEED A FRIEND - BLAZE

GUITARRA   - RAUL

SHOUT IT TO THE TOP   - THE STYLE COUNCIL

PARADE HOUSE   - KOXO CLUB

HOW FAR I'LL GO   - PETER BLACK

LET ME LOVE YOU   - KARIYA

DJOBI DJOBA   - GYPSY KINGS

VOODOO RAY   - A GUY CALLED GERALD

YOU'RE GONNA MISS ME   - TURNTABLE ORCHESTRA

I SHOT THE SHERIFF   - CASTLE BEAT

The above tunes are all totally unignorable. Purchase or
perish and forget all this Minneapolis/P-funk hype. Speaking
as someone who caught the original Mothership tour first time
around, I can sure dig the tunes. But the clobber as well?
Behave! It's a false scene being faked by certain d.j's who
can't handle the open style of the so-called Balearic movement.
Well they've got to work, I suppose, but surely Bootsy would
sound blinding next to Chris & Cosey?!!!...Most of the above
can be acquired from Black Market, Trax and Rough Trade...The
sounds of '88.

KAREN.

FAT TONY and THIN SANDRA.

THE TWO SEXY SACHAS (OOH AAH!)

GRANT, the DUCHESS, BILLY . . .

IBIZA UPS

1. Listening to Fourelevenfortyfour by Pete Wylie as the sun comes up (amyl nitrate an optional extra).

2. Actually getting a lift after sticking your thumb out for two hours.

3. Hot Chocolate with cream.

4. Roy 'Have A Special Sweet' Mills, Wayne, "Free At Last" Sid, Maurice, Northern Jo, Little Debs, Ange, Paul 'I woke up and there were all these bods' Penny, Nick, Andres, the D.J. at Space and last but definitely not least Nina (whose eyes would go all sort of far away.)

5. Getting the photos back from Supasnaps.

BALEARIC BUMMERS

1. Having your apartment burgled by so-called mates.

2. Being mistaken for an 18-30 merchant.

3. Pissed Swedes singing "What shall we do with the drunken sailor?"

4. Hearing the phrases 'top buzz' and 'blinding visuals' every five minutes.

5. People pretending to be villains on holiday.

6. Coming home.

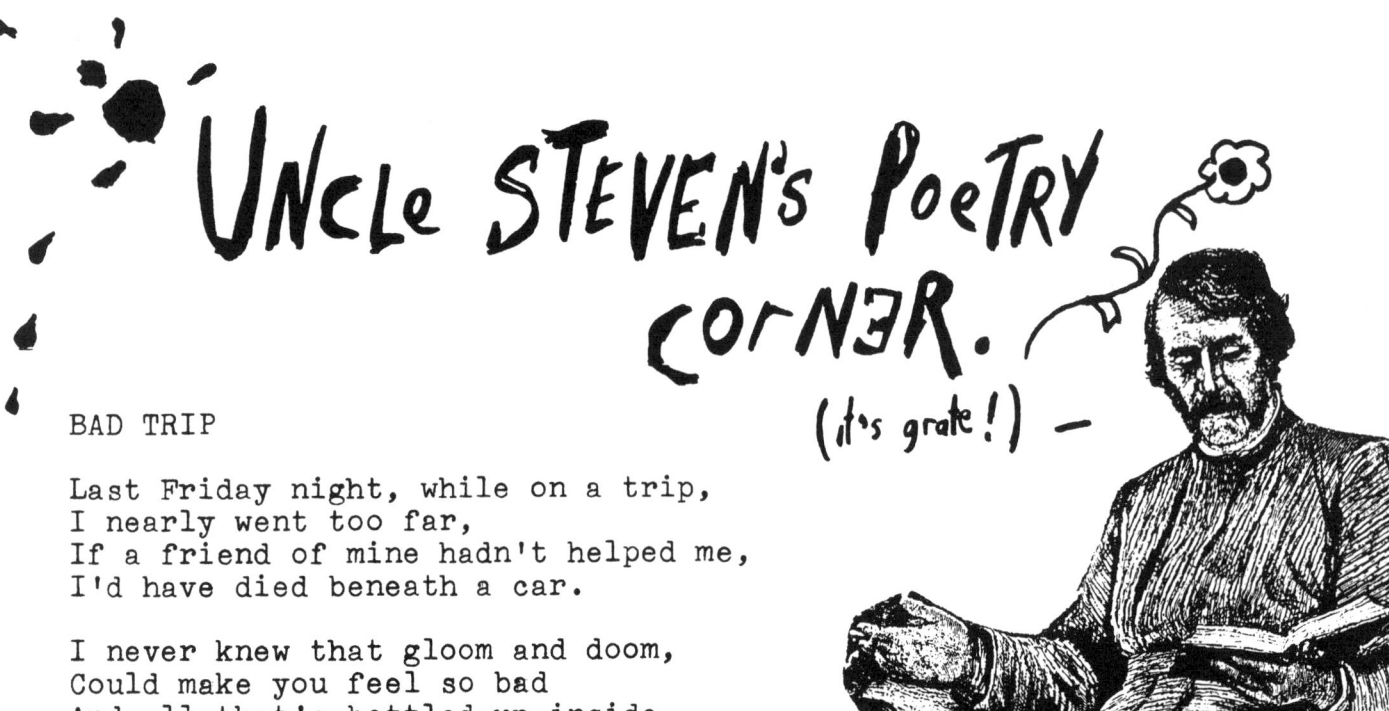

UNCLe STEVEN's PoeTRY CorNƎR.

(it's grate!) —

BAD TRIP

Last Friday night, while on a trip,
I nearly went too far,
If a friend of mine hadn't helped me,
I'd have died beneath a car.

I never knew that gloom and doom,
Could make you feel so bad
And all that's bottled up inside,
Could make you feel so sad.

The lesson's there for all to see,
Be careful when you trip
Or you could end up on a slab,
It only takes one slip.

                MARTYN PASSEY

At the end of my work in the dead of night
I had the misfortune of watching a fight.
The geezers went to do him with bottles if they could
He was going to do them with a lump of wood.
He swung to the right, they jabbed at the left
At the end of the fight he had no face left.
Lying on his back, unconscious on the ground
The fact he was not dead made the angry crowd frown.
They wanted to hear him plead for no more,
Then a wanker ran forward and kicked his head in on the floor.

The sound of leather connecting with head,
The poor bastard must have wished he was dead.
The crowd looked on and in their minds it had to be
'Thank fuck it was him instead of me.'

                        DAVE HENLEY

        That Bloody Woman.

This evil woman, she must be mad,
The things she says have no meaning.
The policies she pursues are greed and dogma,
Right-wing jargon gone beserk
In that dyed blonde head of hers.
She's the woman to cure Britains pains
I don't care what you say, she's not all there.
The way she behaves, refusing to listen to reason
I know best she says,
On what grounds, we say.
Your only care is for businessmen and their ilk,
Who abuse their wealth and power
Your party and you are an amoral shower.

                        STEVE MAYES

WHEN WILL I BE FAMOUS

My mate is on the telly-he told me so today,
Just watch 01 for London and you'll see me right away.
It's going to make me famous in all the clubs I go
And all the girls will shout at me, I saw you on so and so.
But come the fateful hour, the worst nightmare of all,
They'd cut most of the programme and we didn't see him at all
And now he's got to face his friends with dignity and grace
After all, it's not often you see egg on Mark Spits face.

        Jobs For All.

" Never had it so good " is the whine we hear,
  From Lord Young and his merry men.
  What relief that must be to the millions unemployed
  Whose lives are declared null and void
  By policies that have ruined and destroyed.
  But we'll get the figures down, cries the Minister
  With drastic measures for our jobless masses
  Who are press-ganged into menial labour.
  These Tory bastards know no bounds
  Anyone for Y.T.S., J.T.S. or Restart?

        TOP TEN TED CHART.

1. TED MOULT- ALL TIME TED FROM TEDDINGTON.

2. SUPERTED- THE CARTOON BEAR NOT JAY STRONGMAN.

3. TED WESTWOOD- YO! DOWN BY LAW TED!

4. SHOWADDY WADDY- FIRMED UP ACID TEDS.

5. TED RAY- CARRY ON TED.

6. TWO-CAN-TED - BOY'S OWN TED.

7. JAZZY M- (AKA VINCE PRINCE) SAD TED.

8. TEDDY KENNEDY- TOOK ANOTHER TED DRIVING.

9. TEDDY MAYBANK- SEVENTIES CHELSEA TED.

10. TEDDY PENDERGRASS- NEVER HITCH A LIFT WITH TEDDY KENNEDY.

CHRIS AT THE SHOOM

The smiling look upon my face is not there just for fun
It tells the people that I know I'm really right on one.
I'll stomp around the dance-floor to any acid beats
And stand inside the speakers, I hardly move my feet.
Just making lots of circles with fingers in the air
I'm happy as a sandboy and I haven't got a care.
There's nothing bad about it, I wish that you could see,
This is the only place I know where everyone is haaapy!

                                        MARTYN PASSEY

DEUTSCHLAND HOOLIGAN

" It's because we're Leeds, 'cause we're Leeds " young Tony insisted. Cold and wet, with nowhere to sleep, Stuttgart no longer seemed as hospitable a place as when the bars had been open. His friend, John, also Service Crew material, had just spent four months at Her Majestys pleasure domes, after meeting the Headhunters in November 1984 at Elland Road. Both of them had travelled out to Germany on their own, with no real violent intentions but, inevitably, those stories cropped up. How a group of Leeds had refused to fight some Irish, despite the presence of some Thames Valley Chelsea urging blood. How the ICF and the Service Crew ran some German lads, how the press were blowing it all out of proportion, the usual.

Indeed, the European Championships, from an English point of view, smacked of 'the usual'. The usual tales of drunken partying, the usual scuffling, the usual pathetic soccer team, the usual antagonism. It was true that the Germans wanted a few 'meets' with English chaps. It was true that when the German police were let off their leashes they liked to break heads and it was true that the press drooled over the tales of violence but, nevertheless, it all happened because of the English.

Despite a lack of serious chaps from London (apart from a small division of the ICF) England gathered a healthy and reputable 500-strong mob for the game with Holland. But the Dutch were a myth. Their chaps, about 50 in all, disappeared at the end of the game, along with their banner 'FUCK ENGLAND'. How dare they, don't they understand?

THE EUROPEAN CHAMPIONSHIP IN BRIEF

THE BRADY BUNCH and their NEW TOUR VAN.

The Germans, however, were a more serious proposition. Hair short on top, long at the back, with an optional fluffy pencil moustache, knobby jeans and trainers. (Sounds like the 6.57-Ed.) They both looked and acted the part nicely. " Deutschland Hooli-gan, Deutschland Hooli-gan " they chanted, as they roamed the streets of Dusseldorf looking for the English. They had travelled about 50 miles from Dortmund (04 and VSB) to find the English and they did. The battle ensued (yawn) and, really, the English came out on top. On the day of the game with Holland, Dusseldorf was a mess A lot of revenge demolition had been undertaken by England in return for the German lads initiating the violence at about eight o'clock, running the English out of the old part of Dusseldorf, where the majority of bars and clubs are situated.

The trouble is that you can go on relating tales of violence and disorder in Stuttgart, Dusseldorf, Frankfurt and even Cologne, where the English attacked some Danes and Irish (what brave lads they must have been) but it really misses the point and the point is: what a waste of time. For 90% of the time, he's Leeds, he's Chelsea, he's West Ham, he's Man.Utd. and everyone hates each other. For the other 10%, we're all English and we hate everyone else. If the blatant hypocrisy doesn't rub you up the wrong way, then the futility ought to. With fat milky-white beer-bellies hanging over Union Jack shorts, anthem-singing and "Sieg Heils", English fans made one despair. Thoughts that hooligans are really the 'clever ones' disappear as the embarressment sets in.

The English have a long history of sending young men abroad to fight and it's never been really looked upon with any degree of guilt or wrong-doing and now football is paying the price. Today, so many people are guilty of doing this, from holiday-makers to professional thieves to soccer fans that the blame has to lie with our nation.

Unfortunately, talking about soccer violence is like banging your head against Paul Scarrotts' Converse trainers, it gets you nowhere and, ultimately, it's boring. No-one with any power will listen to sensible ideas. If they had, football might be a bit healthier than it is today. The only ones interested are the chaps themselves and those members of the public who like to read about violence, to halt the crushing boredom of their poxy lives.

The European Championships were just a very good example of this set of circumstances coming to a head. If the English could behave them-selves when they go abroad, then all well and good but they can't.

Also, there seemed to be missing the more intelligent and thoughtful hooligan. Taste was replaced by 'Invasion of Germany' T-shirts, thieving was replaced by drunken, Fascist saluting and style was replaced by running from the Germans. Whatever happened to the good old days when chaps were chaps and fat, slobbering nonces just watched?

I tried explaining to John and Tony that it was all such a waste of time. John looked on fairly sadly, bemoaning the fact that he'd had to leave behind his two kids and that, at 24, it would probably be his last trip abroad to see football and that he could imagine getting more 'into peace' because no-one at Leeds Utd. Football Club really gave a monkeys about him. I suggested to Tony that he too would be better off getting involved in some sort of beautiful brotherhood-type communal activities of a more peaceful nature. Tony thought for a second, " Aye, you could be right. I mean, I'd much rather be out 'ere getting me leg over than fucking fighting." Oh well, I thought, at least it's a start.

ADAM PORTER. JIHAD

Football hooliganism died as a laugh in Heysel, it's now only fit for barmy Fascists and Geordies. It's over. Most had the crack, some are still paying for it. This is Boy's Owns last word on the matter. Don't let the gaffers have the last word.

DIGGING YOUR SCENE

"Evenin'."
"How the devil are you?"
"The scene is getting a bit shitty, ain't it. Some right
knobheads turnin' up."
"I know but what can we do?"

Stop moaning. That's what you can do. Picture the scene
twelve to eighteen months ago. It's Friday night and we are
plotting in the front room:

"Where shall we go to-night then?"
"Wag?"
"Fuck all else on. We might as well."
"Down the pub first?"
"Yeah, we can get a bit lagged."

What follows is an evening of Special Brew, Public Enemy
records, not really talking to anybody, a cold Hot Dog, a swift
psychedelic yodelling session and home to a headache.

REPEAT Saturday night, etc etc.

However several months later (If this were television we would
insert a wobbly fade into the next scene).

"Where shall we go to-night then?"
"I dunno. There's a couple of clubs just started that I
wouldn't mind trying. They finish at four and then there's a
couple of warehouses on until nine. Let's just see what
happens."

What follows is an evening of orange juice, records from anorak
indie to deep house, talking & making friends with every man
and his dog.

REPEAT any night from Monday to Sunday, etc etc.

Alright, alright. I know some of the warehouses are a bit
iffy, and to say there are a lot of teds about is an
understatement, but just think of some of the adventures you've
had in the past eighteen months - from all-night parties in
barns to raves in old cafes (cheers, Bobby). And just think of
some of the sounds you've had in the past eighteen months from
solid soulful rockers to mad deutsche metal bashers.

The next time some plank in an E t-shirt grabs you in a sweaty
embrace and shouts 'Can you feel it?', smile politely and say
'I certainly can....But you'll never understand, I'm afraid."

Staying in moaning means that these people have won. In the
words of a t-shirt modelled by a certain Michael Clark...
        "DON'T LET THE BASTARDS GET YOU DOWN!"

letters to ED.

Hello Boys

So yet another search in Manchesters W. H. Smith's for the new Boys Own has ended in tears.
Obviously you've dried up, to help you on your way heres currently whats ''IN and OUT'' amoungst the sounder elements of Manc life.

IN....Chocolate Brazils.... wearing a Snorkle in bed.... pretending to be Muslim.... sing Orinoco Flow at the Match ....being a member of Sinn Fein ....shouting ''Hey Hoe a Diddle ....getting out your TCR Set...

OUT....getting legged by a cat ....Pot Noodle Butties.... Leaving Santa a mince pie.... The Manchester E Possie.... forgetting your alphabet.... saving up for a rainy day.... coming fourth in a Talent Contest....Fred Pontin.... being put on a high fibre diet ....being Roy Kinnears Kid....

Yours

Elton Welsby
MUFC MANC.

Dear Boy's Own
Here's a new dance (Teds take note).
Turned up at an all dayer in Deepest Downham (top secret location). Locals outside fully equipped with brand new smiles and T Shirts to match ("I've Got The E" & "Where's the Acid Party?", currently proving most popular in 8 out of every 10 households).
Forget the other dance's I've seen it all...
One (just joined the 'Acid' Gang half an hour ago) acid enthusiast to another.. "Eer mate av u seen this blindin dance they do at discos now?"
Acid enthisiast then demonstrates by running up and down the road (Ben Johnson stylee) as if he had just been thrown in a bush of 'Poison Ivy'.

'Poison Ivy' see it soon at a disco near you.... or.... do as I did and return home to the comforts of Tea and McV's.

Yours ever faithfully
Informer Of Bromley
Girlies Division.

Dear Boy's Own,
        Thanks for Vol.5. Good stuff, especially 'Rumours'. Don't know about the 'Banana Strikes Back' poem. Anyway, we all know tragically Liverpool never won the double. Also, that Swansea Jack wrote to the 'End'. Are they after world recognition?
P.S. As you will have noticed this is not written in crayon and in joined-up writing.

Stephen Conner,
Waterloo, Liverpool.

THE END OF ISSUE 6 .... THREE YEARS IN the MAKING, THREE MINUTES IN the READING, THREE SECONDS IN the TOILET !

A HEARTY "TA" to all the FOLLOWING .... NORMAN and JOEY JAY, Dave Little For the BLINDING COVER, NORTHERN CORRESPONDANT PHIL THORNTON, CHRIS THE BRUMMY BASTARD FROM BATTERSEA, ROCKA (THE D.J.s FRIEND), GARY 'RENT-A-CHALET' HAISMAN, JONATHON, TRACEY and TOBY WALKER FOR HELP WITH THE MAG, ANYONE WHO ENDED UP CLIMBING THE WELSH MOUNTAINS (MARK, ANDY, ELLIOT, etc. etc.), MR and MRS RAMPLING, GARY McCLARNEN, DOCTOR BLOOMBERG THE ROCKIN' COMMODITY BROKER, SIR CHRISTOPHER BUTLER, COXY THE EURO GUVNOR, PLUG 'I'M HUGE IN MARGATE' O'CONNOR, ALL OUR NEW GOONER CHUMS, ANDY NICHOLLS, STEVE 'LOOP THE LOOP' LEE PUTNEY'S LOVEABLEST, DAVID ROLLS (all GOLD TEETH and THRUPS), JOHNNY MEEHAN (KING KETCHUP), LASTLY AND BY ALL MEANS LEAST THE RICH-ARDS; Ms. SUSAN HARRIS, MS. NINA WALSH, MS LISA GRAILEY .... SORRY ABOUT THE DELAY PLAY-MATES .... HOPE IT'S BEEN WORTH THE WAIT!

American Classics

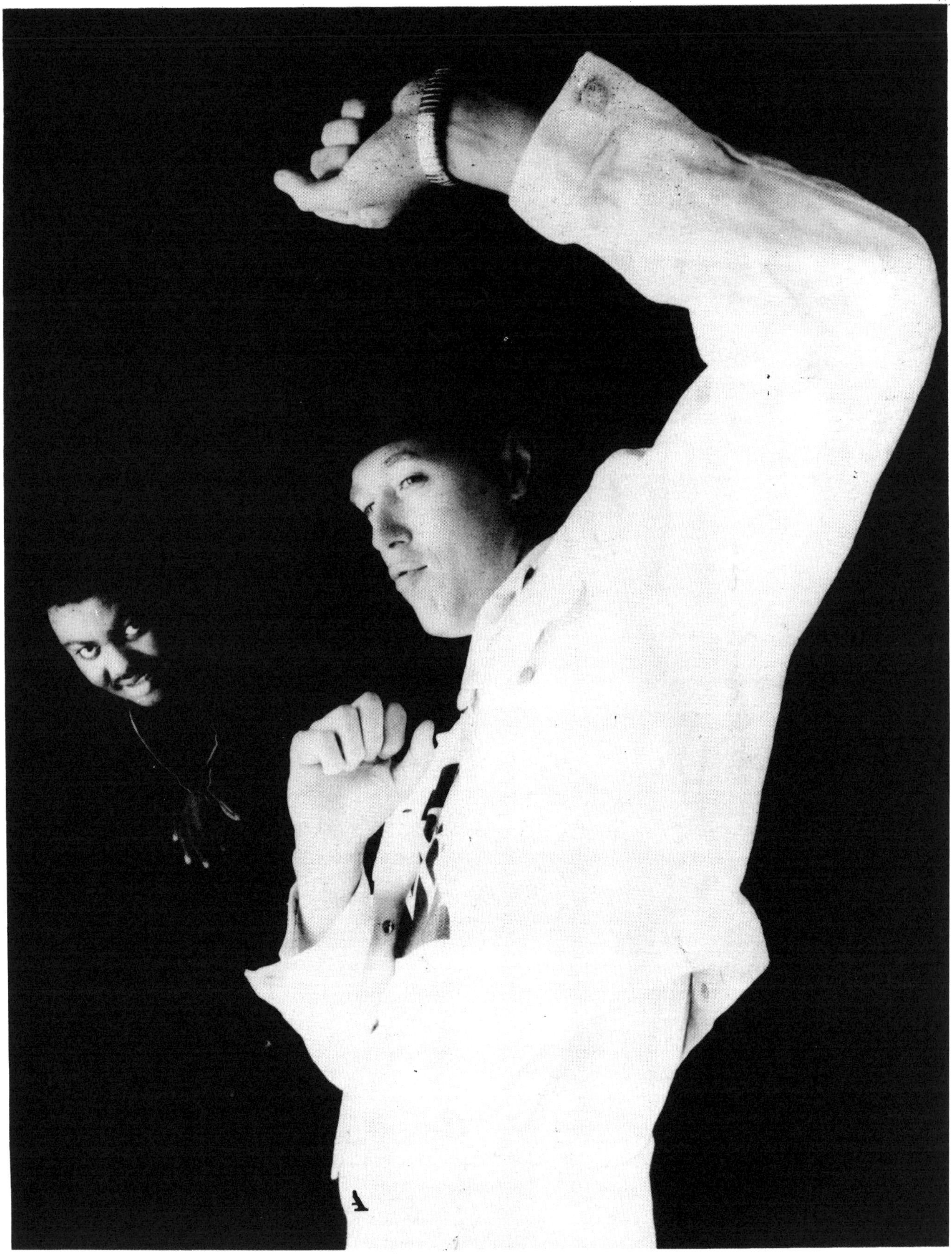

D-MOB

**A NUMBER ONE RECORD
FROM
A
NUMBER
ONE
RECORD COMPANY**

No. 7
Spring 1989

"BOY'S OWN — THE FANZINE THAT 'MISSED the BOAT'! *

'MARNIN'

HEY NONNY NONNY AND AWAY WE GO...
THIS TIME I'M DISPENSING WITH THE
JOVIAL GREETINGS AND BEGINNING
BY WRITING A SWIFT LIST OF DEFINITIONS
OF WORDS USED QUITE FREQUENTLY IN THIS ISH...

① NUTTIN' — TO STROLL PURPOSEFULLY WITH AN
AIR OF NONCHALANCE ... I.E. 'NUTTIN AROUND *
TOWN'.
   SEE ALSO: 'TO BOWL' AND 'OI MATE D'YA WANT
   SOME FRUIT WITH THAT BOWL'.

② LOG — IF YOU DON'T KNOW WHAT ONE IS,
   YOU ARE ONE.
   SEE ALSO: LAMPTON WICK.

③ 'FOUND IT, WASHED IT, AND WOOFED IT' — PARLANCE COMMONLY
USED TO DESCRIBE THE PARTAKING OF BOLIVIAN MEDICATION.

④ LONG UN — MONETARY TERM.
   SEE ALSO: MONKEY, COCKLE, SMALL HORSE, SPONDS AND
   WEDGED UP.

⑤ BLURTMANS — VERB, ADJECTIVE, NOUN. ABSTRACT CONCEPT.
THIS WORD ADDED AFTER ANOTHER IN A RANDOM FASHION.
e.G. 'GIVE IT A BLURT' OR 'WHO'S GOT THE WHIZZ-MANS'

⑥ MINGED OR MINGED UP — RATHER SQUIFFY DUE TO A
COMBINATION OF ALCHOHOL AND MEDICATION.
   SEE ALSO: E-BOAT.

© 89. THE OUTSIDER'S CONCISE LOVEABLE DICTIONARY.

SO HERE'S SAYING TARA...

KEEP ON VOGUEING AND SURGING
YOURS WITH SCANT REGARD FOR NICETIES
   The Outsider
      —X—

* QUOTE COURTESY OF SOUL UNDERGROUND ... CHEERS CHAPS!

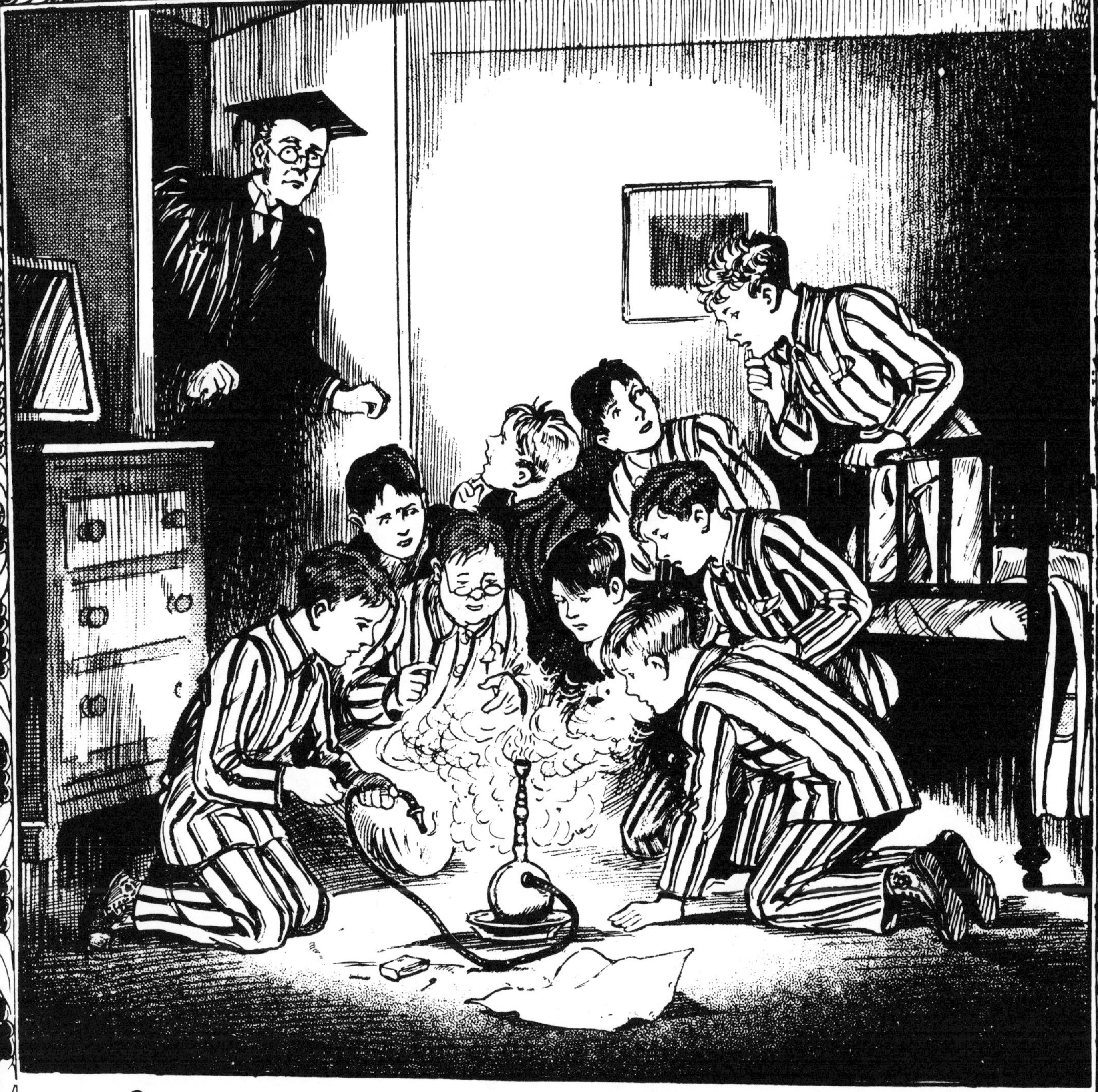

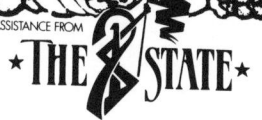

A MIDNIGHT FEAST THAT ENDED SUDDENLY

It was Terry's idea! "Who says a feed in the dormitory to-night, boys?" he called out. "I have two pounds of Moroccan and we can borrow a bong from the cook when she is not looking."

And a shriek of glee went up from the rest of the Third Form.

"But we haven't any Rizlas," said Wheathers. "How can we skin up?"

"Well, we have exersise paper, haven't we?" replied Terry scornfully. "I'll show you how to roll them."

That night the headmaster had been working late in his study. At last he finished and went up to his room. On the stairs, however, he stopped and sniffed.

"Moroccan!" he muttered. "It cannot be spliffing time."

Carefully he tracked that appetising smell to the Third Form Dormitory and listened.

"When the water bubbles, forget your troubles" he heard Terry saying. "We'll have such a jolly feast in a minute. Get ready, boys."

Then the Head opened the door. Oh dear!

ART ASSISTANCE FROM ★THE STATE★

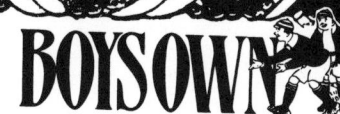

BOYSOWN

WEDNESDAYS at THE PARK...
38 KENSINGTON HIGH ST. W8.
· OPENING NIGHT WED 21st JUNE ·
EUROPEAN DANCE and MELODIC HOUSE
by
DANNY RAMPLING
GUESTS:
JULY 12th · NOEL WATSON
JULY 19th · TERRY FARLEY
JULY 26th · JOHNNIE WALKER.

£5 MEMBERS · £6 NON·MEMBERS

HARRY THE DOG
MILLWALL'S OLD FELLER GIVES IT SOME!!

...oy's Own,

Oi what's happened to my boy Millwall, alright he was ...ways a lost cause, but his carry on recently has been ...ng out of order. Let's face it, little Millwall was ...ver gonna be as hard as me; when I was young you always ...d a couple of wages snatches to keep you busy during the ...ek... alright that's a bit much for him but why can't he ...t by with some simple cheque book, credit card fiddles. ...not him, he's become a fucking journalist, who the fuck ...es he think he is, Eamon Dunphy? Bringing shame on such ...hardworking family.... fucking disgraceful!!!
...Never thought he was mine in the first place. He's a ...ny little shit - cop the mugshot, I mean you see more ...scle legging it around Catford dog track. The wife denies ...of course but I'm sure that Jack Russell down the road ...t at her, he even looks like the little slag. To tell ...u the truth I even tried to kill him when he was a pup, ...ed a couple of paper "Millwall Bricks" around his neck and ...cked him into the Thames. Problem was the paper got soggy ...l he floated to the top. Anyway it was bad enough with ...n shouting the odds in your rag, but I came home the other ...ek to find him minted. Bunging the missus scoves and telling ...to treat herself. Me face lit up, I thought he'd done ...ething to make his old dad proud - a post office blag, a ...of touting.... nah! He reckons he's fucked Boy's Own out ...it and got a job with The Face. He reckons The Face has ...en him a column of his own in which to talk total bollocks ...ut lovable Cockney characters and their ins and outs. ...lwall's even changed his name. He calls himself - wait for ...- Geoffrey Deane. He reckons in a couple of years with them ...ces he'll be able to retire to that great kennel in the ...for suspect journalists, the "Mail On Sunday". ...nat I want to know is what's going to happen to his old ...lwall the Dog column. All those Northern punters of yours are ...ng to be gutted. Now I know tales that would make Adam ...th shiver never mind those Kemp brothers; you gonna give ...to me or wot? Don't fuck me about cos I'm a busy man. ITV have ...ered me grands to write the next series of "Fox" and Euston ...ns, fuck me, Euston films want to do me life story. Go on ...e an old timer a break. Think about it, Millwall only ever ...three paragraphs written about him in the South London press,

me, I've had pages upon pages. This is Big H, writing to you from the Pepys Estate Deptford, a place where dogs are dogs and you would be fucking nervous, sweet!

Big H. (The Guvnor)

P.S. If you're wondering about the titfer it's me old club Woolwich Arsenal. South London's finest, the tales I could tell you (write to the Face letters page instead - Ed). Like the time we firmed up to ambush the Accrington Stanley Adidas München Firm.....not to be continued.

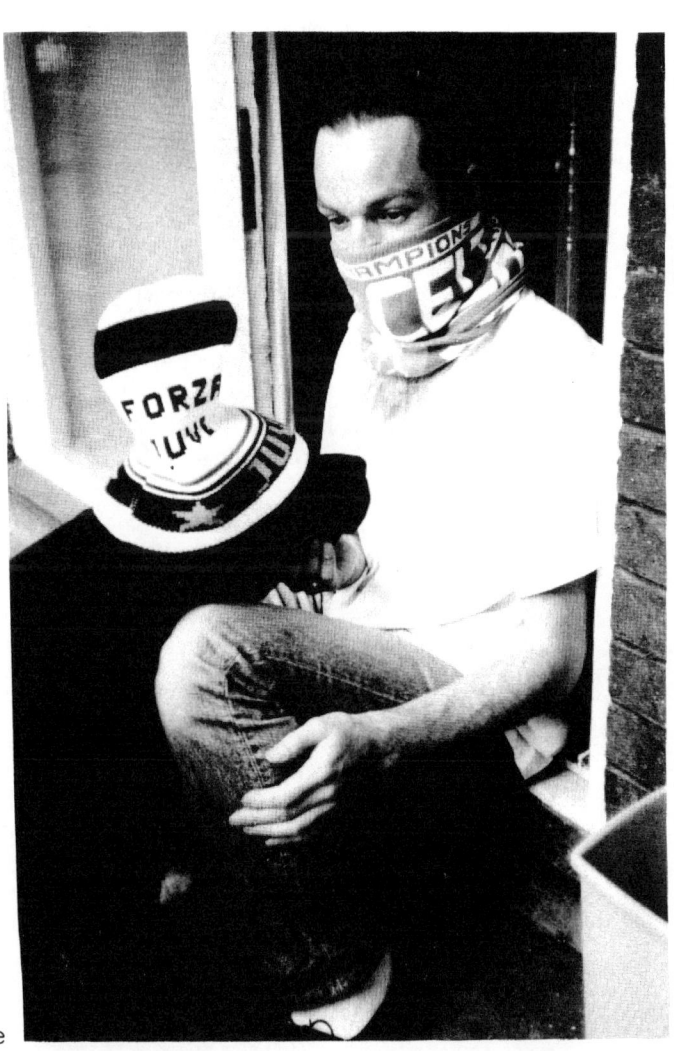

STOP PRESS : " ROTWEILER NEEDS 28 STITCHES AFTER FRENZIED MAISEY ATTACK! "

"WATCH YOUR BACK! ...IT'S THE MORB"

Scene 1

Rupert Urquahart-Jolly, is dressed in his Saturday gear. He's decked out in a full Monty top hat and tails with a Dicky bow to set it off. He and his pals are driving around in his Rolls Royce Silver Shadow. Rupert is the 16th Earl of Gloucester but come Saturday afternoon he is transformed into a croquet hooligan. The lads are members of a notorious gang of yobs known as 'The Mob' or as they pronounce it 'The Morb'.
Rupert is their top boy and they are on their way to meet a rival gang known as the 'Inter-Mansion-Firm.

Scene 2

Rupert and Tarquin Posh-Facker, the IMF's top lad, are arguing about who is to lead a National mob in an orgy of violence at the European Croquet Championship. The two gangs end up yelling abuse such as "Go away you oiks" and "Get the Moet out for the chaps".

Scene 3

Rupert decides to have a meeting with another gang called "The Not Very Pleasant Posse". Six of them are ambushed by a twenty strong mob and Oliver Blink-Dashit is beaten with a Cashmere cardigan. The Morb have been done! They are one-nil down and Rupert is not happy.

Scene 4

Ruperts baby eats a croquet mallet which was left lying around his stately home. His wife slings him out so he goes to stay at Buckingham Palace. Prince Edward is also a croquet hooligan and prints calling cards saying "Congratulations you have just met the Morb, please wipe your bottom before you leave".

LET'S GO AND SEE WHO IS ON THE NEXT PAGE, DICK!

<u>Scene 5</u>

The IMF have been doing the Morb over, so Rupert decides to give it
to them good and proper. They tool themselves up with fountain pens
pocket calculators, and double barrel tippex bottles. They meet
the IMF at a local ballroom on Tarquin Posh-Facker's estate in Devon
The two gangs battle it out and as they work out eachother's
bank balances, Tarquin and Rupert really get stuck in. Rupert is
just about to shout out Tarquins profit margin when he is struck by
a killer blow. Tarquin has pulled out a peice of paper. It is
Rupert's birth certificate and it proves that his parents are both
dockers from Glasgow. He is finished! No longer is he accepted by
his chums as their top boy. He is a No-Mark Pleb.

'THIS IS WHAT YOU
CALL I.M.F. TAKING
SEVERE LIBS ON
THE MORB'S MANSION!'

<u>Scene 6</u>

The Morb, the IMF and the NVPP are being filmed in a brasserie.
They all agree that Rupert had brought them all together. Now they
are united, they could really shit on the oiks.

THE END

HILLSBOROUGH TRIBUTE.

LIVERPOOL FANS HAVE HAD THEIR FAIR SHARE OF STICK
FROM THE GOVERNMENT + T.V. KNOBHEADS THE WORLD OVER.
SINCE HEYSEL THEY HAVE BEEN BRANDED "COLD BLOODED KILLERS",
VIOLENT ANIMALS" AND WORSE. NO-ONE SAID A THING ABOUT ROMA
FANS ATTACKING SCOUSERS AFTER THE 84 EUROPEAN CUP FINALS.
NO THATCHER BRANDED LIVERPOOL FANS "SCUM OF THE EARTH"
BUT NOW SHE'S PLAYING A DIFFERENT TUNE. AFTER HILLSBOROUGH
WHEN LIVERPOOL LADS DID THEIR BEST TO AID DEAD AND DYING
VICTIMS, THEY'RE SUDDENLY 'HEROES'.
        I DIDN'T GO TO THE GAME, BUT A LOT OF MY MATES
WHO ARE LIVERPOOL FANS WENT AND THEY ALL CAME HOME OK.
BUT THERE ARE PEOPLE FROM MY HOME TOWN OF RUNCORN WHO
WERE KILLED AND INJURED. I WAS ONE OF THOUSANDS PHONING
AROUND ON SATURDAY EVENING TO CHECK THAT MY MATES HAD
GOT HOME SAFELY.
        IF ANYTHING GOOD COMES OF HILLSBOROUGH IT WILL BE
THAT STUPID LOCAL RIVALRIES BE IT COCKNEYS, SCOUSERS, MANCS,
GEORDIES OR SCOTS WILL BE AT AN END. I'VE BEEN AS BAD AS
ANYONE ELSE IN THE PAST FOR MATCH MITHER BUT AFTER THIS IT
ALL SEEMS RATHER PATHETIC. I HOPE NO-ONE IS AT THIS
MOMENT THINKING UP SICK JOKES AND CHANTS ABOUT HILLSBOROUGH.
WE'VE HAD ENOUGH OF "MUNICH 58" AND "SHANKLY 81".
        IF WE ALL HAD AN OUNCE OF SENSE WE'D SEE THAT
THIS IS EXACTLY WHAT THE TORIES WANT TO SEE. DIVIDE AND RULE
IS THE NAME OF THE GAME AND WE'VE FELL FOR IT FOR LONG ENOUGH.
        THE BACKLASH STARTS HERE
                PHIL. RUNCORN. LANCS.

MANCHESTER
Centre of the Solar System
(AKA; THE NORTHERN SCHEME OF THINGS)

Before travelling up to Manchester, home of Terry Duckworth, Big Jimmy Anderton and the Barmy Banana Army, there are one or two things you should be clear about.

1. According to Mancs, their city is A1; the absolute centre of everything and all things revolve around it.

2. They regard Manchester as the capital city of England, so be prepared to be treated as a provincial.

3. Unlike their ex-Lancastrian neighbours, the Scousers, Mancs are fiercely Northern in attitude and are very anti-London. Whereas Scousers are anti-everywhere that isn't Liverpool.

Once you've got this sorted, it's pretty safe to roam around the place. But where to go? Well it's a pretty undeniable fact that outside of London, Manchester is the best place in Britain for clubs, gear and footy (ha!). The following is a potted history of all things Manc.....

No. 1: FASHION.

Some arguements will never be settled. Who has the right to govern Ulster? (The Irish – Ed.) Is there life on another planet? And who invented "Scally/Perry" dress sense? The Scals, naturally, claim it was they; the Mancs are equally vociferous it was they. Both agree on one thing, however – cockneys were years catching up.

As an impartial observer who shops, drinks, and watches footy in both cities, I'll give you my memories of this period. It's 1981 and the Scousers had started growing their fringes into wedges and wore baggy jumpers, faded Lois and Dunlop "Green Flash" pumps. They danced to OMD's "Memories", Human League's "Empire State Human", Kraftwerk's "The Model" and Funky disco, such as Rick James and Tom Browne. At the match, the newly-named "Scallies" developed this Northern style of dress to encompass pastel jumbo cords, Keo and Kicker boots and every Scal's favorite garment...... the sheepy.

In the wink of an eye the Mancs has adopted this style themselves and as the rivalry between the two tribes is so intense, they proudly claimed that they originated it. By 1982 the two were more or less mirror images of each other and the style spread throughout the smaller towns and cities of the Northwest. By now however the sporty foreign clobber craze had arrived from "darn sarf" and Hurleys Golf Shop in Manchester became the mecca for the boys and girls who gladly forked out ridiculous prices for Head, Cerutti, Kappa, Fila, Lacoste and Ellesse. The Face told everyone that the type of people who wore these clothes were called "casuals" and everyone up here laughed at these spotty divs with disgraceful haircuts and six pubes between them. As this style remained popular amongst the working class kids around England, Manchester suddenly went into a scruffy backlash in 84 (Scruffy Northerners? What's new? – Ed). Flared jeans and chords were everywhere. This meant you didn't have to spunk £40 on a pair of trainers cos you couldn't see the fuckin thing's anyway. Beaten up cord shoes and suedes now became the big alternative to

Adidas. 84 also saw the "Snorkel craze"; everyone went frantic digging out their old school parkas, because, worn loose with a polo shirt underneath and with 20" flares below, Snorkels were back chummy????

Up until 86 you could easily tell who was and wasn't a student, but in the next year loads of scals/perrys adopted a more studentish style. Fringes got slicked back, polo necks were worn with extra baggy kecks and brogues. The scruffy but stylish Manc style of dress hasn't changed much over the years: the Happy Mondays are probably the best example of this mode.... loose gear, baggy kecks, Rizla's, beards, short hair, tide marks, spunk stains and a don't-give-a-fuck attitude!!

No. 2: SHOPPING.

So where do you shop in Manchester? The Arndale will take you 20 years to find your way around and is full of "Hitman and Her" type crappy gear. St.Annes Sq. is a bit better – Zio, Woodhouse, Bellhop etc; if you're well minted you could also check out King St. Afflecks Palace, however, is a different kettle of fish. This place is three floors of Alternative and casual clothing stalls, mainly ultra-student joints flogging hats, scarves, posters, t-shirts, PLO uniforms and Semtex explosives. It also houses some decent record stalls, a proper Northern Soul stall called "Out Of The Past" and Eastern Bloc records, which along with Spinn Inn and Expansions are the best in Manchester, all with well sound House sections.

Identity Clothing are the Manchester t-shirt outfit; they have three stalls in Afflecks flogging their infamous and provocative designs. It was they who started the "Manchester: Born In The North, Race Pigeons In The North, Eat Tripe In The North, Have A Heart Attack In The North" t-shirt craze. Actually the proper slogan is "Manchester: Born In The North, Exist In The North, Die In the North, England." It is this brand of militant Mancunianism which has gripped the city's youth in a deliberate attempt to fuck London off once and for all. Mancs are sick of cockney football boys humming the theme tunes to Coronation St. and Hovis at them when Eastenders makes Wetherfield look like Brideshead Revisited. Identity Clothes also fuelled last summer's Acid craze. It was they who supplied half the Hacienda with "E For Additives", "Manchester E Possie" and "This Ain't Chicago...This Is Manchester Matey" t-shirts.

No.3: CLUBS

Speaking of the Hacienda, it's time we moved onto the club scene. As we know whatever London does today, Manchester did twenty years ago – just like it was into Acid when London was into three star jumpers and old Blackbyrd records – just like it was into Northern Soul when London was into Slade – just like it was into space before Yuri Gagarrin – and discovered America before Columbus.... yes, Manchester did it first!

Sorry to say it; though Manchester may well have been into House while flare groove ruled the Smoke's dancefloor, but it copied Shoom/Spectrum/Future's Acid culture Lock, Stock and Waterman. Wednesdays "Hot" night at the Hass was solid Acid with the obligatory

HACIENDA TYPES

"LIKE-A PUT ON SOME DIZZY DADDIO! WHO ARE ALL THESE SQUARES? WHY, I BET THEY DON'T KNOW THE DIFFERENCE BETWEEN CHARLIE PARKER AND CHARLIE GEORGE. AND THAT SUIT LOOKS LIKE IT'S BEEN CUT BY CHARLES MANSON. REALLY, I REMEMBER WHEN THIS PLACE WAS INTENDED FOR WE SERIOUS TYPES, ALL 7 OF US!"

"HEY DAVE YOU SAID THIS WAS LEB & IT'S ONLY MOROCCAN. GIVE US A DANCE LATER AND I WON'T TELL OUR MASHER"

"SO THIS TOP CHELSEA TED GIVES IT THE COPPER AND HIS MATE COMES AT ME WITH A SPUD GUN. SO I HIT HIM OVER THE HEAD WITH ME BANANA AND SQUIRT ME WATER PISTOL AT THE ALLY"

THE JAZZ BORE

SKIN-UP SUSAN

KIPPAX KEV

Converse, psychedelic prints, wavey dances and plenty of E-by-gum! Balearic didn't get a look in though as top Manc DJ's John Da Silva, Mike Pickering, Stu Allen et al were suspicious of its fad image — in other words couldn't find a black American connection and so dismissed it as white Euro pop shite!

As we now know too many divs, wankers and trend hoppers hijacked the scene for it to last with the serious clubbers; it was good while it lasted but too good to last.

So what's happening now in our glorious capital? On the clothes front, ethnic print gear is in and the B.A.F movement have taken over the city centre. What does B.A.F stand for? "Baggy As Fuck!" That's wot. Everything's gone baggy — bananas, shirts, kecks, even baggy haircuts, the lot. Identity have a new militant slogan for the city's youth — "061 — State Of The Nation". 061 being the dialing code for Manchester and also the name of the North's newest underground dance label.

On the club-front, the Hacienda's Not night on a Wednesday has mutated into "Void"; with Jon De Silva and Mike Pickering playing Deep and Techno grooves. By the way isn't Deep now getting as cliche as "Acid"? All these two bit tinkly winkly bands knocking out mixes of their crap records, "just stick a piano on it". The Hass Nude Night (Fridays) is still strong though with a more varied soundtrack. Legends, Hysteria and Fizz are also worth checking if you lot dare venture up here. On the Northern side of soul "Landslide" at the Old Steam Brewery and Soultown Promotions have lined up some good looking allnighters in Blackburn.

On the footy front – United as usual bottled it and have been designated a trophy-free zone yet again. City will get relegated next season and United may go with 'em.

Those naughty Man City guvnor charlies have been starring in their own TV serial. Not content in ambushing United at Piccadilly they've taken to performing acrobatics on prime time telly and I thought Elton Welsby was the star of "Kick Off".

Come on boys calm down or you'll end up doing runners from Preston Open Nick or sampling Risleys famous cuisine pretty soon.

There it is then – Manc is a wierd place, the people pronounce money "munneh", they hate Tracy Barlow and without a trained eye you'd think the top boys were total scruffbags... Manchester Born In The North etc..........

IN	OUT
Green check baggy shirts	Surf Automatic beachwear
Breaker through a straw	Charlie through a rolled-up fiver
Getting busted for insider-trading	Getting busted for twatting the milkman
Licorish tabs	Double glazed window-pane heads
1984 20 inch flares (Man City)	1987 20 inch flares (rare groove)
Brummy in fancy dress going loco in Palace-oco	Brummys in normal dress going loco in Palace-oco
Empty spaces at Old Trafford	Empty spaces in lifts
Stone Roses, Happy Mondays & the Manc go take-over	Ian McCullough & the other forgotten 81 Scouse brigade
Getting a propper hiding off a bunch of ice cream men	Getting a proper hiding off a bunch of Wolves fans (cavemen)
Wearing a turban	Wearing a skull cap
Liverpool/Everton cup final National Anthem fuck off	Gerry "who?" Marsden and other assorted cunts cashing in
Twating touts for their tickets	Twatting little kids for their tickets
West Ham and Candid Camera (hide the scrapbooks lads)	QPR on Candid Camera (one man and his brush)
Special constables (YTS gaffers) on parade at the match	Ex-SPG barmys raiding your boozer
Jamie & his magic torch	Wattoo-Wattoo (the bird from outerspace)
Sticking Sugar Puffs up your bum	Getting caught stickingSugar Puffs up your bum
Getting a hard on in a shopping precinct	Not getting a hard on in bed
Loopy bus drivers giving you gyp	Loopy vicars refusing to marry you

Phil Thornton.

ADVERTISEMENT © QUAFF·89·

QUAFF RECORDS · 133 STROUD GREEN ROAD, FINSBURY PK.

THE CHARTS

```
LES NEGRESSES VERTES...........................................THE FLY
STARLIGHT INVENTION GROUP...................................NUMERO UNO
CRY CISSCO...................................................AFRODESIAC
DOROTHY.....................................................REFLECTIONS
FAX YOURSELF................................................SUNSHINE 89
HAPPY MONDAYS...................................WROTE FOR LUCK (HOUSE)
WEST SIDE......................................................IM IN DEEP
MC BUZZ B..............................................HOW SLEEP THE BRAVE
COLDCUT........................................................IM IN DEEP
MARCO MARTINA...........................................JUST AN ILLUSSION
ELLIS, BEGGS AND HOWARD.........................................ROCK ME
WALTER P.P.K...............................................GET ON BOARD
BANANARAMA...........................................YOU GIVE LOVE A BAD NAME
RITCHIE HAVENS........................................BACK TO MY ROOTS
WHITE RABBITT.........................................I HAVE A DREAM
TONY RALLO.................................................HOLDING ON
OHCIOLILI.................................................ZANGA ZANGA
FLASH.....................................................FLASH JACK
STYLE COUNCIL...............................EVERYBODYS ON THE RUN
DIZZY HEIGHTS...............................COULD I FIND LOVE
YAGMAR.......................................................ALI BABA
JIMMY BO'HORNE..............................................SPANK 89
HIGH VOLTAGE............................................LETS GET HORNY
GINO LATINO.......................................................YO
CHAKA KHAN.........................................AINT NOBODY (REMIX)
RENEGADE SOUND WAVE...................................THE PHANTOM
STRETCH..............................................WHY DID YOU DO THAT
BARCLAY DREAM........................................BARCLAY DREAM
G-FORCE......................................................SPICEY
CHARVONI..................................................ALWAYS THERE
CELLI BEE, BUZZY BUNCH.......................................ONE LOVE
K.T.P..........................................................BIG MAN
```

THE ABOVE TUNES ARE ALL ESSENTIAL, COMPILED BY ANDY NICHOLLS, DANNY RAMPLING, FABIO,
FARLEY, KEVIN HURRY, ANDY WEATHERALL AND ROCKY AND DIESEL –
BEG STEAL OR BORROW – TUNES OF THE SUMMER. "REAM".

STOP PRESS :— TOP TUNES continued : THE NEW KISS A.M.C,
CORPORATION of ONE L.P., BANG the PARTY, LES SUN RAE,
etc etc ....

'THE LOVEABLES'

FROM THE TIME THE FIRST COCKNEY CORPORAL DYING IN A TRENCH UTTERED THE IMMORTAL WORDS "YOU TOFFS IS ALL THE SAME" TO WHEN A WIDE-BOY ON THE MAKE ASKS SOME "GEEZER" "COCKLE", THE LOVEABLE HAS BEEN WITH US. THE TWO EXAMPLES QUOTED ARE CINEMATIC AND TELEVISUAL, BUT AS IS ALWAYS THE WAY THEY HAVE AFFECTED THE MAN (OR WOMAN) ON THE STREET.

THANKS TO TELEVISION AND FILM THE 'COCKNEY' HAS GONE THROUGH A NUMBER OF STAGES. THE STOUT COSTERMONGER OR THE DOWN-TRODDEN CORPORAL FALL INTO THE 'SALT OF THE EARTH' CATEGORY. THIS TYPE OF COCKNEY METAMORPHOSISED GRADUALLY THROUGHOUT THE 40'S AND 50'S TO GIVE US THE "CHIRPY" (MICHAEL CAINE, ADAM FAITH).AS THE YEARS WENT BY THESE CHARACTERS WERE BEGINNING TO HAVE AN ADVERSE EFFECT ON THE POPULATION. YOUNG MEN IN PUBLIC HOUSES TALKED OF 'MONKEYS', 'BLAGS' AND 'RICHARDS' AND STAYED IN ONCE A WEEK FOR "MINDER". THIS IS WHEN THE 'LOVEABLE' TOOK OVER, AND THE COCKNEY TURNED INTO THE 'MOCKNEY'.

NOW BACK IN THE MISTS OF TIME THE FILM WORLDS VIEW OF THE COCKNEY WAS STEREOTYPED, BUT AT LEAST THE PUNTER KNEW THAT THERE WERE REAL ONES OUT THERE AND DIDN'T FEEL THE NEED TO GATHER IN DRINKING ESTABLISHMENTS AND IMPERSONATE THEM, BUT WITH THE ADVENT OF DALEY AND McCANN THE DISTINCT LINE BETWEEN THE COCKNEY AND THE MOCKNEY WAS ERADICATED. NOW UNFORT-UNATELY THE REAL AND THE STEREOTYPE ARE MERGED AS ONE TO GIVE US 'THE LOVEABLE'.

SHAMEFUL AS IT MAY SOUND, REGARDLESS OF POSTCODE, SE 16 OR W6, THE FIRST SOUND OF DROPPED H'S AND SLANG BRINGS THE RESPONSE "OH NO IT'S A LOVEABLE", WHETHER IT'S A QUEUE OUTSIDE A PIE AND MASH SHOP OR A PARTY IN THE DEPTHS OF PUTNEY YOU SADLY LUMP THEM ALL TOGETHER AND COMMENT ON JUST HOW 'LOVEABLE' THEY ARE....

THE SERIOUSNESS OF THE SITUATION WAS BROUGHT HOME TO ALL AT BOY'S OWN BUNGALOWS WHEN A DOCUMENT FROM 'THE INSTITUTE OF PROFESSIONAL LOVEABLES'FELL INTO OUR HANDS.

B O L OC
BRITISH **O**RGANIZATION OF **L**OVEABLE **O**LD **C**OCKNEY

~INVITES~

Sir Les of Lig.

"TO AN EVENING OF CHIRPY COCK-A-NEY REVELLRY"

3 course supper
AND
knees up
~

STARTER • SEAFOOD COCKTAIL (MUSCLES, WHELKS, COCKLES ALIVE ALIVE OH!)

MAIN COURSE • PIE A LA BEUF et SAUTÉ MASH et SAUCE de LIQUOR.

DESSERT • PUDDING DE SPOT le RICHARD

apres nosh entertainment • INTERNATIONAL COCK CABARET CHANTEUSE JOE BROWN WITH HIS HOT BACKING COM THE BRUVVERS.

<u>THE LOVABLES TOP ORALS....</u>

<u>LOVABLE CLUB SPEAK</u>

1. "I'LL DO BISCUITS FOR A COCKLE, AN ARCHIE MOORE FOR THE CAPSUALS."

2. "STICK ME ON THE G.L. AND I'LL NOSE UP THE DOORMAN."

3. "ORDER ME A SHERBERT, THIS GAFF'S JANK."

4. "ALRIGHT BABES, JOIN ME FOR SOME DOM."

5. LISTEN GEEZER I'M DOING A RAVE OVER SOUTH."!!!

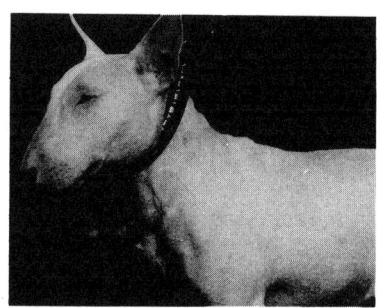

A LOVEABLE CHERRY.

<u>LOVABLE FEMALES - DORIS, RICH-ARD, SORT, SPEAK</u>

1. "I'VE SEEN BIGGER WINKLES ON TUBBY ISSAC'S STALL."

2. "NOB OFF DIV OR I'LL CHIV YA."

3. BUY US A DRINK FUCKFACE."

4. "WHO YOU CALLING SHARON?"

5. "OI MATE PLAY THAT STRINGS OF LIFE RECORD."

<u>HAUNTS OF THE TERMINALLY LOVABLE</u>

1. <u>THE HALFWAY LINE, FRATTON PARK</u> - HOME OF THOSE COCKNEY WANNABEES THE 6.57 (DO THEY
   STILL EXIST?)

2. <u>THE LAMB (PUBLIC HOUSE) SURBITON</u> - TORY LOVABLES: "COR BLIMEY LOOK AT THE F.T, SELL ME
   PORK BELLYS NOW."

3. <u>COOKES PIE'N'MASH SHOP</u> - FORGET JOSEPHS CAFE (AND ITS TINNED VEG), THIS IS THE ONLY
   PLACE TO BE SEEN SCOFFING IN.

4. <u>CHIPIE CLOTHES SHOP, COVENT GDN</u> - THE TICKET TOUTS, POMPEY FOOTIE FANS AND SOUTH LONDON
   POSTIES FAVE PLACE IN WHICH TO SPEND (OR ROB) THEIR "HARD EARNED."

5. <u>FRANK "LOVABLE" WARREN'S BOXING SHOWS</u> - THE ULTIMATE, "DOWNSTAIRS", "BE FIRST",
   "DOUBLE UP", "CHIV THE CUNT": A HIGHER LEVEL OF LOVABILITY CLOSED TO ALL BUT THE
   COMMITTED.

<u>TOP FIVE LOVABLE OCCUPATIONS</u>

1. "ME WORK - I WOULDN'T GET OUT OF BED FOR LESS THAN A MONKEY A DAY."

2. <u>ON THE PRINT</u> - LOADS'O'LOVABLES: "WOT'S YOUR CHAPEL?"

3. <u>ON THE POST</u> - "ON YOUR TOES."

4. <u>BALL BOY AT MILLWALL F.C.</u> - ESPECIALLY IF YOU GET TO STAND ON THE EMPTY TERRACE
   BETWEEN THE RIVAL FANS (FOR UNDER 12 ONLY THOUGH!)

5. <u>EXTRA ON TV HOOLIGAN DRAMAS</u> - GOLF GTI, "NEXT FOR THUGS" JACKETS AND WIMPEY HOMES
   IN SUBURBAN ESSEX ARE SUPPLIED WITH JOB.

<u>RECOMMENDED FURTHER READING....</u>

1. "BILL SYKES: ONE MAN AND HIS DOG" – O. Twist (Bullseye Publications).

2. "WE WERE POOR BUT WE WERE HAPPY – A COSTERMONGER REMEMBERS" – Nobby Lard (Get Off Me Barrer Publications).

3. "REGGIE AND RONNIE WHO? – AN OLD KENT RD. PUBLICAN FORGETS" –'Police Review'article.

4. "HOW DO THEY GET AWAY WITH IT? – A CRITICAL LOOK AT PIE AND MASH SHOPS" – London trading standards booklet.

5. "YOU DON'T GET MANY OF THEM TO THE POUND MISSUS – A HISTORY OF THE SOUTH LONDON FRUIT AND VEG TRADE" – Nobby 'Some As Big As Yer 'Ead' Lard.

6. "OH MY GAWD~IT'S COME ON TOP" – Ronnie Knight (Publicacion Espanol).

7. "THAT'S NO BLAGGER THAT'S MY OLD MAN" – Barbara Windsor (Ooh What A Carry On Publications).

8. "SHADY DRINKING WIDE BOYS – A NORTHERN PERSPECTIVE ON THE COCKNEY PHENOMENON" – B.Tilsley (Tetley Publications).

9. "JACKS, COCKLES, MONKEYS, PONYS AND LONG 'UNS" – Nobby Lard, Financial Assistance Ltd. Brochure.

10. "CRANK UP THE OLD JOANNA MADAM I'M A LITTLE BIT MUTTON – THE LOVEABLE SONGBOOK" – Richard Dido (T.Trinder Publications).

Boys Own Magazine
c/o Andrew Weatherall
216 Goulden House
Bullen Street
London
SW11

25 EFFIE ROAD, FULHAM, LONDON SW6 1EE
TELEPHONE: 01-736 6267 · FAX: 01-736 9861

Dear 'Boys Own' Readers,

Thank you for your donation of £1200 which has resulted from the Charity
Fancy Dress Ball held at Cobdens on 1st April.

The Society is now by far the major funding body for Multiple Sclerosis
research in the United Kingdom and at the same time is being asked to
substantially increase its commitment to welfare and support services for
those families, one member of which suffers with Multiple Sclerosis. As
the Society is not in any way state aided and relies entirely upon
voluntary sources for income, support such as yours is most valuable.

Again, thank you for your support.

Yours sincerely,

Dawn Booth

Dawn Booth
Fundraising Department

THE REMAINDER OF THE MONEY RAISED WENT TO THE MARTINDALE
SPECIAL SCHOOL, HOUNSLOW TO HELP THE FRIENDS OF GRAHAM HOWELLS,
A VERY SPECIAL PERSON WHO PASSED AWAY EARLIER THIS YEAR ...

Yo! Posh Fackers in the Mansion

Throughout the years the so-called "smart set", you know those zany kids with double-barrelled names and single cylinder brains, have liked to dip a tentative toe into the waters of working class youth culture. In the 50's gangs of teddy boys stalked the dorms of Eton de-bagging and shouting "Be-bop-a-lula My Father's an M.P. with a Large Majority".

Later in the Sixties copious amounts of LSD were introduced into the half-time orange drink at Wellington College annual boys versus masters Rugby challenge match. The game had to be abandoned mid-way through the second half when boys stormed the public address system and played "Hole In My Shoe" to an ever increasingly confused mass of masters and boys giggling uncontrollably and holding "Be-Ins" during the scrum downs.

The Seventies saw uncle Malc and the Punk Rock explosion and once more the bastions of top people's education were rampant with working class youth culture influence. However, things fizzled out somewhat when "Holidays In The Sun" was relesaed. The public school punks thought this would be a "rippingly good idea" and it was safety pins in St. Moritz for the whole movement.

NOw as the Eighties draws to a close we see another example of cultural piracy. It's school caps back to front, Troop trainers during gym and "Yo Nigel You're Def!" What makes this movement different, and in our opinion more dangerous, is that actual Recorded material is hitting the streets. What follows is a hip-hop chart published in Harper's & Queen (next to the usual photos of twats in Ball gowns and dicky bows cutting a rug at a charity ball).....

TOP CHELSCENE D.J. DEF-SKI-TRUMPINGTON.

LADY CAMILLA-STROBE LOVETT AND A FRIEND SHARE A LAUGH AND A DRINK AT THE AFTER GIG COOL JEREMY PARTY HELD AT FUN CITY...

SLOANEY HIP-HOP CHART

1. "BRING THE PICNIC HAMPER" : Public School Enemy

2. JUST ICE (WITH MY PIMMS)

3. "FIGHT FOR THE RIGHT TO HOLD A MIDNIGHT BUM FEAST" — The Perfectly Beastly Fellows

4. "SCHOOL FEES PAID IN FULL" — Cedric B and Tarquin

5. "ROCK THE BELLS (OF CHARTERHOUSE SCHOOL)" — L.L. Cool Jeremy

RECORDS SUPPLIED BY THE RECORD DEPARTMENT — HARRODS.

BLAINE AND SIMON '6·57' BECK...

JAK, ROCKA, MEEHAN, SIR LES and FRIEN

DEJA VU ~ TOP PLOT

ANNA, STRIPEY, OS, WALLACE....
YES WE DO KNOW WHO WON THE LEAGUE

STREATHAM GIRLS' ON THE PLOT
JANE, SUE, AND NINA ...

ELLO ANDY ... FUCK OFF TEDDY♪
O YOU CANT HAVE A TICKET FOR JOY.

HOW MANY? STEVE IN THE BACKGROUND
GETS KNOCKED FOR 6

MISTER P. CONS and THE BANANA
BARMIES...

BARRY THE FROG and THE TOMATO
BARMY...

FACES AT THE FANCY DRESS

LAUNCH 22ND JUNE
It's The Future
CHAPTER 2

"BUT NOT AS WE KNOW IT JIM"

NEW DJ's Terry Farley & Andy Nichols

TURBO SOUND & NEW LITES

EVERY THURSDAY £5 10-3.30am

UNDER THE ARCHES
HUNGERFORD LANE
OFF CRAVEN ST.

The Strange Case of THE GARAGE TEDS

THE LOCATION – Black Market Record Shop
THE TIME – Friday Afternoon
THE SOUNDTRACK – House (Surprise, surprise)
THE ACCUSED – London DJ's (Various)

"Alright Geezer, you still playing Acid then?"
"Who me? When, where, never, I've always been into Garage!!"
"I'm sure I saw you trancing out down Spectrum last summer"
"No way matey, oop's I mean mate, I used to check out the Paradise
Garage every Monday"
"What in New York?"
"No the Watford one"

"So what tunes you spinning then?"
"All the Deep House Classics, Style Council, Beats Working, and er,..I
can't tell you the rest 'cos I cover up my labels"
"Do you check out the New Jersey sound?"
"Didn't know they had blacks on the Channel Islands"
"No, Blaze, Adeva and all that stuff"
"Oh yeah, Blaze's 'Break For Love'"
"I had that one ages ago, I play the Yorkshire version"

Suddenly Frankie spins the latest (and last we hope – Ed) Miami Bass
import 12", (AKA Streetsounds Electro Vol.1).
"It's really crap but there's only five copies in the country" cries the
Black Marketer.
"I'll have one"
"Stick it on my pile guy"
"Yo, Miami's the sound of the summer, serve me that tune"
"Yeah Garage was good whilst it lasted but it's gone commercial"

"Anyway I'm having a walk, check out our new club down Croydon"
"It's called 'Tony Montanas Miami Beach Bar' It's in Cinderellas every
Tuesday, 100% Latin Hip Hop Matey"
"By the way, you still serving E?"
"Leave it out, I'm a Charlie man, the E nowadays is well snide"
"Although I remember when me and Alfredo started off the...(boring,
boring, boring – Ed)

The lesson of this story is:
1. Most of us did like Acid House (STEADY LAD... Ed)
2. Very few of us played much Garage in the summer
3. The Charlie Brigade are paranoid, "You talking to me?"
"I neverdid trust those Chelsea, Millwall, West Ham, Gooners"

'40 ST MARTINS LANE W2.

20 ENDELL ST· COVENT GARDEN·

AMERICAN CLASSICS·

American
Classics

400 KINGS Rd
CHELSEA·
404 KINGS Rd·
CHELSEA

HUG

STAVROS

VOICES IN THE DARK

What is it our mothers and fathers, aunts and uncles, grandads and grandmas and ultimately brothers and sisters actually expect when voting for the past and present government? For the last ten years all they have done is run down the NHS, education spending and privatise public services, let aone the stripping of the country's assets (assets that we own) and then put them on the open market so that you and I can have a say in the future of that company. But at the end of the day, how many people do you know that actually own shares in the companies in question, except of course for the fat bastards in slim Porsches (and dodgy Conservative MPs who are caught trying to cook da books).

But isn't this a lovely illusion they are trying to create, the average working man pulling himself out of the gutter and maybe rising to become an ENTREPRENEUR, and maybe being able to afford private health care one day.

But of course there are more sinister angles to this beautifully manufactured vision, and some of those are what happens to the people that are left behind, the people who can't rise out of poverty or sickness... and isn't it always the lucky ones who say "you can achieve whatever you want in life, all you have to do is work for it hard enough." There is also a status symbol element attatched to this, which is, of course, human nature.

All this has seemed to create an "I'm alright Jack" attitude amongst the slightly better off of the working class (ie the chaps in the chapel and superhods etc). Why? Well this again comes down to the present government which is commited to the privatisation of anything that costs money. There are some things that are not meant to make money and never will.

One feasible reason for privatisation of public services is that after selling off our assets, the working revenue has been lessened, but this is not true — the treasury is sitting on £15 billion. So how come cuts in everything from the health service to students grants?

The worst thing is that you always think you're immune from the problems, as I did, until I found myself lying on a hospital bed after an accident. For the treatment I needed there were two options, East Grinstead or Liverpool, and then I had to wait six hours before I could have surgery, because the specialist surgeon needed was already in surgery. All this is hardly condusive to good and effective treatment. This is just one case; there are a thousand others and many a lot more important.

The whole point of this article is to appeal to the people who have taken on this "I'm alright Jack" attitude, which is more than you think, as people have tried to crawl out of this rat race. All I am saying is don't forget those who are left behind, get on and do whatever you want with your life, just remember your voice can help the less fortunate.

So when you hear of NHS cuts and closures, councils selling off homes (homes not just houses and flats), students grants being turned into loans and taxes for the incredibly rich being cut, just think what it's like when you're the person affected. If thousands

of Kent Tory voters can move a channel tunnel just think what the silent majority can do.
Don't turn your back, because one day it will be your turn, and you will scream blue
murder when it is.

Life isn't just about being the first to get that elusive Italian 12" or whether the E
coming in from the Dam is any good or not, there are people who are stuck with their lot,
so use your voice if nothing else.

SIR LES

aka REXEL CUMBERLAND

BOOK REVIEW by ADAM PORTER.

HOOLIGAN: A HISTORY OF RESPECTABLE FEARS : GEOFFREY PEARSON : MACMILLAN : £8.50.

As they say 'history is always written by the victors' and so the social history of
our country is usually written by 'victors' or more obviously those in positions of
power and or access to the public.

The crux of this book is to show up the lies and distortions that are perpetrated by
poloticians/the media over the violent behaviour of young men. The idea that 'hooliganis
is a modern phenomena is a lie. The idea that street robbery is a modern invention
(and by using the word 'mugging' closer association with the post-war British black
community is implied) is a lie. Even the idea of hazardous tube travel dates back to
the latest century and one can find countless examples in this book of the way that
these distortions are carried on in an endless cycle of meaningless fears.

The birth of the industrial revolution in this country gave a spawning ground for
exploitation of the vast majority of the population. People who lived by streets full
of excrement, in fear of the next cholera/typhoid/TB epedemic that could and did kill
thousands at a time. People who lived ten to a room, where the infant mortality rate
rose to seventy percent not syrprisingly found few positive images t identify with
especially when the aristocracy regarded the poor with such distaste. As the book shows
the result of this is, (and this is the important finding of the book), the CREATION
AND IDENTIFICATION of an underclass to be persecuted harrangued and rejected.

The hooligan was merely one of these new industrial age underclasses. Young Victorian
men with 1. Too much money. 2. No parental control. 3. Warped by city life.
4. Violent. The hypocrisy is unending. As parliament in the 1880's brought back floggin
to deal with the menace they were also allowing British troops to run amok accross
the world in the name of 'civilisation'. As the demise of the 'Imperial Race' (does tha
sound dodgy or what?) was predicted wages were cut for the poor, which meant roughly
85% of the population, in order to restrain them and their fanciful ideals such as the
vote, representation etc.

Nevertheless this book also contains good portrayals of the original hoolie and of
other similar forms such as Teds (the fifties ones turkeys) and inter-war strops. So
once you've read this book you'll know what to say to people who think the eighties
has seen a crime-wave/disintegration of morals.
Yup it's 'fuck off'.

On other fun subjects check BIG DEAL - THE POLITICS OF THE ILLICIT DRUGS BUSINESS -
PLUTO PRESS - £4.50 ANTHONY HENMAN. Apart from a really naffo chapter called 'The
cost of Lacoste' which is basically saying 'footie chaps take drugs too - gosh' this is
a pretty decent number that shows the way that international drugs money influences
the world. Did you know for example that, drug money Banks 2 million dollars every
hour or that marijuana is the 2nd biggest cash crop in the USA?   Then again try
MAFIA BUSINESS - THE MAFIA ETHIC AND THE SPIRIT OF CAPITALISM : OXFORD PAPERBACKS :
PINO ALACCHI : £4.95. Pino Arlacci was one of the investigators on the last big
Italian govt commision and he knows the truth, boys, about these chaps. No sentiment
no misinterpretation all fact. An excellent book for all lovers of organised crime.

AS THE SECOND SUMMER OF LOVE (SIC) IS WELL IN SWING, THERE ARE ONE OR TWO THINGS THAT HAVE TO BE SORTED BEFORE THE DRUGS TAKE OVER AGAIN. IN THE LAST BOY'S OWN WE MOANED ABOUT SHITHOLE RAVES THAT CHARGED A NICKER FOR SOFT DRINKS. WELL NOTHING'S CHANGED ON THAT FRONT, EXCEPT THAT INSTEAD OF SHITTY WAREHOUSES, THE MOODY MONEY MAKERS OFFER US SHITTY BARNS COMPLETE WITH HORSESHIT, MUDDY DANCEFLOORS AND OF COURSE THOSE SOFT DRINKS THAT STILL COST A QUID. OUR MAIN MOAN THIS TIME IS THOSE FUCKIN TEDS WHO GRAB YOUR EXPENSIVE DESIGNER "HAPPY SHOPPER" COKES AND WITHOUT A SECOND THOUGHT GULP HALF YOUR DRINK AND REWARD YOU WITH AN "ECSTASY HAND SHAKE" AND HEPATITIS OF THE COKE CAN. THE NEXT TIME YOU GO FOR A BEER DOWN THE OLD KENT RD, WHY NOT GRAP SOME BODS CAN OF RED STRIPE AND SEE IF HE'S "ON ONE MATEY".

TAKE MY ADVICE THE NEXT TIME SOME WANKER GRABS (OR ASKS) YOUR "HAPPY SHOPPER", POINT HIM WITH THE HELP OF YOUR KICKERS IN THE DIRECTION OF THE BAR AND BY THE WAY MINE'S A GROLSCH. IT'S ABOUT TIME THE SENSIBLE PEOPLE ON THE SCENE FUCKED OFF THESE NOBHEADS ONCE AND FOR ALL; I DON'T WANT TO SHARE MY CLUB WITH THESE MUGS LET ALONE MY DRINK, ENOUGH SAID!

TOP 10 FREDS

1. FRED PERRY — Successful former tennis ace and sportswear designer; now running Colnbrooks premier acid house pub.

2. FRED HOUSEGO — So it's goodbye sherbert and hello linkman Thames at Six for this top loveable Fred.

3. FRED "PARROTFACE" DAVIES — zany Seventies cabaret artiste who cleaned up with his outsized bowler hat and interesting budgie act.

4. FRED WEDLOCK — who could possibly forget Mr. Wedlock's immortal gramaphone record "Oldest Swinger In Town"..... answer....everybody.

5. FRED FORSYTHE — made a fortune writing books about men in balaclavas, mercenaries and unsuccessful attempts to off frog generals.

6. FREDDIES REVENGE — A series of crap films about a man called Fred with a pair of specially customised Marigolds and a tricky skin complaint.

7. FREDDIE STARR — not only notable for having the same surname as one of the Beatles, but for also being the subject of the Sun's finest headline... and wearing large pants with swastikas on.

8. FRED GEE — poetry in motion is the only way to describe Mr. Gee as he pulled pints of frothing Newton & Ridley's ale at the Rover's Return.

9. LORD ALFRED DOUGLAS — his dad (the Marquess of Queensbury) invented boxing, and Fred himself was partial to Oscar Wilde's winkle.

10. FRED DINEAGE — did potty things with ordinary household objects and asked us "How?". Currently hosting "My Dog's Got A Secret" or something similar. A bit of an artistic lull but this top Fred will once more rise to light entertainment highs.

ROBOT

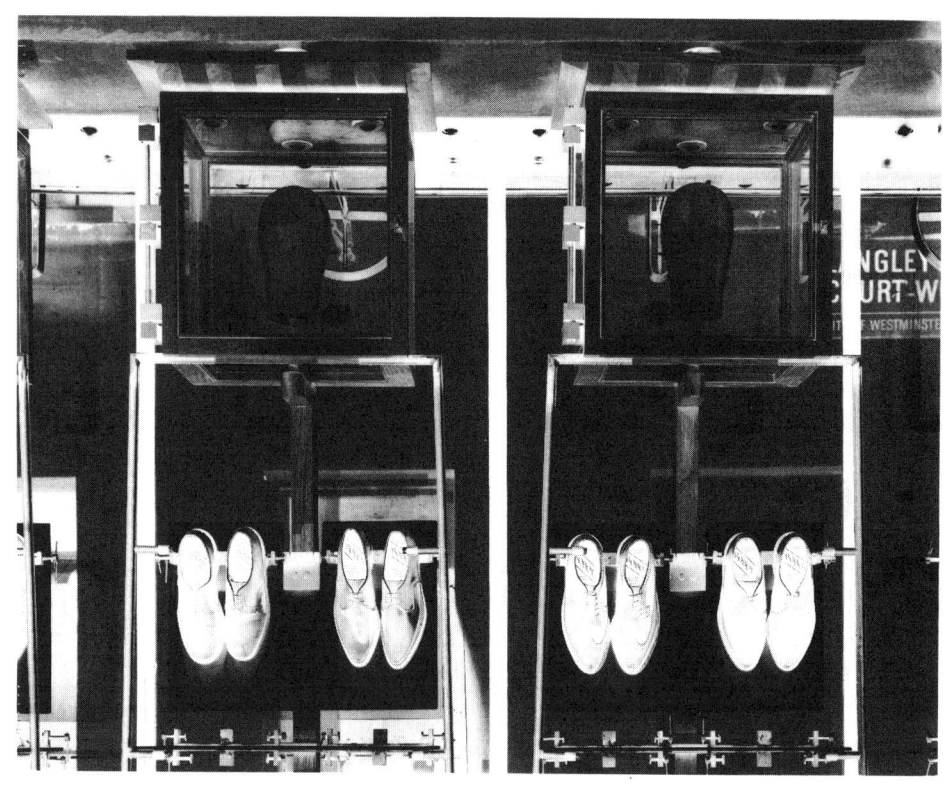

LOCATION~COVENT GARDEN
ARCHITECTS~AO PARTNERSHIPS
PHOTOGRAPHY~PETER COOK

**323 kings rd. 37 floral st. hyper~hyper.
LONDON**

"got Any Skins....?"

"SAY HELLO TO THE SPEAKER OPPOSSITE ALFREDO FOR ME." THIS STRANGE GOODBYE AS I LEFT GOOD OLD BLIGHTY CAME FROM ONE OF THE LAST YEARS IBIZAN VETERANS. I SMILED AND THOUGHT "I'D BETTER NOT DO TOO MANY OF THOSE INFAMOUS PINK ONES IF THAT'S WOT HAPPENS",BUT MORE OF THE SPEAKER LATER. FIRSTLY LUTON AIRPORT WAS TOTAL BOLLOCKS   FULL OF "LOVABLE" COCKNEYS FROM HEMEL HEMPSTEAD AND POTTERS BAR ATTIRED IN THE FULL MONTY,CYCLING SHORTS,BOXING VESTS WHILE THE WOMEN SPORTED THE LEGEND "WHEATSHEAF PUSSY POSSIE" ON FETCHING CAP SLEEVE T-SHIRTS AND THESE PEOPLE HAD BROUGHT THEIR CHILDREN WITH THEM,HORRENDOUS....

ANYWAY THE NEXT DAY AFTER THE USUAL KIP TO GET OVER THE JET-LAG AND TIME ZONE MULARKY WE VENTURED WITH TREPIDATION TO THE CAFE DEL MAR,RUMOURS OF HUNDREDS OF VALBONNE/QUEENS BODS JACKING WERE UNFOUNDED, THE MAJORITY OF THE ENGLISH CLUBBERS WERE HALF SENSIBLE AND NEW AGE WAS STILL THE SOUND OF THE BEACH. THE NEXT FEW HOURS WERE SPENT MAKING SURE OUR AMNESIA OPENING NIGHT INVITES WERE NOT JECKYLE AND CATCHING UP ON THE GOSSIP, TALES OF TEDS, FAT TONY'S DINGO BABY CAPER AND A CERTAIN LONDON NEW BEAT DJ WANTING TO BECOME A BOXER WERE TOLD OVER A WELCOMING GLASS OF COLD CHOCOLATE, IT WAS GOOD TO BE BACK.

BY 12.15 THE CAR PARK AT AMNESIA WAS PACKED WITH TICKETLESS PEOPLE ALL PUSHING AT THE MAIN ENTRANCE, TASTELESS HILLSBOROUGH JOKES MIXED UNEASILY WITH ANXIETY ATTACKS FROM THOSE WHO HAD "DROPPED ONE" TOO EARLY.

ONCE INSIDE LIFE SEEMED TOTALLY WONDERFUL, THE GARDEN-LIKE LAYOUT OF THE CLUB, FOUNTAINS, PLANTS ETC, SET TO A SOUNDTRACK OF IZIT S "STORIES" WITH A CAST OF TOP PEOPLE WAS TO MAKE THIS A NIGHT OF NIGHTS, BY NOW YOU WILL ALL BE WELL FED UP WITH PEOPLE GOING ON AND ON ABOUT WHAT A TOP NIGHT YOU MISSED, WELL YOU DID (HA HA) BUT I'LL JUST SAY THAT MOST OF US OVER-INDULGED HORRIBLY, DANCED OUR BOLLOCKS OFF, ALFREDO IS A GENIUS, AND HALF OF LONDON SPENT HOURS HIDING FROM DAVE SWINDELL'S (I-D, TIME OUT) CAMERA, AS MONGED UP BOATS WERE THE ORDER OF THE NIGHT.

THE NEXT DAY WAS TAKEN AT A MUCH SLOWER PACE, SAN MIGUEL'S AND TOASTED SANIES AND TALES OF THE PREVIOUS NIGHT THAT GOT TALLER AND TALLER EVERY TIME THEY WERE TOLD. MEANWHILE A SPLIT AMONGST THE RANKS HAD OCCOURED WITH "PASSION" AND "QUEENS" PUNTERS DOING THEIR OWN RAVES WHILE THE MORE SEASONED SOUTH LONDON CROWD GOING TO PACHA, ANGELS AND AMNESIA, OF THE "PASSION" EVENTS THE KU CLUB WAS PROBABLY THE BEST WITH A BLINDING THUNDERSTORM AND DJ'S CRAIG WALSH AND FRED PERRY SPINNING WILLIAM ORBIT, RAVEN MAIZE AND DON PABLO YOU NEARLY FORGOT THAT THE "FAMOUS KU" ONLY REALLY LOOKS LIKE BRENT CROSS SHOPPING CENTER BUT WITH DEARER DRINKS............

SAYING OF THE HOLIDAY WAS, "GOT ANY SKINS?" WHICH BECAME TERRIBLY IRRITATING AFTER A WHILE, STILL IT S BETTER THAN ALL THAT "PEACE 'N' LOVE - MATEY" MULARKY.

AS THE WEEK WENT ON EVERYBODY GOT INTO A MELLOWER ONE, THE CHEVIGNON SHOP GOT ITS USUAL "RE-DISTRIBUTION" AMONGST THOSE FROM SOUTH OF THE RIVER, YOU CAN TELL THOSE WHO HAVE BEEN DOING IBIZA FOR YEARS BY THE AGE OF THE CHEVS WORN. ANOTHER PASTIME THAT BECAME POPULAR WAS "SPOT THE SUN REPORTER" ANYONE WITH KICKERS AND A CENTRE PARTING WERE GIVEN A WIDE BERTH. THE FACT THAT YOU COULD GO OUT DRESSED UP AND RAVE ALL NIGHT AND STILL COME HOME CLEAN WAS NOT LOST AMONGST THOSE OF US FED UP WITH LONDONS SWEATY PITS THAT WERE ACCEPTABLE LAST SUMMER, BUT NOW NO WAY. IT TOOK TILL THE LAST NIGHT FOR ME TO UNDERSTAND ALL THAT "HELLO TO THE SPEAKER" LINGO AS ALFREDO SPUN "HILL ST BLUES" FOR THE LAST TIME I FINALLY REALISED WHAT THE CLUB MEANT FOR SO MANY. THE CLOSING NIGHT IS IN OCTOBER, BE THERE OR BE AT HOME.

P.S..Anyone seen Maizie??? Last seen down the Cafe Del Mar with Happy Monday man Bez.......It's a funny old world eh !!!!!!!!!!

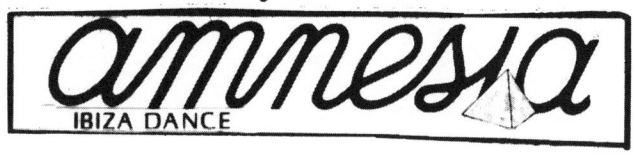

amnesia

IBIZA DANCE

CLUB LINE

0898 662700/01

24 HOUR INFO SERVICE

ON LONDONS CLUB SCENE

FROM 28th JULY

25p Off 38p On

Promote your Rave Tel 317 7765

'LAGGED'

A WORD ON BEHALF OF THE BEER DRINKER by LEE VITOUT.

Last sunday lunchtime, having reposed in that most heavenly of hostelries, often referred to with great affection as "the boozer", I was intent on enjoying the benevolent service of the aptly voluptuous barmaid. The cool reassurance of a medicinal pint in my right hand was enough to absolve the weekend's sins even before the first sip was taken.

After ceremoniously devouring this initial offering and thus feeling totally invigourated and at peace with my fellow regulars, it saddened me to reflect that in recent times the noble sport of beer drinking has been the subject of much criticism and stigma from the intrepid posse of do-gooders, the tabloid press.

We are informed that, upon quaffing a few pints of his his favourite bevvy, your average son of England turns from his hitherto placid endeavours to become a snarling, spitting, neo nazi monstrosity intent on terrorising the local constabulary and dismembering any poor foreigner unlucky enough to stray into his path. This phenomenon has been dubbed "the lager lout", a mutated ancestor of knights of old willing to die in defense of his sexuality ("Did you call my pint a poofta?") and his country ("Eng-errrr-laaaand"), charging fearlessly into the fray should any pilgrim risk more than a fleeting glance at his girlfriend's unfortunately magnetic cleavage.

Of course, the infamous "session" has a place on the calendar of most beer drinkers, but, whether they be steamy, riotous or slapstick they are generally conducted in a jovial and good natured manner with plenty of sarcastic repartee ("Oi! Tell me that one again at bedtime, I'm having trouble sleeping at the moment"). And if they are performed with the requisite style, they do not include the wearing of pastel coloured Fred Perry T-shirts with white toweling socks or drooling on the bar staff ("Cor! Look at the jugs on that") and leaving a trail of broken car aerials and pavement pizzas along the route home.

No, although it possesses undoubted aesthetic attributes, your typical pint is basically a very functional piece of apparatus who's primary purpose in life is to bestow a feeling of well being on the consumer. In this task it can be extremely versatile, whether it be in the drowning of sorrows, celebrations or relaxation. After all, a swift indulgence on the way home from a hard days toil can release just as much tension as 15 rounds throwing saucepans at your partner and for those of us for whom sunday lunchtimes have evolved into a near religious experience, there can be no doubt that convalescing in a public house on the day of rest is heaven on earth.

So, despite the favourite image of the beer drinker as a misguided pillock sporting two clenched fists and an expression of vacant aggression ("Ere, watch it mate your e cruisin for a bruisin"), It is important to remember that at closing time tonight, for every one of those glorified cretins that make themselves apparent, there are a hundred others sliding gracefully from their bar stools to the floor or being stretchered home by helpful and more sober freinds or just swaggering off to bed or a party in a meandering fashion, the smile of contentment playing across their lips, having just enjoyed the finest of the publican's pleasures. For what is life without enjoyment and pleasure. CHEERS!.......

The Tony Benn Funk Force

1974 was quite an exciting time, for my own, musical awakening. I was 18 years old and looking to find a radio deejay broadcasting in sympathy with my own tastes & musical direction. At that time, a young(ish!) deejay called Robbie Vincent, who had up until then, hosted a late night call-in programme on Radio London, started a music show, on the same station, on saturday mornings from 11.30 a.m. until 2 p.m. Robbie Vincent, in my mind, influenced a great deal of soul fans of my generation, who, like myself, love soul music and were excited by it's new developments. We wanted to listen to radio that complimented our own tastes. Robbie offered an alternative to Radio London's other black music deejay, David Simmonds, who mainly concentrated on 'The Blues' and ignored the developments in dance music which were to later dominate even Radio One's airwaves, more than a decade later.

Robbie's show, to begin with, consisted of 1 hour of soul (the last hour) and the rest of the show concentrated on some soul, some blue-eyed soul and some 'soft rock' artists of the time. Those artists included Loggins & Messina, Dr. John, The Meters, Rufus, Steely Dan & Little Feat. Ironically, these artists became popular in the mid to late eighties in some jazz circles. In the mid to late seventies, Robbie's show slowly became all soul as he converted the powers that be at Radio London, to a more soulful sound.

1975 brought Capital Radio. It always struck me as strange that a radio station based in Canada should feel itself in tune with London's streets. Capital Radio.....in tune with Toronto! Anyhow, in between a daylong torture of Bruce Springsteen (yes, I know his politics are sound!) and Dave Cash, we were treated to 3 hours of soul on a saturday night, courtesy of Greg Edwards and his show 'Soul Spectrum'. When I say 3 hours of soul, I actually mean 2! Capital wasted an hour on adverts! Greg seemed to know what he was doing although he lacked Robbie Vincent's main talent. That of spotting a good tune! Capital then proceeded to put him on the air, then take him off the air, then put him back on, finally to remove him permanently. You see, Capital wasn't all that sure of soul music. They thought they had a soul deejay in Dave Cash. In 1978, Dave Cash picked up and played twelve-inchers by such fine soul artists (in true Saturday Night Fever fashion) as Dolly Parton, The Beach Boys, John Travolta, Olivia Newton John & Gerard Kenny. Hot soul sounds, eh? Capital Radio's idea of a crisp biscuit, then, (Pete Tong was to lead them in the right direction later) was my idea of dry bread and water!

Radio London carried on regardless. By 1982, we had recovered from Saturday Night Fever (our temperatures had gone down!) and we were treated (in London) to the first pirate radio stations, like JFM. Now, it's easy to critisize pirate radio. I do on one point. That is, I feel that their priority is to be 'on the air' firstly, and because of that their entertainment suffers due to the poor quality of some of the deejays. However, having said that, they were very similar in one aspect, to the punk new wave. Entirely necessary for the time. What a joy to turn on the radio at 3 in the afternoon and listen to some soul music instead of a M.O.R. deejay like .....well Tony Blackburn.

Feature on Robbie Vincent
Blues & Soul, May-June 1977

Now,didn't he slag off some dance records. Of course,he did have a track record of loving and playing Tamla Motown,but I also remember him giving Positive Forces 'We got the funk' a real roasting on one of his afternoon 'record review' shows. Ain't it funny how the worm turned?

1983 came along and who should pop-up on Radio London,with his 'funky-head' on,but good old Blackers! It was like watching a Labour M.P. get voted in on a Labour ticket and then joining the S.D.P. or the Tories (Yes,I remember you Reg Prentice!).

It was about this time that soul music began to catagorise. Hip-hop, Jazz,Soul,Go-go & House (later). Capital could not cope. Radio London ignored the changes. The pirates did not.

You see,up until this time,the stations could more or less,keep all types of soul on one show,with deejaying going from hip-hop to soft soul. Of course,more soul on radio was needed,but we didn't get that until later.

In 1984,Robbie Vincent went to Radio One,at that time,on sunday nights Jeff Young took over his Radio London slot (this was,sadly,only for a couple of years until those powers that be decided to have a full frontal lobotomy)

Radio London carried on,and was full of surprises. Still reeling from Tony (I think I'll be a head-banger today!) Blackburn being a self ordained club/radio deejay,we now had Super Soul Sister Susie Barnes in the afternoons. Full of useful information was old Suze. Otis Redding is a Woolworths colour dye and Brass Construction is an iron foundry in Deptford! Talk about a case of brain death. Suze knew as much about soul music as Dr. David Owen knows about party loyalty! Come back Johnny Rotten!

Radio London did have two happy accidents,though.Gilles Peterson (Gary Crowley with street cred!) and Andy Peebles (Short-lived) but wise about his sounds. Really,though,Radio London's own street cred went to the wall with the redundancy of Jeff Young. At least you could hear Jeff trying to push back some musical barriers and playing some new types of sounds,such as a new type of dance music out of Chicago called 'House'.

Capital Radio hired Pete Tong to replace Greg Edwards whilst Radio London went from the bland to the ridiculous, G.L.R.! (Radio C.R.A.P.)!

Tony Blackburn put back on his 'Radio One Brain Death Head' and joined Capital Radio's newly formed station for people who know nothing about soul music called 'Capital Gold'. Robbie Vincent went to saturday nights on Radio One (7.30 til 10.30p.m.). Sanity prevailed.

Pete Tong played a lot of House & Hip-Hop in 1988 and won me over in the way he was constantly sending himself up. He and Jeff Young are very similar in style to the way Robbie Vincent was in 1974. Hope for the future.Robbie can still pick a good tune. Tony Blackburn cannot. Pete Tong and Jeff Young can still pick a good tune. Susie Barnes can too....if you like Chris Rea!

In 1989,Maggie is going to legislate against London's Delbert Wilkie's. Pretty pathetic,eh? I resent my taxes being wasted on such a trivial form of legislature. I mean,you ask most women if they feel safe walking around London after dark. They could spend our taxes on better street lighting and more frequent public transport and leave the pirates alone. It seems a bit like getting a steamroller to crack a walnut! I hope we do not lose the KISS F.M.'s of this world. Perhaps we are bringing out the sadistic side of her personality in wanting to enjoy ourselves! Ask any of the vast silent majority of soccer fans who will now not attend their favourite teams ground because it's too much hassle to get in.

My hope for radio in 1989 is that we lose from the airwaves the House music made by stylophone,and we get more House with Soul. More Turntable Orchestra, Adeva,Ricky Dillard & Ten City.

I also hope that we see more little label records getting more airplay. These are independent label deep soul sounds,as you'll hear on Robbie Vincent. Willie Clayton,David Sea,Oscar Perry & Lanier & Co.

ABOVE ALL MORE RADIO WITH TEETH!

Toby Walker.

AIR-A-SOUL

give us a line

BOYS OWN'S VERY OWN LIFESTILE GUIDE
FREE OF NICE PICS OF PAUL SMITH PANTS...

BOY'S OWN QUOTES NO. 61

A CERTAIN LOVEABLE SCOUSE, MR. PETE WYLIE, AT THE
HAPPY MONDAYS ASTORIA BASH: "I'VE SPENT THE LAST YEAR
BEING HAPPY, HAPPY, HAPPY, HAPPY, AND I'M NOT - I'M
GOING BACK TO BEING A RIGHT CUNT."

'OH MY GOD ... A VERSION
OF WORK IT TO THE BONE
BY RYTHM IS RYTHM,
REMIXED BY A GUY
CALLED GERALD!'

FELICITY KENDAL'S TOP TED TERROR TRAX

1. CORPORATION OF TED - TED LIFE.

2. TED IS TED - STRINGS OF TED.

3. LOGGSY T - THIS IS TED.

4. RICHIE RANK - SALSA TED.

5. TED CITY - SIX E WILL MAKE IT BETTER.

NEWS AT TED: REPORTS ARE COMING IN THAT A NEW
CHANT IS BREAKING OUT ACROSS THE BARMIER
DANCEFLOORS OF LONDON.... "MENTAL, MENTAL,
FELICITY KENDALL". WE CAN'T WAIT FOR THE T-SHIRTS.

'NO THEY DIDN'T PAY ME TO WRITE THIS • PT 96'

IT SEEMS THESE DAYS THAT BUYING GRAMAPHONE RECORDS IS
A BIT OF A PAIN IN THE BOTTOM. SILLY ASSISTANTS, BUM
LICKING PUNTERS HOVERING LIKE FLIES AROUND SHIT
WAITING FOR THE NEW SOUNDS WHICH THEY MUST HAVE BEFORE
ANYBODY ELSE, WELL I SAY 'FRACK YOU MUGS', "I'M GOING TO
QUAFF". NOW "QUAFF" IS ON LANCASTER RD AND STAFFED BY
THE LAZIEST BUNCH OF BASTARDS I'VE EVER MET, BUT THEY'RE
ALSO SOME OF THE NICEST GEEZERS I'VE MET WHO LOVE THEIR
MUSIC AND DON'T MIND SHARING IT WITH LIKE MINDS. YOU
MIGHT NOT GET THE LATEST MEDIOCRE MUST OUT-DO OTHER DJ'S
REMIX, BUT YOU WILL GET HELPFUL STAFF WITH KNOWLEDGE
AND LOVE FOR THEIR PRODUCT (P.S. ASK FOR ROY OR PHIL).

SUMMER ENTERTAINMENT TIPS.

1. WATCHING THE LAST SERIES OF GRANGE HILL ON VIDDY.

2. THE SOUTH LONDON PRESS - REPORT UPON REPORT ABOUT
   LOVEABLES MISBEHAVING THEMSELVES.

3. LIGHTNING RADIO (SPEND AN AFTERNOON WITH THE
   DUCHESS).

4. ANYTHING BY VIV STANSHALL

5. LEONARDO DA VINCI AT THE HAYWARD.

6. A LATE ENTRY SENT IN AFTER THE TYPIST
   HAD BEEN SENT HOME • SITTING ON THE
   BALCONY LISTENING TO THE STONE ROSES L.P.
   'YOU DO CALL THEM 'THE ROSES' DON'T YOU?'
   ANTHONY H. WILSON 89

ROBBING THE DEAD, MOLESTING THE DEAD, ATTACKING
AMBULANCE WOMEN - THESE ARE WHAT THE INFAMOUS SOUTH
YORKSHIRE POLICE HAVE ACCUSED THE LIVERPOOL FANS OF
DURING THE HILLSBOROUGH DISASTER. FUNNY THAT ON TV A
WE SAW WAS YOUNG MEN WHO NORMALLY WOULD BE TREATED
LIKE THUGS ACTING LIKE HEROES. POLICE LIES NEVER
SOUNDED AS SICK OR SHALLOW.

SO GOOD OLD MAXWELL'S MIRROR PUT UP ITS PRICE BY
2p TO GO TO THE HILLSBOROUGH FUND.... FUNNY THE F
STOPPED BUT THE PRICE AIN'T GONE DOWN (SURPRISE,
SURPRISE).

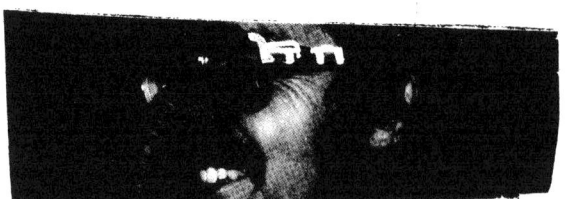

BOY'S OWN FASHION TIPS FOR THE SUMMER.

1. SLING BACK KICKERS.

2. CLOGS, PATCHWORK JEANS, A.C. MILAN BEANY HAT

3. McDONALDS LITTER PATROL ANORAKS.

4. HAPPY MONDAYS BOXER SHORTS.

5. PANTS OUTSIDE YOUR TROUSERS.

T-SHIRT TIP. 'FASHION - I DON'T CARE '

letters to ED.

Dear Boy's Own,

Please help. I feel suicidal, so I'm turning to you; you're my last hope. Seven months ago I was living the life of Riley, I was really enjoying myself. Every Friday I went down to Cinderellas Rockerfellers, paid to get in, drank as much as I liked, a few egg burgers on the way home, yeah a blinding nite out with change from a score.

Sadly those days are over. My mate Ian, fuck me only went and got himself some style. Now every weekend I've got to hit the West End for the trendy "one nighters". The queue's are murder, you then shell out seven sovs to get in, then fifty bob for a can of lager... Ian says it's dear so the clubs can create a warehouse atmosphere! Fucking hell if this ain't bad enough Ian insists that real Westenders don't stay in one club all night.

Now we used to repeat this carry on a couple of times a week, but now Ian rekons real Westenders go out on Tuesdays and suchlike - have you ever heard such nonsense!

I'm at me wits end; six months of this malarky and I've yet to see a drug induced orgy, yet to be offered a recording contract, or been raped by a wild child. I'm shelling out the dosh, so where am I going wrong? Dear Boy's Own, are we getting into these clubs too early? What's the problem? I'm starting to wish Ian had never bought the fucking Sun in the first place.

Yours in fucking desperation,

Gary, Mottingham, S.E.9

P.S. Fucking hell, it's getting worse, Ian reckons he's gonna become a DJ (is this the way to drugs, Argies and birds etc?). He seems to think so.

Dear Boy's Own,

Here's my Spring dreams: the end of acid reign - the revival of two step soul - Sugar Ray Leonard winning another title - West Ham mates still double loyal - educating yourself with books by Tony Parsons and Mario Puzo - plays by Mick Mahoney and Tony Marchant - L.W.R. getting a license after six years as a pathfinder - a Scotch and Coke and a smile from a loved one - my old man said be an Arsenal fan, I said Fuck off (no, no, this is censored cos we're fed up with getting grief - Ed) - you and me on the winning side.

Paul T.
W.H.U. & L.W.R.
Bethnal Green
East London.

Reports upon reports of London's youth nutting about shouting "Up Your Cunt" have been flooding into Boy's Own mansions. This summer's craze is now reaching epidemic proportions; schoolkids are abusing the lollipop ladies, teenagers hiding behind fences are giving it to unsuspecting hedge creeping plod, even old grannies are shouting it at the D.H.S.S counter staff. Boy's Own can now exclusively reveal the Mr. Big behind this evil madness. Mr. Roger Melly, who is also known as "The Man On The Telly", is the instigator of this new term of abuse. Our reporter, who went to Melly's home, asked him to comment on our accusations. His reply - "Up Your Cunt". Will this fad spread up North? Will The Sun newspaper's Bizarre column sell "The Sun Says, Argies - Up Your Cunt" T-Shirts? Will Nicky Holloway's next New Beat classic be a cut-up sample of Martin Luther King's little known speech "Up Your Cunt - Free At Last?" We wait with baited breath.

UPPERS & DOWNERS

UPPERS......

HAVING A MOB OF PET SOLDIER ANTS AS PETS.... WEARING CLOGS INSTEAD OF KICKERS.... THROWING VIVIENNE WESTWOOD VICTIMS UNDER BUSES.... GETTING FRANK BOUGH TO SNEEZE IN YOUR FACE.... SHOUTING "UP YOUR CUNT.... SID THE MANAGER (HELLO BOYS).... TEA, TOAST AND TWO HOURS OF INSPECTOR MORSE.... HAVING A CRY OVER THE LAST EPISODE OF FOOL'S 'N' HORSES.... BRIAN TILSLEY GETTING CHIVED UP IN CORRIE (SERVES HIM RIGHT FOR HAVING A CURLY PERM) ....BILLY CORKHILL.... ZIGGY GREAVES.... JUSTIN (MINDER) ... GETTING LAGGED.... OBSCURE FOREIGN FOOTIE TOPS.... GIRLS WHO SAY "SUPER DOOPER".... WALLACE THE NUTTY K.P. SWEATY.... McVITE'S BOASTER BICCYS, J.P.G. FLOWERY DUNGAREES.... PAT NEVIN (DIXON FUCK OFF).... DOPE SOUP... NUTTING ABOUT TOWN ON A SUNNY DAY.... PERCY SUGDEN'S MAD MANC MUTTERINGS.... DAVID ROECASTLE'S RISE TO ENGLAND STATUS.... THE DOOBIE DUCK SHOW.... PEOPLE WHO HAVE THE CRACK AND TAKE THE PISS.... BULLSEYE, RIPPY, REAM, STAY SWEET....

DOWNERS....

HILLSBOROUGH JOKES (KIDS DYING AIN'T FUCKING FUNNY)... PROFIT AND GAIN MASQUERADING AS PEACE AND LOVE.... GIRLS WITH SEVERE E-BOATS... LIMPING POSSIES... DREAMING YOU'VE GOT A GARY NUMAN TATTOO AND WAKING UP TO FIND YOU HAVE!!.... TARQUIN POSH FACKERS CASHING IN ON YOUR SCENE (FUN CITY).... SCOUSERS WHO MAKE DONKEY NOISES.... COCAINE VIOLENCE.... LOOKING LAGGED AND FEELING SICK.... HALF GLASGOW RANGERS - HALF K.K.K. POINTED HOODS (THE OFFICIAL IBROX CHAMPIONSHIP MOMENTO).... CALLING TEDS, NITS.... GRAHAM KELLY'S LAME EXCUSES... SLOANEY'S WITH JEEPS AND ENGLISH BULL TERRIERS.... SEEING YOUR PET ANTS "THUGGING IT" AT THE MATCH ON T.V.(WAIT TILL THEM LITTLE SODS GET HOME)... LIVING NEXT DOOR TO MRS BRADY OLD LADY.... STAFFS WITH HAIR LIPS... THE NEW "ASTORIA/SIN" DOORPERSON ATTIRE BULLET PROOF VESTS (BE CAREFUL, THE REAL OTIS NEVER MADE IT TO 30 EITHER).... CHELSEA NOBHEADS IN U.D.A. LOYALIST T-SHIRTS (SOME PEOPLE NEVER LEARN)... PEOPLE WHO CRITICISE BUT DON'T UNDERSTAND.................

BOYS OWN BUNGALOWS.
216 GOULDEN HOUSE
BULLEN ST.
LONDON
S. W. 11.

STAFF • TERRY FARLEY • CYMON ECKEL • ANDREW WEATHER
STEVEN MAYES (I WOULD HAVE WRITTEN SOMETHING BUT IT'S
BEEN ON TOP A BIT LATELY)

CONTRIBUTORS • THE OUTSIDER, PHIL THORNTON (NORVEN LAN
RICHARD NORRIS (DEAR DEAR DICKIE), KEIRON KERSLAKE, LEE,
REXEL CUMBERLAND (SIR LES), TOBY WALKER.

IT'S THANK YOU TIME AGAIN...

TA TO ALL THE D.J.'S WHO GAVE THEIR SERVICES FREE OF CHARGE AT THE FANCY DRESS DO ... (SEE BELOW) TO ALL THE PUNTERS WHO MADE A SUPREME EFFORT AND BROUGHT THE HOUSE DOWN ...

COVER STAR • J. MEEHAN • KETCHUP MODEL AGENCY.

AND TO R·M· WEATHERALL • PROBABLY STROLLING ABOUT THE BIG BUS GARAGE IN THE SKY! ...... STRONGER THAN MOST IN SOUL • .... JUST AS GOOD?

LOVE and RESPECT TO ...
DAVE DORRELL, GILES PETERSON, DANNY RUMPLING, TREVOR FUNG, ANDY NICHOLS, THE 2 KEVS (THE COVER-UP KINGS), FABIO, CRAIG (MR BYRITE) WALSH, SOPHIE, LAST AND BY NO MEANS LEAST ... MISTER D·HEIGHTS.

ALSO ...
SPENCER, BLAINE, STEVE and SEAN (DEJA VU), MARK (BIG GREEN ONES) SMITHERS, ROLLSIE, MARK (WESTWORLD), ALL AT LONDON (BUTLER AT YOUR SERVICE), A BIG HI TO BALDRY AND THE 6·57 FROM SIMON, GARY (FALL IN SHITE AND COME OUT SWEET) HAISMAN, ROCKA (ALL TROOPED UP AND NOWHERE TO BREAK), PLUG, STEVE AND TANNY, McGOO AND THE PERFECTS, ARSENAL CHELSEA AND CELTIC, PORTOBELLO Rd POSSEE, AND A BIG FUCK OFF TO ALL THE DEAD CUNTS TOO SCARED TO ADVERTIZE WITH US ... IF WE'VE LEFT YOU OUT ... WE STILL LURVE YA! ESPECIALLY STEVE THE MINISTER FOR TRANSPORT!

ffrr – silver on black

No. 8
Autumn 1989

BOY'S
OWN

Good Morrow my young Succulent Buds,
How's it with you? Survived the summer?
I don't think we've spoken since LAST
we MET ATop A LArge collection of HAY
somewhere IN deepest SUSSEX, where the
CRACK WAS Good and YouR FAces went all
sort of WOBBLY....
A lot of wateR HAS Been PAssed uNder
MANy Bridges sincE; Riots in ReigAte,
Hill St BLues inHackney; and WallaBEES
absoLuTEly bleediN' eveRywherE, but don't
LET it GET you Down; THiNK PoS, Think....
Top tuneS uN-piZ2A stylEE (wrote FoR LUCK
re-MiX, AvALON Sunset, PENGUin CAfE orchestrA,
Foxy BROWN etc etc)
    THiNK.... top T·V·.... Fuck off StandGREANSiE
Hello BESTand MArsh (SEVEntieS cHeeKy cHic complete
With NEW ORDER Theme tune), PARadiSE cLub (the
most 'LoveAble' pRoGrammE EVER), and new PROGS
From ALexei and EdmuND (BlackAdderR)
    THiNK.... nice Nights out, the Black and WhiTE ball,
DiNNeR for Two at SYdneY'S (sw 11's bEst EngLish Nosherie),
THE BAcK Room at KaoS (the one Not sponsoRed by KickerS
and NAF NAF).... GettiNG seriously plottED etc
        OH! BeforE I Go, bewARe the TED TriAngle etc etc
(the AREA of LONDON BoundeD by MASH oxFord st,
TRACKS, and BLACK MARKET) where NORMAL HUMAN
beings nAve stRAyed and come out THE other SIDE
With a BAgFul of Ropey GrAmapHONE RecoRdS, very BAGGy
CallARdS, and a CENTRE PaRTiNG....
        LuRve and LOVEAbility   The OutsideR

THE MARVELLOUS MUSHROOM

1. "Heigho for a picnic in Grinstead Meadow!" sang Terry and Andrew as they helped themselves to the goodies in mummy's pantry. "We are both as hungry as twins, so we will take enough e for four!"

2. Soon they were in the meadow, looking for the nicest spot to lay their picnic. "Oho! Here is a big mushroom!" cried Terry.

3. When they had spread out the goodies on the mushroom, the pixies made a fire to boil the water. "A watched kettle never boils!" said Andrew. "Let's taste the acid now!"

4. But when they looked round they found the mushroom had grown ever so tall—they do spring up quickly! "This is what I call a HIGH tea!" said Terry.

Jolly Japes by dickie

PUCKA CLOBBA

MICHIKO LONDON

Picture this....it's Springtime in Brighton, you've popped down to
the coast for a pleasant nights entertainment with your mates (sounds
nice eh!!!) hold on some lunatic's running amock with a length of metal
piping (or an electric cattle prod, depending on how paranoid you got)
Where are the security you ask, how did this "person" smuggle in such
a weapon? The anwer is easy, he was the security and paid to look
after and serve the paying punters, a job well done?

Bouncer horror stories are nothing new, like the time they gassed the
queue outside Clink, or the bod who sulked all night 'cos the promoter
wouldn't let him patrol the dancefloor with his pair of American Pitbulls
The main problem as we see it is that the bouncers actually don't like
the crowd who they are paid to look after. "Fucking poofs", "Weirdos",
"Look at the state of him", "Alright darling" and that's just what they
think of the DJ's. The answer is to employ people who know the score
and are diplomatic as well as being firm. Now drugs are illegal and
obviously the bouncers have to be seen doing their job but a word in
someones ear and a quiet warning works much better that the "chuck 'em
out" approach, then they gain respect that they need from the crowd.

How can people respect some meathead in marble wash jeans and a Mike
Tyson haircut who spends the night confiscating people's "personal".
The only way drugs should be taken from people is if and when the police
are called. Club security have no legal right to steal from punters, if
you're caught taking the piss over gear then you deserve to be thrown
out, a re-distribution of illegal substances is just not on. "No re-addmission", "No re-addmission" come on chaps the fucking record's stuck,
play it fair and you will find life's a lot easier....respects to the
guys who do a good job.....Big Kevin, Ali, Eric and the others who do
the job properly....

VINYL SOLUTION ⦂

MODERN GRAMAPHONE RECORDS in the DANCE STYLE....

231 PORTOBELLO ROAD.

∘ LONDON ∘

THE CHARTS

```
GARY CLAIL.....................................BEEF
F.P.I. PROJECT................................RICH IN PARADISE
BASEMENT BOYS.................................IT'S OVER NOW
INNER CITY....................................WHAT YOU GONNA DO WITH MY LOVING
THE FUTURE EDITION 4..........................AUTUMN LOVE
FLAMENCO MASSIVE..............................MICORAZON ES NEGRO
EDIE BRICKNELL................................WHAT I AM/KEEP ON MOVING (REMIX)
ROXANNE SHANTE................................LIVE ON STAGE
STING.........................................AN ENGLISHMAN IN NEW YORK
MOD NO.4......................................ZOBI LA MOUCHE
BELOVED.......................................SUN RISING (THE LOVE IS REMIX)
PIANO FANTASIA................................SONG FOR DENISE
STONEBRIDGE...................................JAZZY JOHN'S FREESTYLE DUB
A.R.KANE......................................LOVE IN OUTER SPACE
THE GRID......................................ON THE GRID
TEN CITY......................................I NEED TO BE LOVED
BLAKK SOCIETY.................................JUST ANOTHER LONELY DAY
BIG NOISE.....................................WOAH
LAURENT X.....................................IT'S MAGIC
ISHMAR & CO...................................AMOR SUAVE
ESTER B.......................................THE PLEASURE OF MUSIC
RED BOX.......................................ENJOY
4 TO THE FLOOR................................LOST IT
M.D.J.........................................BROKEN WINGS
LANDLORD......................................I LIKE IT
BIG AUDIO DYNAMITE............................LONDON BRIDGE
GROOVE ROBBERS................................HOW FAR CAN WE GO
BITING TONGUES................................SURRENDER
JAGO..........................................I'M GOING TO GO
SEDUCTION.....................................SEDUCTION THEME
MAD DJ'S BAND.................................SEXY LULLABY
GO-NO GO......................................A PACIFIC STATE
BETTI VILLANI.................................MI AMOUR
RUTH JOY......................................SOUL POWER
BOY GEORGE....................................AFTER THE LOVE HAS GONE
FLUKE.........................................THUMPER
```

CHART COMPILED BY PAUL OAKENFOLD, DANNY RAMPLING, ANDREW WEATHERALL,

ROCKY & DIESEL, KEVIN HURRY AND TERRY FARLEY. COPYRIGHT NOTE: TRAX —

KEEP YOUR NOSE OUT OF THIS CHART.

STOP PRESS: TUNES CURRENTLY DROPPING THRU OUR LETTER BOX AND KICKING ON THE MORE SENSIBLE FLOORS INCLUDE THE FUNKY "CAT" BY THE CATWOMAN; THE BCN ORCHESTRA WITH "QUIEN TUTE CRES"; THE NEW TYREE COOPER HIP HOUSE WORKOUT; NOTHING NEW BUT DOES ANYONE CARE... "OH YEAH"; "OH YEAH"; THE NEW HAPPY MONDAYS "RAVE ON" EP, WITH REMIXES BY OAKEY COKEY AND THE BOYS OWN TEAM; THE NEW MELLOW VERSION OF IZITS "STORIES", THIS TUNE STILL KICKS; THE NEW ROBERT OWEN'S LP AS PREVIEWED BY FRANKIE NUCKLES AT THE OUNCE OF WIZ (AKA LAND OF OZ IS A ABSOLUTE CORKER, REAL SOUL FOR THE NINETIES, REAL SOUL FANS TAKE NOTE; THE NEW ELEKTRA SINGLE IS ALL THAT THE WORD BALEARIC - MUCH RAVED ABOUT BY, MR. RAMPLING INFACT; DANIEL LANOIS THE NEW CAJUN IS A TRIP FROM LOUISIANA TO SHOOM AND BACK; THE NEW GUY CALLED GERALD IS MILES BETTER THAN THE TITLE "TRIP CITY" SUGGESTS; "SHOUT IN THE NIGHT" BY IN-SIDE IS THE BEST ITALY HAS TO OFFER THIS WEEK. FINALLY ON CULT LABEL NUGROOVE DTR PROVIDE HAUNTING MELLOW HOUSE WITH "JOURNEY INTO A DREAM"......

' MORE PICS OF THE GRINSTEAD GRIN !
(HIGHLY CENSORED)

TOP PIC. A SEX PET CHILLS OUT.
BOTTOM PIC (OOH ER!)
CLIVE AND ONE HALF OF THE SPROCKET AND UNLEADED DISC JOCKEY TEAM....

In the run-up to Xmas, things are looking up. Take last Monday for instance. The much knocked Land Of Oz (aka Land Of Wiz) had New York's FRANKIE KNUCKLES spinning on the main floor while upstairs Amnesia's ALFREDO kicked a rammed club on a wet Monday night - not bad, eh?...SHOOM has our fave Euro DJ NELLO from Pacha playing in November: well recommended. QUEENS Sunday lunchtime session sees BOY GEORGE and MO KINKY along with FAT TONY playing out also in November. After the successful Black & White ball, PASSION have a top-looking New Year's Eve bash on the cards. Despite competition from THE FUTURE, THE SUB CLUB down Ladbroke Grove continues to be a top plot and rumours of the much raved about DEEP JOY playing on 14 December for the club's XMAS party are true. Back at THE FUTURE look out for an appearance from FLOWERED UP around the Xmas period.

"MONKEY DRUM" AT 4 GRAYS INN ROAD, WITH JOHNNY ROCKA PLAYING TUNES STOLEN FORM THE GRANGE HILL END OF TERM PARTY THIS DRUM DOES ACTUALLY KICK (CLICHE NO 41) SEE CHART; MONDAYS 10-3 AM 5.00.

MONKEY DRUM CHART.

1.   SPECIALS
      BLANK EXPRESSION

2.   STONE ROSES
      WATERFALL

3.   PRINCE
      LETS GO CRAZY

4.   MONKEES
      I'M A BELIEVER

5.   HAPPY MONDAYS
      FREAKY DANCING.

TOP PIC : MR SWINDELLS
.IES OUT HIS NEW
UTOMATIC CAMERA....

TTOM PIC : MRS LEA GETS
N THE TABLE INSTEAD OF
NDING UP UNDER IT !

MOODY DO'S

an audrey witherspoon exposé

How do I start? What can I tell I tell you that you don't already know? You've all seen them, you've all had them in your house, you've all ripped bits off them for various purposes, you've all avoided people giving them out. You've all laughed heartily at the spellings, you've all questioned whether what they advertise will actually take place. You all, by now must know of what I speak. Crap flyers advertising crap 'parties' (members only, sorry about last months cancellation old tickets still valid...)

Do you need to be reminded? I think so, because in months and years to come you'll wish you'd kept them. Take it from me these are historical documents, acid house ephemeria destined to be the subject of a Victoria and Albert retrospective, a reminder of the potty late eighties, these bits of throwaway cardboard sum upthe whole mentality of the latter years of this decade, and thats what the V and A will realise, and that's why the exhibition will be called "GREED AND STUPIDITY" two attributes common to 95% of current club and party advertising......read on and weep.

Here it is then music fans, this weeks top 5 moody flyers brought to you by several dodgy geezers in a rented limousine wearing track suits and brandishing voda-phones.

Noise: Double Trouble, Ron Pickering (Hacienda),
Raw-D and The Rhythm King (Quartz), P. Anderson, T. Fung,
M. Duncan (Roxy, Amsterdam) D. J. M★A★S★H

Attractions:
No Funfairs, No Bouncy Castles, No Gimmicks!!

NUMBER FIVE

"THE ETERNAL DREAM"

In at five, a classic this one. Standard 'mysterious' artwork 'borrowed' from a record sleeve. (in this case the first Electribe record). Nothing strange you say, but just hold it a second, turn it over and check out the disc jockey line up. Billed as 'noise' the alledged record spinners include (surprise, surprise) Paul Anderson, Trevor Fung, DJ Mash and last but by no means least, we have Ron Pickering. Now I thought old Ron was earining a fair wedge from the whacky world of athletics and wouldn't really need to risk his chances of a New Years honour for services to track and field by getting involved with the acid house craze, but then again Eddie Edwards was billed as playing at Subterrania so maybe 1990 could see a big house music sporting crossover. Stop Press: Ten City produce New England Football Team World Cup song. (A rousing garage version of "Back Home")

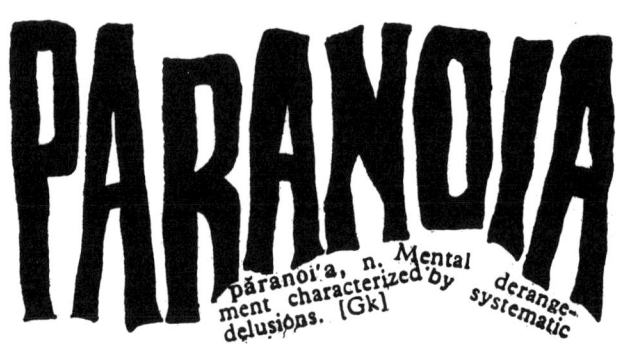

"SUMMER OF LOVE (GOES TO THE MECHANICS)"

Quite a rarity this one, spotted only once, but well worth a mention all
the same. Obviously it had to happen, an event called "Summer of Love"
nothing wrong with that I suppose (if done properly) but this "Summer of Love"
is a different kettle of teds entirely.
The front of this pink A1 thin card extravaganza has an entwined couple
snogging the wotsits off each other. Turning over brings the real delights,
you know it's downhill allthe way when greeted with the words "What else is
there to do on a Sunday but Get Mental!" If you want my honest opinion
fellows, and call me an old stick in the mud if you like, there's a myriad
of better things to get involved with on a Sunday afternoon in this fair
land. Things like staying in bed, going to see ya mum, tucking into Roast
Beef, Yorkshire Pudding, Roast potatoes and two veg, and a nice cup of tea
and a grin at the Sunday Sport etc etc etc etc.
If you did decide to forego the usual Sunday delights and wanted to "Get
Mental" then reading the rest of the flyer will tell you how to do it, and
who will entertain you and aid you in the art of reaching ultimate 'mentalness'
To get to this event you must gather at a meeting point, in this case that
mecca of youth culture 'Arding and Hobbs', Clapham Junction. Oh I can picture
it now, hordes of kicker clad youths gathered in a field shouting, no not
"Mental, mental, radio rental", but "Arding, Arding, Arding and Hobbs!"
I almost forgot to mention 'this event will be filmed for future viewing'
Oh really, and where prey tell will this event be viewed? The organisers front

room? Thames at Six? Or even by the local enforcers of law and order when
they raid the place and confiscate the equipment. "I recognise that one
handing over the money Sarge. I nicked him a while back, but he didn't have
a pony tail then......."

NUMBER THREE

"AMEN"

A subtle charmer this one. Pseudo-mysterious graphics depicting a human
face mask being held aside to reveal a skull. There's quite a few of these
'mysterious' pictures used, the reason? Just picture the scene, the venues's
been sorted, one of the chaps knows a printer, all we need now is the artwork.
"I know, Steve did C.S.E Art, he's a blinding artist, does all these well
trippy pictures, he's almost as good as that Tony Hart geezer"
The trouble is these people have got no brain under normal circumstances,
soaked in L.S.D. Things deteriorate even further. Blockheads like the dark
side, and it shows.

If you do get past the O-level horror movie graphics there is another delight
to be had we're told that there will be "No bouncy castles, no funfairs, no
gimmicks" Why is that I wonder? Well apparantly "Gimmicks attract LARGER
Louts" This just confirms my suspicions that the people frequenting these
events are louts, but what I didn't know was that having the odd bouncy
castle or candy floss vendor meant that louts of an increased size would
show up at the gates......The DJs for the night? Well I think you can probably fill that in for yourselves.

NUMBER TWO

       "THE NEW BEGINNING, SWEET SOCIETY"

A classic of the horror genre this one. A jolly piece of party advertising
based heavily, sorry that should read, copied directly, from the 'Alien'
film poster, using the emerging alien pod as its central feature. The DJs
(yes you can guess them again!) and not actually billed as DJs they are in
fact "Dangerous Demons". The things which attract the 'larger louts' (lasers
coloured smoke, bubbles etc, etc, etc) are called "Evil Features". Sounds Fab!
This one also features a 'Hot-line'. An aquaintance of mine phoned the number
to enquire about the concept of using such grim visuals and wording, and
whether the overall ambience might not be somewhat menacing, leading to what
is called in psychiatric circles "HEAD-FUCK" The bright spark on the end of
the 'hot-line' informed the caller, "Well that's what tripping's all about
that evil stuff, if you can't handle your acid, don't come" Delightful I
must say.
This one's also a real family affair with one of the attractions being a
'buggy park'. Does this mean you can take baby Ted, drop him/her off, drop
a tab, drop out, and get back in time for the early morning feed? (Amyl with
your rusks anybody?)

NUMBER ONE

       "FREAK OUT FOUR"

I'm afraid this one will be at the top forever. The ultimate moody flyer for
the ultimate moody do. In fact this one's so moody I had a niggling suspicion it could be a very well perpetrated situationist type hoax, until asked
'would I like to play some gramaphone records at the event.' When I explain the
concept behind 'Freak Out' you'll know why I shouted "Go Away Quickly!" and
requested he leave the building and not to come within 50 miles of my personal
space.

The Wording on the
'KEYBOARD WIZARD's'
LABEL SUMS IT ALL
UP REALLY....

Firstly the graphics, a very jolly cartoon of two ample bosomed maidens
entangled in the tentacles of various monsters and demons. Apparently these
cretins have held parties in the U.S.A and promise us limeys "THE BIGGEST,
LOUDEST, TRIPPIEST, MOST SCHIZOPHRENIC MEGA-RAVE THIS WORLD HAS EVER SEEN"
and "A HURRICANE OF LASER AND SOUND TO SIGNAL THE END OF THE WORLD. THIRT-
EEN DEMENTED HOURS FOR YOU TO PANIC AND DIE SCREAMING" !! Yes please I'll
have 10 tickets, I'd love to have "A NIGHTMARE IN HELL".

No surely it can't get any worse, but just when you thought it was safe to
read on ...... "IF YOU DON'T FREAK OUT, YOU'RE ALREADY DEAD" Ho hum, followed
by a delightful qoute from revelations (the chapters of the bible dealing
with a prophecied holocaust and world destruction), featuring the following
words, 'Nightmare', 'Posessed', 'Frenzy', 'Burn', 'Scream' and 'Die'.
The piece of resistance however is the catchphrase "IT'S NOT JUST MENTAL, IT'S
EVIL". Good Grief it gets worse. I've just tried the hotline where I was
promised a seance, a graveyard, a lunatic asylum open nearby, horror films
on twenty-foot high screens, and to hurry up and buy the tickets because
the scarcer they get the higher the price goes. Pathetic I know, but then
our I.Q does actually get into double figures (I hope). However funny we
may find this it would be even funnier had the blockhead factor not picked
up on it. Rumour has it that certain pirate radio stations have picked up
on it and are informing their listeners that in the world of Ted the word
'Mental' is passe. The new word on everbody's lips? Yes you've guessed it
'EVIL'! Double sad I know, but also a little disturbing. Our advice to
you, phone your local constabulary ..... immediately.
So there it is spot pickers, just a few fave flyers from the Boys Own filing
cabinet (a waitrose shopping bag in the kitchen). A few classics may have
been overlooked, partly because they were consigned to the waste bin, but
mainly because if we were to mention the lot it would result in a Boys Own
special made up of over 20 volumes.
Although these events should be treated with the contempt they deserve
please spare a thought for legit club runners and D.Js who through no fault
of their own are being effected by these moody goings on. Hopefully the
bubble has burst and the change in weather will dampen the spirit of Ted
(Don't count on it. Ed)

Thank you for reading and may you never spend an evening or
any money at this kind of "party" for want of a better word.

TOP FIVE MOOODY D.J. NAMES   TOP FIVE MOODY TICKET VENDORS

1. Darren and the get Mental Crew
2. Reg. E. Reg   1. Black Market
3. Mad Axe   2. Black Market
4. Rodge the Dodge   3. Black Market
5. Jim the Music Man   4. Black Market
(Where's Balearic Mick - Ed)   5. Black Market
                                          (Wot no Black Market - Ed)

M E T H O D

A I R

GUEST DJ'S

NOV 3RD   DANNY RAMPLING

NOV 17TH   ANDY WEATHERALL

FRIDAYS FORTNIGHTLY   £7

66 GODING ST   SE11

TAKE some
TIME OUT

About this time last year I was the only person around that had a "real job". Everyone I met seemed to be either knocking out a bit of "gear" or delivering Mountain bikes to order. I know some people do make their living from DJ'ing, doing the door at a club etc, but you couldn't walk through 'Future' of a Thursday evening without tripping over twenty bods claiming this sort of work as their only means of support.

Whenever I've dipped my toes in the murky waters of Maggie's "Black Economy", I've always looked at this avenue of earning as closed to me. Since leaving school I've always worked and never really liked it but I'm old enough now to know that if I didn't I'd be lost. How being born in Ladbroke Grove or such like areas enables you to spend entire days 'nuttin' about is a mystery to me and a feat to be admired. I find it hard enough to fill the hour between Neighbours and Top of the Pops now Nationwide isn't on anymore. It is sad to say but clocking on gives my life a much needed structure.

Luckily for me though things seem to have taken a turn this summer. Either unemployment has become a thing of the past or some of you out there weren't telling the whole truth last year. The 'duckers and divers' are still around but people are now coming clean and admitting they can't go to Shoom on a Wednesday as they've got to be up in the morning. I'm not saying we've all got career minded over night but last year Acid House, 'the summer of love' and all that old caper seemed enough. This year we've all realised that you've still got to pay the rent and you'd like to put a bit aside for that trip to Goa we've all been planning.

Something that has amazed me though is the variety of jobs we all do. It has become a favourite game of mine on meeting new people to indulge in a bit of "What's my line". The answers often leave me laughing but sometimes horrified that responsible, important and even dangerous work is being carried out by the nutter in front of me. I once met a bloke who put himself through medical school making sulphate and L.S.D; a fine fellow to have along on a night out but would you like to wake up in hospital one day and find he'd just removed your tonsils?!

Pre Acid House the world of nightclubbing was predominantly the home of hairdressers, fashion bods (be they designers or sales assistants) and assorted media types. I suppose you'd call them Robert Elms type people. Now it's great to see that the top bod on the scene can be a looney glazier with a liking for fancy dress costumes. You meet girls who leave Joy to take Jane Fonda workout sessions after 3 E and half a trip. There's even a certain 'House Music' promoter and "haute couture" salesman that has given up Sunday trading because he can't manage to put his stall up!

Lastly a few words of warning to you all. It's great to go out for a night and get off you're head but not so great if you loose your job over it. If you hate your job then what the fuck-do what you want, it doesn't matter but I've heard of people losing good jobs from too many nights of excess. The balance isn't hard to find, anyone with half a brain can see when the excuses for not turning up for work have worn thin. You can only pass off the bloodshot eyes, sweaty forehead and shaky leg as flu symptons so many times. Try and make sure the odd "mad one" in the middle of the week stays just the odd one. Boys Own writer and day time gas fitter says "I only need a cheeky half for a top night".

Don't ever let work stop you from going out but don't let going out stop you working (whatever that is) ! ! See you in Goa.

Steve 'Jobsworth' Hall

LAND OF OZ

THE LAND of OZ

HEAVEN
EVERY MONDAY
DJ'S
PAUL OAKENFOLD
COLIN HUD

phoneys

Have you ever sat down to watch a programme on the telly and cringed with embarassment as some posh nonce delivers his lines in a stunningly inept accent? Yes, more and more it seems, these phoneys are taking over the broadcasting world.

Worst offenders seem to be shows which are based on scousers. Scousers, it seems, aren't an acting breed, so all scouse parts are taken by tootal nobs who end up sounding like a cross between the cartoon Ringo and Joey O'Rouke - one of the first laughable accent killers in the ace 70's kids serial "Rocky O'Rouke".

Every programme about scousers ever has included in the cast at least one phoney. "Bread" is entirely populated by phoneys which isn't surprising as it has as much to do with Liverpool working-class life as does Neighbours. In fact almost all Carla Lane's sit-coms from the Liver-Birds to Bread have been about as credible and realistic as Spurs winning the League. She should stick to middle-class suburbia like Butterflies as she obviously hasn't been anywhere near "De Pool" (phoney pronounciation!) in the past 30 years.

Even cred serials like 'Boys from the Black Stuff' have had their phoneys ie Loggo and Yosser who are both Mancs. Brooky has sufferred too, remember Gavin Taylor, Doreen's mam and George Collins?

Ok so you get the picture, but what abaht yer cockerney shows like Fools and Horses? Well being a Northern chap I can't tell the difference between an Essex, East Ham and a Surrey accent. To us they're all cockneys! But I'm sure some of you London types go red in the face when Del Boy or someother cliched wide-boy spiv gives it the old rhyming slang and diamond geezers in Eastenders come on like a Dick van Dyck gorblimey pearly king.

And what about Corry? All types of accents in the same fuckin' family! No-one in Manchester says "Happen" or "Nowt" (Newht, yes!) York-shire dicks say things like that.

It's not only TV programmes that employ phoneys, advertisements are bad as well. It must be some kind of marketing concept that to sell any product to the under 25's you need at least one chirpy loveable and a down-to-earth witty scouser.
ie. OXY 10 advertisement:
Witty scouse disco girl 1.   "Did yer pearm go wrong?
Witty scouse disco girl 2.   "No zits!"
                         1.   "E'are try dis it really wearks"
                         2.   "You cheeky friggin' meth, I'm gonna stanley you!"
Street level cockney voice over: "Blitz those cheeky scarse cars wiv OXY!"
                                                        (cows)

And just look at 'yoof' TV shows, they are chockabloc with loveable scousers and street cred cockneys. There's even an ultimate phoney puppet dog called 'Scally' for fucks sake!

So do us a favour TV people, if you must have parts for these people why not be daring and get the genuine article instead of useless rada dickheads.

P H O N E Y   T O P   T E N S

1. Bad Bri Tilsley: "Just going down tut Rovers mam", we may never see his like again, thank fuck!
2. Def-Jeff Young: The big beat phoney, how to go from suburban jazz funk mafia DJ to a down by law with the possie's brother in one easy pay-rise!
3. Norman Tebbitt: His old man used to pal it with the Richardson mob a true blue working class boy.
4. The Grange Hill gooner: A shout of "E-I-E" and more hair gel than fat boy Gazza and twice as much lip.
5. Scally the dog: Stick him in a park in speke and he wouldn't last 30

6. Ian Beale: More wooden than "Yus M'lady" Parker from Thunderbirds (see No.10 for his aul fella)
7. Cartoon Beatles: 3 aristocrats and a mental retard.
8. Tarby and Ted Rogers: One a scouse, the other a cockney, both phoneys both tories, both right knobheads! "Where's Brucie" "Alright my love"!!
9. Joseph Stalin: Wasn't fucking Russian at all. Came from Canning town but blagged his way to the top.
10. Pete Beale: The Dick van Dyke of Albert Square, no wonder Cathy had a guy (loveable speak no 254, Guy Fawke= Walk)

QUEENS'

queen mother rsvoi
horton road, colnbro
(near slough)

SUNDAY LUNCHTIMES

12 › 4 pm   ENTRANCE £3

"QUEENS"

RESIDENT DJ: PHIL PERR

NOV 5 th   ...   TERRY FARLEY

    12 th   ...   ANDY WEATHERALL

    19 th   ...   KEVIN HURRY

    26 th   ...   CRAIG WALSH

girl's own
NIGHTMARE

Drop the acid (gulp) scare headlines, forget about peace and lovey housey types belting the police in their frenzy to reach the latest 700k turbo-charged-WC-chill-out-lounge-and-blinding-visuals party, far worse things happen, under our very noses. Here are 8 nightmare scenarios that Boy's Own's girls risk on the average night out.

1. Death by asphyxiation

It's a well-established behavioural fact that when boys get excited they sweat. When they get really excited, they forget all about that nice can of Brut de-odourant that Auntie Trottie off-loaded on them by way of a tacky Christmas present. Standing in rows, the herd instinct compells them to strip to the waist, displaying inelegant post-pubescent torsos, and bellow along to Chaka Khan's 'I'm Every Woman' as they wave a sea of arms about, a move known as the Sin (as in Astoria) Surge. Modifications include trousers at half mast (be still my heart) and waving soaking t-shirts, so smelly they hum, about.
Scotching all rumours about their naturist inclinations, Shoom now require male torsos to be dressed. The Ramplings haven't said anything about the girls, though.

2. Death by Amyl Nitarate

Bleuuuchhhh. Equivalent of a football sock nosebag. The gormless use it as aftershave and the stupid as a reviver for those you've fallen in love with strobe lights and had an epileptic fit. Gives everyone else instant migrane.

3. Death by sisterhood

The chappies aren't the only offenders here. Give a gal eight tabs and she'll come straight for you. Nothing, not even a crater suddenly appea-ring in the dance-floor will stop her. "Be Happeeee" the gibberish monologue goes, as stubby little fingers reach up to re-arrange your face into a smiley "I am, and I don't even know how I'm getting back to Romford tonight........ hee hee hee. I wish they'd play 'Break For Love' .... you know, it goes, BREAK uh uh FUR wheeze wheeze ... ere? do you want to meet my mates?"

4. Kissy Kissy

Kissy kissy is a time-honoured ritual in clubs, but like all rituals, there exists a time and a place for cheek rubbing, or the studied air-kiss to the side. This nuance has proved a little difficult to grasp for those complete strangers who hurtle towards you, licking their lips in anticipation of touching tonsils, probably because they think you live in the same postal district as they do. Solution? take classes in a deadly martial art.

5. Mouth out of gear with brain problems

A number of possibilities ... the men'al boys ... those who rush round with a megaphone announcing "I'm on one!" Pass The Sun hot-line, and be quick about it matey.

6. Surviving the loo queue

Less of a quick wee, more of a way of life for the girlies, which is maybe why so many blokes love to congregate in the ladies' lavvies. Conversations range from the sublime ("I'm going to be sick") to the ridiculous (" 'Ere Trace, we've already got five in the cubicle ... go on, let me try on your plastic flower, pur-leeeese").

7. Handbags

Beloved of Balearic secretaries who've made the transition from the Cat's Whiskers to something more exotic because they know the bouncer at the door and giggle when he fingers his bulge (more often than not, it's a blackjack, girls ... don't be fooled). They pile PVC handbags up on the floor like sacks of potatoes and look suprised whenever someone breaks their neck falling over them.

8. DJs

A strange and pale breed who sleep all day and want to be fed at odd hours. Often DJs only present problems when they insist on playing their 'Hits Of House' record, and warnings about personal contact aren't required. DJs like versatile girls - those who can turn their hand from whisking up meals at 5am to lumping boxes of records around without turning a hair.

66 I SWEAR, SOME SWEATY GEEZER GRABBED ME, TRIED TO GIVE US A FRENCHIE ... AND NOW LOOK ... JJ

66 DON'T WORRY ... THE SWELLINGS BOUND to GO DOWN ... JJ

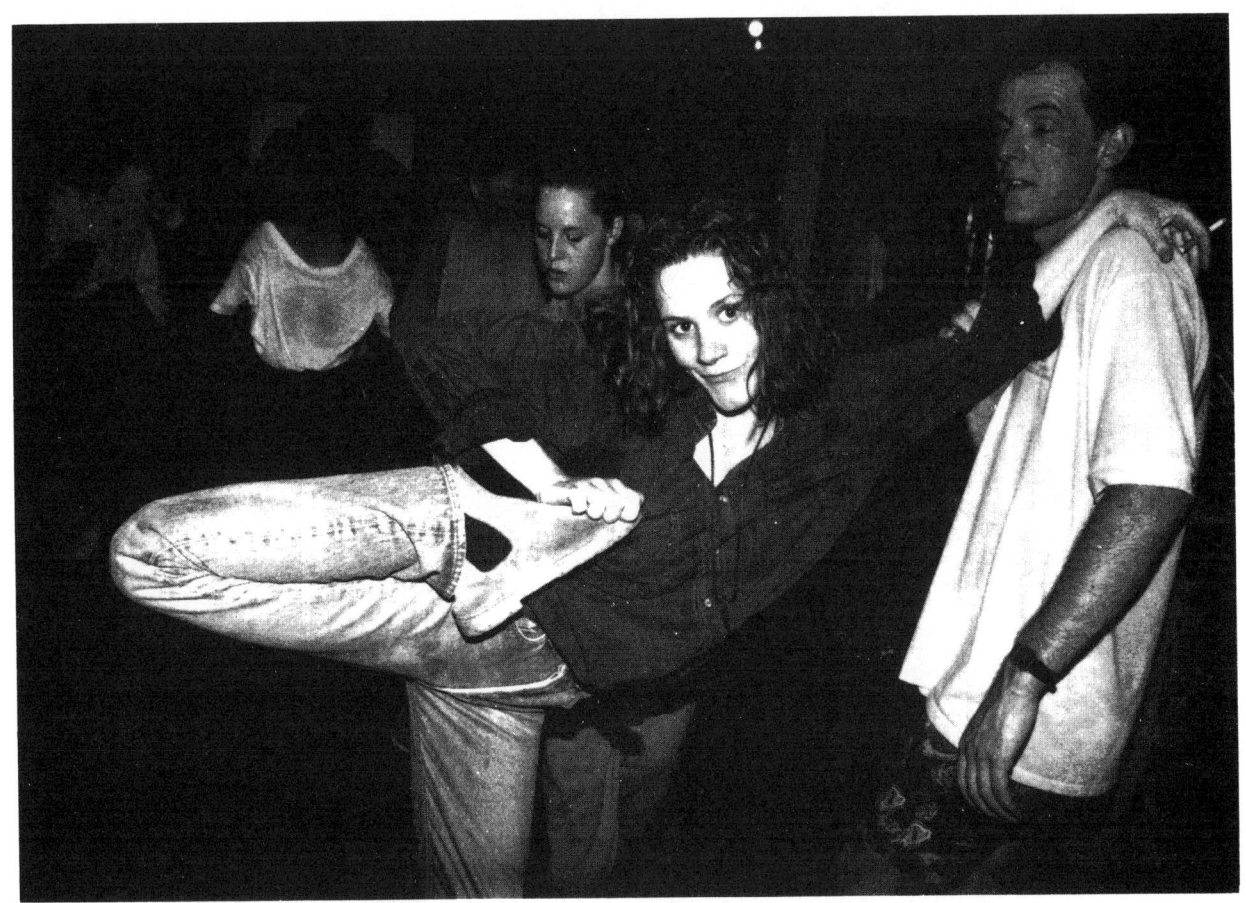

" REMEMBER KiDS, CAROLINE iS HiGHLY TRAiNED .... THiS SORT OF THiNG SHOULD NOT BE ATTEMPTED AT HOME ! "

To help the sensible clubbers amongst you, the following is a guide to see you through the smoke screens put up by the less reliable promoters and leafleters .....

THEY SAY	THEY MEAN
"MIXED CROWD"	"FULL OF RAGAS"
"NICE CROWD IN TONIGHT	"THE GAFFS EMPTY"
"NICE GIRLS"	"TOP KNOT SHARON IN THE HOUSE"
"V.I.P. LOUNGE"	"TOILET FACILITIES"
"NO DRESS RESTRICTIONS"	"KICKERS + SUEDE WALLABYS WELCOME"
"TOP LAZERS TOP DJ'S"	"£20.00 TO GET IN"
"CAR PARK FACILITIES"	"2 MILE WALK ACROSS FIELDS"
"GUEST DJ'S	"MY MATE DAVE AND HIS "WAREHOUSE RAVES" LP"
"NO TEDS	"LOADS OF 'EM"
"VENUE IN THE ENGLISH COUNTRYSIDE"	"HACKNEY MARSHES"
"TOP LONDON DJ"	"JUDGE JULES"
"SAFE SECURITY"	"ANIMALS WITH ANIMALS"

FL❀WERED UP

EVERYBODY'S LOOKIN' FOR THE LAST GANG IN TOWN

This is probably a point for raging debate, but what the fuck let's debate. I put it to you that there hasn't been a band which says 'LONDON' loudly in everything it records, says and wears since the days of "Sten Guns in Knightsbridge" ...... Come on lets hear it then "ACCENT" you say, do me a lemon, Lois, Filas, Gabbiccis and pimples, it cut no ice with me and besides sounded like Big Country. "BIG AUDIO" I hear shouted from the back, nearly I suppose. Their long players are like a cab ride around the capital, but 'ave a look at the look..........sideways baseball caps and surfing shorts more West Eleven wet fish than anything else. No, no, no, no, no.............

What's needed is a band of thugs, it's always been the case. The best pop groups in the world have always had the name Herbert attached to them somewhere along the line. Two prime examples are also two of the best groups England has produced in the past ten years. The trouble is we're talking 'North of Watford' here. Don't get me wrong, I've had some of the best nights of my short but interesting life in Manchester and even better times sweating, shouting and indulging in the odd frack-arse at NEW ORDER and HAPPY MONDAYS gigs, but London they ain't........

"SO WHERE HAVE ALL THE HERBERTS BEEN"; skulking about in clubs that's where. The last eighteen months eclectic music mix has meant that the good old soul boy (with no thoughts of forming bands) has been well and truly knobbed off from the world of real people (they still gather in enclaves, usually in Welsh caravan sites) and a rock edge has crept into club music. The time is right for a bunch of bods to harness that sound and represent London in all its splendour;.....The Future; Shoulder length or cropped hair; Talking with a whistle; Walking with a purpose; Deja Vu Fisher athletic; John Moore shoes; Wearing bins without lenses; G-force jeans; Moving to Muswell Hill after you had a big one; Living in London and not apologising for it;......You haven't heard them, I haven't heard them but something tells me we need them.........."FLOWERED UP"

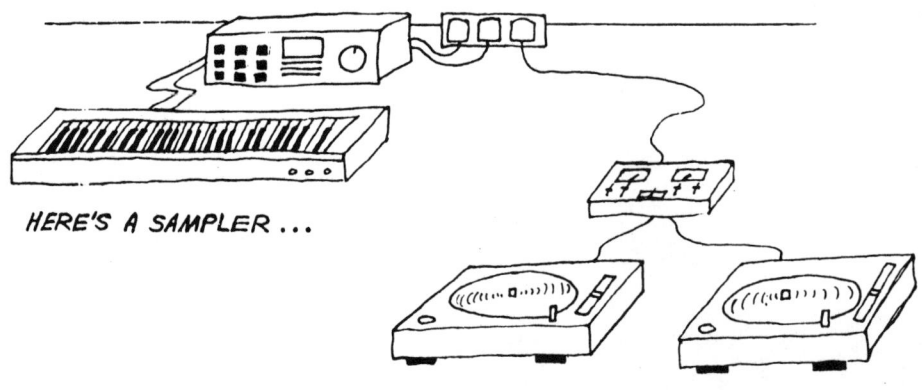

SNIFFIN' GLUE REVISITED...

HERE'S A SAMPLER ...

HERE'S TWO DECKS...

NOW GO AND FORM A BAND!

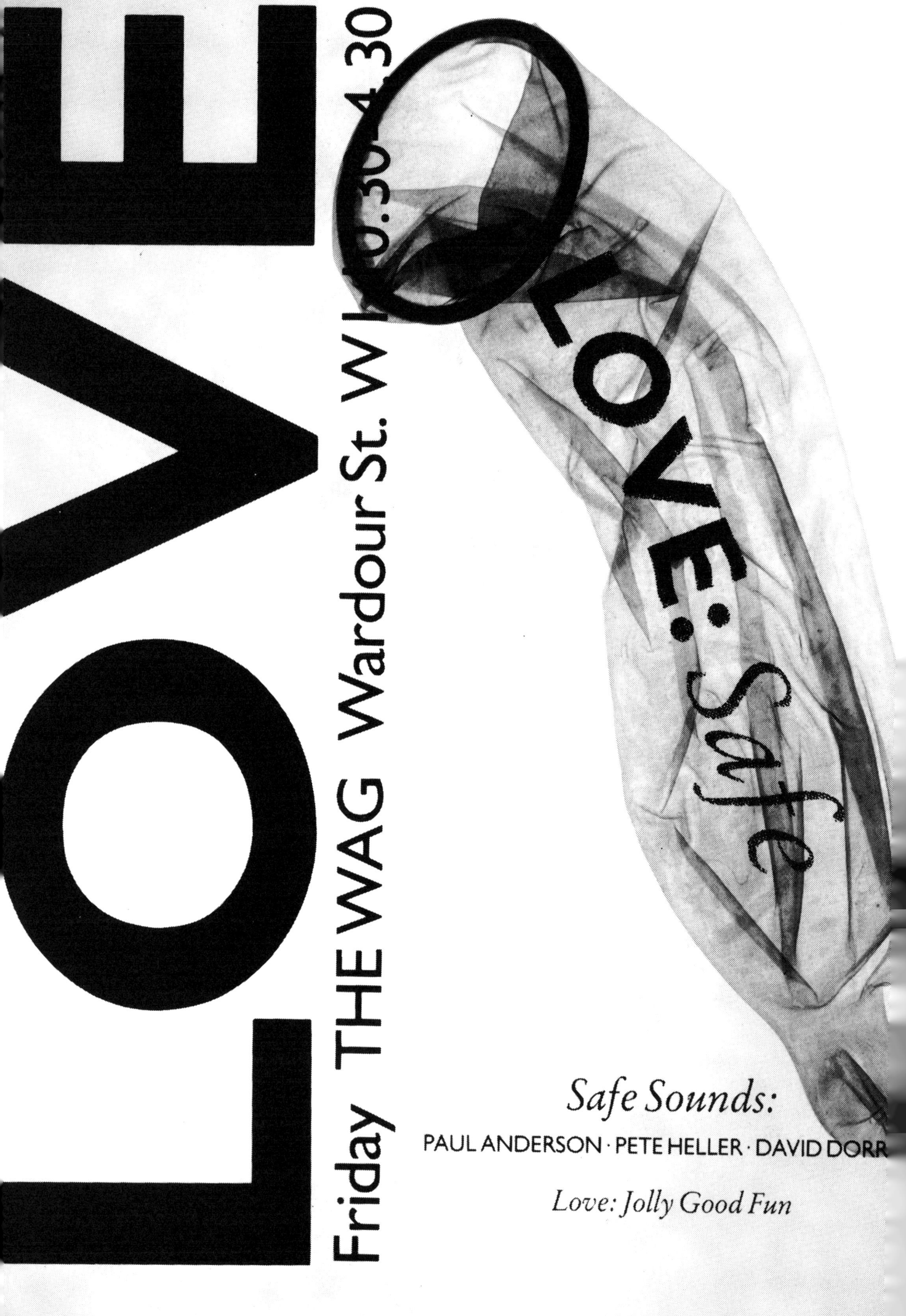

LOVE

Friday THE WAG Wardour St. W1 10.30-4.30

LOVE: safe

Safe Sounds:
PAUL ANDERSON · PETE HELLER · DAVID DORR

Love: Jolly Good Fun

BOXING UN-CLEVER

Listen, we all know that sometimes you find yourself in a position where a bit of the frumpy fisting seems the only way out of a sticky situation. It does happen, it can even come out for the best - very very occasionally. But when you start to live your life by it ....well.

Ronnie and Reggie Kray, natives of Vallance Road, Bethnal were still getting it on top with Irish chaps from their local manor well into their twenties, hence a certain break in the idea that they were upmarket-men-of-the-world-Gawd-luv-ya types from an early age. Their rows were not carried out exclusivly by top chaps in nice sta-press, but often by themselves....and often with a savage relish.

Their lives revolved around the desperate, scrambling, sense of 'community' that hung (and hangs) over each separate East End hamlet fused together in the 1800's under the pressure of emergent consumer capitalism. A sense of community that pervades all economically deprived areas all over the world, a fear of outsiders (Not The Outsiders of course' - Judge Pickles), as fear of authority and a fear of the future. They also had perverted ideas of what it took to be a 'man'. I think I'm a man because I've got a dick - that's it basically. The Krays thought they were men because they could instil fear into sections of the populace, because they thought they could avoid the attentions of those 'outsiders' and because they gave off the air (like the orig--inal nineteenth century Mafia philosophy in Sicily) of always being able to control their own destiny ... they were all untrue.

As we all know their time inside has been marked by occasional intense press attention as the call for their release picks up pace as the years go by and by several books. The best of which is the classic 1970 job 'The Profession of Violence' (Penguin). Straight up, concise, unemotional. The funniest is 'Our Story' by Fred Dineage (the twins mate) which is inaccurate, rambling and utterly sentimental. The rest? About as factual as the Kemp twins stubble and almost as interesting.

The public opinion about the Krays is confused, ranging from 'Moors-hang 'em-Hindly' to 'they-were-honely-Heast Henders-your-honour' according to the latest, and always sensationalist, article. Recently the Daily Schmurn (I can't remember which tabloid it was) had a phone-in vote which resoundingly called for their release ... in the cold light of reason all those who voted them out should be sent a copy of 'POV' to read, immediately.

It is difficult to write about the two of them without resorting to personal opinions on the matter in hand. Between the lines of all the books about them you'll see that the Krays were victims themselves, nevertheless they were not nice people. They ruined and scarred the lives of many around them as well as allegedly ending a fair number as well. They were dirty, bullying fighters who understood the power of physical aggression without ever really being in control of their own. They were not 'businessmen', they liked fiighting, they enjoyed fear and their own unpredictability. However, if one looks at them in reality they were never 'mass' murderers, they never 'owned' London's underworld, (especially with the emergence of Brixton's 'middle-class' Charlie Richardson and firm, plus the Italian and Maltese influence in Soho) and they never even got near the scent of 'real' power, ie: big money or political clout.

The thing which annoys me most (and which is balanced heavily by Ronnies disturbed but actual love of violence) is that in reality they were just 'playing the game'. They were super-capitalists climbing out of the utter pit they were born into, and they chose to do it in any way possible. They were created by a system that showed them the way out was via wads, big wads, they were just more open about it than most. If they had been owners of filth-producing death-spewing chemical plants that had blown up in a country full of brown people they wouldn't have spent twenty-five years in jail. Oh no Vicar, they'd have been on the make from the insurance and dining with Thatcher or Kinnock to explain what had gone wrong. But they came from the wrong direction with the wrong method and they paid. They paid off a good five minutes worth of conscience-time for the morally bankrupt West who, whilst disowning them as 'social deviants', were freely murdering woman and child worldwide for the strength of the dollar.

Like any capitalist 'working class' (I hate the phrase 'working class') grouping such as Trade Unions or football clubs or certain pop music bands, they hoped to eventually join the oppressor via bug bucks. But like their social counterparts they just didn't understand that it ain't just cash you need it's also where you're coming from that counts, and if you refuse to come in dressed right then you ain't coming in at all, ever.

ADAM PORTER

PARADISE LOST

These amassed words of wisdom, borne both of observation and cautionary
tales, begin months ago when a certain Boys Own editor interupted one
of my more pleasant reveries at Joy. "Ere!" the little figure before me
said plaintively as it flickered, yes, unmistakably flickered, in the
intimate hum of the strobe light-stand that was giving me moral support.
He gestured towards a typing pool full of Balearic secretaries who, having
painted their faces with those fluorescent pens you find in the better-
equipped office, were dancing in a circle around a pile of handbags,kicking
their sling-backs out on every fourth beat. "You've got to do something
about this" he continued, "I mean, there's such a thing as decorum ... and
you don't do that" - the girls were now hand-jiving - "to Ce Ce Rogers".

Nodding, to signify assent as much as to allay doubts that my head had
detached itself from its supporting vertebrae, I went away and forgot my
enounter. Until now, that is. Stuck in a six-floor cold-water walk-up
somewhere on the wrong side of Manhattan, my thoughts turn towards those
who need guidance as they traverse through the dance-floors, dodging the
cries of "men'al! men'al!", trying to avoid the beats that numb the nation.
Even here, the tales of the Satan-inspired acid raves thathold Britain in
thrall are old news.

One year ago, I would have wiped a happy tear from my eye and presented club
debutantes with aluminium whistles as they jostled to throw themselves onto
the first guest-list they could find. Those were the hlycon days of clubbing
where, for the first time ever, posing, boozing and prettifying took a back
seat. People from the most heterogenous backgrounds were transformed by a
single entity - music - which for a few brief hours every night gave everyone a common language, a common cohesion. Although acid house has been subject to a process of criminalisation since last summer, let's not forget that
a lot of people liked it, and were changed by the glimpse of new possibilities that the sound's configurations offered. Many of you are thinking that
I perhaps reminisce about nights at Spectrum or where-ever, after a tot too
much of Cherry B and Brandy (is that what young things drink nowdays?).
Hardly ... consider it another way. How does music work? by a statement of
what it's not. The structure of sound operates through a continual state of
change, it describes an abstraction for emotion, for perception, within its
own architecture. The changes need not be immense - a new fall of light, the
sweep of a glance - but it's enough.

What does this actually achieve? on the most mundane level, it gives a language, devoid of the act of compromise that verbal mediation essentially is,
to peoples experiences. It allows a moment to catelogue and accept the seen
through means of the unseen.

So why the hell are clubs so boring at the moment? The language I speak of
is not limited to any particular format of music. Some would say that last
year we were spoilt for choice. Short of the occasional one-offs like Life,
Joy and (dare I say it) Boys Own's parties, it's only Confusion, High On
Hope and Shoom that come anywhere near to approximating the exhilaration of
RIP, Hedonism, even Trip and Heaven. The people haven't changed, nor have
the DJs. The answer lies in a simple point. From tabloid hysteria, from
music critic fundamentalists, from those who collected party t-shirts like a
Brownie does badges, clubland is under siege. More than this, it is fragmen-
ted and directionless, it has lost it's language. At its conception, acid
house was a new development of musical expression unparalled by any other
popular movement short of punk 12 years ago.

Paradise Lost Cont...

The Cheap technology with which house records could be made created, as did punk, an entire breed of non-musicians, ready, through an extensive process of trial and error, to fit a soundtrack for their particular world. Much of this was haphazard, but the fact that there existed an experimental platform was of fundamental importance. Although these new producers/non-musicians/creators had not attended conservatoires or studied composition, and are therefore unable to give anything other than a limited theoretical explanation of their work, this in no way lessens their significance.

My purpose is not to describe a pre-Fall idyll, some sonic paradise towards which we should wander as do unreconstructed hippies to Glastonbury or thousands in search of total mind-fuck to the current orbital utopias, those turbo-charged, candy-floss and WC-available mega-parties, rather to lament the way clubland has so quickly become self-conscious and unspecial. Acid house was not the be-all and end-all, but it was a beginning, and something that was stamped out before it was allowed to develop. Policing crowds is one thing, criminalising creativity is another.

In New York, DJs like Frankie Knuckles have to compete with prats crowding the dance-floors for chats, damn it, people who line up little ski jumps of coke along their index fingers and look ready to kill anyone who jogs them. The club has become a continuation of the thrust and riposte of street life, and little else. You couldn't imagine anyone dropping their agrandised notion of cool long enough, to offer, say DJ Tony Humphries, the ovations he received in Shoom months back. As NYC's Manor Koch extends the curfew hours applied to clubs, and the City Hall departments militate against more and more liquor licences, London should be fore-warned. The politics of club music extends far beyond establishing personal boundaries and points of interaction. Death disco isn't far off.

TRUE PARADISE iNNA GRiNSTEAD STYLEE !

.... BARRY MOON-CULT'S CUNNiNG RURAL DiSGUiSE....

UPPERS & DOWNERS

Cut throat razor shaves at the barber
a potent mix of terror and ecstasy.

Laughing like Mutley and dancing like
Desmond Tutu.

Singing 'Filleting fish' at the match

Shouting "My dear fellow I am a valued
customer here", in Dunn & Co.

The 12" mix of Leslie Granthams 'Winn-
ers and Losers'.

The spam fritter revival.

Becoming a born again cynical bastard

Tony Humphries back at Shoom.

Your mum dressing like she's in S-Xpress

Having a potty grandad who wears braces
on his false teeth.

Putting an ad in Exchange 'n' Mart
for your old motor saying "It's a fast
one, good for jobs".

'Knowing the apple'.

The Happy Mondays 'Freaky Dancing'
T-shirts.

Getting loved-up.

Getting pissed up at 'Eggs, Bacon
Bubble and Two Slices'.

Shakey, chattering jaws for girls
(AKA flu-boats).

Being a rascal.

Calling Teds - Rarsclarts.

Being true to your mates and fucking
the rest right off.

Shouting George Bush "Get Your Nose Out Of
My Nose"

24" flared jeans by Joe Bloggs

Clubbing it in Rimini next spring

Looking at the schoolies at Hammersmith
Broadway around 4 o'clock

Looking a right knobhead in I-D

Sticking chewy in your nans hair.

Being caught out as a top fibber.

Ted the T.V gardener in the yellow pages
ad (sack the old git).

England barmies on acid playing 'Walk
the Plank'.

Baby tone-locs limping about the Carnival
playing 'N.W.A'.

Dressing like the Prince Regent down
your local.

Bunging your doley brother a ching.

Dungaree wearing top-knot acid Sharons
from E10.

Charlie violence actually breaking out
all over town.

The QPR boys who still think it's 1981.

Watching happy bods pissing up your
profits.

Having flu in Ibiza.

Winter's back.

All the Tarquin posh fackers who called
us hooligans, but lurve us now 'cos
they fink we are trendy (what with them
haircuts - Ed).

Whistling in the station bogs.

Sam off Brooky's car crash.

Giving up the match to do the shopping.

Centre Force radio: the discoverers of House
music, Ibiza, the drug ecstasy, the Planet Zog
and Lime Green Wallabys.

Onion Bhargis and custard.

Corry youth.

Getting caught looking at the schoolies at
Hammersmith Broadway at 4 o'clock

Getting caught bollocking up the typing
at 4.15

THE FUTURE

DJ'S TERRY FARLEY
& NANCY NOISE
TURBO SOUND
NEW LITES
EVERY THURSDAY
£5 10-3·30AM
UNDER THE ARCHES
HUNGERFORD LANE
OFF CRAVEN ST.

ear Boy's Own,

Pissed off? Isn't everybody nowadays?
'm sure the latest issue of your slanderous
ag is going to be chock full of moaning
innies and bolshed-up types complaining
bout
) the scene being wet-fished
) how the best thing going is "The Hitman
 Her" with a handful of mushrooms at
am Sunday morning
) the ever-expanding mass of teds/ragas/no
ecks in wanna-be boots etc etc ad-bleedin'
auseum
ut.... maybe a few more people ought to
top to think why this sorry state of affairs
as come to pass.
   The usual excuse you could offer for such a
oor show of late - the tabloids, the cash-ins
he unwashed masses - do hold some degree of
ruth, but let's be honest.... thge one thing
olds it all together is the music. And it's
een seriously lax this year.

For me the downfall started earlier this year,
nat with the rise of Trax and other half-assed
fforts some would call "Record Shops". Such
stablishments made it so easy for any two-bit
ickerkid with a wedge in his dungerees to own
 decent set of tunes. The result? Early evening
ocks playing their just-bought copies of Richie
avens, rather than building up a whole night's
ntertainment, that's what. Whatever happened to
oing out, hearing a reputable slab of vinyl and
ninking "oh my gosh dearie me I never thought
'd hear that one out...."??? Whatever happened
 "I never thought I'd be dancing to......"
ill in the gaps)??? It's much too easy
wadays and too safe by half. The Gary Davies
ow is just as eventful as any club you care
 mention.

bviously there are exceptions, but you've
t to admit that most clubs are turning into
ther giant A&R departments or watering holes
r scabby media folk.
nyway my advice is pop down the Record & Tape
th a fiver and look out for a bargain - no
ey won't have Italian import stamps on but
u won't have to queue three teds deep in Soho
ther!

e only reason me and you ever went out was
r something different than the usual... let's
t back to some adventurous music planning,no?

urs with the cotton wool,

ck Mouthoff
ndon W10

Dear Boy's Own,
      After reading your Manc article I must
tell you about a rather worrying trend that
is occuring up here at the moment. People
are suddenly buying the "scally" dress sense
in kits, flared jeans, trainers, Stone Roses
t-shirts and claiming to have been there
from the start.
      Now having been to see both the Happy
Mondays and The Stone Roses, it seems to me
that the Mondays are the real thing while
The Stone Roses are simply a replacement of
the Smiths to please the N.M.E reading
Manchester students now that their Morrissey
t-shirts have worn out.
      The real boys in Manc relate much bet-
ter to State 808, Inspiral Carpets, MC Buzz
B and T-Coy. For me the old Manc identity
could well be lost forever and a new one
that separates us from the South will have
to be found.
                JAMES.   CHORLEY, LANC'S

Dear Boy's Own
      Loved the recent issues but what's
happened to our fave series, "Great Firms
of History". You lot are mixing with the
wrong sort, you're going soft, to help
here's five more mobs that terrorised the
world:
1. The Sunrise Kickers Firm: Destroyed clubland in less than a year, ruined Saturday
night raves with their marauding. From Kent
to Brum, they have left a cultural wasteland
2. Leeds Utd Service Crew: They loved Pring-
les and Filas and a bit of Seig Heiling,
rioted at Barnsley and Shrewsbury but legged
it when in London (Piccadilly '81, Highbury
'80, London Bridge'83)
3. The Charlie Brigade: The Vietcong not the
nose up possie, with top boy Ho-Chi-Min they
wooped Uncle Sams arse and chased him off
the manor
4. The Paradise Gang: Dirty Den, a blackman
in a Gaultier bowler hat and a priest who
"knows the apple" its camp and a right
giggle, they couldn't run a fruit stall but
we give them 10 out of 10
5. The Metropolitan Police: The Gaffers, the
William, the Rozzers, Plod, the Filth, whatever you call 'em they go in hard and certainly not fair......ask the print workers,
miners etc. If you see 'em coming have a
walk (also see rhyming slang with "James
Hunts").

                        Cheers Jamie Wilson
                             Acton London

Dear Boy's Own

In my quest for higher highs, I've never said
no to a few mushrooms. I've always been able
to handle my drugs but this was a grave mis-
judgement.

At the beginning of the week, I went in
search of the Libeerty Cap, covering a good
few miles of cow-shit splattered meadow in
the process. On finding what I was looking
for, I was over the moon and greedy for the
buzz.

Monday night I had a hundred & seventy in a
brew and everything was sweet. Come Thursday
I took fifty in a brew and ate twenty small
fresh specimens and what happened next is in
the On Top category.

Sitting in the woods coming up was good. In
fact it was brilliant; watching squirrels and
cats whose form were shadows and trees that,
got up and walked. But then it hit me that it
was so strong that I may not be able to handle it . Anyone who's ever dabbled in psilo-
-cybin knows it works on whatyou are think-
-ing at the time and that was the turning
point - the start of a journey I will never
forget.

I was suddenly gripped by fear and had the
irresible urge to take my clothes off and
have a shit. I tried to fight it as I didn't
want to found naked and covered in pony on
Wembley High Road. I headed for the sanctuary
of Rosewood (Institute of Cosmology) but no-
-body was home. This really sent me off because I thought I was the only person in the
world.

Continuing to walk my sight became worse and
the sky lowered itself. Just to throw me off
a bit more, things were right on top. Reeling
through the streets hearing Movement and see-
-ing Sound - suffering pandemonium of the
Mind. Then, at last, I found someone - a friend
just in from work.

I walked into house and freaked out the occ-
-upants to the extent that they left. By now
I didn't know who, where or what I was. My
body was letting me down while my mind was
going into disneyland. In a world of spinning
spheres of light and holograms, the tracking
was so heavy that using my hands became con-
fusing. I started to feel really ill about
this time

nerves and cells twitching and grimacing
and burning. I thought I was going
to snuff it. I ran downstairs into
the kitchen and asked someone to call the
Funny Farm (St. Bernard's). No-one took
me seriously until I managed to spell it
out. My mate was very good and took me
straight to casualty at the local Bone
Shop.

I walked in at one with the wall. They
asked me what I had taken but I couldn't
talk so my mate filled them in. They then
rang Guy's Hospital Poisons Dept; which
got me really paranoid. Thinking I was
close to the end I could hear God or
whoever it was telling me to leave the
hospital room and my own body and make
the leap into astral existence. I wan-
-ted to, but couldn't, without closing
my eyes and giving up the fight to stay
sane. The doctors started testing and
suggested I stay in over night for obs-
-ervation. I refused because every one
was melting and the floor was getting
sticky as it undiluted under my feet.
I sat down and things got weirder. My
body turned inside out and split up into
symmetrical forms. My saliva was singing
and my head had completely disappeared.
I lost all knowledge of my own existence
and form. At that moment, I was just a
collection of cells in a world that didn't
fit. All very hard to comprehend when
four hours later I was back to normal.

On leaving the hospital I felt a complete
fucking doormat. It's all very nice when
you're having fun and in control but
when you are given the option to either
stay in normality or go totally Nean-
-derthal, the mortal mind can't quite
suss it out.

Needless to say, I know better now. My
closing words to those who think it's
clever to take more than the next man are
you are walking a fine line and when it comes
on top you'll know which side your bread's
buttered on.

This hasn't been written to put anyone on
a bad buzz but if its happened to you,
you're not alone - you know the apple.

May I just add that I'm not your Land
Of Oz Dayglo Barny but consider myself
a hardened user of hallucinogenics for
many years.

BETTER A LIGHTWEIGHT THAN A DEADWEIGHT.

                    RICHARD, WEMBLEY

give us a line

BOYS OWNS VERY OWN LIFESTILE GUIDE
FREE OF NICE PICS OF PAUL SMITH PANTS...

WE ARE TALKING TOP NOSH

Dear Boys,
        If you like your grub and you find
yourself nutting about in this great city
of ours, here's a short selection of scof
shops where the food is good and the
prices are not a bolt up.

1. The Nicosia Grill: Bethnal Green
    Right next to the underground station
    this is one of the only cafés I've
    been to where two plates are needed
    to manage the mixed grill, it's not
    the Ritz but the food's topper and
    there's lots of it. Five sovs for
    the T-bone steak with the works, so
    get down there and get on it.

2. The Noshery: Hatton Gardens
    A Jewish sandwich bar with a pucka
    salt beef on rye well worth a visit

3. The Tatlers: York Road, Battersea
    Had the pleasure of going here after
    a night out, a fine way to wake up!
    A lovely gaff with Roast Lamb, spuds
    and two veg weighing in at £1.90,
    blinding!

4. The Stockpot: St.James W1
    You'll find this chain all over town
    but I like this one best, good café
    food at cheap prices, the beef goul-
    ash is a lovely little number.

5. Uncle Ernies: Temple Fortune, Gold-
                                    ers Green
    Kosher deli diner, the salt beef's
    very cheap and a fine selection of
    chopped liver and latkas.

6. The Riviera: Holloway Road
    A boom café with top selection of
    home-made pies, clean 'n' tidy well
    recommended.

All the mentioned cafés are grease and
dog hair free, write and tell us some of
your faves, letters from Greasy Bill 'n'
Lil not excepted.

                            MARK SMYTHE
                    Good Café Correspondent

TUNES TO MAKE YOU THINK MORE CLEARLY

1. C'EST LA OUATE: Artist unknown
    A corker of a track with a little bit
    of Lou Reed and Electrica Salsa.
    (It's by Caroline Loeb - Top spotter Ed

2. KIPSY: Boy George

3. BREATHE LIFE INTO ME: Mica Paris
    (Frankie Knuckles remix)

4. Any of the ballads from the New
    Primal Scream long player

5. WORLD PEACE: B.D.P.
    Records on this subject are usually
    total crap (Stand up Paul Rutherford
    and ABC) but this throws away the rose
    tinted specs and tells it like it is

BOYS OWN WINTER FASHION TIPS

1. THE NIGERIAN PIMP LOOK: Suede Gucci
    .loafers, flared silk strides, flowery
    shirts and a right rascal of a hat (a bit
    like Ron Atkinson)

2. VINNY JONES T-SHIRTS: Capped sleeve
    tight fitting, bearing the logo 'Just when
    you thought it was safe to go to Elland
    Road'. Fashion victims queue here.

3. BOYS OWN J.R BALACLAVAS: Knitted by
    our nan in lambswool, tri-coloured without
    the holes cut out, big amongst Battersea
    Park military organisations.

TEN OBJECTS THAT ARE IMPOSSIBLE TO FIND

1. Toilet paper in an acid house warehouse
2. A tune that ain't Ted in Trax
3. A spare pit bull pup in Brixton
4. A legally obtained mountain bike in W1
5. A decent pair of jeans in Manchester
6. A decent parcel down the Limelight
7. Anything but a kebab to eat in Camden
8. Any spare parts for XR3i motors in
    Bethnal Green
9. Hacksaw blades in Wandsworth
10 A decent pair of shoes in the boot
    store

BOYS OWN : 249-251 Kensal Rd, London W.10.
Telephone : 01-968-8459.
Editorial : Terry, Andrew, Cymon, Stephen.
Contributions : Louise Gray, Dicky Norris, Phil Thornton,
Steve Hall, Jane Bussman, Adam Porter.
Photos : David Swindells, Pete Heller.

THANKS to....
FIRSTLY ALL THE YOUNG LADIES on the SCENE who put up
WITH SO MUCH.... DAVE CHIPS, BILLY the BIKE, PLURG,
The P.O.P. GROUP, The RAMPLINGS, OAKEY COKEY, The LOVELY
NANCY NOISE, SPENCER, SEAN, STEVE, ROCKA, HAISMAN,
TWO KEVS ON LAGER, JAK at VICTORY, TOSH N' PHIL at VINYL
SOLUTION, THE FAMILY TRIBE, STEVE 'I'LL TREAT YA' LEE,
BLAINE, RUTH at B.C.M, DESMOND, TERRY (INA BRIXTON),
SPARKS; ALL THE LADBROKE GROVE BOYS — "THIS SPACE GAFFS
A TOP PLOT INIT!", SMITHERS and ROWLES, Little LIAM,
McGOO, AND ANYONE THAT KNOWS Me.....P.S. Beware the HOOTER FIRM.

No. 9
Spring 1990

BOYS OWN

SPRING EDITION

Afternoon; MY Little Love CHILDREN,

I KNOW YOU'RE PROBABLY ALL 'UP' AND 'OPTIMISTIC' ABOUT THE 90's AND DON'T NEED ANYBODY MOANING... BUT... NEVER HAS THERE BEEN A Greater NEED FOR A MOANY OLD Git... WHY?... Well HERE'S ONE REASON WHY (MUCH MORE TO COME THOUGH kids)

GURU JOSH: 'HE'S A LOAD OF OLD TOSH' MR and MRS JOSH'S BOY, GURU has BEEN rather VOCAL RECENTLY ON A variety OF TOPICS RANGING FROM prophecies of forthcoming violence and bloodshed At 'Raves' (You MUST be expecting SOME CHOICE BOOKINGS GURU), to How He's the FIRST REAL 'personality' ON THE SCENE, A SCENE Which he CLAIMS is A 'REVOLUTION'... YEAH!... SUCH A Revolution That 'Mister Buywrite' And 'NEXT for MEN' NOW sell YIN YANG sweatshirts, and OTHER ESSENTIAL ACID FROCKS, COMING SOON, the 'GURU Collection': RUBBISH INDIAN TROUSERS, stick on taches, And Sticky UP HAIR-do. LOVE That TEDDY BEAR T-SHIRT!

don't GET Me WRONG MISSUS, I don't MIND THIS sort of WAFFLE The Rantings OF a TOTAL TWAT are RELATIVELY har!LESS.. BUT.. WHAT REALLY is ANNOYING, IS that EVERY time I Have the MISFORTUNE to read tHE 'PHILOSOPHIES' OF MR. JOSH he SLAGS A CERTAIN MR O'DOW And I Quote...

" what doES BOY GEorge KNOW ABOUT HOUSE MUSIC, he DOESN'T KNOW HOW to go Mental " .. OR..

" IT'S A CAREER MOVE to MAKE SOME MONEY out of the SCENE, he's JUMPING on the BANDWAGON "

O.K. You PYJAMA CLAd Git, Let's deAL with YOUR 'ARGUMENTS'.... BASICALLY, GURU me old CHINA, BOY GEORGE has GOT MORE to do with the REAL club SCene than You will Ever hope to HAVE; he's BEEN clubbing it FOR Fifteen YEARS; and correct ME IF I'M WRONG; I don't remember seeing The GURU's stan LAUREL hairdo bobbing And TRANCE DANCING at the Fitness centre, I do REMEMBER seeing GEORGE...

" JUMPING ON a BANDWAGON " do Me ONE enormous citrus fruit

" MR O'DOWD; did You OR DID You Not used to BE iN a rather GOOD PoP group that EMerged OUT OF, And Reflected, the Look and FEEL of CLUBLAND "

" MR GURU; did You, or did You Not used to BE iN An extremely Ropey new wave/PUB Rock band called 'JOSHUA cries WOLF'

So Rests The CASE For the defence: GURU JOSH, 'LEIUTENANT PIGEON' for the 90's and REMEMBER kids the white clothes Trend IS JUST A conspiracy instigated by LAUNDERETTE OWNERS ... And anybody Who BUYS OR SELLS CRYSTALS iS A TWAT!

Not MUCH Love ✗ The Outsider

" Haul it in, my lucky lads, it's
the flyers!" cried Anton.

THE pirates of " The Saucy Do " are very brave and daring,
   You'll see this by their flyers and the clothes that they are
   wearing.
They sometimes have a vip lounge, and rigs of fifty k,

Oh, yes, they are a reckless lot, these pirates, so they say !

One morning when the ship was off the coast of Basingstoke,
The Captain cried, " I spy a plot, me merry pirate folk !
It's fifty miles to North-North-South, or there around,
   Let's get ten thousand in and charge them twenty pound. "
To tell the truth, the do was crap, not worth the time of day,

Oh, yes, they are a reckless lot, these pirates, so they say !

SOLARIS

4 GRAYS INN ROAD, LONDON WC1
SUNDAYS 6 P.M. – 12 A.M.

UPPERS & DOWNERS

UPPERS

HAVING A MAD BUDGIE CALLED LEEDS...

SAYING THERE "REALLY CLEAN"....

SLOUGH Vs MIDDLESBOROUGH DEBATES...

THE BASSETT JELLY BABIES, "THEIR IN A WIBBLY, WOBBLY WORLD OF THEIR OWN".....

CENTRE PARTINGS IN YOUR PUBIC HAIR..

PEACE IN ITALIA '90....

BEING A HARMONICA WIZARD.....

TELLING RIPPING YARNS.....

BEING THE PROUD OWNER OF A GREEN SKUNK....

A MAN WITH THICK GLASSES AND A BASTARD ANORAK SHOUTING "IT'S NOT MY TROLLEY"....

GAZAPACHO SOUP....

GETTING AWAY WITH IT.....

SPENDING TIME GIGGLING WHEN YOU SHOULD BE WORKING....

SAYING "COME ON BILLY LET'S GET BOOTLEGGING"....

EXTREMELY LOUD GUITARS.....

THE RETRO-CASUAL TRAINER REVIVAL (AKA ADIDAS OLD BASTARD)....

BEING A RIGHT LIBERTY TAKER....

MICKEY MOUSE CUP FINALS...

MAD CRISPIN GLOVER HAIRCUTS SHOUT-ING "GET THAT GANGSTER OUT OF MY CLUB"

FRED KRULL'S MAD POLL TAX DODGE (CORNISH TIN MINES)....

FEEDING POLICE DOGS AT THE MATCH...

GOING ON A POTTY LAGER FRENZIE....

HAVING AN E-BOAT INSTEAD OF A CHARLIE SNARL....

DOWNERS

DRUG GUARANTEES (IE. THESE MUSHROOM ARE SAFE).....

FINDING OUR YOUR PET ANTS HAVE BECOME BASS-HEADS...

ACTUALLY LIKING AN ADAMSKEET RECORD

BEING THE TOTTENHAM GOALIE....

PEOPLE WHO SAY "GOT ANY OATS"...

STUSSY CLAD - POSH FACKERS

GETTING A NIGHTBUS...DRIVING A NIGHTBUS...BEING A NIGHTBUS...

THE RISE OF GERMAN FACISM.....

RADION ADVERTS(LOVE THE T-SHIRTS THOUGH)....

BEING A KEYBOARD WIZARD (IE. MR. WET MONDAY MORNING AND LOAD OF OLD TOSH)...

YOUR UNCLE SID LOSING HIS SEAT IN THE NICARAGUA ELECTIONS.....

GETTING CAUGHT...

SAYING "THINGS AIN'T WHAT THEY USED TO BE....

LONDON Vs MANC DEBATES....

KNOBHEADS CALLED WILBUR...

TARQUIN POSH FACKERS INTO HIP HOP WHO PUT "SKI'S" ON THE END OF THEIR NAMES.....

BUSES FULL OF OLD PEOPLE....

HOODS WHO WEAR HOODS.....

HEAD FUCKS....

CHARLIE CULTURE....

CLASS WAR SOAP DODGER'S DOING THE SOCIALIS CAUSE NO FAVOURS

GIVING YOURSELF A LOVE BITE....

CHARLIE CHESTER GIVING YOU A LOVE BITE...

"Guess who I had in the back last week"...

THE SCENE: A WET 'N' WINDY WEST END SATURDAY NIGHT, HOME AND OVALTINE BECKONS.

"FUCKING SHLAGG"!!! is screamed loudly across Old Compton Street, "Paarrp" goes my bottle as it drops severely. I look over my shoulder, expecting to see some lunatic tearing down the road at me, shouting "Didn't you kill my brother?" but no, it was just another irate clubber tearing his hair out and going crazy, apeshit, bonkers about yet another cabbie (salt of the earth -ED) who had mugged him right off, leaving him looking a complete pleb.
Why he was mugged off? I don't know. He was dressed to the nines in his latest Rock 'n' Roll, Indie, dance, euro ambiance-crossover fashion - in the bods opinion "pucka" - to the cabbie a complete "Soap dodger." Being rejected by London's finest in front of his pals, who then completed the humiliation with jeers of "You Nobhead, you couldn't catch a cold let alone a cabbage."
The next perspective hailer mooche's up to the sidewalk (gutter to you and me), he has a more mature air about him, short hair in a Ian Brown stylee, mandarin style jacket (black of course) nice strides, Dirk Battenburg shoes, that are a bit unspirited, but nice n' easy on the feet. Slowly nutting up to the top of the road ahead of his waiting droogy pals, he sights a cab, "light on - sweet." His pals are hedge creeping in an attempt to keep out of the moody monty - cabbies sight, on your own chances are always higher. The cab slows, our bod starts grinning to himself, the promise of warm cab leatherette and a double speed fan heater seems like heaven.
Basically it's a game of wits and cunning, the usual ploy being, getting in the sherbert, telling him you want to go to Holland Park, then at one of those crucial corners telling him, "No, I've got to get to my girls gaff, South of the river".
Those last four words to Monty Sherbert are like garlic and a cross to vampires or soap and water to a geordie. At this, Monty wants to tear out your heart with his bare hands but realises there's a ching on the clock, money talks.

— GOD BLESS PRINCE WILLIAM, HE'LL MAKE A GREAT KING!

— YOU'VE NEVER LIVED UNTIL YOU'VE TASTED ERNIE'S PICKLED KIPPERS

— YEAH, 'COURSE YOU HAVE TO GO VIA MILL HILL TO GET FROM WATERLOO TO THE WEST END!

— I HAD OUR ENERY IN THE BACK LAST NIGHT! HE'S NEVER FORGOT HIS ROOTS! YEAH I WAS TAKING HIM TO SANDRINGHAM!

— MAGGIE'S RIGHT TO STOP THESE SKIVING BASTARD'S DOLE. THEY'RE NOTHING BUT A LOAD OF PARASITES WHO'VE NEVER DONE AN HONEST DAY'S WORK!

— I LOVE THE ROYAL FAMILY!

CABBY GAB

Anyway, back to Old Compton St. Our Ian Brown look alike smiles at the cabbie now doing 5mph, when suddenly Monty spots his shadowy pals, FOOT DOWN, LIGHT OFF. "SCHLAGG," echoes through the cold London night air yet again. This problem is all to clear to those from the South, where getting a cab home is like stuffing a whale up ones bottom. On the other hand if you are of afro caribean ancestory then forget it, also if your black and from South of the Thames we hope your trainees are comffy.

Like any good investigative reporting fanzine, we sent down club reporter Rex Cumberland to the public carriage office to ask about these chosen Monty's.

He told us this story, "On walking through the door I was punched squarely on the nose, and told to mind my own buisness." Fair enough I thought and the word "Schlagg" once again, came to mind.

This article came from Sir Les, one really pissed off, wet and tired patron of good nights out.

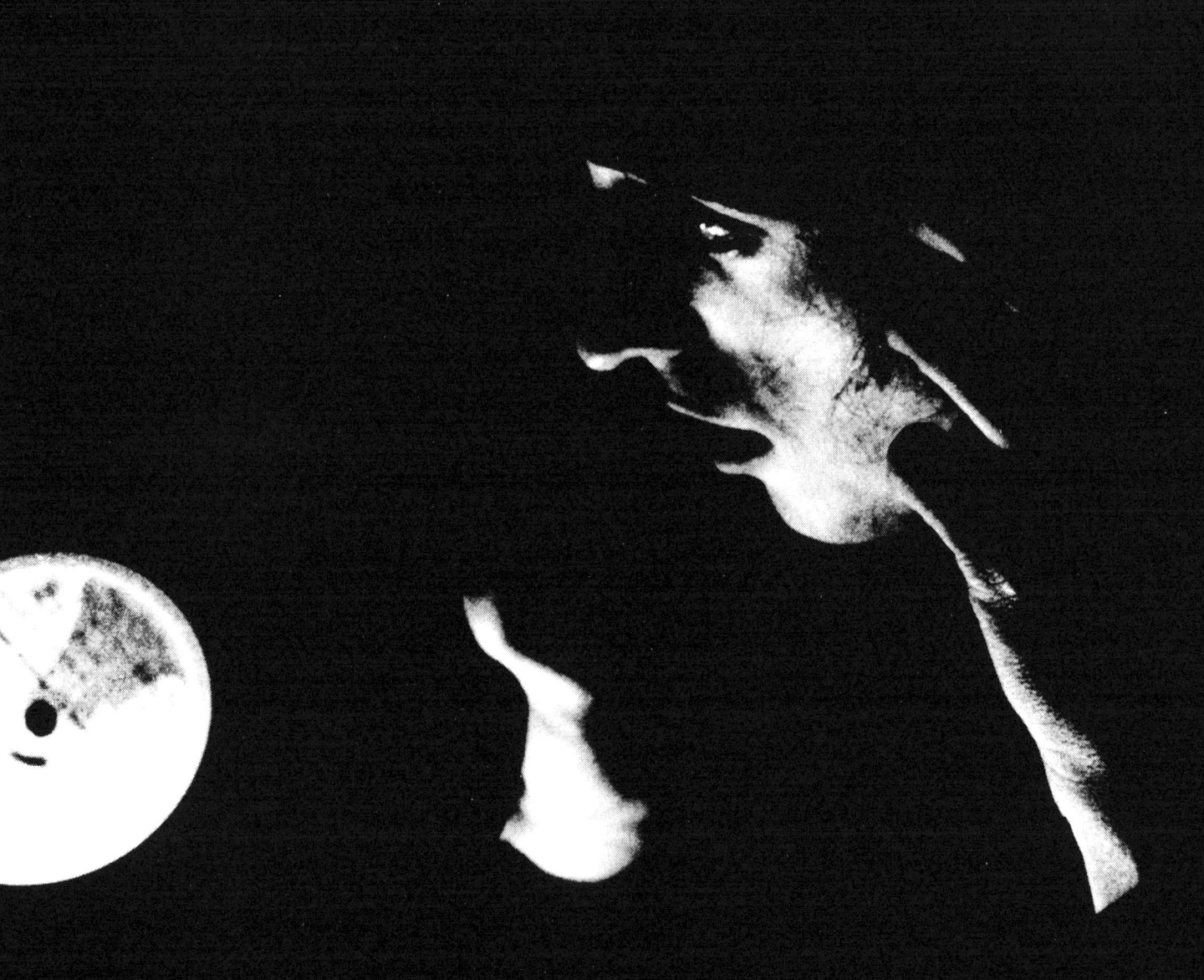

PHUTURE RECORDS
THE GARAGE 350 KINGS ROAD LONDON SW3 TEL: 352 0141

TOP TUNES: THE SOUND OF SPRING.

ST.ETIENNE.....................................ONLY LOVE CAN BREAK YOUR HEART

FLUKE...JONI

WAY OF LIFE...................................TRIPPING ON YOUR LIFE

SATOSHI TOMILE................................AND I LOVED YOU

THE GRID......................................FLOATATION

TRANCE DANCE..................................YOU'RE GONNA GET IT

SISTER SLEDGE.................................THINKING OF YOU(90 REMIX)

LOVE CORPORATION..............................PALATIAL(RAMPLING REMIX)

NATURAL EXPERIENCE............................DON'T LEAVE ME

COURTNEY PINE,SOUL II SOUL....................COURTNEYS BLOW

FRAZIER CHORUS................................CLOUD EIGHT

LEFTFIELD.....................................NOT FORGOTTEN

FOUR TO THE FLOOR.............................AFREAKADEAKY

DIANA ROSS....................................I'M STILL WAITING (90 REMIX)

CO DEPENDANTS OF KNOWLEDGE.....................THE LIGHT SIDE

THE FARM......................................STEPPING STONE

JESUS LOVES YOU...............................GENERATIONS OF LOVE

JAMIE PRINCIPLE...............................DATE WITH THE RAIN

SINEAD O'CONNOR...............................STRETCHED OVER YOUR GRAVE

MIXTRESS......................................DO WHAT YOU WANT TO

AFRICA..HISTORY

SUBLIMINAL AURRA..............................NO STOPPING

SLY 'N' LOVECHILD.............................THE WORLD ACCORDING TOO..

MORSE CODE....................................THANK GOD

PAPA WINNIE...................................ROOTSIE AND BOOPSIE

JOEY NEGRO....................................DO IT,BELIEVE IT

7th LITANY PRODUCTIONS........................BRING ON THE LUCIE

MIKI HOWARD...................................TILL YOU COME BACK TO ME

CHIMES..STRONGER TOGETHER

FOXY BROWN....................................FAST CAR

MOCCA SOUL....................................RYTHUM OF LOVE

WEST BAM......................................SWEET 17,SAXAPHONE

RYTHMATIC.....................................TAKE ME BACK

RHONDA MOORE..................................PREFACE

SOUP DRAGONS..................................MOTHER UNIVERSE

AKWABA..SOUTH AFRICAN MAN

KAREEM..YOUR IN LOVE

CARLTON.......................................DO YOU DREAM

BIG BAD GROOVE................................SNAPPINESS

RUBBERMAN.....................................RUBBERMAN ROCKS THIS HOUSE(REMIX)

THE LAND OF FIB

PRINCE OF PORKSTERS

Let's face it chaps and chapesses, we all know them well. Sometimes
they've got us out of trouble, sometimes they've turned a mess into a
disaster. Most of the time they're embarassing to be involved with,
though occasionally they can be so funny that it just dosen't matter.
What are we talking here? We are talking PORK PIES.

Great fibbers have historically led lives as majestic as the highest
ranking soldiers, politicians and drunkards. The same is still true
today. If you are a prize Porkster, a legend with the lie, then the
world is your oyster. Literally. Where as we all despise those shifty,
lacklustre compulsive liars, who go on endlessley about their sexual
prowess, their feats of daring at football, their epic voyages overseas
and their bulging bank accounts, there is a place in all of our hearts
for that master craftsman the seamless Porkster.

Before analysing the technique and success of these kings of fantasy,
let us take a moment to distinguish between him and the slug-like compulsive spinner. Compulsive bullshitters only really want to be liked
and accepted. They go on about it in a curious way. They rave on about
fights at the match, for an example. Usually they've details second-
hand and embellish the bare facts with massively improbable extras which
generally reflect well upon Benny Bullshitter himself; Benny leading a
troupe over the fences in the Ilderton Road End to rout, the Halfway
Line Potsmokers; Benny riding all the way to Aston Villa in the First
Class seats from King's Cross. He's even better when sex and drugs and
clubs come into it, as the drug-taking element gives him license to talk
complete crap. When you suggest to Ben that he might not have known
sexual congress with three models from the Select agency, on the
hammocks at Spectrum because Spectrum didn't have hammocks, he can look
you in the eye and say, "Better E, man, thought I was swinging there."

The point is that he has complete disregard for the charm of the natural
storyteller. He dosen't give two figs for entertaining people, it's all
about building up his ego instead. Consequently he never checks facts,
he just spews forth bollocks, regardless of whether there is a fence
at The Anfield Road End or whether you can get to Birmingham from King's
Cross (the BBC's The Firm was based upon his exploits).

Your Prince Of Porksters, though, he's a very different crock of
neuroses. He dosen't care whether people love him or not - he just
wants to give them a laugh, or suprise them. Or simply tell tall
stories as a straightforward challenge, to see if he can get people to
believe his far-fetched utterances. Therefore he does his homework. If
he's going to tell a story about his friend, (he rarely throws the spot-
light on himself) being kidnapped from Amnesia by a Czechoslavaian
Princess who took him to the hills to subject him to drug-induced sexual
experiments, then at the very least he;
            will have been to Amnesia,
            has undergone a Linguaphone course in Czech,
            has abused himself physically for a minimum of three weeks.
This way he can take you there. He can take you on a flight of fantasy
in which you too, can feel the sharp tang of cocaine inside your
Japseye give way to the narotic throb of her tongue....ENOUGH!!
You no longer care whether he's telling the truth or not. It is

irrelevant. You are in the company of a master, perpetuating one of the oldest traditions - holding an audience spellbound by his narrative skills. You want to hear the outcome of the story. And then, holding on to the image he has implanted in your mind, you hasten to a locked cubicle and get to work, fist flying. Only the Prince of Porksters can do this for you...
When we mentioned before that the world is Prince's oyster, this was very much the truth, leaving the way clear for dodgy puns about his Rolex and his champagne lifestyle.

Suffice it to say that the Prince of Porksters is not averse to profitting from his silken tongues. You'll see him in the best seats in the Olympic Stadium, Roma 90, enjoying the World Cup Final. Not by merit of some blouse "Gary Lineker's second cousin" sketch, but by convincing Sophia Loren that he is David Puttnam with tales about the traumas he had getting extras for Chariots Of Fire. He's actually in Italy to recce a major TV drama series for Berluscohi..... "female lead? Not yet."

You've all read the proposterous Richard Allen "Skinhead series, de-tailing the unlikely stories of one Joe Hawkins and his sometime buddy Benny The Jew. You may also have dabbled with the equally laughable but irrestible Absolute Begginers by Colin MacInnes, in which hip dudes drink loads of capuccino. In a world where craft is being replaced by assembly-line and output is prized higher than skill. We leave it to you, dear reader, to deduce which of our heroes is Richard and which is Colin.

(Benny Bull stories gratefully accepted).

THE GREAT DEBATE: *Pie n' Mash Shit or What?*

The great debate, the press is full of it. Who's lionel's are the
silliest? Who won the war in 1964? Yes, the old Manchester Vs London
rivalry is back on the agenda, stired up by a fashion press who normally
wouldn't entertain either faction in their clubs. Can you imagine
The Paris Angels having a quiet drink down Browns or Freds with their
I-D sponors - I think not.
Anyway back to reality, the real debate of our times - Food and to be
exact - PIE 'N' MASH.
"The food of the people," "It got us through the blitz," just two quotes
gathered from bods passing the Boys Own office. "Complete crap," "A
cockney myth," just two quotes from a certain Andrew Weatherall - Food
Correspondant for this publication. Who's right? Read on to find out..
....Sitting in Albert's Pie 'n' Mash just off of the Caledonian Rd, the
debate gained momentom. In the corner of cockney tradition, Liam
(singer with London pop combo "Flowered up") in the opposing corner a
certain Mr Peter Hooton, (singer with "De Farm" - Scarse pop stars)
mediating Mr Suggs, (Ex-nutty person about Camden).
"The gravy's shite, that's all I've got to say on the matter," coming
from the Northern side of the table. What could you expect from people
who put curry sauce on their chips!
Liams answer wasn't audable, half a mincemeat and onion pie in the gob
left our boy in the corner quiet. So it was all down to Mr McPherson to
cast the winning vote.....
"My earliest recollection of Pie 'n' Mash also co-incided with my first
encounter with drink," recalls suggs. "My mum's boyfriend had entered
himself in a pie eating competition and had spent a whole morning in a
Fulham pub, primming himself with pints of mild and pickled onions, in
an attempt to stretch his stomach." (Suggs orders another cup of tea,
Liam scoffs another pie and Hooton looks a bit Tom-dick). "I was a
mere eight years old and was given a couple of half's of cider by the
would-be Pie King". "This intoxication coloured my view of Pie 'n' Mash
giving it an almost surreal effect, which last's until this day."
(Sugg's "Uncle Tommy" necked eight pies of the traditional variety and
was on his ninth when he was saved from certain death by being declared
the winner). "The sight of this gluttony put me off it for years"
slurped Suggs.
Liam was still scoffing and Hooton had left in search of mushy peas
with curry sauce, no doubt!
"A quick revival ensued with Chelsea's promotion push in '78, when Pie
'n' Mash, football and beer drinking seemed to be inextricably linked."
Nowadays, the slightly older and wiser, Suggs has grave concerns over
the quality of meat (or lack of it) in the afformentioned pies. "Gettin
mad cow disease, won't get me back on Top Of The Pops, where I truly
belong," cried Suggs. "Then again it hasn't done Shaun Rider's cause
any harm has it!" We thanked the inn-keeper for her hospitality and
left Liam happily chomping away.
So there you have it, complete bollocks or Top-Scoff - who knows, who
cares - no-one....but then who gives a fuck about opening old London/
Manc football wounds, I suggest the fashion mags either SHUT UP or
SCOFF UP!

ALBERTS

PIE & MASH (SMALL)
PIE & MASH (LARGE)
JELLIED EELS
EELS & MASH

MASH & LIQ
Apple pie ~ Ice cream
COCKLES (PINT)
PRAWNS (PINT)
CRAB STICKS (7)
TEA ... COFFEE...
ORANGE SQUASH
MILK
CANNED DRINKS

KAZOO

SATURDAY'S

9pm - 2.30am

BASEMENT
GREAT WESTERN ROYAL HOTEL
PRAED STREET, W.2

D.J's (ALTERNATIVE WEEKS)

TERRY FARLEY · KEVIN HURRY

STEVE BICKNELL · ANDY WEATHERALL

STEVE LEE · ROCKY & DIESEL · RUSS POTTER

Friends, Fools n' Lovers.

Boy's Own is for those of you with brains and humour. In the last ish, the "Girl's Own" section appealed to your sense of humour. In this ish, it's yer brain we wanna engage in thought over matter which is always being pushed under the carpet leaving broken frienships galore...

There's a lot of crap written in those, "womens magazines" about men. Let's face it, in the eyes of those magazines, all you "loveables" out there can never do anything right - in bed, out of bed, down at Sainsbury's, their always picking fault with you. Have the writer's of these pathetic articles, ever actually been out with someone for a length of time? I often ask myself or do they just bump into some poor blokes trolley down at Sainsbury's, whisk him off to bed and then analyse him for their next issue? I say this because they never raise the point about sex and friends.

We've all been there. It's the problem with sex. "Problem with sex? Not me mate! "I hear you all you virile young men exclaim. No, not in that way chaps, it's the problem when sex rears its head between friends of the opposite sex. Let's face it, having a screwed up (metaphorically speaking) love life is one of the more unpleasant aspects of life, but if the person concerned also happens to be a close friend who you've known for years, then the situation becomes even more complicated. Whoever said getting loved-up was simple?

I'm not saying don't go out with friends, I'm just saying bear in mind that when it does all end you might be losing not just a lover but an old friend as well. There's just too many tales of woe circulating around London Town at the mo' concerning old friends turned to lovers turned to ex-lovers/ex-friends. To all you out there contemplating taking a friendship one step further, just stop and think whether it's because (due to previous bashings of the heart in the love stakes) deep down you just love the security of already knowing that 'she' has a sense of humour, cares, will listen to your probs and means you won't have to think of any blinding chat-up lines, "Ere, I'm Dave, how 'bout it?"

All is not doom and gloom though. For all the disaster stories you and I hear, there are exceptions when old friends come together (ooh er) and stay together. If you're brave enough to take the risk and your closest female friend suddenly starts making your trousers bulge in the right places, then go for it, bearing the following few points in mind (for those of you in the "hard of thinking" category of life) which have arisen over many nights contemplating the behaviour of you lot (don't deny, you do it too) at "Girl's Own" all-night analytical sessions.

1. Okay, because you're friends there's alot of emotional int-imacy between you, but if you're trying to prove this point, pick a pleasant scenario. "Ere, d'you remember when you threw up that night? I was with you wasn't I? Your puke was so strange that night, all sorts of.... This is NOT the way to a woman's heart boy's.

2. Likewise, just because you get on as friends all the time, don't make the mistake of thinking any moment will do to proclaim your feeling. Walking up to them woman of your (wet) dreams and giving her that, I'm a new man - let's talk it through "garbage" at 3am in a crowded club is not likely to produce the response that you want.

3. Finally (and predictably) just be yourself. As mums all over the country say with their funny ol' phrases about love, "A leopard can't change it's spots" and we all know how mums in the end always turn out to be bloody right. Despite what you might read in your sister's/ girlfriends/mum's magazines, we girlies don't want highflying career men or sensitive "I understand the problems of being a woman" wimps. We just want our men to be full of cheeky charm, have an intelligence above that of a Ted (not too difficult) and most of all to be a good friend. If you understand what Boy's Own is about then you're half-way there already......

MICHIKO LONDON

PUCKA CLOBBA

SHOP NOW OPEN

70 NEAL ST. COVENT GARDEN WC2

TEL: 497 0165

A Safe Journey Home

When you've lived in the suburbs all your life as I have, London will always be able to shock you. After a splendid night in one of our great capital's nightspots many a simple soul from the country has been known to gaze about the shit strewn streets and ask "Who the hell are all these looneys?"

Strolling the streets or driving home any time after midnight, strange folk of all shapes and sizes will spring from behind every pillar box and phone booth hurling abuse, at you or anyone else within a 120 yard radius of you. To those of you born within the sound of Bow bells or even the unaided sight of the Post Office Tower these strange nocturnal creatures are a common sight and go almost go un-noticed, but for those of us from out in the Green Belt, where the red buses fear to go, a body spreadeagled across the pavement, quoting from the New Testament and swigging from a bottle of Bulmer is not something that can be ignored or simply stepped over.

So let me take you on a trip around the West End on a Friday/Saturday night, leaving no cardboard box unturned. Many of thee characters you will undoubtably have met yourself, others you may have just laughed at from the warmth of your passing cab, but now read on and next time you see one of them ask yourself this question, "Is London after dark just a huge nuthouse?"

There is only one place to find hordes of sorry states after midnight (not including the que for Sin), the land of the night bus, Trafalgar Square. All manner of men sweep across this famous landmark at night reducing it to no more than a massive rubbish tip. Fighting, spitting, swearing, pissing up walls, pissing in doorways, pissing on eachother. All the lowest forms of human life seem to come together in Trafalgar Square, and have you ever noticed that they all seem to want to travel on the N96 with a Doner Kebab in one hand and a can of Skol in the other.

I have never quite managed to workout what you have to do to travel on a nightbus but it looks to me like you have to have a turn of speed like Seb Coe and a right hook like George Foreman. Crowds seem to rush around from stop to stop waving empty Burger King cartons at each other. They push one another onto the buses, off the buses, under the buses until finally, ram packed, the bus moves off creaking down the street. The bus departing then seems to signal the start of yet another great stampeed, to any other bus stop on any other side of the square. There must be some method in all this madness but I'm yet to see it, then again it could be some old pagan ritual that's been taking place since Adam was a boy and who am I to know, a mere lad from the sticks.

Thus far we've just looked at the Square as a whole but sometimes if you're either on foot or have had to stop the motor for that can of Fanta or a packet of skins, you have a wonderful chance to view the Squares residents at close quarters.

The Friday night boy's are a real favorite of mine, dressed in Next for Men, carrying plastic brief cases. When Friday night comes they all seem to become axe welding, raging homicidal maniacs. A mere nudged elbow in the pub can lead to an orgy of violence and almost certainly to some young Accounts clerk spending a night in the cells and another to an appointment with his dentist. Peace and love obviously never reached the City last year, and who said that the most dangerous place to go last year was the terraces of Millwall.

After the "Thank God it's Friday" crew the next largest group to be found chilling out by the fountains, has got to be those wonderful friends of the family, the drunks. It is possible to sub-divide these fellows into all sorts of smaller groups but however you do that, they still seem to fall into one of three types.

The first of these groups are the singers. How these fellows know the words to awful hit's from the seventies is a mystery to me, and how they manage to sing them pissed out of their minds is nothing short of a miricle. A friend of mine and I once decided that no-one could possibly remember all the words to "Knock three times on the ceiling if you want me" and not be one of the original members of Dawn. This line of thinking then led us to believe that the hopeless idiot dancing round the lamp post infront of us, must infact be Tony Orlando fallen on hard times.

It's even worse when there's a bunch of them because they always seem to insist on running through the whole of Paper Lace's greatest hit's and will ask for an audience participation.

All in all though the singers are great, they're harmless, they're having a good time and the worst they'll do to you is ask for a request. The same can hardly be said of the next type, yes you've guessed it, the fighter.

The fighter will scream insults at everyone, take a swing at most of the men and give a Westminster Council dustbin the worst beating of it's life. He's not a man to tangle with by any means as he's always pissed himself at some stage during the evening so avoid contact with him at all costs. The fighter is easily sidestepped when necessary as his span of attention is very short, move out of his line of vision for a couple of seconds and he'll turn on someone else, hopefully a police-man. The fighter usually meets his match with one of his own, which can be as entertaining as one of Frank Bruno's contests. The fight will be a noisy, one of them could split their trousers and more damage will be done by a trip over the kerb than a crafty upper-cut. At the end of the bout both boys will declare undying love for eachother, discover they were both in the Scrubs at the same time and share the same dead mother.

Last but not least we come to the sleeper. These chaps are usually found sprawled on the grass infront of the National Gallery, they don't take part in the usual rushing about in search of transport home and are quite content to let all sorts of people go through their pockets, removing fags, money or anything else of value. These lads are very quiet except for the snoring, seem able to sleep in any position including standing up and are loved by all the other nightbus users as they never attempt to get on the buses.

Further out heading for suburbia the spottings of your "right raver" become less common but some of the varieties on view are far more exotic. The more upwardly mobile areas seem entirely populated by Sloanes swearing at cab drivers that refuse to stop for them. If they could just stop for a minute and look at themselves they would see why the cabbie would rather pick up the four black kids going to Dance Wicked, than have them in the back of his motor. Abigail will be slumped on the kerb, head between her legs, staring at the chicken Kiev and a bottle of Cotes du Rhone, she had earlier at Alister Little. She'll have ladders up both legs of her Christian Dior tights and one of her Gucci's will be halfway down the road, stuck in a manhole cover. Then there's her beau, Todd. His lightly greased hair is sticking in every direction, his shirt covered in claret (the real thing), he started out the evening looking like Michael Douglas a la Wall Street and has ended up more like Jack Duckworth from Coranation Street. When will these people learn that just because you've got a few bob and a public school accent, dosen't mean you look good with vomit down your blazer.

You know, the more I think about the strange people that appear in London's streets at night, the more I realise this piece could go on forever. I haven't even mentioned acid teds jackin' to the sound of zebra crossing, the men that walk their dogs at five in the morning with their slippers on, the women at five in the morning with a pint of milk in their hand, miles from the nearest shop, let's face it we could all name hundreds.

Hopefully my rantings won't have upset any of you out there because I'm sure that some of you might just of recognised yourselves somewhere along the way. All I have to say to you though if you do, is don't worry about it, nearly everyone I know falls into one of the categories at some time and a certain fellow called Anthony into all of them.

BOYS OWN PIN UP, SAMMY ROGERS (COR — ED)

THe SUndAy SessiON

QueeNs

sunday afternoons 12-4
dj phil perry & guests
£3 before 1 o'clock £4 after

queenmother rsvoir
horton road colnbrøøk

FLOWERED UP FACT OR FICTION

FLOWERED UP - An invention of Boys Own's imagination or the next big thing? That was the question being asked all over town, and mainly amongst the 500 or so bods locked out. Firstly let it be said that the "doo" wasn't a Flowered Up gig, but Dance Hall Daze" featuring a couple of London DJ's (of ill repute) and around 300 of the Monkey Drum/ Future crowd. Although once word of F.U.'s "secret" appearance "leaked" it was a free for all with "Muso" types and trendy bandwagon hoppers all demanding entry.

The African Centre (original home of Soul II Soul) isn't the best venue in town when it comes to packed crowds and by the time F.U. had appeared many a toe had been trodden on and more than one parcel split (oh, what a shame! ED).

Musically up until then we had been treated to the DJ debut of Sarah (Girls Own bod) spinning Edie Brickel, Talking Heads, This Mortal Coil and Depth Charge. Terry Farley had followed by playing the Monday's, A.C.R, Gary Clail and other London Underground faves and suddenly it was the turn of King's X's favourite boys.

Decked out in Michiko bar Liam (I new that boy had taste) the band gave the ecstatic crowd 3 tunes (don't know the titles). Plenty of Fuck off strobes, a few lobbed beer cans, a bit of this and a bit of that and no-one shouted "London vibe in the area" thank fuck! The general con-census of the band was great, but then if your home fans don't like you, who will?

The charge to the bar and the ensuing crush, proved to much for the weak hearted and many left to the strains "Road to Nowhere" (via Mr Dean Thatcher). Leaving the people who really wanted to be there and not just to be Mr "Next-big-thing-nosey-parker!"

Catch Flowered Up at the Boy's Own "All day affair" and up at the Hacienda in the Spring,with bands popping up from Bromley, and all points sarf of the river, It looks like being a singer will be this years alternative to "serving up" and why not it's alot less harmful to your health.

                    Flowered Up 1   -   The Rest 0

FUTURE

EVERY THURSDAY
WITH
NANCY NOISE
JAM MC'S + SPICE
MEMBERS ONLY CLUB
MEMBERSHIP ENQUIRIES ON 01-267 8885
HUNGERFORD LANE OFF CRAVEN ST. WC2
ADMISSION £7.00

THETA

THE EFFORTLESS ACTIVITY AT
KONSPIRACY
WITH D.J.'S

TOP TUNES:
THE SOUND OF SPRING.

The sounds of young London part 46, Giles Peterson vital "Vibra Zone" show
on jazz FM — Saturdays 3 till 4, the sort of vinyl selection that the word
balearic was invented for.........

1.ROY AYRES.................................WE LIVE IN BROOKLYN BABY

2.RAMP......................................EVERYONE LOVES THE SUNSHINE

3.YUSEF LATEEF.............................BROTHER JOHN

4.LENNIE HIBBERT...........................MIGHTY

5.AUGUSTUS PABLO...........................EAST OF THE RIVER NLLE

6.THE MYSTIC MOODS.........................COSMIC SEA

7.GRADEY TATE..............................MOON DANCE

8.OPAFIRE..................................WALK LIKE RAIN

9.GENE HARRIS..............................LATIN FUNK LOVE SONG

10.YZ.....................................TOWER WITH THE POWER

11.LINDA WILLIAMS.........................ELEVATE YOU'RE MIND

12.STEVE WILLIAMSON.......................VISIONS

13.ANDY AND THE BAY SISTERS..............A TASTE OF HONEY

14.STEVE SOUL............................POPCORN WITH A FEELING

15.FAZE O................................RIDING HIGH

GANGSTERS, GUNS & PONYTAILS

The slimey pony tail and blazered world of the T.V and film executive,
has always had a major problem getting it's head round reality. That's
because virtually everyone who works in the medium is an expense account
worker - too wrapped up in their own mediocrity and four hour lunch
break, to remember what life is like for everyone else.

Of course this dosen't stop these boozed-up male losers thinking that
they can write decent scripts about violence. Take gangs. Those appar-
itions that appear out of sidestreets in Newcastle, Cardiff and Commercial Road, that chuck dodgy homemade sugar 'n' weedkiller devices at
Ajax, that kill for fun in Madellin, Columbia and East LA and stab you
pronto for anything Adidas on housing estates in Moscow and Kiev.

The fear (Euston Films 1988), despite encouraging Inter-Borough reg-
ionalism within London (Gawd 'elp us) and basing itself too loosely on
the 'designer' ethic, was in my own humble opinion not a bad lil'
feeler. The last episode was bollocks and they never seemed to do
anything, to make all that money to buy their nice clothes with but
they did behave like utter cunts on occasions, which is always nice
to see on a Tuesday night with a cup of cocoa and an attitude hard-on.

Banana splits (Hannna Barberra 1971) delved deep into the psyche of the
violently disposed youth and came out with Fleagle, Beagle, Drooper
and Snork. Four of the furriest mayhem merchants to drive beach buggy's
since 'Scorpio Rising', (a 1960's Gay Biker gang flick, well worth
catching - after you've eaten). Drooper was, of course, top boy. He
may have looked like an Elephant with a vocal problem but in yer actual
had served eight years hard labour in Space Family Robinson, another
gang show.....and what a bunch of pricks they were.

Let's face it we all want to be cuddled. Just 'cause we have a lil'
stubble and the odd tooth missing it dosen't mean we aren't in line
for some tickling, as t'were. Indeed, many of the modern day gangs
such as The Cockney Inspiral Teds and the Cardiff Sheephunters are known
to have modelled themselves on The Double Deckers (BBC1 1973) and especially Doughnut - yes you remember.....the fat bastard that everyone
was very size-ist about. Doughnut loveable?....I nearly fell off my
video of Fox (Euston Films again 1981). The bit where the very hard son
was crying on the shoulder of the very hard dad, the dogs or what?
However unlike Deckers, Splits and The Robinsons 'Fox" had some really
over the top pre-cencorship vio. Big Fuck off rows in pubs and gyms, on
pavements and tables. Perhaps a bit too much of yer Cocker-nee fackin'
'ell nobwash but all the same nay bad.
On the vio front perhaps it's best to look in a celluloid direczione.
Scarface (Brian de Palma 1981) and the original Al Capone 30's flick
are both pretty cheeky on the deaths. Let us not forget the bathroom-
and-chainsaw-to-the-head scene in Al Pacino's remake. Then again for
a really down-on-yer-lucksome gang try Scum. Out on 'sell through'
video as we speak (why 'sell through' you barsts?) this luckless film
says more about growing up young and male in the UK than anything
else I know - as Tim Westwood would say if he were at one with the
animal kingdom....'respect is gnu'.
Old timers out there will remember The Lavender Hill Mob (1951) and
The Ladykillers (1955). A real set of rascals in both, with Fat Alec
Guiness getting sponds from both paychecks. Both expert comedies with
an almost painfull sense of naivitee, plenty of 'Gawd Luv Yuz' and good

plot. The Ladykillers showed out a real brat pack of British comedy.
Frankie Howard, Kenneth Conner, Guiness, Herbert Lom and Peter Sellers
were all on top form, a kind of feature length black and white
Minder'.
Talking of Minders, as we were, one would have been handy standing near
Frankie Warren on the night of his enforced body perferation. No doubt
when the whole Marsh/Warren thing has blown over they'll be pulling out
a few tired script writers and doing a film version. What money on,
Dill The Dog as Terry Marsh and a bamel of lard as cuddly Frankie
Warren.
Perhaps it's true that gangs aren't really cuddly, that real gangs cause
so much antagonism that any redeeming qualities we might give them
('loveable rogues' etc) become meaningless. Certainly we've seen a
London gang situation insired by Charlie and it's economic power
increase in importance in the past months. But in the world of low
level violence there is always going to be someone harder, someone more
disturbed, someone with a bigger firm at the right time. On the level
that we all live, gangs are nothing. They only effect those who choose
to participate and as far as living your life by them and actually
profiting from them.... Well, do you know any chaps who haven't been
fucked by it at one time or another? Think for yourself - believe in
cause and effect - cuz if don't you'll cause it and the effect will be
right on your fucking head.....promise. That's life.

TOP BOWL'S

Great walks of the eighties. Along side fashion and music, the way you walk has always been a way of telling quite alot about a person. A footie bod in Comme De Garcon whistle, still walks like a bod - whilst a Wet Fish in trainers is still most certainly a Wet Fish. Here's a quick glance at some of the more pottier walks of our time.

No 1 - THE HANDCUFF STRUTT

This started around 1981 and involved clasping your hands behind you back, as if handcuffed, and strutting about with your head held back at a 45 degree angle, which prevented the fringe of your wedge from obscuring your vision. Scallys everywhere could be seen in their wooly gloves, jockey jackets, ski jumpers and legwarmers all walking in this style. However when Brummys started doing it, it really became a joke.

No 2 - THE BORSTAL PENGUIN (also known as the D.C.swagger)

This took over in Liverpool as the handcuff strut faded out, around 1983. The new walk took off as car swipers fresh out of D.C. couldn't get to grips with civvy swaggers. The drill marching so beloved of Her Magesty's penal institutions, forced these crew-cutted, cord-jacketed, bovril-blowing nutters to swing their arms out alarmingly. Not only that but they also wobbled from side to side like deranged, hardknock penguins, (only they didn't have bits of grass growing out of their ears or talk like Johnny Morris).

No 3 - THE POLIO LIMP

This was more of a Manchester based gait which entailed walking as if one of your legs had severe gangrene. In 1984 wearers of 22inch flares and golf jackets (beige and tartan lined) were all perfecting a decent convincingly realistic limp in shop windows across the North-West However, souped-up wheelchairs soon became trendy and limps were regarded as half-arsed.

No 4 - THE RAINMAN TWITCH

This particular walk is fairly new and is a direct result of the footy/clubbing crossover. Long-haired kicker louts and shadey, short back 'n' sides merchants can be spotted outside Anfield, Old Trafford and Highbury, coming down from last night's bash. Their legs don't stay still for longer than 3 seconds, their eyes don't focus on anything and they shiver and sneeze into their circus tent sized sweatshirts.

No 5 - THE SOHO SLOG

A mince rather than a bowl or strutt, this walk was usually practice between the Soho Braz and the Wag around '82-85'. At chucking out time bottles of Grolsch would be discarded and the bright young things of Soho charge down Old Compton Street en masse, many a mincer never made it, falling fowl of drunken sweaties, an pre-acid house footie fans.

No 6 - THE LONDON BOWL

Perfected in the early eighties by gangs of South and North London dressers" pouring of the 125, this larger than life walk usually consisted of clapping your hands wildly in front of you shouting E-I-E", "War,War,War", and other pleasantries at the startled natives. This London based bowl spread like wild-fire to country Hamlets like Portsmouth and Bristol although the pretend - cockneys never really got it right, usually falling over their moody extra large trainees. (This walk was usually accompanied by the shout of "Oi, d'ya want some fruit with that bowl)".

IBIZA JUNE 3 - 17

DJs

DANNY RAMPLING · ANDY WEATHERALL · PAUL OAKENFOLD · TERRY FARLEY · MIKE PICKERING (HACIENDA) · DEAN THATCHER · PHIL PERRY · STEVE LEE · KEVIN HURRY · STEVE BICKNELL · JOHNNIE WALKER · BEN & ANDY · ROCKY & DIESEL · CRAIG WALSH · BOB JONES · HARVEY · SCOTT JAMES · ORD MIEKLE (GLASGOW) · GARY ALLEN (LIVERPOOL) · TONY ROSS (MANCHESTER) · GLEN GUNNER   + LIVE PA'S

CLUBS

KU (3 NIGHTS) · **SUMMUM** (3 NIGHTS) · **ES PARADIS** (3 NIGHTS) · **PACHA** (1 NIGHT) · **AMNISIA** (1 NIGHT) · **IBIZA 92 CONCERT** AT **KU** (LIVE ACTS TO BE CONFIRMED)

HOLIDAY DETAILS

1 WEEK **£199** (3-10 JUNE/10-17 JUNE)

2 WEEKS **£230 - £240** (APARTMENTS)

2 WEEKS **£269 - £299** (LUXURY VILLAS)*

£50 DEPOSIT + 2 PHOTOS REQUIRED TO ENSUR HOLIDAY — ACCESS/BARCLAYCARD ACCEPTE THROUGH TRAVEL AGENT · PHONE STEVE 876 111

*BASED ON 4-6 PEOPLE SHARING PRIVATE GARDEN SWIMMING POOL

HOLIDAY INCLUDES..

ACCOMMODATION · FLIGHTS · COACH (TO & FRO IBIZA AIRPORT) · CLUB PASS (FREE GUARANTEE ADMISSION TO ALL CLUB NIGHTS LISTED

ALL CLUBS & DJS HAVE BEEN BOOKED AND CONFIRMED FOR THIS HOLIDAY
ALL ACCOMMODATION HAS BEEN CAREFULLY VETTED
FOR FURTHER INFORMATION PHONE **CHARLIE** ON 01 845 1695/0344 860778
OR WRITE TO **NIGHTLIFE** · 89 DALCROSS · CROWNWOOD · BRACKNELL · BERKS RG12 1JU

GIVE US A LINE (OO-ER!)

Dear Boy's Own,

I am writing with reference to the article "Take some time out" in the last issue.

Steve "Jobsworth" Hall points a pretty picture of the Mountain-bike re-distribution system in W10 Well let me tell you it's not all coffees and spliffs. Getting a brand new Muddy Fox was a "result" I thought. Someone had bent over to do up their laces and two hours later the bike was mine.

Only now do I realise these things have a nasty habit of coming back. Around six months on I am riding home along the canal, in the dark, with no worries and a headful of tunes, when suddenly this bush started shouting "Muddy fox coming through." "Strange" I thought then noticing 4 posse boys in front of me, and looking back the talking bush revealed another 2. I carried on thinking nothing's going to happen," 2 years of mind-benders had left me totally un-prepared for this. Before I know it I am shown a ratchet, which more than sways the decision to part with the bike!

There I stood "bikeless and gutted," easy come, easy go maybe but it bought it home how that unfortunate, unsuspecting charec-ter, who bent over to do up his laces must have felt, when his bike first entered the re-dist ribution system.

I only hope the system continues and hopefully by now they will be without wheels.

                    Billy The Bikeless
                    Ealing London

Since the late 70's the training shoe has been the standard footwear of the chaps. The fashion standing of a town fell or shined on what was being worn by who and when. Nowdays all manner of bods are on the trainee bandwagon - sloanes (wet-fish to you) ragas, hoolies even plod. Here's the Boys Own guide to the good, sad and the ugly of the training shoe.

THE BEST
1. Adidas Munchen - First robbed in Switzerland (Circa'82).
2. Diadora Borg Elite - A kangaroo skin classic.
3. Puma Minotti - A scouse fave from '79.
4. Hi-tech Squash - The South of the river footwear.
5. Adidas Samba - Much sought after amongst the retro-casual fraternity.

THE SNIDE
1. Travelfox - Worn by Tarquin Posh Fackers all over London (see Sub-teranian club for reference).
2. Adidas Kick - Still worn by Brookie' Barry Grant (say no more).
3. Troop - Anything on this Jeckyle label is a nuisance.
4. Puma-sad - As worn by Quentin "Housemartin" Cook - Big on the fror line in Brighton.
5. Converse-Hightops - Big bad and sad, only for non-trainee wearers.

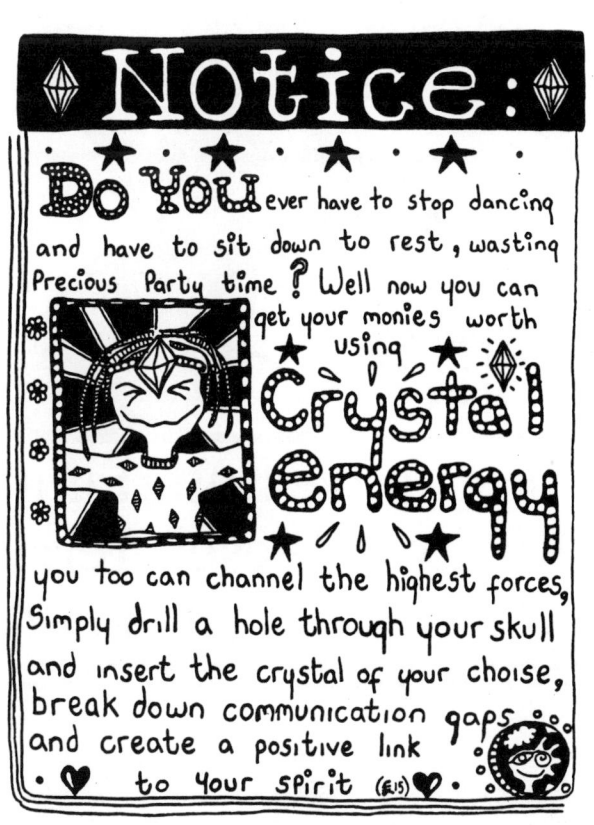

Notice: DO YOU ever have to stop dancing and have to sit down to rest, wasting precious party time? Well now you can get your monies worth using Crystal energy you too can channel the highest forces, Simply drill a hole through your skull and insert the crystal of your choise, break down communication gaps and create a positive link to your spirit (EIS)

The Yellow Book

The Rock Garden, Covent Garden.

From Friday 20th April 1990

Alternative Entertainment 8.00 till 10.30
Rocky & Diesel Terry Farley plus guests
10.30 till 3.30

Price
£8
Net

<u>Five good reasons why it may be preferable to just go out and get drunk
instead of spending a large part of the weekend in a chemically altered
state!</u>

1. Money

Pounds, Dollars, Roubles, Yen, Zlotys. A pint of Holsten Export will
set you back approx 1.50, you do not need a degree in pure mat,
to deduce that this is Ten Times cheaper than one dose of your favourite
club-time pick-me-up. Twenty quid well spent at a suitable hostelry,
with the right company, buys you a night of good companionship, ribald
humour and unrivalled Political Commentary. With enough change left
over to purchase a revered Greek delicacy of your choice (kebab).

2. Work

Suddenly finding yourself at 8.30am Monday morning, perched 60ft atop a
builders scaffold (*) with a still slightly expanded conciousness and
no-one to share your recently fractured perception of the world with,
is a bummer.
If your hung over, Monday morning we'll see you sitting in a tea hut(**)
with half a dozen or so like minded Smirnoff casualtys holding your head
in your hands and ruminating sadly on the weekend events. You will
suffer together - you will survive.
*NB- If you work in an office substitute with (*) Xerox machine and
(**) canteen.

3. Parents

If you are particually unlucky enough to bump into your mum and dad the
morning after a rather "good" night, sunken eyes, askew face and
generally frayed demean - all can be explained by saying "I must of had
a couple of beers too many." Your dad will express outward disaproval
but is inwardly thinking "That's my boy," your mum will be "concerned"
rather than "suicidal".

4. Food

No matter what you have been doing to yourself the night before, a good
English breakfast is NEVER, NEVER a wise idea. However come 4pm and a
trip to the local "Pizzaland" is probably looking more likely. If you
consumed a crate of continental lagers, cider, cheap red wine and
assorted spirits the night before, then a baked potato is going to put
your world to righ   till
the wee hours" then anything you eat will taste like earwax and have
the texture of a cotton wool pleat. No contest.

5. Concience

By way of conclusion it may be worth nothing that drinking rarely has
much to offer in the "Head fuck" dept. After a weekends boozing you are
much less likely to experience moments of maudlin and desperate self-
analysis than you are with "other" stimulants.
I would just like to point out however, that there are other constructive and meaningful ways to spend your time. That dosen't involve
doing anything to excess. Look out for a future article entitled "Model
railways for the dedicated enthusiast." Peace I'm outta here.......

LETTERS-VOICES OF REASON

Dear Boy's Own,

I don't want to be seen as just another whinger but someone has to do something before it's too late.

Back in the old days everything was amazing. We had new clubs, new DJ's, radically different music, new mags, new people.

Now it's all turning shit right in front of us and nobody is doing fuck all to stop it.

All the clubs are the same. The DJ's are all either "names" to pull a crowd or the club runners mates, the "first one down the import shop."

Mentality has returned and you bump into the same bloody people wherever you go. In short, no fucker is making an effort anymore.

What is needed is fresh blood, some new DJ's, loads of new faces and alot more effort or it's all over. While your at it, it wouldn't be a bad idea to clear out some of the dead-wood, the dickheads who go to clubs to sell a few onces and a bag of E, we don't need 'em they are just fucking parasites bleeding the scene dry.

It's up to you lot with the power and influence to kick this all off, otherwise nothing will change.

Do yourselves a favour, look outside Labroke Grove for a change, there's plenty of writers and DJ's who know the apple outside the W10 postal district.

I should imagine that this letter has pissed you off no end but someone had to tell you. Just cos you lot at the centre of attention are all a bit famous and are on a nice little earner it dosen't mean everything's rosey.

By the way, I'm not going to sign this (just in case) but you all know me and I'm not the only one who's got the 'ump, ask around, you could be shocked.

ANONY - LONDON

ED - Instead of telling us, why not do your own club! We know Boy's Own isn't the be-all in club world and evrything is far from perfect in our garden, but at least we get off our arse, try it yourself........

Dear Boy's Own

Heard it before how we are taking a big step from the Design con-cience 80's into the caring 90's. From hi-tech design to designer drugs. Exit the decade in which a large chunk of your youthful mem-ories are held. So here we are young adults with a whole fresh decade to play with.

Even though the first summer of love was over 20 years ago when most of us were mere toddlers or a wink across a dancefloor, while the folks twisted in their purple mohair and satin stiletoes.

But what does the nutty nineties have in store for us?
Here we are a generation of Born Again Bohemians, (never trust a hippy) who'd like to be gween and well into peace love and harmony. So how did we get to the stage when 20yrs after Woodstock, (U.S.A. not M25) we ran around in sunset colours comfortable if not slightly bulky footwear and lots of long hair. The headbands can stay in the 60's along with the stiletoes thank-you.

Well with a little help from
our friends Sid and Ernie,
Purple Popeyes, Yellow jokers,
Pink Bernard Mannings.
How many are you on Matey?

So there we all were wandering
around with Kalediscope eyes and
horizontal jaws, ahhh didn't we
look fine. All lovely mind expanding stuff, but how are your
brain cells? Not to mention
your spinal fluids - or lack of.
For the most still in tact but a
few unfortunate ones wibbled
along the way.

Here enters a decade in which
it's time to grow up. Me? No,
never, I'm Peter Pan. Watch out
for those Crocs. As we take on
responsibilities both heavy duty
and rewarding. Time to take it
easy, dream of Jet Pacs and a
mode of transport.

But we don't want to be responsible
for our chums in wheelchairs or
horror of horrors babies being born
with deficiencies due to our self-
indulgence. E babies, perish the
thought, who knows though because
anything and everything is possible.
Watch out boys you might be dealing
with your potency as well! Not that
this is very likely, as we are a
sound and level headed generation.

Why not try the ozone friendly theory on ourselves. Ease off the old
chemicals and expand that expanded
mind. It's up to our generation to
save this planet that we play on.
Not much of a challenge when Sains-
burys does most of it for us. The
challenge for us lot of wild, weird,
wacky humans is not to take the
Accident and Emergency option.

Sarah Barker
London S.W.15

Dear Boy's Own,

It seems to be the thing to do to
slag off "Charlie casuals" at the
moment - and why not? - most of
the thugs ask for it.

But something else springs to
mind that also slows down our
scene at the moment.

Your favourite DJ has spent all
week preparing a killer set to
blow us all away. He finds new
(or old) tunes that are different,
danceable and even some have
lyrics to listen to. He chooses
his timing with precission - it's
a "doo" we've all been looking
forward to and talking about for
weeks.

So when the moment arrives for
those records to work their magic
on the floor-there is only a half-
hearted response.

Why? - because most of all the top
bods on the scene are sitting in a
semi-circle, on stairs, on the floor
in the bog, in the kitchen, behind
the bar, in the guvnor's office....
Wherever - passing the 35th joint
that hour.

Now far be it from me to slag off a
good smoke - we all love it. BUT,
why not get into it round your
mate's flat after the "doo" is over?
There's always one 'session somewhere!

I present these as personal opinions
and you're right in thinking, people
can do whatever the fuck they like
in clubs, but don't all moan about
the atmosphere not being what it was.
It's you, us that create that feeling that "buzz" (sic).

Sitting down all night does not
create a buzz, (apart from a selfish
one in your own mind).

Get dancing - support your DJ's. I
believe they're playing better, more

varied records now, than ever.

The best is yet to come!

Richard Elliot.
Middx.

THE LAND OF OZ
RETURNS

EVERY MONDAY
FOUR ROOMS OF DANCING
D.J.s
PAUL OAKENFOLD + ALFREDO

NANCY NOISE + TONY WILSON

JOEY JAY + LEPKE

THE ORB + CARLOS
AND HIS LANTERNA MAJICA

+ GUEST D.J'S + P.A.S EVERY WEEK
MEMBERS ONLY CLUB – 10 TILL 3:30
MEMBERSHIP ENQUIRIES ON 01-267 8885
ADMISSION £8.00

BOYS OWN: 249-251 KENSAL Rd. London. W10
Contributions: STEVE HAUGH, KEVIN SAMPSON, TERRY,
PHIL "FLARES" THORNTON, FLEUR, SIR LES, Audrey Witherspoon,
Adam PorTER: PHOTOS: PHIL PAIN....

THANKS to: New BOYS OWN bod 'SPROCKET', BARRY
MOONCULT, CHIPS, BILLY, NORMAN JAY, BLANE and CLAIRE,
STEVE and DALE, PeTER HOOTON and DE FARM, SUGGS,
PLUG, Pete "I'M 32 and ME RECORDS CRAP" WYLIE,
GREG and JUSTIN (OOH Spicey), FOXHEAD BARRAT,
SOLARIS BOYS, STAN, SPENCE, BARRY, STEVE,
SMithers and ROWLES (Very big DOWN UNDER), Nick COX,
JOHNNY O', OAKEY COKEY, PHIL and Tosh (THANKS for the BreakBEaTS)
TWO KeVs and ONE Ricky on GUARANA...

and NoT FORGETTING
Rocky's Mate CLIVE,
DesMond, Paul McKEE,
ROckA, Stevie Lee,
SPARKS, MUGSY
and R.H. Weather ALL
the Rockin'
COMPANY director!
and JoSEPH's DAD GARY.

BOYS OWN,
a buttock
clenching Read!

SCARED STIFF

The GIRLS — LURVe and X's to
SUE and E.T, GLORIA, EMMA, JACKIE, HANNAH,
LindA, MIFFY, MandY CREWCUTS, Sue, JANE and DEBBIE,
CATHY, TONSEY, SARA, NANCY NOISE and JEAN,
VANESSA, CAROLYNE and LUCY...

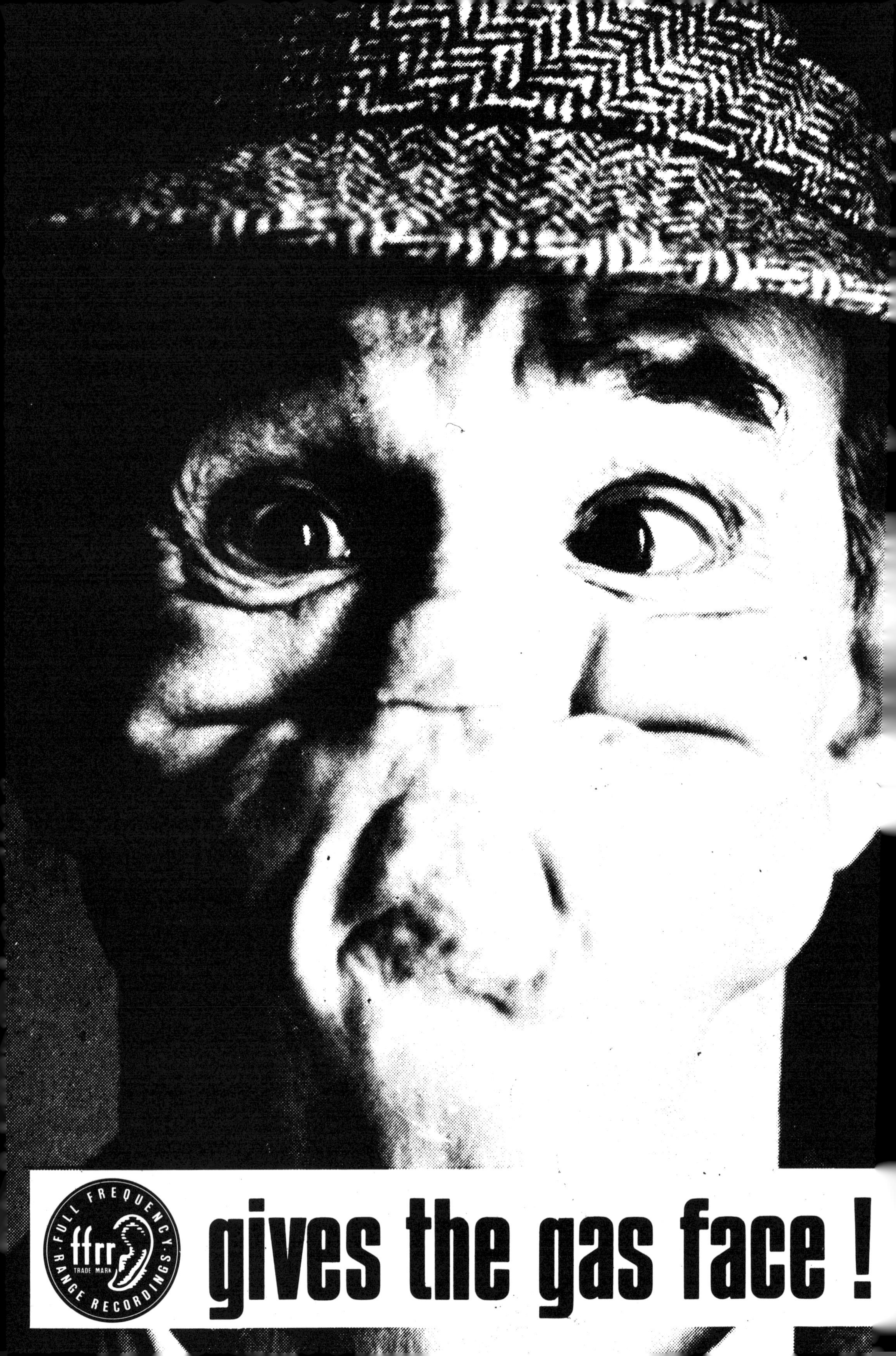

gives the gas face !

No. 10
Autumn 1990

BOYS OWN

AUTUMN REVIEW

MORNIN' CAMPERS,

and WELCOME to the outsiders HELPFUL
HoLiDAY Hints (part one in a SERIES of SOME MORE)
LOCATiON one ... THAiLAND ...

TO RECREATE tHAT MAGiC AtMOSPHERE DESCRiBed
iN the RECENT I.D. ARTiCLE ON the NEW 'RAVERS PARADise'
FoLLow these SiMPLE steps ...

1. TURN UP YOUR CENTRaL HeatiNG AS HiGH as it WiLL GO ...

2. ORdER SoME COCKROACHES oR SiMiLAR EXOTiC
   iNSECT LiFe FROM the LoCAL PeT EMPORiuM ...
   and LeT THEM LOOSE ARound YoUR HOUSE

3. iNViTE SOME PASSiNG PuKKA PURPLE PeoPLe
   iNTO YOUR ABOdE and ALLOW THEM to PLAY THEiR
   FAVOURiTE 'SUNRISE F.M' TAPES EXTREMELY LOUD
   ALL NiGHT and ALL DAY.

   est VOiLA the THAiLAND 'FRENZY' EXPERiENCE
   at a FRACTiON OF the COST and AVOiDiNG
   DiVVY GiRLS FROM the MiDLANDS and their pals in
   the FiRiNG SQUAd.

   NEXT TiME How to CONVert YoUR LOFT iNTo A
   ScaLed DOWN RePLiCA OF GOA USiNG ONLY
   2 U.V. LAMPS, SOME STRAW and A BaR OF LAXATiVE CHOCOLATE.

   And NOW some pop MUSiC NEWS : FORGET aLL THiS
   DiSCO NONSENSE and GO PURCHASE The FoLLowiNG
   GRAMAPHONE RECORdS. The NEW LP by 'PoWER OF DREAMS',
   'RiSiNG STAR' by NORTHSiDE, The EXTREMELY LoUd 'LARd' L.P,
   'BLACK SHEETS OF RAiN' by BoB MOULD, and Re-DiSCOVER
   YER OLD 10,000 MANiACS RECORdS ...

P.S. ANYONE OVER THE AGE OF 13 owniNG OR RidiNG
   a SkateBoard is extremeLY CHURLiSH !
                         LOVE ... The OUTSiDER x —

CLUB GANGS NO. 1. .....SPICE..... MANCHESTER'S FINEST BACK ON SUNDAYS, PURE BALEARIC FOR THE HAPPY OF HEARING. DJ'S JUSTIN ROBERTSON AND GREG FENTON.

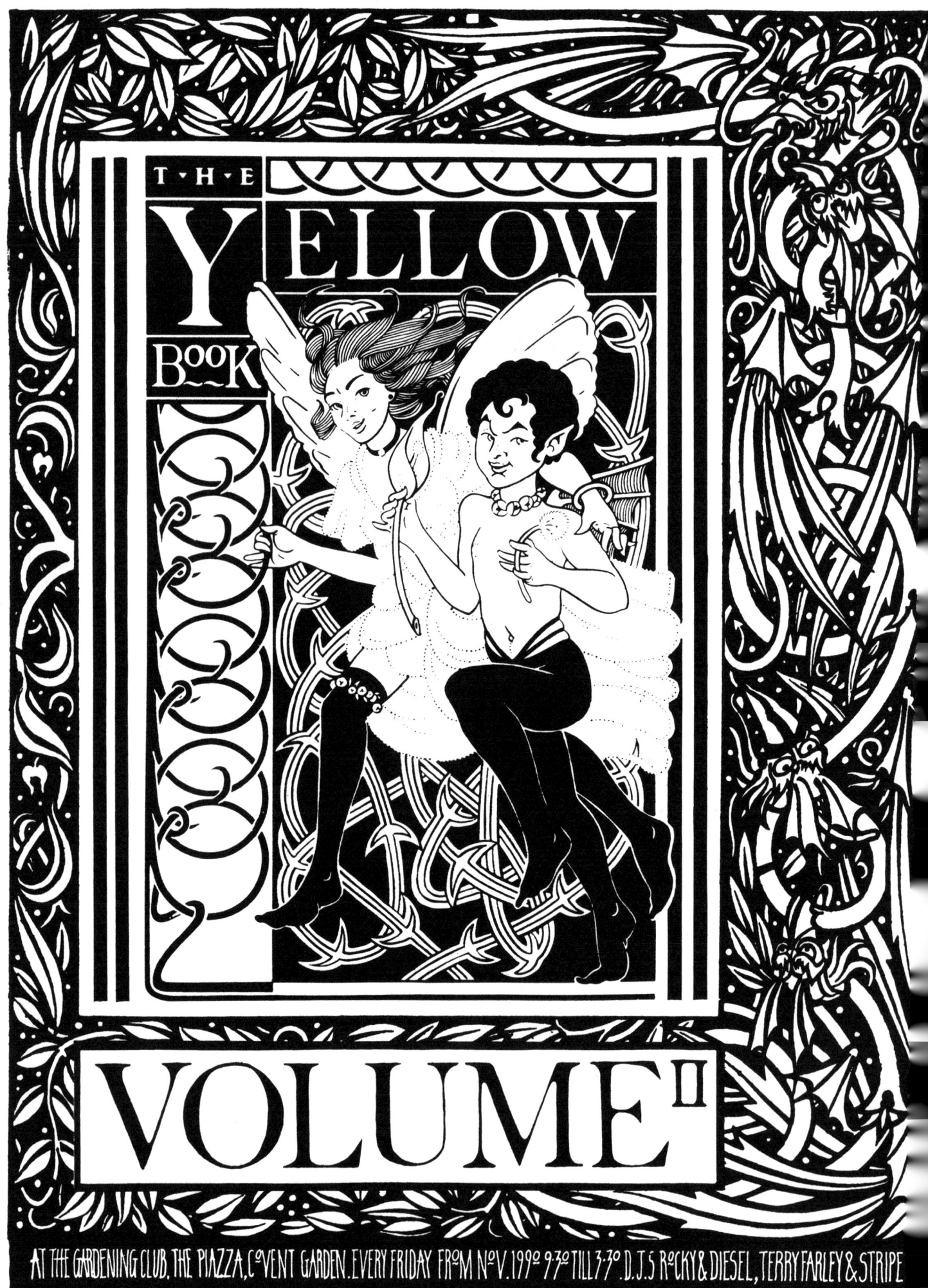

THE **YELLOW** BOOK

VOLUME II

AT THE GARDENING CLUB, THE PIAZZA, COVENT GARDEN. EVERY FRIDAY FROM NOV. 1990 9·30 TILL 3·30 D.J.S ROCKY & DIESEL, TERRY FARLEY & STRIPE

STAND UP FOR YOUR 'LOVE' RIGHTS

"A holiday home for you and the missus, two weeks August for the rest of your natural. A grand deposit the rest easy instalments..." Just the sort of line you're likely to hear echoing around the bars and cafe's along the Costa Brava all summer long. But would you believe a timeshare shark?

"Honest pal, the mileage is that low 'cause the last owner was a vicar. Only took it out on Sundays". Another bog standard claim from one of the fellows from the forecourt, would you fall for that one? I think not.

"Their blinding capsules, from Goa. I broke one open and did half with a mate", I was screaming. Hook, line and sinker I've swallowed it, not a second thought. I've cleaned out my wallet, tapped a mate for a tenner and bought four!

Why on earth do I do it? Time and time again I fall for the worst sales pitch this side of Wembley market. Whether it's 'brown ones' from Liverpool, 'burgers' from Brighton or the legendary 'white ones' with doves on the back, I just can't seem to stop myself forking out for gear that I suspect to be nothing more than salt tablets. On the countless occasions I've been let down by my chosen brand, I have told myself never again will I be foolish enough to give my hard earnt dosh to a moody looking geezer dishing out stuff in the darkest corner of a smelly nightclub. But I do, so do my friends and so do complete strangers who ask me where I got mine from.
To some of you out there buying from strangers may sound risky, but they usually come with some-one's seal of approval and besides how many times have we all been let down buying gear from friends?

The quality of gear being pushed upon us at the moment seems to have reached an all time low. I know some people have grown somewhat immune to the effects of MDMA and a degree of tolereance may have built up but I think the real reason the "rush" isn't there anymore is more to do with the chemical composition of the drug than our bodies new abilities to absorb it. How many times whilst buying off some-one you know do phrases like "they're good for a top-up" or "you need a couple" seem to crop up in the transaction? Let's face it, what they're saying is these E's are shit and that's why they're on special offer at fifteen pounds.

For far too long we've accepted all sorts of things masquerading as ecstacy, we've swallowed them, sucked them and snorted them but most of the time just puked them straight back up! We've
taken LSD disguised as E and spent the next day unable to work and talking to the toast rack, we've taken speed disguised as E and sat around talking the biggest load of drivel this side of "Call my Bluff!" There's even tales of people buying sleeping tablets disguised as E at the bar of Pacha then promptly nodding off in their gin and tonics. (God bless you Nicky Holloway). All this isn't good enough and something has got to be done about it now!

The time has surely come to rise up against the evil drug barons and cast them out from amongst us. The time is right for someone to stand up for the poor consumer in his fight against trippy E's and chalkdust. The time is here for the Roger Cook of the acid house scene to reveal themself to us all and lead us in a crusade against permed centre partings, baseball caps and hippies that take their scruffy dogs in nightclubs!

The fight need not end at dodgy drug dealers; all aspects of the club scene could be investigated. Just as Esther and the "That's Life" crew exposed the perverted headmaster at some overpriced public school, there must be a wealth of warped clubrunners out there waiting to be shown in their true colours. A free drink here, a name on the guest list there, who knows the price young, innocent, unsuspecting punters are paying? Who knows how many lives have been ruined in Soho basements, fields in Hampshire and converted warehouses in Manchester? There are so many questions to be answered before any of us step inside these sleezy pleasure palaces again...

Who questions the girl on the till that never has change of a tenner and never finds you later as promised? Why is your jacket always on the floor in the cloakroom? Why are the toilets always overflowing? Then there are the deeper darker questions that are only spoken of in whispers. What goes on in the VIP lounge and why is Dirtbox Phil always involved? Why can girls under 18 and in lycra walk to the front of the queue at Yellow Book? And why is Terry Farley DJ'ing at a rubber club?

We've almost had a Clubbers political movement before, of course, with the Freedom To Party mob, but this time we can do it properly. An underground network of clubs and fanzines already exists. We could even start by lobbying Parliament to extend the Consummer Protection Act to cover shit drugs and Acid house raves. Think of it, cases going to the small claims courts because the parcel you bought was light or the promoter promised 40k turbo power but you only got 25k. Get this going and there could be car stickers, t-shirts, World In Action exclusives, even questions in the House. Imagine: "Can the honourable member for Putney East please explain why a Mr.Tommy Mack, Acid House promoter, is opening a nursery school in Bracknell?"
Or: "Parliament believes the reason everyone wears a hat at the Brain is that they're all under cover Iraqis".

The reason I've ranted on in this way is to try and stir someone into action. We need a Leader, a Spokesperson, a Voice and we need him now. Right now, we're at a crossroads with one way leading to good times, true friendships and value for money and the other way to something like the Energy Docklands All Dayer. A few years back I could have been the man for the job but after a serious badminton injury and a bout of worms I've been left unable to give it a hundred per cent.

So for the sake of all of us who suffer in silence at the hands of cads, rotters and bounders, some-one please speak up now and lead us forward long into this new decade.

"Ive got big brown ones from Bermondsey, Pink ones from Peckham, Capsuals from Clapham, Love Doves from Hayes, Speedy crap from the Dam, C'mon swop you for your Dairylea.....
...Remember kids, it aint big and it aint clever.
Say no to crap cheese...

CLUB GANGS NO. 2. .....PURE SEXY..... LONDON'S BEST NIGHT OUT, EXPECT TO SWEAT AND SMILE.
DJ DANNY RAMPLING AND FRIENDS.

THE BOY'S OWN AUTUMN CHART.

CHUNKY TUNES TO MAKE YOU GO OOOH!

EVE GALLAGHER	LOVE COME DOWN.
LESS STRESS	DON'T DREAM ITS OVER.
SOUND OF SHOOM	I HATE HATE.
ACTION A.J.	ACTION.
JOEY WASHINGTON	WERE ON THE MOVE.
FRANK K	EVERYBODY LETS SOMEBODY LOVE.
DYNAMIC TWO	DONT LET LIFE GET YOU DOWN.
DEEP JOY	FALL.
PARADISO	HERE WE GO AGAIN.
CRAZY EDDIE	NENA DE IBIZA.
LENNY WILLIAMS	GOTTA LOTTA LOVE.
LUPO	KEEP IT UP.
PLEASURE INC	SEXY DANCER.
SHARON REDD	BEAT THE STREET (REMIX).
OFFSHORE	I CANT TAKE THE POWER.
ST. ETIENNE	KISS AND MAKE UP (REMIX).
ARTHUR MILES	HELPING HANDS.
SHOCK FEAT EQMC	NEVER TOO LATE.
JAH WOBBLE	BOMBA.
RIO RHYTHM BAND	CARNIVAL DE CASA.
RAW SEX	SUCK IT DEEP.
NOMAD	DEVOTION.
KING FOR A DAY	KICK THAT RHYTHM.
FLUKE	PHILLY.
CE CE ROGERS	JOIN HANDS.
JOE SKI LOVE	I KNOW SHE LIKES JOE.
NITRO	ROCK SKOOL.
KORTEZ	PUT YOUR BODY ON (REMIX).
BE BIG	THATS WHEN ITS GOLD.
BACK TO HOUSE 2	FEEL THE SUNSHINE.
BETTER DAYS	LOVE IS THE MESSAGE. (REMIX).
CARTOON CUTS	CULT OF BLEEP.

Geese Royal Exchange Manchester *Not* Madchester

Plus!

London Paris New York
Barcelona Tokyo Milan
Darwen Blackburn Oslo

Los Angeles Dresden
Penzance Rio De Janeiro Belgrade
Wellington Mexico City Aberdeen Calcutta
Bonn Grimsby
Lima Sydney
Giggleswick
Abergavenny
Washington DC
Warsaw Goole
Birmingham
Washington
Moscow Vancouver
Buenos Aires
Leningrad
Geneva Athens
Montevideo
Blandford Forum
Mobberley Clacton-on-sea
Osaka Santiago Crawley

Kiev Istanbul Cockermouth Reykjavik
Lagos Hamburg Mountfitchet Pontefract Jakarta
Perth San Francisco Havana Chicago Ankara Glasgow
Wick Amsterdam Billericay Caracas Philadelphia Louth
Montreal Torino Stanstead Eastbourne Winnipeg Brasilia Ullapool
Helsinki Madras Littlehampton Manila Stroud Houston Maltby
Brussels Casablanca Bagshot Cleveland Melbourne
Dungworth Saffron Walden Bogota Tangier Oswaldtwistle Cairo
St. Louis Bangkok Madrid Toronto Filey Mold
Stockholm Cardigan Nairobi Delhi
Crewe Detroit Salford

ON THE TOOLS

A Boys Own Observer Guide To The British Building Worker. (BBW)

Builders. Who? What? and Why?
Many of us will have met builders, some of us may have sat next to one on a bus or train. Lads, you may have been punched in the face by one, or girls perhaps it was a builder who screamed "Tits Out" at you this morning whilst displaying three inches of ample bum cleavage and a tattoed beer gut.
This brief but effective cut out and throw away guide tells you all you need to know about the BBW. Read on and learn!

1. Carpenters (Chippies).
Yes Mate! Complete and utter top boys on site. Smooth and suave, educated and politically sound, stylish and good to their mums etc, etc. Every other trade on site wants to be a chippie 'cos it's clean, creative and cashed. Young chippies are cheeky and lovable, old ones are wise and avuncular.

FACT: American women view carpenters as their No 1 sexual fantasy (A recent survey revealed). Basically the dogs bollocks.
WEARS: Anything that looks bloody good and workmanlike although the older boys are fond of aprons and 1/2 round specs.
READS: The Guardian - Proust, N.M.E, Brendan Behan, The Bible,   Steinbeck and very complicated building plans.
SAYINGS: "Lovely bit of Rosewood that, madam"

2. Bricklayers (Brickies).
Only serious contenders to chippies for mantle of Top Boys. May even surpass them in 'lovable' stakes. Energetic and volatile nature means that they are good fellows to have around when it "goes off", but not when trying to watch Luis Bunel's top Mexican surrealist epic 'L'Angel Extermidor' on Channel Four after a curry. Could substitute any arty film here.
WEARS: Unsubtle combo of high leg docs and tight tracksuit bottoms. Often reveals a 'Morning Glory' in newsagents at 7.30 am. No points here.
READS: The Daily Mirror - The Ring - Back of Holsten Can
SAYINGS:"Course its not a load bearing wall."

3. Plumbers ('erm plumbers).
Quiet men of site (boring), spend all their time in toilets and kitchens on their tod. Have little idea of what the outside world is really like or any personality of their own. (Bit like Prince Edward with a gas bottle - ooh satire!)
Earn stonking great wads of cash due to the fact that they can charge your gran twenty bloody quid for changing a washer!!
WEARS: Have the dubious honour of being the most likely blokes on site to wear a boiler suit.
READS: Anglers Weekly and most obituary columns.
SAYINGS: "That'll be twenty bloody quid for that tap washer please poor little old lady."

4. Electricians (Sparks).
Never get dirty, spend too much time at college, never lift anything heavy, drink lots of tea and knock off early. The sexual predilections of this trade can therefore be called into question. Name one famous electrician go on!
WEARS: Probably his best trainers 'cos they don't get dirty
READS: Ohms Law, Daily Star
SAYINGS: "I was on a thousand pound a week over at docklands"

5. Groundworkers/Labourers (Paddys).
Due to the seasonal nature of groundwork, (drains, footings, etc), Groundworkers can be divided into three categories:
A. Irishmen
B. Alcoholics
C. Both!
Consumption of alcohol amongst this group of lads is legendary. About April/May every year, they all get big tax rebates and the sites close down. Work will not start again until all the money has been right royally (and religously) pissed up the wall. They will also buy a new pair of boots about this time.
WEARS: Stunning ensemble of three piece 1974 Burtons chalk stripe suit, maroon bobble hat, string vest and wellies. Donkey jacket if cold.
READS: Sporting Life and the back of Jameson whiskey bottles.
SAYINGS: "It's just medicinal, y'understand."

6. Plasterers (Spreads)

Quite simply, the devil scum dogs of the site. Harry Enfield's "Loadsamoney" was a frighteningly accurate pastiche of today's plasterer. Sexist, Racist, Homophobic, violent, psycopathic, anti-socialism, boorish, loutish, vulgar and crude. The average plasterer (and there are exceptions to every rule lads!), will verbally abuse everyone that does not fit his perception of how everyone should be. So that's everyone but himself, if you see what I mean.

WEARS: Tacky, wacky, Wicked Willy t-shirts or Union Jack "These colours don't run" pro-violence sweatshirts. Sergio Tachinni track trousers and karate slippers. The whole lot is then (mercifully) covered in bonding.

READS: The Sun, The Sport, pornography, the Test card.

SAYINGS: "Look at the jugs" etc etc. "There ain't no black in the Union Jack." "Who you screwin' up?" etc etc.

So there you have it, kids. An all too brief and innaccurate journey through the minds and hearts of a basic but vital section of Britain's working class. If you are a builder and you feel that your trade has been misrepresented in this article or you were disappointed by the non-appearance of your trade in this piece, please write and tell us as we have run out of toilet paper!!

UPPERS (ITS REAM)

LOYALTY AND LAUGHTER...

BEING "IN THE PINK"...

CHOCCY MILK AND BRANDY...

FRUIT BATS CALLED KEVIN...

WINTER HOLS IN SELSEY BILL...

KER PLUNK TOURNAMENTS...

AUNTIES THAT LOOK LIKE
BARBARA WINDSOR...

D.J. RODNEY TROTTER:
(SWEET, AL)

ROOFTOP PROTESTS AT
THE LOCAL INFANT SCHOOL...

APRICOT TURNOVERS...

SHOUTING "LOOK OUT SOAP'S
ABOUT" AT HIPPIES...

JOHNNY ROCKA SINGING "MIDNIGHT
COWBOY"...

HAVING YOUR EAR WAX REMOVED...

TELLING EVERYONE YOUR GRANDAD
WAS IN THE INTERNATIONAL BRIGADE.

DE NIRO, PESCI AND SCORSCESE
"THE GOOD FELLOWS"...

PAUL SMITH SUEDE BROGUES AND
C.P. DUFFLE COATS...

FRIENDS, LOVERS AND FAMILY...

DOWNERS (ITS SHIT)

SADAMSKIS BARMY IRAQ ARMY...

TELLING EVERYONE YOU ONLY GOT SKY FOR
THE SIMPSONS (TORY FIB)...

GLASTONBURY - SOAP DODGERS, SCRATCHERS
AND PEOPLE WITH SCRAWNY MUTS...

THAT FAT GINGER NOB ON GRANGE HILL...

YOUR TORTOISE BEING KIDNAPPED BY GIPPO
KIDS...

OLD TEDS BECOMING NEW MODS...

CILLA BLACK FINDING YOUR LONG LOST
COUSIN ERIC IN AUSTRALIA...

PRE-MED TABLETS (OO-ER I'M IN TROUBLE)

OLD SKOOL - OLD HAT...

CHARLIE CHESTER IN PAM HOGG LEGGINGS...

TRENDY SHOPS THAT STILL SELL ZULU
PENDANTS (SCUM, VIVA A.N.C.)...

WINTER HOLS IN THAILAND (A.K.A.
SOUTH LONDON GOES MAD ON ELEPHANTS)...

ROCKY ON STAGE WITH DE FARM (2 YEARS
TO GET A REPUTATION, 2 MINUTES TO LOSE IT)...

BLAMING BAD FARTS ON YER MUM...

TOP GEAR IN IBIZA WHEN YOUR IN AMSTERDAM.

KISS F.M. THINKING SWING-BEAT AND RAP IS RADICAL.

MISSING AIRSTREAM AT THE KU BUT CATCHING A COL
MANC'.

CLUB GANGS NO. 3. .....HIGH ON HOPE..... LONDON'S ORIGINAL GARAGE NIGHT, A SOUL OASIS. DJ'S NORMAN JAY AND RICKY.

PURVEYORS OF BESPOKE STEREOPHONIC VINYL

FLYING

FLYING RECORDS
KENSINGTON MARKET • BASEMENT
KENSINGTON HIGH STREET LONDON W8
MAIL ORDER ENQ: 071 938 4407 FAX:
071 938 4409

LOVE THUGS OR PURIST MUGS.

In recent months the music press has declared a Jihad against the two great satans of the day: Indie Dance and that new tribe of infidels The Love Thugs. Suprisingly the champions of this Holy War are not, as you might expect, the Black music press or Soul men such as Jay, Jones or Searling but rather it is the White rock press and it's cohorts namely one Paolo Hewitt and a certain Quentin Cook. (Norman to you, Normski to his mates - Ed).

Now this debate has been raging for fifteen years. However whereas then the issue was whether White boys could/should play Soul, now it's whether someone should be allowed to make dance music if they've a history of wearing dodgy leather collards and bowsers and/or once swore undying allegience to a certain Mr Ian Curtis. Personally, I find the Accused guilty on both charges but would add let them make dance tracks only if of the highest order (ie; Loaded, Pacific State, etc). First we should accept the fact that a lot of people had their minds opened to dance music via the Smiley Culture (sic) of '88 and if, as a result, some White kid wants to make a dance tune, far better to sound like Primal Scream than Rick Astley. Let's face it, Liam of F.U is never going to sound like Ce Ce Rogers so maybe IT'S ON isn't such a bad compromise.

The Black v White arguments that White middle class muso jurnos such as Mr Hewitt put up are no longer relevent; Black America has gone pop and for the big buck called Swing-Beat. Black Detroit dances to L.F.O and old Depeche Mode records while New York's gone completely potty on Nelle Hooper's breakbeats. Only in the Southern states is there any real quantity of Black Soul still being made. Yet despite all this, Norman Cook is still calling for musical purity and telling us that DJ's such as Oakenfold have "never played much black music anyway."
Coming from some Brighton based posh facker who wears Jeckyle Puma trainers and did a patronising Black Muslim salute at the end of his musically pure video, that's a bit rich! Oakenfold was breaking Def Jam and early Hip Hop in this country when good old Normski was having a happy hour laugh all the way to the Indie bank, which takes us on to ..... THE LOVE THUGS.

The Love Thugs, it seems to me, are basically plain old TEDS in another guise. Paolo doesn't like the fact that clubland now has white working class kids dancing to House music, especially when they are on gear and may have gone to see a Brentford home match way back in the '70s. The House scene in all it's forms - Shoom, the Shock Sound System, Confusion and even Sunrise etc - has done more for racial understanding amongst today's younger kids than ten years of racist door policies at the Wag ever did. Back in '88 at a Clink Street RIP party, I was nearly cuddled to death by an extremely large and loved-up Black man and saw White ex-hooligans dancing in a manic style to Kid Batchelor.
   Even if it was down to drugs, if just one of these people retained the tolerance of that night, then it was worth it.

Normski and Paolo should go down to the YELLOW BOOK, a so-called Alternative Club, where the biggest whoops are for Candi Statton, or to PURE SEXY where Ce Ce Rogers is played next to Primal Scream in fine style. Who needs musical purity along a racial line when the mix is so good and rewarding?

Bob Jones once commented that at the Blackpool Real Soul
week-ender, a prominent Soul DJ told him that a Richard Rogers record had no place in the Soul room.

If these blinkered people had their way it probably wouldn't...

'rubadubdub'

EVERY THURSDAY
10.00 TILL 3.00
AT THE SOHO THEATRE CLUB
(BEHIND THE ASTORIA) W1

RUB-A-DUB DUB
3 MEN IN A CLUB
WHO DO YOU THINK THEY ARE
STEVE LEE, DARREN EMERSON
AND DON'T FORGET DOMINIC MOIR

IBIZA EVERY PICTURE TELLS A STORY

"BIG ERIC" BLAGS A SAUCY SPANISH RICH'ARD

" BRENDA " LEE AND SPROCKET DISCUSS THE MISCHIEVOUS ANTICS OF ONE PEPI (KU CLUB NUISANCE

ALL THIS WAY AND IT'S LIKE FUCKING LEIGH BRIDGE ROAD.....'' MR. RAMPLING DOESN'T LOOK HAP

IBIZA IS the above picture........

IBIZA IS NOT ......Tommy Mac and a lump of melon floating in a swimming pool claiming to have discovered Ibiza in 1945. (Which one was the lump of melon? - Ed).

IBIZA IS NOT ......Some knob shouting "Manchester forking vibe in the area." This is Europe not Hulme, Hackney or Huddersfield. Please leave your warehouse mentality back in Britain.

IBIZA IS NOT ......four hundred English clubbers on a Jnr Gaultier style 18-30 trip.

IBIZA IS NOT ......Some Ted playing K-Tel's twenty greatest acid raves around the pool all day.

IBIZA IS NOT ......Coming off your moped at forty MPH.

IBIZA IS NOT......Paying five mill for a big brown 'un and feeling like you had a result.

IBIZA IS NOT Cesare and Pepe turning your music down at the Ku.

IBIZA IS NOT ......About theorising and writing articles. So we'll shut up and go back next year with just a couple of close friends and share a spliff and a chocolate and brandy

Keeping the Faith. 1990

SUBBUTEO A KICKING GAME

The name Adolf hasn't exactly set the world alight with anticipation over the last forty five years. It's not really the name that inspires visions of children frollicing, arguing, smelling really gross and doing all the other things kids like to do. Indeed no m'lud. But back in 1947 some chap by the name of Peter Adolf who lived in Tunbridge Wells patented a game. A game all groovy kids like ourselves came to know, love and fight over. Yes, Subbuteo was invented by someone called Adolf.

Perhaps it was the enormously bad kharma of being British and having the surname Adolf in 1947 that energised his spirit and imagination to invent such a perfect table top passtime. Being as Adolf managed to invent a soccer game with such exact detail it meant that all the little extras you get round real-life soccer grounds could be added to the Subbuteo realm. The catalogue is never ending, and when you add the ingenuity and imagination of soccer crazed kids, then it's more than never-ending...it's just Subbuteo rools OK, or whatever kidspeak stretches to these days.

The best way of finding out how much Subbuteo has affected the life of Brit kids is to ask people about their memories of it. Soon they are ghosting off watery-eyed into a highly selective good-times nostalgia about how they used to have eight of their favourite team in their England side and of course that terrible dilemma over how to propel the little plastic players. You could play for hours on your own, practising free kicks, letting Chelsea win the cup again and again but when you played someone else, another human, there were always endless rucktions about who was flicking/pushing/being a twat generally.

Then there is the ball. The only thing violently out of scale with the rest of the game, titchy it wasn't. The ones that came with the game were on a scale with a transit van and the special smaller ones weren't much below a Triumph 1500. Kicking one of those in real like would have meant instant hospitalisation and they would have needed the skin of an entire herd of cows to make.

Accesories were always the key to the real oddballs. I had thirty three Chelsea players, no doubling up for me, no fank you. Then there was the TV gantry that was constantly being polaxed by the ball, the scoreboard that was more fake than a cockney Van Gogh, the fantastically useless green fence complete with adverts and the incredibly fiddly bench complete with individual 'backroom boys'. None of whom looked remotely like Eddie McCreadie much to my disappointment. However the stands were the major flop in my book. They just weren't BIG enough.

I remember collecting loads of bits of wood from school/skips/the road, in order to make the first true-to-scale replica of Chelsea's East Stand. If you've ever stood on/run on/fled from the pitch at Chelsea, you'll know that right up close that stand really is fucking tall. Mine was bigger.

I can remember it not being appreciated in the slightest by my mum - it was that big - probably due to the fact that it was prone to collapse, yet was not something anyone else was allowed to disassemble. It was huge, crap and held together precariously by sello and glue, rather like the real thing - tee hee.

One Boys Own person was telling me one fine day, about how he used to tape the Kop Choir competitions from Sportsnight with Coleman and play them back during some Subbuteo bouts. Now that was real ititiative. I also remember my mate Izzi improvising the Stretford End (for he was a youthful Cockney Red) with a variety of cardboard boxes, (I laughed at his primitive building materials) whilst I had a series of secondary stands which were used as Chelsea's North stand.

Here the schmooligan interest starts. Whenever things went wrong for Chelsea or England (virtually the same team in my case) the North stand would suddenly be found to be holding all the non-participatory players (Leeds, Man Utd, Brentford, Coventry etc) who would gradually slide onto the pitch until they encroached, at which time everything would be sumarily called off. In fact Subbuteo violence is something that has increased with age, as mentioned in 'Boys Own' #3. Indeed a renewed bout of game-on fervour only a couple of years ago had to be abandoned as increasing violence (treading, throwing etc) threatend the safety of my remaining squad members. I had to take my set back to my Mum's cupboard from whence it came.

Non-interested parties will at this point be squirming at the self-indulgent reminiscenses of the grown-up child, but I am unapoligetic. Subbuteo, (it means hobby in Latin) is a self-contained game, it's built to last, incorporates the imagination and is played by over five million people worldwide. Thirty countries have national associations and whilst that stuff that was on TV recently is a bit too serious for me, those figures mean lots of people get lots of enjoyment out of it. What's wrong with that? Go on - get it out the cupboard.

ADAM PORTER.

KNOCKING ONE OUT

It's Saturday night, Sunday mornig. Some drunken oik decides he wants to goad me into violent combat, so what does he do? Punch me? Call my mother a whore? No readers, more often than not he will call me a "tit" or a "cunt", two things I'm inordinately fond of, or he'll twist his face into a merciless pit of venom and snarl the words: "You wanker!!" Why's he so surprised then, when I shake his hand and say: "That, sir, I am"

It couldn't be less insulting. I love wanking. Ever since the discovery that if you tug your maleness up and down for long enough it will cause a mildly pleasant sensation followed by a pert burst of jism in the area, I've been addicted.

Early adolescence was a period of obsessive masturbation. Finding a new place to do it was the challenge in those days. Not a corner of the house went unfertilized - in the wardrobe, under the bed (difficult to get a good rhythm going), into the icebox in the fridge. Glorious days!

We had a room where most things used to take place - eating, playing records, watching telly. One day I was able to add juvenille ejaculation to the list. I noticed that there was a gap between the record-player and the curtains, a gap just wide enough to accomodate a small youth - so long as he removed his trousers first. I concealed myself behind the curtain and immediately set abut masturbating very, very quickley. Agreeable images of enormous-bosomed actresses raced through my fevered mind to such effect that the clarion call of orgasm was never far away. Intriguingly, I heard the front door key in the lock, a door only used by one of two persons. It was Mad Glad, my mum. A quick assessment suggested that I could get out, get my kecks on and escape out the back door just in the nick of time, but by now the very reliable combination of Barbara Windsor and Diana Dors had brought me to the brink of splashing. There was no choice. As my mother and aunty came in to sit down and have a cuppa, their youngest relative was unloading both barrells a mere 12 feet awway. Surely they could've smelt something? And if not, what were my troos doing on the floor? Half an hour I had to sit there listening to them, with crusty evostik hardening on my thighs and stomach all the time.

The next progression was to become more extreme in the choice of subject matter. Wanking material of the busty blonde/ Playboy spread calibre was no longer up to scratch. Relatives, Martians and persons from the sub-continent were regular visitors, but the real trick was to change storyline as often as possible in one bout. One youth claims to have used 154 different subjects during one brief wank. He is now one of the guitarists in a popular musical combination hailing from the Liverpool area, but journalistic ethics forbid me from naming which. If we were to say Keith from The Farm it would already be saying too much.

By now you're older, of course. You've messed about with girls, which makes the challenge of the ultimate wank even more acute. The tales relating to young men in pursuit of the self-induced superwank are nothing less than depraved. In the interests of scaring off impressionable but inexperienced "tosseurs", I feel that I must name a few game-casualties.

Let's quickly get the hospitalisations out of the way: broken hip trying to nosh himself off; vaccuum cleaner surgically removed; numerous milk-bottles, test tubes, glass and china recepticals which have burst under the pressure of anxious erections, stabbing shards of glass into the member; weirdest of all, though, has to be the yokel who contracted listeria by embedding his knob in an Edam Cheese and proceeding to shaft it enthusiastically. Ignore well-meaning advice that beating off is Safe Sex.

Then there are the orgasm-aids, little bits and pieces that help jaded tossers to get there. Liver is a recommendation that comes up time and time again. Take a substantial offcut of thinly-sliced liver in order to effect one "velvet mitten". Only the gentlest stroking action is then required to reduce participants to a state of groaning, churting ecstasy. When relieved, fry liver. Delicious. (Samson, you pervert - Ed.)

For those thrilled by a little bit of danger, even the suggestion of mild pain, the following helpful hints might lead to satisfaction. Exquisite pain can be realised by halving and coring a grapefruit to approximately one-third the girth of the penis. Pop the old man in there, push the melon towards you so that the fit is nice and snug then squeeze the fruit hard sending jets of tangy juice bursting all over your bell and up your Jap's
eye. Excruciating, but most rewarding when the inflamed member is doused in The Old Faithful, the icebox in the fridge. You have now constructed a human ice-lolly, ready for concerned lady-friends to lick and comfort.

On reflection, it would be irresponsible to commend the Dangerwank to a wide and impressionable readership, as there have been (albeit unsubstantiated) horror-stories of exploding scrotums and permanently embedded plastic straws. So no - I shan't tell you that one.

Other folk swear by freezer-bags filled with Marmite, tubs of Swarfega, monkey wrenches for weird types who can't bear to touch their thing. But the most common plaudits and the ones I find most difficult to understand are those which claim to "make it feel like a bird's doing it".

Who wants it? It's common knowledge that girls are willing but ineffectual wankers. All that is required of them is that they take command, grip the aching penis in a sturdy manner and pull it vigorously and rhythmically, up and down until deposits have been made in places. Instead, fuelled by the deranged fantasies of Jackie Collins and Jeffrey Archer they scrape, tickle, juggle and scratch your knob until it dozes off through boredom. Tug, girls, TUG!!

Nonetheless, I did succumb to a persistent recommendation to lie on my good arm until it went numb at which point I was to set about masturbating "as if a bird was doing it". Unfortunately my arm went so numb that it lost all sensory functions and I was unable to direct it even to the tip of my knob. A ludicrous sight, I feel sure, when a grown man with an erection is flapping his arm from one side of his body to the other, vainly trying to grab hold of his tumescent organ. No more girlie stuff like that, thanks.

No, the simple things are best. Just store up a good sackfull of sperm over a few days. When your Towns are heavy with discomfort leave off for yet another day. Yes. Then go out and get very very drunk and take some speed. This will have a dual effect. You will stay up all night slaving frantically over a limp dick which will not offer the faintest promise of a result. However, the next day you will feel excessively "sensual". There is nothing like a spree for inducing the advanced stages of Wank Fever. Then, and only then, go to it. Find a comely subject and take the tiles off the wall. There's no harm in it.

* Have readers got amusing masturbation stories?

* Next week: Are you a frotteur?

* The above article was written by a certain Liverpudlian called Kevin Sampson and confirms our suspicions at Boys Own that all Scousers are wankers. Personally we have never interfered with our privates in any manner and consider that wanking makes you go deaf.

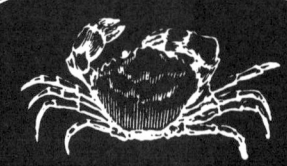

From the people who brought you the slogan "Better dead than an acid Ted," the next bit (like the Nathan McGouth and Adamski story) will be a bit hard to swallow. Two and a half years on from the House Revolution, a few of us are having to make a few clubland decisions. In the left hand corner we give you the revival of the spirit of '88. Clubs such as PURE SEXY (as good as Shoom ever was), brown and pink ones and one-offs such as BLUE SOURCE. Lots of sweating, lots of dancing and house music nearly all night long. In the right hand corner we have last year's slow-down and the funky alternatives, mooching, Charlie, and lots of pony tails and going home dry and clean.

Clubs such as Yellow Book Gosh etc have a little bit of both in them, but it seems to us that as attitudes get polarised and violence breaks out at several London clubs, many people will have to choose one or the other. If the 'alternative' to Ted is violence, then many of us may be forced, or be happy to decide that a little bit of Ted's good for your health.

QUEENS CLUB 1988 - 1990.....WHEN IT KICKED IT KICKED

.............WHEN IT DIDN'T WE ATE POXY HOTDOGS...........

....QUEENS R.I.P...................................

UGLY AS FUCK SWEET AS A NUT

A few people I know still follow the criminal theories of Cesare Lombroso, matching the distinct physical features of people to their crimes. They have pain-stakingly built a small national network that operates discreetly in its reverence of the italian scientist. A newsletter appears every month with long columns of arguments about new evidence. A recent issue raged over how large the ears are of sexual delinquents and also over what proportion of bouncers did have an odd-shaped cranial structure. I can list all the recalcitrant developments with relative ease. Not that I believe. But I see less of my friends now. On certain streets in Manchester I do meet one or two, shadowed in doorways, writing notes into small books that have edible paper. They are a very excitable lot, almost spitting on you as they explain rapidly their new discoveries.

Recently though they have begun to speak more clearly, relaxing a little, sometimes only whispering. Old Cesare has been resurrected to look deeply into the diverse and distinct scallie faces now around us, only to be laid finally to rest. Striving for attention from the shimmering surface of the media, these young working class provide ready material for the Lombrosians.

The Farm have managed to capture the Scallies central feature(s), the "ugly as fuck" motif. With faces that crawl onto our screens, they provide a sense of depth that upsets the sleek surface. A style of ugliness is born. Shaun Ryder's nose displays the underworld obtrusiveness of the shady drug deal. It was possible to say, "Oh yes, he looks the type." But fame and fortune came like the celestial dove and shit pure gold into his lap. Alas, his nose may not after all determine his life. Lombroso it seems was wrong.

In the early eighties your average scally would have been pleased, happy no doubt to verify any of your Lombrosian assumptions. The Giro was never enough and so you had to do a bit of wheeling and dealing to get money for your smokes and your weekly stash. Clothes posed few problems, people a plenty selling hot stuff "Hitchens" sold flared cords cheap, your old man always had a dusty tweed blazer stuffed down the back of the wardrobe covering some old porn mags. And however lazy you were, however much of a clown you looked, it didn't matter; and if it did who would complain to a half-grade crew cut and bulldozer face?

Today your average rag-tag scally has pressing matters of careers in hand. You could sit comfortably over half a Chester's mild and chatter towards the night about the Acid House catalyst. Or else shift unsatisfactorily around the varied effects dole changes had. Whichever, you still remain with a few problems about the new scallies. Across the north it is a definitive fashion moving well outside the inner city.

The dozy I-don't-give-a-fuck style can't whistle us away from seeing the basic eclecticism. The whole scouse originated look mixed itself with a dreamy Woodstock trip. How long is it before ageing "Rolling Stone" journalists with their dope fried brains eventually recognise the second coming of Jim Morrisson in Ian Brown?

Sure enough the past is there to be exploited, granted even that it will be at the cost of depoliticising it. Nostalgia led fashion round the late 80's and is already providing the post-scallie 90's style. But eclectism becomes damaging when it takes the Black dance beat, gives it a White face and sells it to a national public. The list of Black rap and soul groups in Manchester is long but ignored, like their talent. Take it down as a fact that every White-boy pop phenomenon can be traced to Afro-American roots. It begins in white working class subcultures and gradually dissolves into mainstream music.
Glenn Miller, Elvis, the Mods, Teds even Punk.

And if the scallies are spinning delightedly upon the music world's discovery of Black dance music, it is certain to keep it for the lads. I can only really think of Jane Gill from the Paris Angels to represent women. Yet again, for whatever reason, the boys make it their own. I know loads of scally girls, so whose fault is it? Racism and sexism are what the music business is built on.

It's a long way the scallies have come, proving themselves tricky entrepreneurs. Despite the cynicism a smile is possible at the reservoir of youth creativity that promotes itself outside major record companies influence. More interesting now for being outside of London and for once firmly rooted in what is left of the working class. In the end they play those riffs for the Man but upset His hearing problem doing it.

TWENTY THINGS NOT TO DO AT 8 O'CLOCK ON A SUNDAY MORNING AROUND YOUR MATE'S AFTER CANING IT ALL NIGHT.

1. A THOUSAND PIECE PUZZLE OF THE QUEEN MUM SITTING NAKED ON FRANK BRUNO'S LAP...

2. WATCH WEEPY FILMS INVOLVING SICK CHILDREN AND CLEVER DOGS...

3. VISIT YOUR RICH GRANDMOTHER (YOU'RE OUT OF THE WILL NOW LADDIE)...........................

4. GO TO A SUNDAY MORNING FOOTIE MATCH INVOLVING WEST HAM FANS ON HACKNEY MARSHES..........................

5. RUN OUT OF PUFF AND TEA BAGS..................................

6. DECIDE YOU FANCY YOUR MATE AND TELL HIM.................

7. GET RELIGIOUS...

8. GET OUT THOSE OLD PICCYS OF YOURSELF IN KICKERS AND PONCHOS......................................

9. DO CLUB PEOPLE IMPRESSIONS: ..."HE'S MAD THAT STEVE LEE"............................

10. TELL FIBS ABOUT OLD FOOTIE RUCKS: ..."HONEST IT WAS 30 OF US AND 400 BORO......................

11. QUEUE FOR A BUS...

12. HI-JACK A BUS...

13. KNOCK ONE OUT ON A BUS...

14. HALLUCINATE THAT YOU ARE A BUS AND THAT OLD LADIES ARE SITTING ON YOUR LAP SHOWING YOU THEIR BUS PASS.

15. ASK IF ANYONE CAN CUT HAIR.....................................

16. RIDE YOUR BIKE TO BRIGHTON....................................

17. GO TO CAMDEN MARKET AND TALK TO SOAP DODGERS..

18. ADD UP HOW MUCH YOU'VE SPENT THE NIGHT BEFORE.

19. GET ALL GUILTY ABOUT DOING GEAR................................

20. NECK MORE GEAR. (WHY NOT - ED.).................................

BOY'S OWN - BROADSTAIRS, OUR REAL SUMMER PARTY

.....................SHEILA AND KERRY GET REAL....................

..............." OI,TAKE OFF CHESTER'S LEGGINGS, ".............

'FALL'

Remixed
by
Andrew Weatherall

Out Mid October

" audio sensory stimulation "

..........................BOY'S OWN SUMMER PARTY, TACKY VENUE, DIDN'T KICK, ENOUGH SAID..........................

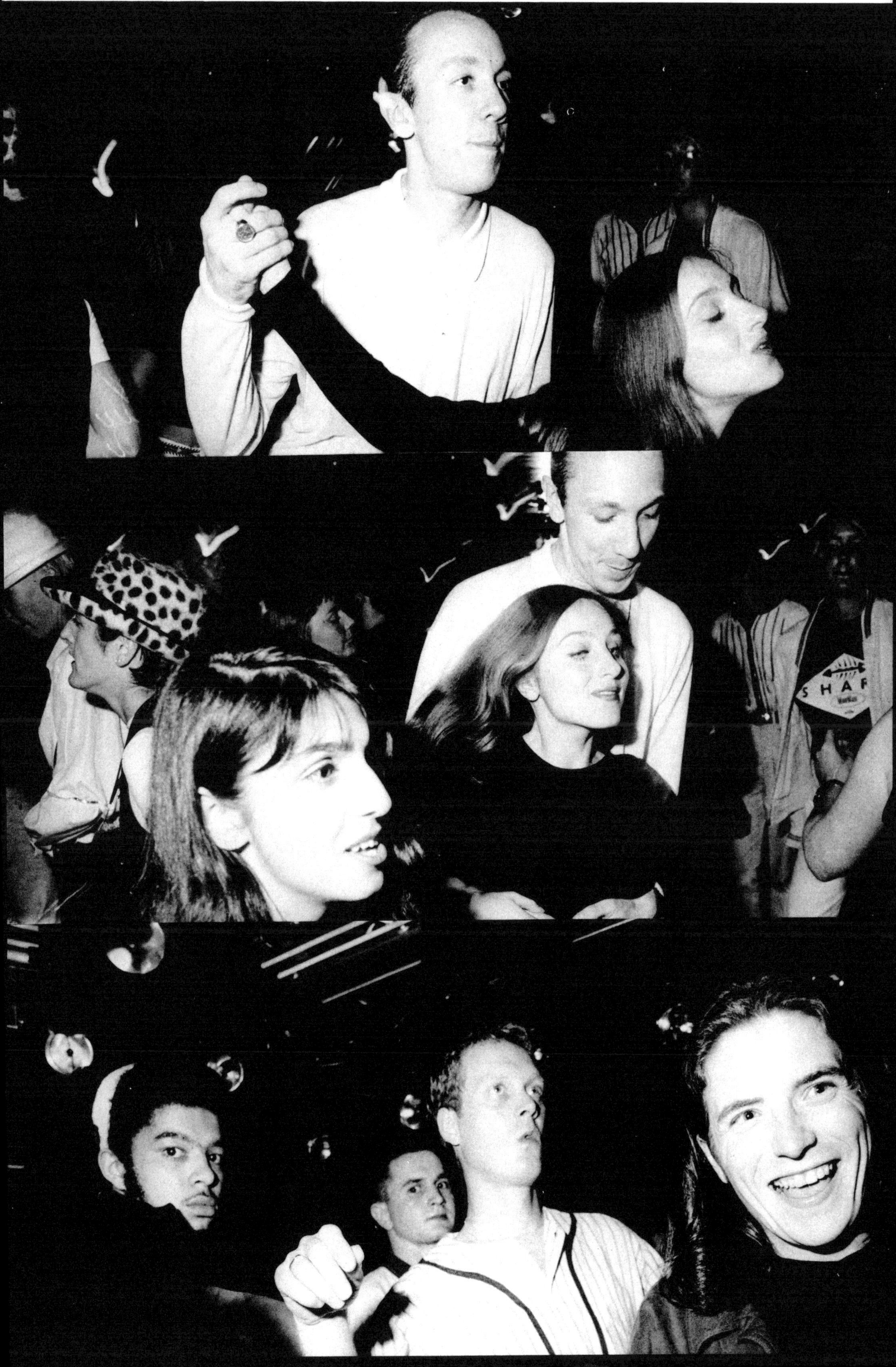

BEGGARS BANQUET
MAN, OUR STORES BE KICKIN'!
C.D.S - ALBUMS
CASSETES
INDIE-DANCE
TECHNO
HIP-HOP-JAZZ
ROCK
SOUL-HOUSE
NEW RELEASES
BASS HEAVY

CLUB GANGS NO. 4. .....ORIGINAL LONDON FUCK OFF POSSE, ORIGINAL OLD SCHOOL.....
FEAT MC KINKY, GEORGE AND STEVE....." YA LARGE "

LETTERS TO THE CHAPS

Dear Boys Own,

I was reading the magazine (Spring Edition) when I got to your letters page - Voices of Reason? What a load of crap ANON, LONDON...Sarah & Richard, please tell us something that we haven't heard before: bad clubs, Save the World, puff is bad...yawn, yawn.

Firstly to answer (the brave) ANON, who won't let his name be published, there are 'loads' of 'New' people out there doing good, interesting projects. Where I live in Walton-on-Thames, there's two new fanzines being produced, at least three new bands and half a dozen new DJ's! There are scenes happening and new blood coming along. Unfortunately you have to be involved to realise all the happenings and you obviously aren't. I suggest if you want to see how the scene may develope, read a book called Pump House Gang, especially 'Noon-day Underground.' Does the story sound familiar? Of course it does. All the best ideas are stolen. Boys Own - New Boy Network, coincidence? I think not. Right on to Sarah and the 'E' babies scare. Oh dear, oh dear. You have more chance of damaging your unborn baby by eating eggs, beef,cheese and drinking tap water than by taking E. Let's just sit back and contemplate what's been happening since the last Boys Own:

1. Reprossessed meat such as bones, offal, fat, scrap that have been declared unfit to eat have been blasted, reheated and then fed to vegetarian animals! This 'suprisingly' has lead to Mad Cow
disease, but it's OK, they've stopped feeding this stuff to cows. Now they're feeding it to pigs! What a wonderful World! And what about the rest of the 'waste' from meat production. Where does this go? Well into pies, pastries, cheap mince - but we know that, that's OK. Let's get back to the babies shall we? They've just revealed that lovely Robinson baby food contains it. Let's face it, the occasional use of drugs is OK. The only problems can occur when prolonged or habitual use occurs. Worrying about E babies is ridiculous. All I've got left to say is be positive and do things for yourself not someone else it's the best way to go. Start your own business, fanzine, even charity. Instead of using your energy time to complain and knock, use it to improve and advance. If you can't think of anything that needs improving - kill yourself!
> Love Mark
> Walton-on-Thames
> The New Manchester

Dear Boys,
Footy tops have been popping up here, there and everywhere this year. Maybe it was the world cup which was to blame, but for some reason footy tops became the No1 item of clothing for both footy boys and fashion victims alike. Even Teds International got in on the act on Top of the Pops as they mimed along to their top choons. Then there was the Derek Dougan look which came in during the Spring. You know those two colour, round-collar long sleeved jobs which George Best and Charlie George did their stuff to in the late '60's/early '70's? About a year ago I met this Manc clubber called Darren whilst on a bootleg t-shirt flogging jaunt to Cardiff. He was wearing a purple prototype of this style of footy top which, he assured me, he was going to mass produce. So either the Duffer of St. George stole his designs or Darren is a very rich man. Seeing as it's topical at present to goon and on about the significance of the soccer jersey, I thought Boys Own might as well jump on the bandwagon.Let's go back to the mid '70's when the traditional Derek Dougan jobs were going out of style. There were some really toss brands about in those days. Anyone remember UWIN, Forest's ace kit supplier which was an ICI subsiduary? And then there was BUKTA, the brand with the mad acid logo. The big two British makes, Umbro and Admiral had a virtual monopoly on British kits but they soon had competition from that huge German sporting war-machine, Adidas. The Adidas logo became a mid '70's youth cult as spotty 12 year old urchins perfected the famous design on bags, school desks and crap Keynote Easter special t-shirts across the land. Instead of using cotton, Adidas used a silky material which was typically puffy and continental. Astonishingly they poached Liverpool from Umbro and Man Utd from Admiral so our big two fought back. Admiral came up with their famous mad curvy line design which incoporated two vertical lines, studded with admiral logos that bent alarmingly at the top of the shirt. Umbro copied this design and stuck Umbro logos down the sleeves of all their kits.

They also started producing glossy brochures which we used to browse through for hours on end in local sports shops. The main teams around our end were Liverpool, Everton and Man Utd but only Teds wore those so we used to order Le Coq Sportif, Hummell and asics brochures for all those obscure European kits which yourmam and dad had to import direct from the Czechoslavian Embassy. Remember LokomotivLeipzig, Grasshoppers Zurich, Young Boys Berne and Paedophiles Lisbon?

Of course, the Italians, Spanish, Dutch andGermans always had ace kits and you were an instant celebrity if you could lay your hands on a famous continental kit. I always hated the kids who used to go Spain on their hols and came back with flashy Real Madrid pennantsand Athletico tops.

The 80's were a dull decade with regards to footy kit design and no one really tried anything adventurous, although Scotland became a laughing stock with their hilarious blue and white shorts. At the end of the 80's Adidasbegan to do some really sad outfits.

They gave Liverpool a stupid snow blizzard look which only nippers and retards thought was good. Also Adidas ruined the Dutch and German national kits by doing an insane Cubist job on the formers and a potty Aladdin Sane zig zag on the latters. And the new Celtic top became a schooly favourite. Personaly I hope the new French kits come into style - the nouveau-Stanley Matthews look of Marseilles with their ace knee length shorts and no-nonsense plain shirts. Even if Umbro, Admiral or Puma do get around to designing some decent clobber they will always be regarded as plop second raters. With the new craze for old school Trad brands such as Nike, Adidas and er, Adidas again we should finally piss off the wet fish in their British Fox plimpsoles, Karl Lagerfeld shell suits and South Molton St. Panthers basey caps.

Paul, London, NW7.

Dear Boys,

Let's face it, Teds have never posed that great a threat to the area of clubland you and I know. A tribe is emerging that could be a threat though...As yet, this oh-so-charming clan haven't been given a nice colloquial sociological title i.e. The Face/ I.D haven't picked up on 'em yet, so for now dear reader, you and I shall refer to the species as the Attitude Apathetic Apes! or "apes" for short (referring to their primitive attitude to life -look after number one and a big fuck off to anyone else.) Spotting one of the herd can be difficult. They frequent the same clubs as you and I - Eat the Worm, Gosh and the like. An ape cannot be judged on their clothing either - he/she tends to look like you or I. "Ho, hum,' I hear you ponder, 'Could I be mistaken for an ape?" That, my dear bods and bodesses, depends on your attitude and what your gob says when it's open...The top gob of the apes is known simply as 'Anony.' Ring a bell? That's right 'Anony' of Boy's Own letter writing fame. (The first typed letter to arrive in the office, what a sophisticate - Ed) Look back at the last ish to check for yourself the complete flowing prose of this total and utter whirging twat, but the following few phrases are ones that should be noted carefully. It is such phrases that maketh an ape. "I don't want to be seen as yet another whinger but..." "It's up to you at the top." "You with the power and influence have got to make the changes." Now forgive me if I've decoded this letter incorrectly but to my old grey matter, it reeks of "YOU gotta do this and YOU gotta do that"...What about yourself, my dear Anony? What exactly are YOU doing about the "Shit in front of our eyes?" The answer is simple: FUCK ALL. Press an ape about this line of non-action and you'll get a low defensive murmur along the lines of "I haven't got the time/money/contacts." I can assure you an ape will never admit "I haven't got the guts to make an effort." Don't get me wrong, I'm not saying each and every one of you should become a club runner / DJ / promoter / producer or the like. Hell no! - Do whatever you want to do. I'm just saying instead of slagging someone else's life, try getting your own in order first. Try appreciating what you have clubwise instead of always putting it down, to take another ape's phrase,"Yeah, last night was alright, but I remember the nights we had at ...(yawn, yawn) nothing can beat that". Going out is what YOU make it - if you go out with a negative attitude, it's likely you'll return home with one too. Surely, the most important thing is to ENJOY yourself - do write in and correct me if I'm wrong. Things aren't all bad though. An ape can easily be transformed, despite the ticking off I've given our pal 'Anony.' At least He/She cared enough about the scene to say what they thought was wrong. It's surely better to be passionate about something - love it or hate it - than just passively drift along, lethargically accepting anything and everything. Just slagging off anyone and everything won't do though. It's action that's needed, not hot air from your gob. Action, not just from the DJ's/promoters, but from every single person. Everyone has to be prepared to make an effort. So, next time an ape is standing next to you being a moaning minnie, there are two things you can say: "What do you intend to do about it?" or the more direct line of "Fuck 'orrf home." P.S. For all you questioning cynics out there, no-one told me to write this, I made the effort 'cos I'm sick and tired of everyone slagging off the scene and never saying anything good about it. Hopefully, I've made a few people stop and think, 'cos we're all guilty of the 'ape' syndrome, now and again

April Stevens Purley, South Of Roundshaw.

FORTY BRILL THINGS ABOUT BEING A KID.

1. Getting four fish fingers, chips and mushy peas for Saturday tea.

2. Sending in your younger brother to swipe all the hubba bubbas because he's under age.
3. Robbing loads of sports equipment from the local comp and having your own mini-olympics.

4. Burning next street's bonny down on the fourth of November at 10.30 pm.
5. Lobbing bangers through letterboxes.
6. Watching your mate get kicked to shitin his not-very-convincing penny for the guy disguise.
7. Playing top trumps for money.
8. Camping out on summer holidays and robbing everybody's milk.
9. Pretending to be with the psychos at the match.
10. Getting a backy on a Chopper.
11. Chasing mad people down the street.
12. Finding a load of Strop mags in a field.
13. Saying "Bagsy I'm Mario Kempes."
14. Playing three and in 'em for seven hours on a Sunday.
15. Getting a pair of Tesco Birmingham bags for Xmas.
16. Getting caught smoking in the bogs by a soft teacher.
17. Going to see Close Encounters twenty seven times.
18. Doing bombers off the high board at the baths.
19. Staying up late to watch Vampire Virgins when your Mum & Dad have gone out.
20. Terrorising the specky nobhead who keeps threatening to call the police.
21. Covering your bedroom in football '75 stickers.
22. Buying a Screwball off the Icey.
23. Heinz beans 'n' baconburgers.
24. Letting everybody's tyres down.
25. Making a pair of Bruce Lee numchackers out of a wicket sawn in half and a chain.
26. Shooting sparrows with a gatgun.
27. Farting dead loud in Assembly.
28. Going on the spud van and selling one bag all day.
29. Coming off a stolen moped at forty mph.
30. Playing footy with a pregnant hedgehog.
31. Adapting the game of Knock 'n' Run to Steal fence and Run.
32. Acting hard with a flick knife.
33. Going Carrol singing in mid-October.
34. Bashing scouts doing Bob a Job.
35. Getting legged by a lad with ginger hair, tartan trousers and an Everton scarf.
36. Having Gary Glitter versus Slade gang fights at junior school.
37. Getting a job on the fair as a hook the duck bod.
38. Starting ten grass fires a day for a grin.
39. Going on mad forty mile bike rides.
40. Robbing the kid in calipers dinner money.

BOYS OWN AUTUMN 90 : CONTRIBUTORS :
FLEUR, SAMPSON, HALL, PORTER, WEATHERALL,
FARLEY, THORNTON and LEGGITT......
PHOTOS : MARTIN CULLIVER, RICHARD VARNDEN,
  SWINDELLS and JAFFA .....
BOYS OWN MANSIONS : UNIT 2, 249/251 KENSAL Rd W10.

MANY THANKS to.... BILLY and CHIPS, SPROCKET
the LOVE ROCKET, WEASEL the SNIFFER, CLIVE 'in the pink' HENRY,
STEVE 'BRENDA doin it FOR THE kids' LEE, THE POP GROUP,
RAMPLING ON YOUR RADIO, PETESKI HELLER,
  TOSH and PHIL (THE BEATS GO ON), LEWIS at BLUEBIRD,
FIONA and FRAN (SIGN of the times), JANE at PINK SODA,
NINA FOR SORTING ALL THE LABEL GRIEF, OSMAN,
The STAFF of DUCK CALL, WIZZ, PLUG 'big at weddings' O'CONNOR,
PAUL McKEE, ALAN 'Rodney' TRIBE, MICKEY STACEY,
MR BARRY MOONCULT, The VICTORIOUS BOYS OWN FOOTBALL TEAM,
The Chaps at FLYING and PHUTURE RECORDS, MAX the BOAT,
LITTLE JASON BUCKNER .....
  AND A SPECIAL THANKS to EDDIE GORDON at POLYDOR
FOR ALL his ENCOURAGING COMMENTS about the
  BOYS OWN RECORD LABEL ....

MICHIKO LONDON
KOSHINO

100 mph

Autumn / Winter Collection
90/91

"TUNE UP AND DROP IN"

70 Neal St. London WC2 9PH
Tel. 071 497 0165

No. 11
Summer 1991

Pt 10... iN WHicH the OutsidER goEs all RogER cook...

Good DAY RecESSioN VictiMS,
TiME to gEt YouR NoSES RubbED iN it.....
StRuggLiNg to MAKE those Re-PAYmENTS oN the
RadiogRaM ANd iNSTALmENTS oN the NEXt 'K.A.O.S.'
WeekENDeR??
WELL it's OFFiciAL , 'Boys owN' couldN't Give
A flyiNg FaRT iN A RoLLiNg DougHNUT! HeRe ARE
juSt a FEW ReAsoNS WHy...

1) SoMe of THeM EARN £10,000 PER remiX (it SAid So iN '1.D.' So
it MUSt be TRUE...)

2) THEY HAve A RECoRd coMPANY 'SANcTioNed' BY A
   MAJoR LAbEL (SEE brAckets in PoiNT 1) ...

3) THEY MAKe oBSceNe AMouNTs oF WedGE HoldiNg
   LoAdS oF Acid HOuSES ... (it's A kNowN Fact that
   MESSRs FARLeY, MAiZE, weAtheRALL MAdE NEARLY
   ONE HUNDred POUNdS FroM A 'RAve' TWo YeAus AgO)

4) They ARE GoiNg TO MAKE EVEN MoRE cAsH By
   iNcReASiNg THe PRice of theiR PERioDicAL ...
StHouts of "SHAME , SHAMe" FRoM the BACKbeNches
   \TRAcked THe editoRiAL STAFF dowN iN +heiR
   PLuSH iNdustRiALLY cArPeted office coMPLEX iN WeSt
   LoNDoN To SEE if theY could JUStiFY THiS outRAgeous
   TuRN oF EveNTS..... HeRe ARE a few of the
   MoRe PRiNTAbLE "JUSTiFicaTioNs"

" I NEED SoME SERioUS scHooLweAR FoR the ANkLeBiTER ,
   WELL iT iS A PriVATE oNE , You'VE GoT to GET all the GEAR"
" THE NEW FlAt NeedS A FEW coATS oF viNYL SiLk"
" THE NEW YeSPA NEedS A Re-SPRAY"
" Do You kNow the PRicE oF skuNk-WeeD?"
        REMEMbeR WHeRE You REAd iT FiRSt ... THE —>
        KEEP YouR PeckERS oN THE UPside! Outsider

UPPERS AND DOWNERS

Toppy Top Top

Being a born again raver.

Cheeky halfs that open the surgery doors
for mass piggery.

Saying, "Corkie O'Rourkie," "Nitts," and,
"Get right on one matey."

Girls that are deep in vogue.

Colonic irrigation, a right royal
rim-up.

Chinese Burns contests

Spaghetti and garlic prawns
from M&S.

Top air biscuits on the firm after the above
(A.K.A. dodgy Newingtons).

Blackhead removers from the back of the
Daily Mirror.

Jack Duckworth - a real man of the 'nineties.

Taking Rolf Harris style-a-phone's to nightclubs.

LONDON - footballing capital of England.
(No-one cares about the sweaty's).

Norman playing Thin Lizzy's, "Whisky In The Jar,"
on Kiss FM. (Now that's what we call balearic).

Flirting not fucking.

Your old feller being a ringer for Homer.

Trade - essential Saturday night clubbing.

Fluffy pillows and fluffy cuddles.

The new DJ duo's:
Fabi & Porky (Menace)
Lofty Loud & Clumpy Clive (Bones).

A bag of pickled onions with your chips.

Looking at life thru the eyes of a child

That moment during a top night when you think to
yourself, "YES."

Jeckyle

The words, "Is that as big as it gets?"

Coming last in the Boy's Own/Butlins,
Mr. Wet Y-Fronts competition.

People who say, "Oo-er," "Pucka,"
and "Scream-up."

That poll tax summons.

Dressing on the left and only your mum noticing.

Charlie Chester - Hayes' no.1 church usher.

The demise of the ream McRibs.

Your old feller thinking he looks a ringer for,
"Storming Norman."

Billy and Chips, bootleggings answer to
Cannon and Ball.

People who think DJ's double up as
cloakroom attendants.

The word "balearic" when spoken in alien accents.

Des' sad sidies, Vic "Geordie posh-fackers" suits,
Gazza's sad Milky Bar barnet.

The re-opening of the Limelight, home of all
things para and the noidy buzz.

The nights when it's ,"Your turn to drive..."

Walking on the wild side and stepping in a puddle.

The Gabichi revival - more Ronnie Corbett than
Robert De Niro.

Sweaty pools on your pillow the morning after.

Your little brother turning Queens in his infant
school dinner money scandal.

London's racist/radical radio station.

The letter decoding skills of The Face and
I-D's editorial staff.

The day after the day after.

Good For A Top Up

Whilst reading a recent issue of "The Face," I came across an article about some new designer drugs being used in the States. Obviously my interest was awoken and ignoring another really interesting piece about Icelandic street fashion I settled down to read about these new bits of merchandise my local dealers would be offering me shortly.

The three page feature was about something the writer called, "smart drugs." From what I could gather they were supposed to increase your awareness and heighten perception, thus making your memory clearer, recall quicker and make you a general all round smart-arse!

Now from what I know about the sort of fellows who like to indulge in chemical abuse all that sort of nonsense is the last thing they want. I know most of my friends would feel badly short changed if the class A they were partaking in didn't reduce them to a state of blissful confusion for a number of hours, hopefully with the IQ of a stuffed toy.

I carried on with the article only to learn that these "smarties" were being developed by some of the more reputable drug companies and not, as I had first thought, in abandoned farm houses in deepest Essex. The aim of the drug companies, apart from making a packet, was to produce something to help people with mental problems, learning difficulties and even the elderly that suffer memory loss (Hang on Mo Butcher, help's on it's way!). With this knowledge I realise this wasn't a new street drug and the letter I had considered writing to the manufacturers giving the idea the thumbs down wasn't necessary.

The excitement and anticipation of a new chemical experience had now gone and as I put down the magazine and sat back in my chair I realised this wasn't the first time this had happened. I began to think back over the last couple of years and remembered that magazines like "I-D" and "The Face", newspapers like "The Sun" and "The People" and friends like British Bill and the Brighton Boys had raised my hopes many times with tales of strange new concoctions only to let me down when it actually came to sampling them.

Cast your mind back to some of the strange, almost mythical substances we've been promised... then, how many of them ever found their way into your grubby pockets? How often were you told that someone would have some next week or why was it they only appear when you're having a Saturday night in front of the box? Some of them could possibly exist but it's sort of like the Loch Ness monster or the size of Steve Lee's wallet, unless you see it with your own eyes it's pretty hard to believe in it!

The following are just a few of the "new" highs I've searched out at one time or another, maybe you've found them, more likely not but if you have and still know where to get more, I know plenty of buyers.

MYTHICAL MEXICAN MUSHROOMS

I've read the books, been to Cafe Pacifico and seen "Altered States" three times but short of heading down Mexico way, where do I get some? On the night of the last Shoom at The Park, I thought my quest had ended. Purchasing my bag of fungus I retreated into a darkened corner to inspect my ticket to another dimension. Inside my little Nat-West money bag were some of the sorriest little mushrooms I'd seen in years, you know, the sort you used to crawl around in low fields looking for while you were cross country running during P.E. at school. My heart sunk, an out of body experience with ancient Aztec Gods, house music and Danny Rampling was definitely out of the question that night.

ICE

The tabloid press were the first to inform us about this sulphate based product so everyone thought it couldn't be true. Then one night in 1989 at the "Future Xmas Party," the stories became facts. A bag of the stuff was passed around and huge quantities were snorted by a South London crowd out for kicks. By all accounts, they got them as well! The stuff was so strong it felt like your nose was about to collapse, people's tongues felt swollen and no-one slept until way past Boxing Day. Needless to say Ice never really took off after its ill-fated debut. Rumour has it there's still a sack of the stuff sitting in a garage south of the river waiting for a second chance.

M25's

The orbital drug taken by ravers in fields around the home counties. This stuff must have been good because those chaps were out in all weathers. Once again the tabloids first alerted us to this one and once again I've never been offered the chance to buy it. Most people in the know seem to think that M25's were really those dodgy E's, half speed, half acid, you know, the one's with the texture of a fisherman's friend. Come to think of it I've bought loads of them!

LIQUID E

This one seems to be the latest in a long line of scams. Stories first began to surface from down on the south coast a couple of months before Xmas. Even though the word around town was they were nothing more than pre-med there was definitely a demand for the stuff. The buzz began to grow, people were claiming to have tried them but still not one emerged for sale on the open market, at least not anywhere near me!

Just like super love dove's, crystal MDMA, and 90% Charlie, liquid E seems to be no more than a figment of some sorry souls imagination.

Maybe the last word on the subject should go to a dear friend of mine who when asked if he'd tried liquid E answered, "No, but if it comes in pints I will!"

MEXICAN MUSHROOM MADNESS WITH A GEORDIE BASTARD, DAVE HENLEY, THE LEAD SINGER OF AIRSPRAY, AND "CLUB LEGEND" SKEET.

—NO U.K. REMIX AVAILABLE!

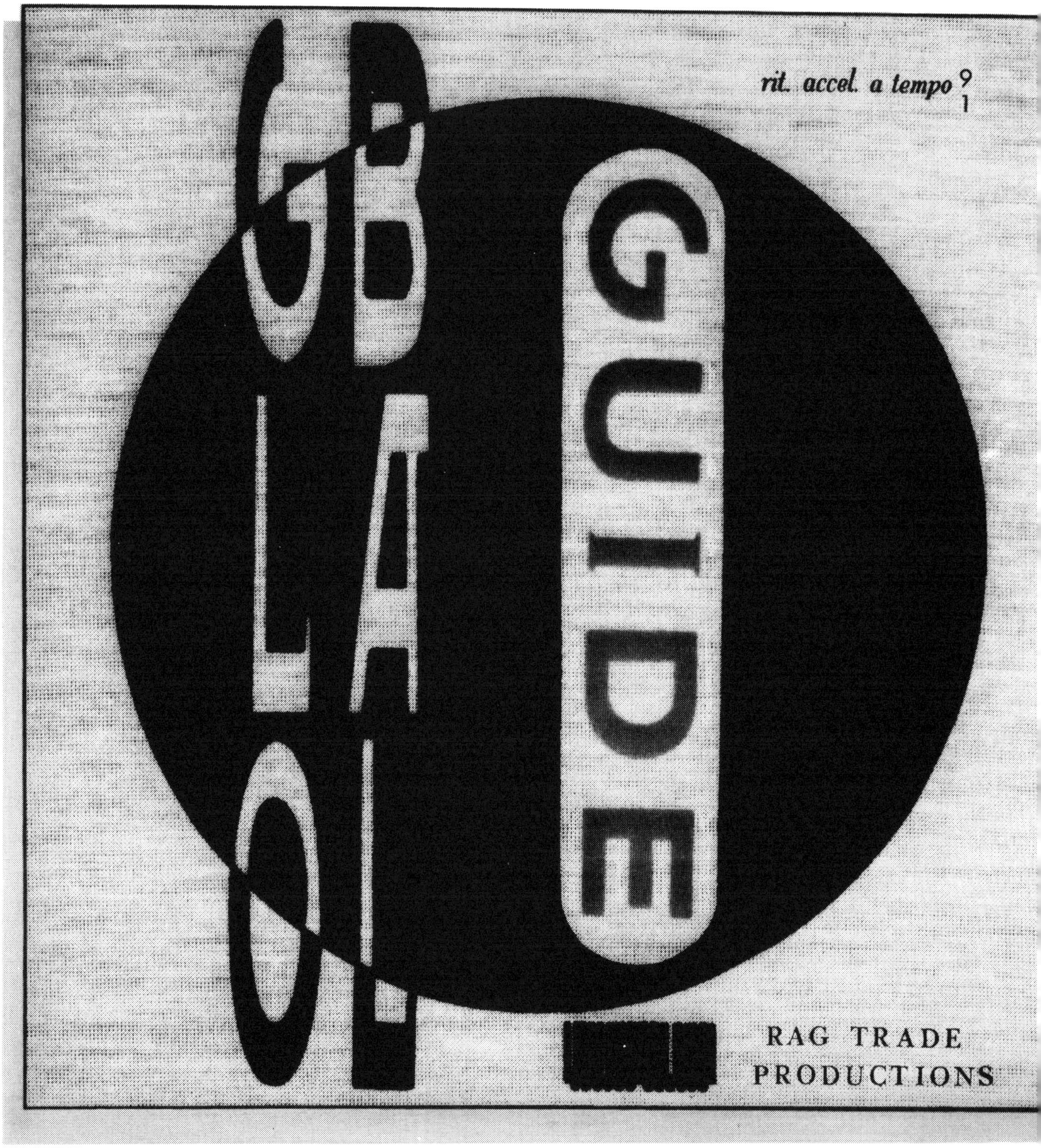

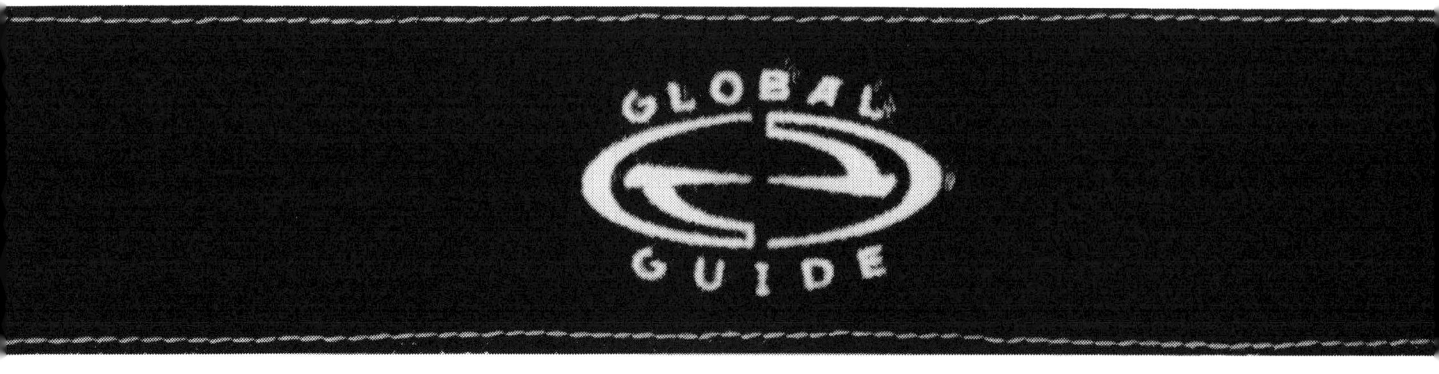

GB
LA
O!

GUIDE

rit. accel. a tempo $\frac{9}{1}$

RAG TRADE
PRODUCTIONS

TAILOR-MADE SPORTSWEAR

The Boy's Own Sounds Of Summer

Tammi Payne — Take Me Now
Trans-plant — Heart Of The World
Leroy Burgess — Heaven
The Pet Shop Boys/David Morales — So Hard
D.F.K. — What Would We Do?
(Steve Silk Hurley Remix)

Phoenix — Plaything
Brainstorm — Help Me To Believe
Primal Scream — Don't Fight It Feel It
Arnold Jarvis — I Want To Have Your Love
Dupree — A Brass Disk
Mental Cube — So This Is Love?
D.O.P. — Future Le Funk
(Left Field Remix)

Aretha Franklin — Everyday People
Tyrell Corporation — Grapes of Wrath
State 808 — Oops (American Remix)
The Transglobal Underground — Temple Head
Finni Tribe — 101 Sonic Shuffle
The Stone Funkers — Come With Me
James — Come Home
(Youth Remix)

Yolanda — Living For The Night
L.U.P.O. — So Sad
The End — You Drive Me Wild
Circuit — Shelter Me (Remix)
Morris Joshua — Sweet Rythm and Harmony

Titiyo — My Body Says Yes (Dub)
Munda Muzique — The Trans Techno EP
Rose Windross — Living Life Your Own Way
Airstream — Follow Through
(Weatherall Dub)

Irving and Romeo — Brighter Day
Hustler's Convention — Now Freedom
Dub Federation — Italian Jazz
Alex Lee — Take it/Minute By Minute

MAN RAY
119 CAMDEN MEWS
LONDON NW1 7AH

TELEPHONE: 071 - 284 0600

AVAILABLE NOW!

On The Tools Too! The Sequel!

Greetings, salutations, devoirs and wotcha! Much rubble has been thrown into the mini-skip since last time we spoke, the time is now right for us to once again don our hard hats and stout boots, pick up our parcel of cheese and pickle sandwiches and head off on the final leg of our thrilling and critically acclaimed "Heart of Darkness," type journey to the throbbing bowels of working Britain!! Yes, that's right readers, it's the last instalment of your very own cut-out-and-keep sociological pamphlet, "The Boy's Own Guide To The British Building Worker."

1. Apprentices

The sight of a pimply adolescent mooching his way to a large building site carrying a bag of lovingly prepared sandwiches and sporting a pair of Dr. Martens finest is a pitiful one indeed. Traditional methods of apprentice initiation were relatively innocent japes that involved sending the bemused sprog to the builders merchants for a variety of non-existent objects. (Indeed, a member of the Boy's Own editorial staff once confided in me, in a moment of drunken shame, that he had spent a whole afternoon standing at the counter of his local Sandel Perkins after being sent there for a long weight - a long wait! Geddit?). However in recent years there has been a drift toward initiations of a more physical nature. By the end of his first working day 1991's apprentice will have had industrial strength adhesive smeared on his gonads, his thermos flask will have been pissed into, the food lovingly prepared by his mother will have been nicked, eaten and replaced instead with a steaming Douglas (Douglas Hurd - Turd). Indeed, his mother's good name will be sullied by a string of foul, perverse and physically impossible insults. Then, when the boy tries to defend his family honour he will be stripped naked, lashed to the top of the scaffold and the words, "I am an uphill gardener" will be daubed on his chest in luminous paint. The early working days of an apprentice are a watershed in his young life.

Wears:
It doesn't really matter what the apprentice wears, because the plasterer nicks all his clobber and shits on it before flushing it all down the site toilet.

Reads:
Smash Hits, Sven Hassel novels.

Favourite Sayings:
"Ouch!"/"Oh no, not my EMF T-shirts"/"Whose pinched my Waggon Wheel?"/etc.

2. Site Agents

Also known as "That fat shit in the office," the site agent will be a former top boy (Chippy or Brickie - see last issue) who can, for one reason or another, no longer cut it on site. He therefore takes the rather foolish decision to defect to the management side of things. He will now have his own little site hut, the walls of which he will decorate with girly pin-ups and rib tickling slogans such as , "You don't have to be mad to work here but it helps," or, "Sex instructor, first lesson free!!" The fact that he is now management and has the 1.6 Ford Sierra company car to prove it does not go down well with his former workmates. Sensing their resentment and also feeling a little emasculated by the nature of his new job the site agent will often try to ingratiate himself with the lads by regaling them with far-fetched stories of his manly capers. It is worth noting that the site agent has the power to hire and fire staff, therefore most of the workforce when listening to these monster flights of fancy will simply nod and express approval at suitable intervals in order to curry favour with the deluded fool. Many site agents turn to drink.

Wears:
The site agent may think that he looks pretty sharp in his grey Farrah slacks, tank top and pin collar shirt, but he is wrong. He looks stupid.

Reads:
"How To Make Friends And Influence People" by Dale Carnegie. (A classic '50's personality manipulation guide, bookspotters!!!)

Favourite Sayings:
"So I decked the big one first, that's the best way, drop the biggun', and then these other five blokes came for me, so I said, 'If you know what's good for you...' "etc., etc., ad nauseam.

3. Architects

The dictionary definition of an architect is, "A person who is qualified to design buildings and to superintend their erection." Apart from the rather obvious merriment to be had from the double entendre, this is an obsolete definition. The days when architects were men of drive and vision, the possessors of great artistic and creative talent are long gone. Today's architect drives a BMW, wears red spectacles and dines in bistros. His job is either to extract as much money from a piece of land as is possible by designing vast housing projects for the upwardly mobiles (his peer group), housing projects whose sales brochures cleverly use the suffix "ette" to disguise the fact that all the flats are runty and over-priced (Flatette, kitchenette, dinnette, gardenette, toilette, etc). Or, he is involved in the serious business of creating shopping centres of such monolithic clumsiness that they appear to exist for no other reason than to seriously piss off our future king. (Carbuncles!) From time to time the architect will visit the building site and in the event of him meeting any of the boys he will generally drop a few H's and call them all "mate" in a vain attempt to prove that he too is one of the lads. This does not stop the boys from calling him a nonce and saying that he doesn't know his arse from a hole in the ground, when he is out of earshot.

Wears:
Cheaney brogues (office), green wellys (site), Paul Smith cords, Barbour jacket, red spectacles.

Reads:
Daily Mail (Tucked inside a copy of the Independent), Reader's Digest Book of Home Improvements).

Favourite Sayings:
"It's a study in rhythm as opposed to symmetry, a nuance in glass and steel. It may look like a concrete bucket but it's making a vibrant, living statement, mining a neo-classical shaft if you like."

4. Labourers

Bit of a raggle taggle bunch these boys, this is probably due to the unskilled and seasonal nature of the work. Interestingly enough, labouring is the only truly classless building trade. This is due to the fact that come summertime assorted college and university bods on their holidays or, "taking a year out" work uneasily alongside the wastrels and alcohol sodden Celtic types that are more traditionally associated with the labouring fraternity. Indeed the possibility of having a future airline pilot, army officer or head of a multi-national corporation sweeping away the debris that has just been made by a vegetable with 'made in London' tattooed on his head is one that fills me with hope and makes me believe that a classless Britain is only just around the corner. It is also worth bearing in mind at this point that the current Prime Minister of this fair country was once gainfully employed as a site labourer in the Brixton area. In fact it is believed that despite the obvious perks of his new job he really misses being able to use the van at weekends.

Wears:
Regular labourers appear to be swathed from head to toe in post-apocalyptic rags, 'a la Mad Max.' The college lads tend to wear rugby shirts and trainers (much the same as they wear down the pub).

Reads:
Ranges from The Sport, to Solzhenitzyn's Avlag Archiepeligo, depending on the time of the year.

Favourite Sayings:
Once again difficult to pigeon hole. In the summertime it may be possible to listen in on two discussions taking place at opposite ends of the tea-hut, one trying to define the allegorical significance of "piggy" in Golding's Lord of The Flies, and the other wondering whether Cathy Lloyds tits are real.

Conclusions?

Well that's about the size of it (fnar, fnar). There is still much more to be said about many of the trades on site that have not been mentioned, but in these last couple of issues we have tried to give you a glimpse into the hearts and minds of the more seminal and numerous trades. It is our hope that the next time you are punched in the face by a dusty hard-hatted neanderthal (boys) or verbally abused by a lecherous blubbery thug (girls) you will instantly reach into your back pocket, pull out your, "Boy's Own Guide..." and be able to recognise your assailant straight away. (If the attack is a brutal one it will almost certainly be a plasterer). Till the next time, may your trowel and bubble remain always clean. (Oh, and don't forget to clean out the mixer).

BLUE SOURCE
PRESENTS

FISHTIQUE

**INFREQUENT OCCASIONS OF EXTREME
MERRIMENT IN THE COMPANY OF LARGE FISH**

THROUGHOUT 1991

081 877 9912

CLUB GANGS NO.5
DELUXE/ECLIPSE
"THE ORIGINAL SCREAMERS"

Softy Walter To Prime Minister

So why should you care Mr. Fronty bastard? That dopey slow twiglet-body who used to be at school with you. The one who sat near the front smiling at the teacher. The only one in the class that the teacher hated when he smiled. The one who ate egg sandwiches, had green teeth, whose nose dripped when it was cold. The one who could never have played football, even after an intensive five year course with the great Eddie McCreadie. The stupid one, the sad one, the one with the oral botanical garden ... the fucking annoying one. You remember. The bullied one.

To see him out of school in his mustard Millets anorak was a crime. It made you angry it made you want to hurt something. But to hurt him would have been a great mistake, what is the point of hurting people you know you can hurt? You must remember your honour after all you silly old sheepbrain.

When you were forcibly entered into the highly complex and tight-rope existence of secondary school, violent brownie points were very much part of life. The ability to express yourself through violence was a great gift at that age. It also came with the added bonus of showing deference to weaklings, a way of gaining respect - by not hurting those at the bottom of the pile. Yik.

Then there were those odd times when the "other kids" bullied him. The "other kids" were the ones who would grass you up and then hide for a month. The ones who actually liked Maths and Science, the ones who didn't fuck around and who grew up to be accountants, bank managers, record company parasites and/or people who sell you things.You know them. Maybe you are one. Anyway, twiglet was already behind a year because he'd had a bad ear infection when he was twelve, yet he was still bottom of every subject. He was over a year older than you, yet half your size and he was a target. The "other kids" were the ones who would wantonly slap the back of the twiglet's head. Wantonly I ask you.

Occasionally you would see these occurrences and you'd stomp across the class and stop it. Like some sort of American in school uniform, making the rest of your class take note of your love of order. You'd fucking crack heads, a couple of your mates would back you up - in order to protect the twiglet. The same twiglet you held not just in contempt but in a kind of hatred-filled awe.

But perhaps the key word here is "order". You would do all these things to preserve order. You'd quash rebellion amongst the "other kids" to preserve order. By protecting twiglet you would belittle him, frighten the "other kids" and preserve your poorly founded reputation as an all round strop with a mission. What a load of cock, m'lud.

But how could twiglet get up every morning? What were his parents thinking of? What sort of insensitive mad cats were they? Kids three years younger than us would bully him, trip him up, take his things, laugh at him, take his money. He was a legitimate target for those kids - you couldn't do anything, those kids were four or five years younger than the twiglet. The worst thing was he'd always give in.

Now what is he doing? Is he dead? Is he still trying to get some exams? Does he live with his Mum in Pinner? Does he shave his tongue? He didn't have any friends. Does he work? In a stockroom? As a BP garage attendant? In a concrete-park industrial estate in Perivale? Is he on the dole? Inside? Institutionalised? He was the bottom of the pile and you helped to keep him there, he couldn't even have climbed the social ladder to cannon fodder height because he wouldn't grow any more. If you ever see him, he'll still be wearing that mustard Millets anorak and you'll feel so guilty you'll try and buy him tea or an egg sandwich ... or a new anorak.

You fucked with him in safety, you cuffed his greasy mop in the certain knowledge you were apart from harm. But you weren't, laddies. You were wrong. If you fuck with other people you are never safe, it will come back worse. It's called guilt or karma (bollocks!) or life or Michael Ryan or Mark Chapman or Vietnam or Son Of Sam or feminism or Broadwater Farm. You cannot break a twiglet, you cannot fuck with people ... oh no you can't.

JOHN MAJOR GETS IT FROM THE BRIXTON CLASS OF '45 POSSIE.

A QUALITY **FLYING** VINYL PRODUCT

EST. 12 45

PURVEYORS OF BESPOKE

STEREOPHONIC VINYL

FLYING RECORDS
KENSINGTON MARKET BSMT
HIGH ST. KENSINGTON
LONDON W8
TEL: 071 938 4407

FLYING RECORDS
4 GOOSE GATE
NOTTINGHAM
NG1 1SF
(Opens early in June)

FLYING EVERY SATURDAY 10-3
SOHO THEATRE CLUB FALCONBURGH COURT
DEAN THATCHER & GUESTS

3 SUMMER CRAZIES TO BE RIGHT UP FOR

1. Spent On Sunday
Abuse yourself in all manners the previous night and then lay still, "necked up," "flaccid," and "spent," while sipping gallons of M&S breakfast brand tea and scoffing lots of rhubarb and custie sweets. (But how do you explain the geezer with the muzie in the swimming trunks sleeping next to you, "Well mum, that gaffs trade's a bit mad).

2.Reliving The Summer Of Love
Yes, pretend it's 1988 time at Clink Street again. Simply pick a right sweaty hot Sunday afternoon on Clapham Common and run up and cuddle the first person of Afro-Caribbean parentage you see walking his devil dog. (Note. He has to be at least six feet tall and shirtless). For total realism, shout those immortal words into his shell-like, "Release it."

3.Butlering
Simple. Neck 21 red and black capsules in 48 hours. For the first 47, sway side to side with a salty old sea dog grin (Throbbing temple veins an optional extra). The last hour will be spent around Darren Pricey's house with your head in your hands muttering, "It's all gone Pete Tong,

3 SUMMER CRAZIES THAT SHOULD BE NITTED WITHOUT HESITATION

1. The Partaking Of Ecstacy Via The Rectum
(The old wives tale is that the rushes are cleaner and that you never feel sick). Believe us, it'll end in tears, plus Newingtons of the sorest nature. Ask Billy and Chips for confirmation.

2. The Wearing Of Gabichi Knitwear
Only one step from buying Frankie Vallie records, fiddling with your nudger while talking to people in the street and adding "The Fish," to the end of your name. Remember kids, Bobby De Niro never shopped at "Stuarts" in The Bush.

3. Vaugeing
Now unless you are either a black homosexual or a "little darling" any attempts at vogueing should be avoided. You'll simply look like another contestant of the Hayes Comprehensive old boy's rubik cube contest.

Fetishlike Smiles!

There are certain aspects of human nature which are seldomly spoken about. Mannerisms we have adopted and habitual tendencies we would prefer not to have. To speak openly about the following could be compared to skateboarding to work in order to save your bus fare ...! Can everyday habits and mannerisms be that serious? Well, the extent to which we try to conceal our true inner personalities would certainly suggest so. It doesn't really matter how but like it or not we all do things which we know full well we shouldn't, should be ashamed of and more importantly, would never own up to!

Take a typical social gathering - the pub. Just a normal mundane evening down at the local. Imagine yourself standing at the bar with friends, amusing one another with relative or perhaps not so relative trivia. Just by chance you happen to glance towards the floor, and there in the middle of four pairs of feet lies a five pound note! What do you do? Do you pick it up, wave it about and ask if anyone has dropped it? Or, just to eliminate any argument do you ask the barmaid to put it in that strange plastic box shaped like a guidedog? No, of course you don't, you strategically manoeuvre a foot until it conceals the fiver, beg pardons whilst you adjust your shoelaces and stand up five pounds richer!

Anyone reading this who is at this point saying to themselves, " I wouldn't have done that - I wouldn't have acted dishonestly towards my friends," give yourself a pat on the back, I promise I won't call you a liar. Ok, this type of behaviour is not honest but it certainly seems obvious. We simply love getting away with things, almost to the point of fetishism! Anything to put a crafty grin on our face's - naughty but nice.

How many of us have gone out for the evening with your spouse claiming that, "Tonight love, we'll have to hang out a few beers and make 'em last," and then decided that the night in general would be much more interesting experienced from an altered state? You can't own up to spending twenty quid because you've already told her you were skint, besides, she'd want half and a half as opposed to a whole sounds fucking unappealing! So you find yourself in a condition of controlled elation. Desperately trying to suppress any kind or form of unusual behaviour, but loving every minute of it. Dancing in one corner of the club like, "The man from Del-Monte," knowing full well she's in the opposite corner dusting cobwebs from her bottle of Sol! It's quite pathetic really, but we still do it. We love doing it. This strange idiosyncratic behaviour that we can't even begin to explain.

Ok, let's take another situation. Once again, you're in a club. You light up a cigarette even though you've just put one out, when you realize you've only got a couple left. You've caned all your money so you can't buy any more and at this rate you'll run out well before the end of the evening. Even worse, you'll have none to smoke on the way home. So, what do you do ? You stick the few you've got left in your pocket and you start ponsing the fucking things ! Your twin brother could ask for a fag but you still wouldn't own up to having those two cigarettes in your back pocket because you couldn't bear the thought of going without yourself.

Alternatively, stand up and be counted those of you who have been in the middle of a packed, throbbing dancefloor with barely enough room to root your feet to the floor and gyrate what is by now an extremely damp body, and then found yourself in that situation whereby you're not sure whether you're about to shit yourself or possibly escape with a slight follow through - either way it's going to be far from normal with a stench to match its ferocity. You're not embarrassed though, why should you be? You're far to bollocks'd to care and besides it could have been any one of twenty equally sweaty gyrating bodies within close proximity. So "Bosh" a guff with enough bollocks to singe even the healthiest of nostril hairs followed by a most confident grin and a look of dismay at anyone who happens to look your way - That's what I'd call situation farting at its best!

So what's been the point of bringing these taboo subjects to your attention? Far be it for me to make anyone out there feel guilty. I'll openly admit to committing all the crimes I've mentioned and more. Feeling a perverse sense of pleasure from vacating a Little Chef with my pockets jammed with those little free lollies meant for the under fives, or convincing myself that I've had the biggest half of a shared 'chemical.'

They are after all, relatively trivial dishonesties and personally if the end result of a dishonesty is a smile, it can't be all that bad can it? So, carry on lying, ponsing, stealing and farting your way through life. Just don't get caught. And remember, fetish can be fun!

ABOUT AND NEARLY OUT

Geese Royal Exchange Manchester *Not* Madcheste

Plus!

London Paris New York
Barcelona Tokyo Milan
Darwen Blackburn Oslo

Los Angeles Dresden
Penzance Rio De Janeiro Belgrade
Wellington Mexico City Aberdeen Calcutta
Warsaw Goole
Bonn Grimsby
Lima Sydney
Giggleswick
Abergavenny
Washington DC
Birmingham
Washington
Moscow Vancouver
Buenos Aires
Clacton-on-sea Geneva Athens
Montevideo
Blandford Forum
Mobberley Leningrad
Osaka Santiago Crawley

Kiev Istanbul Cockermouth
Lagos Hamburg Mountfitchet Reykjavik
Perth San Francisco Havana Pontefract Jakarta
Wick Amsterdam Billericay Chicago Ankara Glasgow
Montreal Torino Stanstead Caracas Philadelphia Louth
Helsinki Madras Eastbourne Winnipeg Brasilia Ullapool
Brussels Littlehampton Manila Stroud Houston Maltby
Dungworth Casablanca Bagshot Cleveland Melbourne
Saffron Walden Bogota Tangier Oswaldtwistle Cairo
St. Louis Bangkok Madrid Toronto Filey Mold
Stockholm Cardigan Nairobi Delhi
Crewe Detroit Salford

CLUB GANGS NO.6
THE OPHELIA/YELLOW BOOK
GIRLS 'N' BOYS

AT SIMPSONS NIGHTCLUB, THE RING, BRACKNELL, BERKS.

EVERY SUNDAY 8.00 — LATE

SCOTT JAMES
WITH GUESTS

ANDY WEATHERALL, TERRY FARLEY, ALFREDO, ROCKY & DIESEL, CRAIG WALSH, KEVIN HURRY, MARTIN MADIGAN, FABIO PARAS

FOR FURTHER INFO: TEL. 0344 860778

2 DRINKS FOR THE PRICE OF 1 FROM 8.30 TO 9.30

BALLOONIC FOR BEGINNERS

Parlez-vous Balloonic? Vot iz zis stvange langvidge vich ze vacky, vay out kids of zer baloonic zene speak in? I, Professor Helmut Frankfurter, have cracked zis stvange dialect and can reveal zat it is a hybrid of Shakespearean English, game show host speak and eccentric phrases vich zer baloonic kids use to communicate with each other.

Below is a qvick glossary of Balloonic expressions vich vill instantly gain you access to von of Chester Cheetah's cheesy parties.

1) "Gadzooks good sir, 'tis a blustery night to be ironing yer longjohns."
TRANSLATION: "There's an all-nighter on outside my granny's bungalow."
2) "Good game! Good game!"
TRANSLATION: "You should see the queue for kebabs."
3) "Oh woe is me, for I have seen the face of "Old Nick" himself."
TRANSLATION: "It's the rozzers."
4) "I'll name that tune in one."
TRANSLATION: "This DJ's playing a predictable set doncha fink?"
5) "Hey nonny nonny my Sapporo's done one squire."
TRANSLATION: "Take care, there's a minesweeper about."
6) "Gather round brethren gather round."
TRANSLATION: "Time for cannabis communion."
7) "Up a bit, left a bit, right a bit, fire!"
TRANSLATION: "You a virgin or wot?"
8) "Blimey young Alfie's caught a terrible cold."
TRANSLATION: "Quicker to walk home than wait for a Joe."
9) "Billy Bunion come on downnnnnn!"
TRANSLATION: "A thoroughly enjoyable evening's entertainment."
10) "Climb aboard me heartys 'tis a moon tide on which we set sail."
TRANSLATION: "Sorry mate, it's a private party."

BALEARIC BALONEY

Balearic Baloney, after last year's less than top Ibiza '90 trip, you would have thought that lessons would have been learnt. Obviously not. "Balearic Breaks," "Art and Clubland," "Black and White and The Ku Presents." Yes, it's organised trips to Ibiza time again, take your own D.J.'s, four hundred of the same boats you see everywhere and you've got home from home. No, no, no. Wait until the East London invasion is over and go in August. It may even be like a holiday then. Anyway, Balearic was always a period of time namely summer '86 to spring '88, rather than any mystical musical style.

Ophelia

Every Saturday at The Gardening Club, The Piazza, Covent Garden, 10.00 till 3.30
D.J.s Steve Lee, Glen Gunner, Nancy Noise, Shane Gibson plus guests.

Keeping Frogs: The Steve Mayes Way (I Ain't Happy)

In a previous Boy's Own, I talked about how two common frogs of mine had died in mysterious circumstances. Although I hadn't suspected anything at first, a letter from a reader I received raised some suspicions. This fellow frog keeper told me that some frogs of his had died and had displayed similar symptoms to those of my deceased duo. They were a difficulty in jumping, lack of food intake and a distended abdominal cavity full of fluid, exactly the same as my frogs problems. My fellow froggie suggested two reasons why he felt unable to maintain his specimens. Firstly, a far too low temperature, and secondly because of keeping them on peat.

I doubt whether the first was the reason for my frogs early bath as they were kept at room temperature (60-65F). However the peat was a different matter. I had been keeping frogs on a floor covering of peat for most of their lives, could the high acidity of this material have been the cause? Although, my frogs usually fed from hand and their food did not often come into contact with the peat. In fact, the newts and salimanders I keep, regularly feed from the peat flooring and they are as right as rain. So could it be that peat is only unsuitable for anurans? On the other hand the common British frog is often found in parts of the country where peat is prominent.

No, the main cause of the frogs untimely death was surely due to a calcium deficiency in their diet. My frogs ate mainly earthworms with a vitamin supplement, whereas the natural diet is made up of snails, beetles and other insects with hard calciferous shells. Our Boy's Own reading fellow frog keeper suggested to me that his frogs also had a diet of solely earthworms, so this seemed to confirm my theory. To be fair, it could have been a combination of both factors, a lack of calcium further aggravated by the peat.

I would be interested to hear from anyone with similar problems in their frogs, especially those suffering from fluid retention. Remember stay off the peat, see you soon chaps.........

10 Reasons Why I Moved to West 10...

What they say...	*What they really mean...*
It's so Bohemian.	You can get puff really easily.
The people are very spiritual.	Acid too!
The architecture is very inspirational.	They've painted my building a funny colour.
There's so many good second hand shops.	It doesn't matter if you look dirty.
It's a 'classless area.'	People sleep in doorways.
There's always something to do.	There's quite a few kebab shops and the 'Sub' stays open 'till 2!
There's so many interesting people.	I saw Wendy James in our chippy.
The accommodation is so interesting.	Hendrix posters rule ok.
It's really lively.	I always carry a kosh - just in case
I wanted to make the break to somewhere different.	Mum's only 10 minutes up the M40.

GOOD READS FOR BEDTIME

At last have come along a couple of clubzines that aren't Boy's Own part 47. Firstly, it's comic time with the *London Illustrated Chortlers Companion* , a pictorial look at the fertile plains of London's club culture with cartoon strips such as, "Moody DJ, he's a bit offish," and "Doing it for the kids." The only drawback seems to be the involvement of club legend (Thank you Clubland magazine, what journalism!) of Johnny "Skeet" Rocka. Draw cartoons? He couldn't draw a bath. More details on 081 877 9912. Next is *Gear,* a wonderfully designed fanzine, very Solaristy, sort of like I-D, for people who go to clubs, as opposed to I-D, for people who go to motorway service stations. Reminds us (visually) very much of the old Manc fanzine Debris. Available from Sign O' The Times. New ideas at last, thank fuck. Buy both.

ABOUT AND NEARLY OUT
BONES PARTY LONDON

Sign of the Times

✳ funky clobber for Madfuckers.
✩71·376✳762
kensington Mkt.
ken High St. London W.8

Leather Collards Around Your Ankles
A Female's Point Of View

Apparently there are various male parties in and around London very much interested in the happenings in girls toilets in nightclubs. Even though girls have no hesitation in using the Gents when they can't be bothered to stand in a queue, can't stand, or can't stand it ("Are you alright?"), it · seems that boys are willing to curb their curiosity temporarily for the sake of convenience, a far cry from the usual head first (Or is that dick first?) behaviour of a normal, healthy, adult male.

The girls toilet is an escape, a release, somewhere where you can collect yourself, and try and get a grip before entering out once more into the fray. Sit down, take a deep breath,   get your head together, have a line and then get out.Average time spent by girls actually on the toilet is a minute longer than boys. Nightly turnover is equal, if even a little less than the boys next door, length of time being due to the law that once you sit down, it's more difficult to get up, or the fact that two people in the toilet takes longer than one. However, despite popular belief, latent insecurities that make for girls who go to the toilet in pairs are caused only by the fear of losing your best mate to the time tunnel in the mirror.

Getting up off the toilet isn't made any easier by current fashion trends, weighed down by folds of PVC and leather round your ankles. I don't know about you, but I often find myself sitting completely naked for several minutes with my head upside down between my knees (Uncomfortable positions are, of course, always the best in situations like these).Tittifying yourself is the last thing on anyone's mind here. Handbags and lipstick rarely exist in this world and yet beauty abounds. Isn't it a strange phenomenon that Ecstasy enhances female beauty but makes boys look like they've been smacked round the head with a baseball bat? ("No way is it bad for you. How can it be? I never get any side effects").

Reasons for going to the toilet in the first place are manifold. Despite the obvious useful little shelf on the back of the toilet, there are reasons unique to the female gender such as the fact that a few girls actually go to clubs purely to sit in the toilet all night. Maybe this is because this is the only place where they can see past the cotton wool. I don't think I ever remember a specific conversation going on in the toilets, though funnily enough they seem quite hectic places. This place is a different, if monosyllabic level of understanding. Most of the time, the walls are physically (or maybe that's mentally) shaking with an e.s.p. buzz let loose and out of control. No-one needs to say anything but you still feel like you're on Mars.

The toilets normally stay reasonably clean, (unlike the Gents) even after the toilet paper has run out and even after the inevitable falling out of one's insides. The Sunday Sport really thought they had a one-off when that woman's intestines got sucked out through an aeroplane toilet, didn't they? Poor deluded journalists of safe middle-class newspapers. There wasn't anything wrong with the plane - she'd just dropped a top E and came out half a stone lighter. Honestly, don't they know anything? Sinks, however, are redundant as a means to hygienic living conditions, more often than not falling victim to the ejaculation of everything else in your body. Just when they'd got used to being ashtrays, they become sick buckets, and then they are ashtrays again, but this time you don't need to run the tap to put the cigarette out.

Depending entirely upon the size of the sub-establishment, there are from time to time sightings of boys in the larger more comfortable rooms (Passion at Valbonnes was always a favourite for men who love women), though this style of toilet has, for some reason largely gone out of fashion nowadays. Personally, I think this is a great shame and it begs me to therefore ask the question, "Wouldn't it be easier to knock down the wall between the two? " After all, this is a natural bodily function and talking about it suddenly isn't embarrassing any more...Sometimes girls don't need to go to the toilet all night, but it's guaranteed that for some reason, we'll see the inside at one time or another of an evening. So boys, don't be shy, Boy's Own, Girl's Own, who gives a shit anyway? After all, doesn't it sound like fun?

"Poverty and tatters and hollow eyed and high, sat up smoking in the supernatural darkness of cold water flats floating across the tops of cities, contemplating jazz."

(Alan Ginsberg)

Time to think again, park your arse, give life to a joint and talk and not about nothing. The marginalisation of the black musician, the black poet, the tragedy of Parker and Holliday, social facades crumbling, an obsessive right, a left in contradiction. Consciousness is back and angst haunts faintly in the jazz clubs opening their smoky doors. Djangos at The State in Manchester has overtaken the Talking Loud mantle, sharp dresssers, a live set and plenty of goatee beards that look like girlies tuftys cut off blow up dolls and stuck on.

Recently over a lager sherbert at the pub my cousin, a sad victim of the old school with a wondrous wardrobe of many acrylic delights, found a great deal of jocularity when I corrected him on his comment that Mod's back is it? Dude it's Mod-ernist I said, politics and intellectual music. Right on. Maybe it goes as he says, that '60's Italian design and American Beat style is the only way to find a degree of stylish sophistication outside the mainstream Mecca palaces. Perhaps new styles can now only be (re)discovered in a past that still had alternative styles to be explored. Sales of Kerousac, Burroughs, Malcolm X will rise, along with Coltrane and Gillespie. Gaillard's Vout Oroonie, that incredibly humorous rhyming language could return and with some of the M.D.M.A.'s that are knocking around right now it will probably appear sooner than you can say shabby da doo with your booties on a kicki-kicki up the dust.

It's easy to glide comfortably along with many of the present style magazines promotion of jazz/rap. The black experience, political expression and a clever use of modern technology that adds a new meaning to the word Beatnik. But it is the media that forge its representation depicting it as a subversive group with social challenges to be gleaned from the surface. For now. And then it must pass as they move cheerfully on to unearthing more spectacular subculture. I-D like The Face constructs many glorious definitions of fashion movements, it draws together disparate and sometimes contradictory elements and smooths all discrepancies. Excess baggage is handed out, heavy with meanings to justify. It's part of the circle that generates its own meanings and own survival on the precarious job of predicting style changes or reporting on the next biggie, a job fraught with huge embarrassing traps.

I remember Reportage claiming Country and Western as the next big thing after Acid House, a happening event that shaped its way on Tuesdays at the Wag. Here I am now, with a rooting tooting wardrobe a-heaving with over sized stetsons, handsewn chaparajos and more leather belts than a bondage fetish. Without meaning to boast I can still lasso a Yorkshire Terrier from twenty feet, though I no longer carry my scribbled out kidney donor card that begs for me not to be allowed to head on out to the ranch in the sky with my boots on. It all comes over like a game where risk is the thrill that allows a giddiness, an excess that only cons, misleads and bamboozles. Recently hype has spread itself around

Quadrant Park in the peaceful Liverpool suburbs that never mentions half the crowd are under eighteen, that to be 'in' the latest Top Man lines have to be sported, that most of the lads become tripping, twitching psychotics who commandeer every good inch of dancing space and any girl who enters this domain must give free reign to gropes. To get an understanding of any article you need to read between the lines and never once hand over belief to the informed tales of apocalyptic visions we read: Madchester backlash, post-house music scene. Events slip into each other, resist easy categories and just ease away in time. Jocks recently took to playing the game claiming a reaction against D.J.'s was on its way, proven apparently in Oakenfold moving from Land of Oz (Mondays) to the Milk Bar (Fridays). This was stood up proudly as a waning of enthusiasm for club nights and D.J.'s. Yet a D.J. like Sasha is near mobbed when the screaming crowds of mini-teen ravers spot him, all trying to rip off his clothes. (Though rumour has it crowds have been seen running away from Justin Robertson, such is the cruel lot and short straw of life that the Bally-Eric D.J. must endure). A real reaction against D.J.'s would be clubbers turning up clutching their own instruments demanding a democratic control on the selection of what was played, ensuring they accompanied.

Me, I've had enough of all the cranked up lauding homages to cockeyed clubs, dicky D.J.'s and two bit bands who are by all accounts experimental. Sycophancy sums up the too many articles that can pass only as generous advertising. My Dad happened by accident on the answer, using my Record Mirror cover when I ran out of bog paper. Nice one Bob!

BONES PARTY - LONDON

PHUTURE RECORDS
TEL. 352 0141

PHUTURE

THE GARAGE
350 KINGS ROAD LONDON

SORT ME OUT!

Guest lists... Either you're on 'em or you're in the queue, but is it fair or just an old relic of that wanky mid-'eighties "West End Trendy" mentality? Basically, it's about time that everyone paid a fair price and the people who only go to a club if they're "sorted" stayed at home, because if you look at the dance floor, it's packed with the payers whilst the guest list packs the bar moaning that, "It's full of kids in here." The ending of GL's will only work if all clubs, D.J.'s and club runners work together, but in the end it's everyone who will profit.

CLUB GANGS NO.7
FULL CIRCLE
"SPENT ON SUNDAY" POSSIE

LETTERS TO THE CHAPS

H. M. Remand Centre, Feltham.

To Boy's Own,

Well, I'm banged up for the summer and I'm roasting for a copy of my favourite magazine. I was out in IBZA for IBZA '90. Saw the bods had a mad time. I would appreciate if you could send me a copy as I am unable to go and get one myself. I've been in since the last sumer well September really. I would love to have a reply.

Hold It Down.

Maurice Small.

PS. Could you send some flyers with the reply?

Respect.

London W6

Dear Boys.

In the last Boy's Own, you had that lagging boat of a scarse explaining the do's and don'ts of masturbation. The one thing he missed out on was where on a Saturday night you can get a good old firm but fair British wank free! Yes free, just get yourself down to Paddington Station and join a large queue of bods and mods and simply wait your turn. In no time at all your privates will be in the hands of a professional. The wank is certainly not tender and it can be quite embarrassing when it's administered in front of countless others but you get the added bonus that once both parties are satisfied you get let into quite a good scream-up (Oh no! That's spoilt it-Ed.) called "Menace" and although the masturbators doing the door search don't wear rubber of laytex, they do answer to the names "Madame Winston," and "Caribean Lovely seeks D.I.Y. merchants."

J. Arthur Rank.

It begins innocent enough, usually a joke or bundled as part of a trippity-whiz conversation at 5.00 a. m. Then I let it all get out of hand, not meaning to. Sure, it all smells roses packaged tight and neat as an idea. Your very own club night, your very own music. But now it happens nearly every month, regular as bank statements, periods, the latest Manc band, or a bath. The future suddenly begins towing away those nine to fives, the court summons on bills, the damp rush hour bus journeys, the uselessness. There was a world of music looking a little too complacent, quite happy with itself and by turns elitist. It needed some beatings, some malicious digs to knock it into odd shapes without a balance, so over, up, and onto its head it could be turned, spun round, with a quick coy tickle between the legs. But there are things that don't necessarily enter the reckoning, good old Mr. Bastard for instance who chooses to sit out any hasty blueprints. Instead he munches on many a ruse to give the vulnerable club runner a good slapping. I'm not here to deter, never that, to moan, maybe, or perhaps weave a quick guide.

Many people would look first to the different and challenging methods of obtaining a night in the first place. Intricate details of how to approach the manager, hard sell attitudes, assurances. There is sadly only one bleak way. Search out the club owner, kneel behind and lick like a dog with worms. This is by no means the only licking. Asking friends means half the people there are on the guest list. So, it's out to freezing streets at closing time giving leaflets to cheery sweaty people who can't feel the cold, or their body for that matter. And what do they do with the flyers? They make paper aeroplanes, fan themselves, decorate the pavements, write each others 'phone numbers on the back, make roaches or shitty little trumpets to go parp parp down and there's always an origami expert who makes one into a china tea set. Only aromatic Albert, the local tramp puts them to effective use wiping his arse.
There are more tricky and technical problems though. The D.J. partner always proves a bit saucy, an unexpected crisis to the troubles. they're usually nice people, though admittedly talking too much of, "Doing it for the kiddies," and blagging of dodgy bootlegs that cost them three mortgages and a pint of fresh blood from every first born child. But

what is most deceiving in their general attitude is a cunning ability to hide that latent mental health problem. It arises in a muted form of catatonic manic depressiveness brought on by the apparent lack of any one dancing. they sulk, muttering about Riding On Time, Whitney Houston, even E.M.F. no less. It's best to stick them with a copy of Chris Rea's "Josephine" a pop star with a surprise, or Talk Talk's original "Such a "Shame. That fools them a treat and calms the situation, only for a minute. Then it's back to the incessant question, "Not a bad mix eh?" It is devastating how bad it is, but this is a person who thinks B.P.M. stands for Bloody Perfect Mixing.

And if there was good mixing who does give a shit? The bar staff, the mad bouncer who call me "Pal," winks a lot and insists on being my body guard? No, not really. The punters? The kiddies "To do it for" stay away in droves and I always find myself placating Tom Git the local dealer whose pockets bulge with near £500 of gear. The only invite to show, but I owe him money. The road dips from here on. The manager, a self-confessed amnesia sufferer looks rather shocked and quite sternly pooh poohs any notion that there had been talk of a probationary period for the night. Suggestions are made of more accessible music, excuses that theirs is not that type of underground club. 'Phone calls aren't returned, you're left waiting at the door, people smile and say "not to worry."

Makes you wonder sometimes if Old Jack Luck will ever be persuaded to whistle your song. There are D.J.'s I never really cared for who could turn up at a club, fart in a general rhythm down a mic and receive rousing applause with commendations at the night's end. Perhaps it is best now to put that crusade on the musak biz to the back burner, pack up my old kit bag and head off to the rainforest where I can help the First International Green Brigade beat off the Guarana users.

Dave Barker.

All letters to Boy's Own Mansions, Unit 2, 249-251 Kensal Road, London. W10.

CHAUVINIST

32 Mill Road Cambridge
Tel: 321372

Premadonna Records

Contents Include:

Heavenly
Flying Irma
FFRR Underground
Strictly Rydbym
Urban NUGroove

UVINIST

Ingredients

Baylis
& Knight
Simpson
Raymai

...l Road Cambridge
Tel: 321372

E CELLAR

D OR DEAD
RED10
DOC MARTINS

20 Jeckyle Things About Puberty

1) Sharing your bedroom with two younger brothers and waiting until 4.30 a.m. to have a wank.
2) Hiding your crusty bills the next day.
3) Swapping your scaletrix for a copy of Anal Sex at 14.
4) Being a bumfluff bobby.
5) Discovering that your foreskin is three sizes too small for your knob.
6) Offering your dad out.
7) Growing pubes ... on your feet!
8) Always having a gap between your kecks and your Kickers.
9) Getting a hard on in double history.
10) Pouring gallons of Old Spice all over yourself.
11) Pissing the bed after a bottle of Woodpecker and two cans of Black Label.
12) Waking up with a strange tingling sensation in your bell end.
13) Shower dodging after triple games.
14) Spending approximately £2562.00 per annum on Clearasil lotion.
15) Ugly birds fancying the arse off you.
16) Fit birds always KBing your advances.
17) Convincing yourself that you've contracted syphilis by knocking one out once too often.
18) Coming home from a party with thirty-six lovebites in various places.
19) Offering your grandad out.
20) Getting twatted by your grandad.

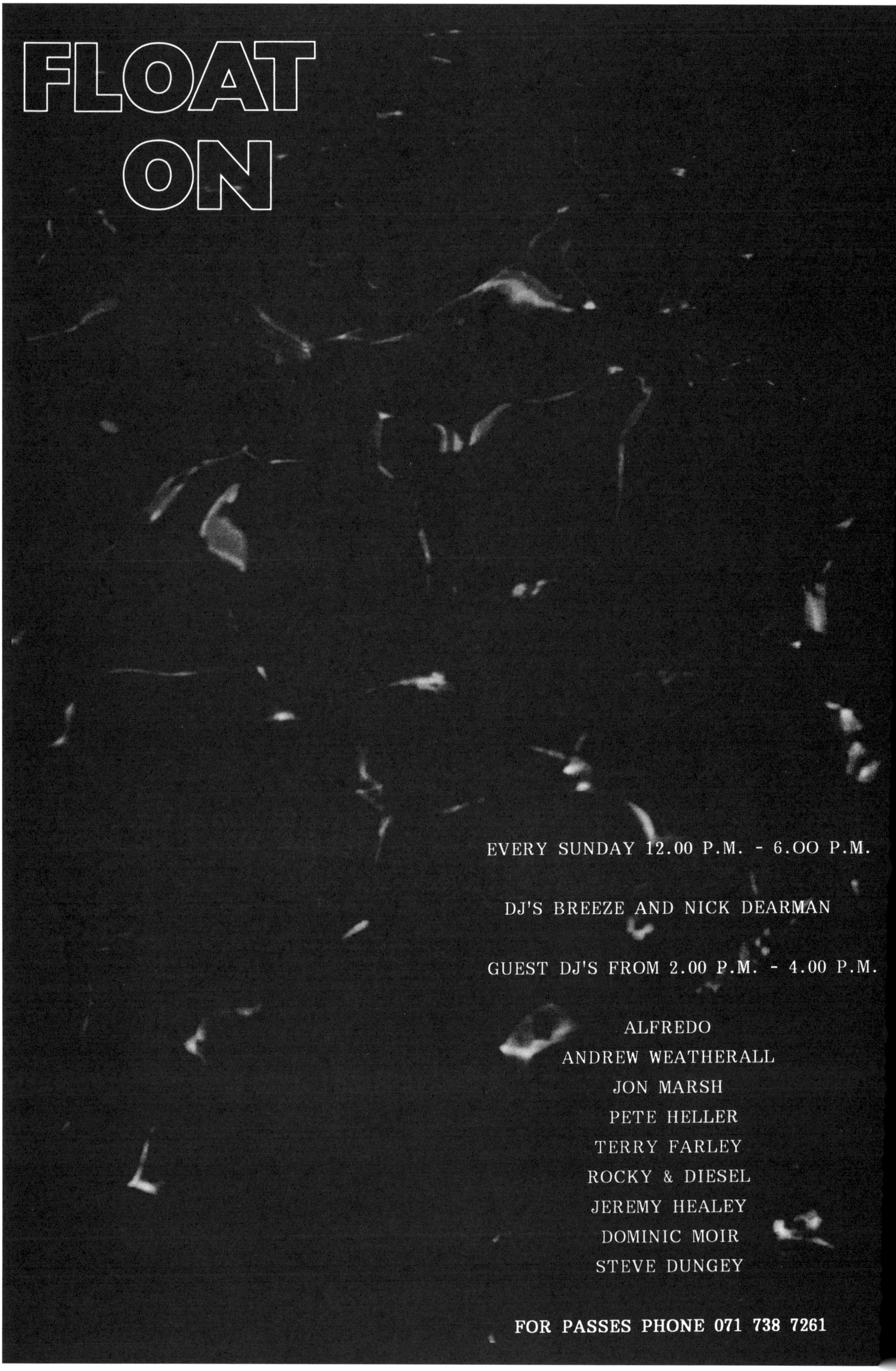

FLOAT ON

EVERY SUNDAY 12.00 P.M. - 6.00 P.M.

DJ'S BREEZE AND NICK DEARMAN

GUEST DJ'S FROM 2.00 P.M. - 4.00 P.M.

ALFREDO
ANDREW WEATHERALL
JON MARSH
PETE HELLER
TERRY FARLEY
ROCKY & DIESEL
JEREMY HEALEY
DOMINIC MOIR
STEVE DUNGEY

FOR PASSES PHONE 071 738 7261

BOYS OWN - SUMMER edition :
Editor · FLEUR . CONTRIBUTORS · TERRY FARLEY, STEVE HALL,
DEAN 'NOB OUT' O'CONNOR, DAVE BARKER, PHIL THORNTON, PHILIPA GRANT,
ADAM PORTER, MAZIE, ANDREW WEATHERALL .
WRITE TO or RING UP : BOYS OWN MANSIONS 249·251 KENSAL Rd.
LONDON W10 · 081·968·8459

THANKS, RESPECT And SNOGS TO . . .
FLEUR, COS WITHOUT HER YOU WOULD NOW be sitting on the toilet
with nothing to read. COVER STARS, JOSEPH HAISMAN And JACK ROCKA.
COOPER and LYNCH (AKA The Mitchell Brothers) The REAL Mick STACEY.
SPROCKET and DISEASEL ("He's always at it), The EXTREMELY RIPPY GARY
HAISMAN, JOHNNY (Club Legend) ROCKA, PETESKI HELLER,
STEVE (Houswives Choice) LEE, FABBI, FRAN AND FIONA, MR and MRS RAMPLING,
STRIPEY and LINDA, NORMAN JAY, UNCLE BOB JONES,
PLUG (AKA 'DIRK VON TINGLE-TANGLE', BELGIAN NEW BEAT DRAG QUEEN AND
PART TIME VAN COURIER). The MOST EXCELLENT JUSTIN N' GREG,
PHIL N' FIONA, 2 KEVS on PUFF, DAVE HENLEY, GRAEME PARK, ROD, WAYNE and
the REAL SCREAMERS, VENUS, KINKY DISCO, PURE SEXY AND FLYING,
DORRELL and SOPHIE, DEJA VU, CHARLIE and KAREN, GINGER MICK (ISLINGTONS
ANSWER TO JOHN MILLS), ALI, MOIRA and SCOTT, BUTLER and PRICEY,
MAX ("He's on a quiet one), 'GEAR' and 'DUCK CALL', OAKEY N' NANCY,
LOFTY and CLIVE, JACKIE N' LITTLE JASON, PLUS ALL The CHAPS
WHO Are UP FOR IT AND ALL the GIRLS on the FIRM.

"IMITATION IS THE BEST FORM OF CRAP"
GENUINE MICHIKO KOSHINO CLOTHING AVAILABLE AT 70 NEAL St. WC2. 071 497 0166

No. 12
Spring 1992

BOY'S OWN

iley not snidey

It's with great sadness (and a slight smirk) that I must announce the death of The Outsider. Details are currently sketchy, but police were called to his Berkshire country residence late last Tuesday, and found the great man lying amongst a pile of discarded Boy's Own back issues, King Tubby gramaphone records, lengths of rubber hosing, bacofoil, and a collection of substances that have yet to return from police laboratories.

Born : Audrey J. Witherspoon.
Exact Date : Unknown.
Educated : Sporadically.
Writing Credits : Full details are sketchy but prior to Boy's Own, it is thought that he was involved with a small group of cynics known as, "The Blatant Whingers," and edited their bi-annual manifesto, "Let Them Eat Cake."

Discovered by Boy's Own, ranting to absolutely nobody at an acid house in 1988, he was quickly put on the payroll.

Boy's Own editorial staff were too upset to comment.

Late news : Police this afternoon raided a travel agent's in Hackney today, after threatening calls were discovered on Mr. Witherspoon's answering machine. The calls relate to an Outsider article regarding Thailand. The men arrested include the owner of "Leggit Sharpism Rave Hols Inc.," two Thai Embassy officials, and a man known locally as Growler.

My Mate's New Friend

So neat and clean and witty, he used to be such fun,
He always got a welcome when he walked into the
pub
He ran and he played football
He never even smoked
He had a lovely girlfriend
But now he's just a joke.

His new friend is called Charlie
It's become his favourite word
It's all he ever talks about, its's making him absurd
He's dirty and unshaven
His nose is always running
I sometimes have to turn away
When I see him coming.

He's borrowing to do his deals
He's pushing drugs and selling pills
Up to his neck in debts and bills
All for the sake of Charlie.

He's stealing now to get a snort
Him who used to be the sort
That you could turn to for support
If you were in trouble.

It's made him think that he's elite
He'll walk right by you in the street
Because it makes him feel so neat
Arm in arm with Charlie.

I tried to tell him what I thought
I told him he would go to court
We argued and we nearly fought
It made me feel so helpless.

He's changed so much, he's gone so thin
I don't know what to do for him
He said 'Fuck off' and with a grin
He walked away to Charlie.

INDUSTRIA

L O N D O N

Café

BAR

CLUB

OPEN
12 NOON — 3.30AM MON - THURS
12 NOON — 6AM FRI - SAT

INDUSTRIA
9, HANOVER STREET, WI
INFORMATION ✦ HIRE ✦ BOOKINGS
CALL WAYNE/ROD 071-493 0689

"Plotted Up" - The Real Chill

The "Art Of Chilling." Much has been written about going around your mates for a "sesh, " both instead of, or after a club. Most of what's been said is crap. Wet fish tales of sipping warm ribena, eating popcorn and listening to arty farty music - all this in an equally crappy suburban Manc flat - whatever next? The truth is more ugly, more vindictive, more real. Read on ...

1.00 AM.
The club's bollocks. Too many odds and sods bods who were vauging last summer, now trying to be outrageous. I feel another middle class punk revival on the cards - it's time to nitt. Everyone's up for it, off to the plot.

1.30 AM.
Everything's going well. Everyone left at the club is getting slagged by our bunch of friends. We have a common enemy - them, and for a while we are all - us.

2.30 AM.
The decks have been hijacked by the up and coming DJ. Every sesh has one and he's proving that he too has every Leftfield remix ever commissioned. "Chill out music?" - No way Pedro, that's for squats in Ladbroke Grove. We're all "Up for it," and it's pumping house time y'all.

3.30 AM.
By now the DJ's and music know-it-all's have fucked off the deck destroyer and are picking holes in the careers, style and sexual habits of every other DJ in town not present. The rest of the people who don't give a monkeys about music are talking (quickly and loudly) about everybody else's drug problem. "This is my first one for ages" - is the most common quote of the evening.

4.30 AM.
The DJ contingent are now in deep debate about who first played "Bridge Over The River Kwai"(On Italian New Music) or who first did the MFSB "Love Is The Message," with the Poll Pott "Dig Deep Cambodia" speech over the top. The non-DJ's neck up again to relieve the boredom.

5.00 AM.
By now there is always someone who's lost it badly and sadly. Kodak instamatic photos of them are already on the mantlepiece and everyone laughs just in case the chirpy banter turns your way. The plot has split into two. The people with dosh are sitting with the people who matter, while those without money (To be called the have-not's from now on) are starting to feel a bit uneasy. Things have started to go a bit Pete.

Every Thursday

Millionaire Club
West Mosley Street
Manchester

DJ Justin Robertson
and Guest

MOST EXCELLENT

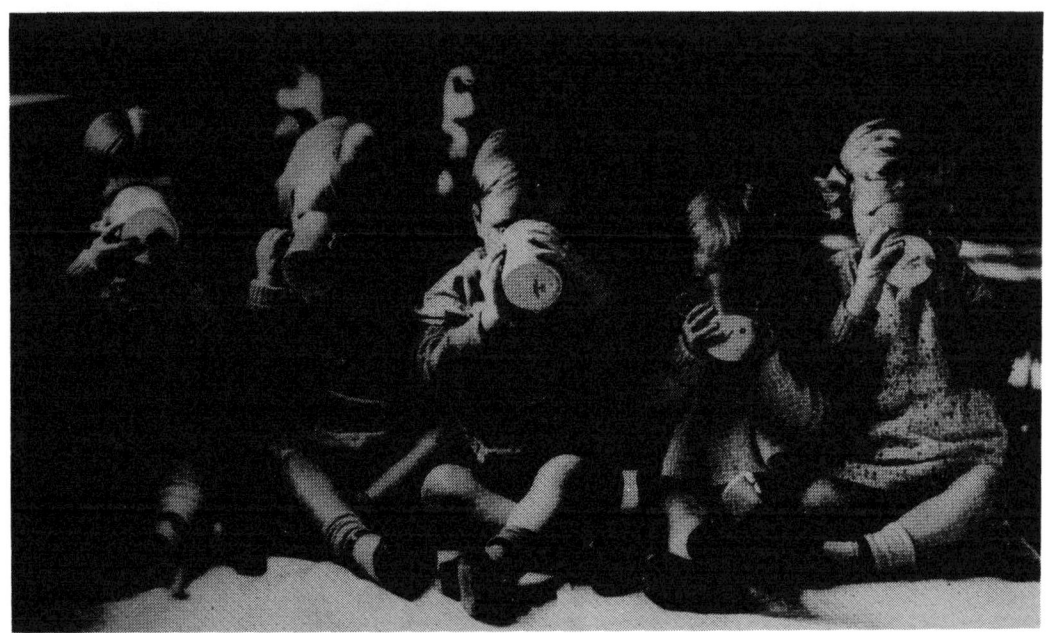

The have not's
get on a para one.

6.00AM.
The stick is now squarely aimed at the have-not's. "Look at the state of you." Old Mr. Noidy has settled into the small bunch of skint and grey looking people huddled into the corner on the other side of the room. It's time for another, " ... and have I told you I always thought you was a top DJ?"

7.00 AM.
The have-nots would leave but that would draw further attention to them and "What would they say about me when I'm gone." Better to ride the storm.

7.30 AM.
The stick's still coming fast and furious. The have-nots try to get a couple on tick and so get back on the firm. Ever heard the words, "No way matey"?

8.00 AM.
Most of the have-nots have now left our friendly "chill out." By a rule, all post-club sessions have to be at least ten miles from where anyone lives and under no circumstances anywhere near public transport. As for taxis, if you couldn't afford a cheeky half then what chance of any sherbert fare? The Marks & Sparks shop girls on the way to work look at you knowingly. You feel empty, look shit and wonder why this always happens to you.

8.30 AM.
Back at the sesh, our heroes have opened that bottle of Moet, saved for a special occassion, sent a cab out for a gram of charles, built another spliff and generally find life splendid. "It's better now that that lot have gone, the real firm's left now."

9.00 AM.
Poor old have-not walks through his front door. His girlfriend says fuck all, but the look on her face says so much more ... the art of chilling.

Sign
O'
The
Times
Party
London.

Distorted Disco - The Sound Of Spring

DJH Feat Stefy	Hey Boy (Larry Levan Remix)
Lemon Interupt	Eclipse/Big Mouth
Sunscream	Love You More (Fire Island Re ..)
Martika	Spirit
Outrage	Drives Me Crazy
Ankamano	Funky Guitar
Voices Of 6th Street	Call Him Up (Slam Remix)
Jus Friends	As One
Love Quartet	Ethos Mama Survives In Dub
Dayeene	Good Thing
D.O.P.	Groovy Beat
Guy Costley	Somebody Here
Mass Order	Let's Get Happy (Remix)
Smells Like Heaven	Rythm De Londres
Ralphi Rossarrio	An Instrumental Need
Kingdom Come	Jungle Bliss
Rase	Say It Loud
We Kill Love	Ten Men Dead (Fabi Parras Re ..)
The Todd Terry Project	Holding On
Rythm 3 Request	Desafinado

You Still Up For It Or What? : Part 36

There's more than a few miserable bastards out there, spreading doom and gloom around London's club scene. It seems their one role in life is to tell as many people as possible what a shit time we are all having. What these people's problems are, I'm not quite sure ... the lack of "pucker bumbles," no decent girls on the firm, a lack of classic tunes. Apart from the bumble problem, the only thing wrong with London clubs I can see are these people's attitudes. If you can't put energy and positivity into clubs then stay at home with your memories of Spectrum and a grubbly half a gramme of charlie, we don't need you. The summer's coming and if all that people can do is moan, then it's time to move on from them and let some people with energy onto the scene - any club or party is only as good as the crowd's attitude. It's not drugs or the DJ that makes a party (Although they can ruin it - Ed.), it's the crowd, so let's get pumping.

Disco Revival Pressure (Part 1)

The George Bussey Experience	Disco Extravaganza
Machine	There But For The Grace Of God
Paris Grey	Reach For Your Dreams
Ecstasy, Passion And Pain	Touch 'N' Go
Sylvester	Just A Feeling (Disco Edit)
First Choice	Double Cross (Larry Levan Re ..)
Loretta Holloway	All About The Papers
Brainstorm	Loving Is Really My Game
Juggy Murray Jones	Inside America
Esther Williams	I'll Be Your Pleasure

Sign O' The Times Party London.

The Illustrated CHORTLERS
Companion

"You can stick it right up your arse for a start!" *S.Wells N.M.E*

Buckle up! Issue 2 out soon

Uppers and Downers

Smiley Culture

Happy shiny people, if you
ain't happy, you ain't shiny.

The new bagel bar at Spurs - top scoff
for the home boys and hours of fun
from the away enclosure.

Cape Fear, AKA "The Steve Mayes
Story."

Resting your beer on Kylie's head.
Pouring your beer on Danni's head.

Shouting "Leave it out Pat,"
in a Pingu The Penguin voice.

The backlash against the house
backlash. We love it.

Weatherall's barnet hanging
next to Billy Wyman's guitar at
The Hard Rock Cafe.

Liza Minelli, live in London.
The top London crime family
night out.

London - the best!

Being able to sell Camilla Deakin's
'phone number for loads of money
to her enemies.

The George Power show on
Kiss. More please. Disco
boogie from an originator.

Toppers - top post-suedehead shoes,
ready for a summer revival. Also
coming up, Converse.

Being a sunny Jim.

Snidey Culture

Miserable, moany nose-up nauses
(Fuck off and stay in)

The anti-E brigade. "I haven't done
one for months." You ain't fucking
danced or smiled since either.

Rugby - a crap game for poshfackers
and rozzers.

The strange stripsearching habits of
the"doorpeople" at Kinky Disco.

All the London DJ's who fell for
Tony Humphries' Cuba joke.

The same old colour of the new
South African cricket team.

Not being able to find anyone who
will admit to being a "sycodelic
skinhead."

Posh facker humour - "The Mary
Whitehouse Experience," and
"Whose Line ... "

Germans - The lot of 'em.

Ministry of Sound - London needs
it, but no real clubbers like it.
Shape up please.

Knobhead American DJ's and their
wanky attitudes, silly vests and
London lackeys.

John Major's road from Brixton to
Westminster. "It ain't in our A-Z
mate."

E-deafs (Pardon - Ed).

Cherish. The Diorama. London.

WARNING : This piece has a raging case of stereotypitis, as it is assuming that all DJ's, bouncers, drug dealers, etc., etc., are male. Unfortunately, most of them are. However, luckily things are changing. Take me, for instance. I've got these pure MDMA capsules, if anyone wants them. I've got to charge a score though, because the bloke that I got them off ...

PULL THE OTHER ONE!
A GROUPIE'S GUIDE TO THE PULLING POWER OF CLUB TYPES

Why are there so few really good looking DJ's? Well, as Freud was wont to say, "Let uz look back to ze personz childhood for ze answerz to zere prezent behaviour." Remember the good looking boys at school? The ones who were tall, athletic and square jawed. The ones who always had girlfriends. They were the ones who were busy going out on dates, juggling relationships with a couple of different girls or out on the pull with their mates. All their pent up sexual frustration didn't stay pent up for very long. They didn't have much time left for introspection.

Now, picture another less well endowed teenage boy. Spotty, greasy hair, sunken chest, massive insecurity complex. What does he do (apart from wank)? He thinks to himself, "I'll show them, I'll be someone. Then they'll all want to know me. Then they won't laugh at me any more." He stays in, partly because he's never invited anywhere, and he spins his records, or plays his instrument (and his musical instrument as well), or he sits and reads everything he can get his hands on, from Nietzche to porno mags. So, when he grows up, what does he become? A DJ, a musician or a journalist. And where are all those good looking boys now? Probably married, with half a dozen kids dotted around the place.

Admittedly, this is a rather over-generalised theory, but it has a nugget of truth in it, and might possibly explain the motivation behind the actions of those who actively seek the limelight, be they DJ's, journalists, politicians, or whatever. After all, if you've got a good record collection you can always listen to it at home. Why deliberately seek to stand up and impose your taste on hundreds of others? It couldn't possibly be for the fame and glory, could it? Let's not pretend that this is a purely unselfish gesture, nobly bringing good music to the kids. One thing we're under no illusions about is that fame and fortune, power and influence are all very attractive. In other words, they give you pulling power.

Now, most people are obviously sensible enough to see through a little fame and judge a person for what they really are, but for those of you who are determined to go ahead and snare a prize anyway, here is a quick guide of what to expect from a selection of "desirable" club crumpet.

Main DJ's
These lot usually get a strange, shifty look in their eyes whenever approached by a stranger, because they're anticipating the sweaty hand

shake and mutterings of, "Great set, mate. Great set," which is a standard line, even when Mother Theresa on acid could have played better. (Incidently, she's on at the next Bob's Full House, isn't she?) Not always the best dressers, owing to the fact that they've always spent all their spare dosh on records and have only recently been able to afford designer gear. This means they've usually developed odd tastes and go for fake fur Vivienne Westwood trousers and Hawaiian shirts from Jones.

Pros : You get to go to all the clubs he's playing at for free. If he starts his own club, you can take over as door person and have fun fucking off all those people you never really liked anyway.

Cons : He's always off playing the Banana Club in West Kilmarnock, or some other obscure venue, thus making it very easy for him to be unfaithful.

Nob Potential : Superb thrusting members size.

"Biggest willie gets the pucka dove."

Warm-Up DJ's

These tend to be the mates of main DJ's or club promoters, who have given them their big chance to prove themselves. Nearly always from a London suburb, their first gig was probably a mate's birthday party in the back room of a pub somewhere in Essex. Now that they've scaled the dizzy heights of success, they're playing some club in the back room of a pub somewhere in Essex. They often work in record shops during the day, and are well known for being sullen and grumpy. This may be because of all the dick heads they get in the shop, or simply because they've so far failed miserably to make it big time as a DJ. Chat up lines go something like this, "I'm playing Peel Your Eyeballs in Slough next month. If you want I'll put you on my guest list."

Pros : He might hit the big time with you by his side, giving you endless cred points - that is, providing he hasn't given you the elbow in favour of a sixteen year old blonde.

Cons : He may not hit the big time and that sixteen year old blonde will let you keep him.

Nob size potential : Small nudgers. (No value girls).

FLYING & VOLANTE
RECORDS
KENSINGTON MARKET
LONDON (BASEMENT)

MONDAY-SATURDAY 10.30AM-6PM
PURVEYORS OF BESPOKE STEREOPHONIC VINYL

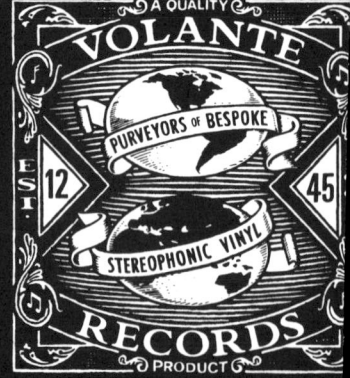

ALSO **FLYING RECORDS BOURNEMOUTH** *PALACE PARKING · HINTON ROAD · BOURNEMOUTH BH1 2EJ*
TELEPHONE OR FAX : 0202 319297   MON-SAT 10AM-6PM   THURS 12AM -8PM

 mailorder
VISA AND MASTERCARD ACCEPTED

TECHNICS SL1210 WITH CARTRIDGE £330 INC VAT + CARRIAGE!
ALSO . . . enquiries · flying records t-shirts · slip mats
despatch bags · to be added to the shop mailing list
for regular charts and newsletters regarding releases
or any further information
phone : 071-938 4407 (2 lines)   fax : 071-938 4409

RIMINI 92
in association with cause 'n' effects
24th JUNE - 8th JULY

DJS: Andrew Weatherall · Terry Farley · Paul Oakenfold · Dean Thatcher
Sasha · Phil Perry · Rocky & Diesel · Kevin Hurry · Glen Gunner
Craig Walsh · Dave Dorrell · Orde Meikle · Stuart McMillan
Darren Emmerson · Fabi Paras · Lisa Loud · Rosko · Justin Robertson
Scott Braithwaite · Clive Henry · Lofty · (TBC) Brandon Block · Ashley
CLUBS: Peter Pan · Pasha · Cocorico · Baia Imperiale
PARTY NIGHTS: Including Kinky Disco · Most Excellent · Venus · Slam
FOR FURTHER INFORMATION / BOOKING FORMS /
CLUB PASSES: Please call the office on **081 848 8802**
between 9.30am and 6.00pm and speak to **Julie**

FLYING AT THE ARENA
208 NEWPORT ROAD, MIDDLESBROUGH
SATURDAY MAY 2ND

DJS: DEAN THATCHER, ROCKY & DIESEL, SCOTT BRAITHWAITE, CLIVE HENRY
FURTHER INFORMATION CALL **0642 251854** OR **081 848 8802**

Doormen

They always have a lot of friends around them at the beginning of the night, but these seem to disappear mysteriously once everyone and their mates have got in OK. Often the cause of 'flu and colds, because to chat to them, you'll have to hover around the door in a draft. They seem to have a limited taste in clothes and probably go down their local in a dinner jacket and bow tie, or wear their embroidered bomber jacket in bed. Remember, you might fancy him on three white burgers, but would your mum's weak heart hold out if you brought him home?

Pros : Copping off with one will ensure a smooth entry (to the club they're working at that is!) . They can protect you in a scrap, so you can safely go around starting on anyone you don't like the look of.

Cons : They tend to be overweight ("No, it's relaxed muscle!") so you may find you have to go on top to avoid premature middle-age spread. Not much of a conversationalist, their best chat-up lines are sleep inducing antiques like, "Are you a model?" or "What's a nice girl like you ... etc. ?" (Yawn).

Nob size potential : Bellheads as big 'n' black as Newgate's knocker.

Club Promoters

They usually have night club tans and deep rings under their eyes, due to the thorough research into their rivals' clubs, that they're forced to do. As with doormen, they attract many friends just before their club is on, so to get their full attention, only call them mid-week (but not before 12). There are two main types of promoter - the hands on, "I'm out there with my punters" type (E-monster) or the aloof, "Keep a low profile," businessman (Charlie head).

Pros : You'll always get into their club for nothing.

Cons : You've got to go to the same bloody club every week to see them.

Nob size potential : Usually too off it to raise a smile.

Drug Dealers

This lot are really the top dogs in a club scene that relies on stimulants for its inspiration. They never dance, despite having an enormous capacity for drugs (because you can't be seen to be losing control - someone might try and rip you off!), but prefer to hover in the corner, looking wildly around the room like Jack Nicholson in The Shining. You can choose between the long haired, "I spent the last four summers in Ibiza," type and the, "I bite the heads off pit bulls," friend of The Krays variety. Top chat-up line, "Do you fancy a nose-up in the toilets?"

Pros : Pretty obvious.

Cons : They are usually noidy from too much charlie, and therefore can be sneaky. They might also encourage your already excessive drug habit. (Who me? I can handle it. It's just a cold).

Nob size potential : Charlie shrivelled weenies.

Queer Nation
Club Gang No. 8

VENUS♥VENUS♥VENUS♥VENU
6 STANFORD STREET NOTTINGHAM   TEL: 0602 410780 - 585054

292
161

The Boy's Own Book Review
Sullivan's Survey

For this book review I have chosen a book that should in my opinion be prescribed on the National Health to old and young alike. It's name is "Ringolevio," and it's the autobiography of Emmett Grogan, malcontent, prince of adversity and ultimate hipster.

One of the purposes of these reviews is to save you the reader, time and the inevitable grief of reading a book halfway through before you discover you don't like it. As for this book I couldn't think of a better way to spend a weekend than to read it, and on that note hoping that you'll take my advice, I shall expand.

The book's title Ringolevio is a New York street game rather like our, "Releasing in the Den," or, "Foxes and Hounds," where two teams chase and physically restrain each other, depositing each other in the den. The game is won when either team holds all the opposite team in their den. This however, is not as easy as it may seem as they can be released by their team mates who only have to enter the den of their own accord and shout, "Free for all." In New York 1956, the games took place in Manhattan and gangs from all over N. Y. C. took part, Flatbush v Harlem Chaplains, Bed-Stuy v The Bronx. The gangs featured thirteen combatants, there were no barriers and no time limits and pride of the highest order was at stake.

The book opens with (as Grogan claims) the all time classic ringolevio game, the Harlem Chaplains v the Aces Wild of Brooklyn. As the book unfolds Kenny Wisdom (Emmett Grogan's nom de plume or alter ego for this work), as one of the best ringolevio players achieves star status and submits to the charms of intravenous heroin addiction, slipping into a life of crime to support his habit. In an effort to save the otherwise intelligent Wisdom, he was granted a scholarship in one of New York's most prestigous and pretentious prep. schools where the sons of Manhattan's rich and famous bided their pre-inheritance time. Wisdom uses this as an opportunity to garner information as to who of his classmates was on holiday whereupon with this knowledge firmly in his grasp he robbed their houses, pulling off a series of outrageous jewel robberies that Raffles in all his fictionalised splendour would have been proud of. Still a teenager, Grogan leaves New York's boys in blue cold, but runs up against a few problems when trying to dispose of the merchandise. Problems in the form of a local fence which was not exactly enamoured by a fifteen year old. This fence wanted his blood and being a good reactionary Kenny (or Emmett) boards a boat to Europe together with his earnings and begins a life that forms the bulk of this book.

It is this life, which in some ways is a travelogue, that makes the book so interesting, one feels that if Grogan had been a successful actor or musician it would have been a waste. He leaves for Amsterdam on a ship and ends up in Italy where he takes up with some local hustlers bobbing and weaving in Rome 1960, being at the right place at the right time. From there he went to London, living in Soho earning a crust writing libidinous pornograpy soaking up Charlie Mingus.

The rest of the book is spent in San Francisco and New York. In San Francisco, he was a big wheel in the Haight Ashbury flower power generation, although never a hippie (he was never an "anything", he was always the wise observer critically dissecting the scene at hand), never adopting the flower power style of dress but chose instead what he called his IRA cap (a smaller Hovis cap), chinos, check shirt and U.S. Airforce leather jacket, an outfit still pretty hip today. Emmett didn't see the groovy, flower power love and peace side of the San Francisco Haight Scene, all he saw were thousands of disaffected mixed up youth, on the at times cold northern Californian streets, under-nourished and under-dressed.

He then started free soup kitchens, free food centres, virtually invented the tie dye grandpa vest, taking thousands of out-of-date under garments dyeing them cheaply and selling them to rich day trippers to Haight Ashbury, the centre of the hippy universe. The difference with Grogan was that his profits in this venture went to funding a centre for the arts and the homeless, free concerts for thousands of people (The first big outdoor pop festivals of their kind) in Golden Gate Park, featuring Janis Joplin and The Grateful Dead. "Rave," organisers (I don't think there're any reading) take note : He never made a penny but churned it all back into the scene and its victims.

Via all this exemplary work, Grogan became involuntarily infamous in San Francisco. He was interviewed and photographed and was asked to appear on TV chatshows, although in typical Grogan style, he persuaded friends to dress up in his clothes, purporting to be him, therefore baffling the press and TV, inspiring the headline, "Does Emmett Grogan exist?". (The enigma of Emmett Grogan - what a geezer).

Grogan championed the poor and crushed the hypocritical commercial hippies cashing in on the trend of love and peace yet espousing greed and envy. Alienated by his own peers, Grogan revelled in his isolation, at times exacerbating it. In one instance, he received a standing ovation for a speech at the conference of, "The Dialectics of Liberation," in front of the leading radical hippy intellectuals of the day such as Abbey Hoffman, Timothy Leary, Allen Ginsberg, etc., only to announce after several minutes when the ovation died down, that the speech was in fact last delivered in Nuremberg in 1934 by none other than Adolf Hitler.

Anyway, he survived that only to upset many more people along the way and towards the end of the book he speaks of various contracts that are out to get him.

The one thing that this book leaves you with is admiration for Emmett Grogan. A damned interesting chap who basically did not give a flying fuck about anything except basic morals, fair play and doing the right thing. He travels through life swimming against the tide, upsetting the establishment and making enemies, and why not? The book does leave one wondering exactly what happened to Emmett? He did write another book after this one although I don't think it achieved the status achieved by Ringolevio. Towards the end of the book an amount of paranonia creeps in, but in the light of later events, this seems acceptable as he was found dead on the New York subway (The A train to be exact) having travelled back and forth for two days. The cause of death was a heroin overdose which friends and relatives claim he hadn't taken for fifteen years. The circumstances certainly are suspicious and taking into account Grogan's behaviour hardly surprising but one cannot help feeling more than a twinge of sadness as another truly great man bites the dust, while millions of wankers live on. It seems the trend in the USA and hardly an encouraging one, Martin Luther King Jr. dead, Jesse Jackson lives, J.F.K. dead, Nixon lives, and the list goes on.

Well that's about it, I think you'll know now whether it's your kettle of fish or not. I think it's integral fodder but I'm biased as I seem to empathise with Grogan quite strongly but then again I think many of you will as well.

Do or die Bed-Stuy
British Bulldog Champs
1965

The Balearic Network

With the recession biting across the land, holidays to Rimini, Ibiza and alike look like things of the past for some this summer. But, as Mixmag and I-D repeatedly inform us, the balearic network they've discovered could hold the answer. Following up information leaked to us by a "mole" deep within these trade magazine's ranks, Boy's Own present you with the Mixmag (In association with, "Wish You Were Here") UK holiday guide to the balearic network.

A.
Closeness to France and the ferry port have kicked **Ramsgate** into overdrive! A definite Gallic feel prevails partly due to the regular visits of French DJ partnership Jean-Paul and Marie-France and partly the channel tunnel workers and their duty free Stella. Top tunes? Anything by Les Negresses Vertes or Sasha (Distel).

B.
Even though land locked, the balearic influences can be felt in the pubs and clubs of **Grantham**. Tambourines, inflatable rafts and surgical instruments are waved gayly above drinker's heads everytime a Hurley mix is heard on the jukebox in The Fox And Hounds. Best nights? The last Sunday of every month with thirty one days. The place? Sexy Rexy's. (All spirits £1 before 11). Kickin'!

C.

With a beach front caressed by the warm waters of the Gulf Stream, **Saltcoats** is an almost ideal holiday location. A happening scene revolves around McKiven's Caravan and Camp Site on a Thursday night, with housemaster Hanley at the controls. For beachwear with a highland dash, try local designer's surfing sweaties. Pumpin'!

D.

After years suffering in Bognor's shadows, from the days of Sean French's seminal jazz funk bashes, "You drop your trousers, I'll start the pyramid," to the recent Boy's Own do's, **Littlehampton** is finally coming into its own. Two clubs are spearheading the movement. Paradise (above the Littlehampton chipery) on a Tuesday, and Lucky's at the rear of Bob's boat yard every other Friday. Regular visits from top DJ's from around the country, supplement the mix 'n' match skills of Fishbone and Driftnet from the, "Aye, aye, Captain, " collective.

E.

Holiday heaven just north of the English Riviera. Palm trees in the winter and summer temperatures to rival parts of the Hook of Holland. **Tintagel** has a vibrant scene unaffected by the ravers from the rest of the West Country. The DJ's at Oceans instead of mirroring current balearic tastes are championing their own sound, drawing influences from the skanking Bristol scene, the Newquay surfing fraternity and their own local morris dancing heritage, the house sound of scrumpy! All around my hat ...

Do It Yourself Balearic Network Club

1) Find yourself an obscure tacky venue, in an equally obscure and tacky town. If you're having trouble locating such a town, they are usually cold and windswept and come complete with crap third division footie teams. The club will usually be called, "Ruby Tuesday's," or "The Bird's Nest," but you can think of some happy cuddly name to change it and so help create that balearic feeling. (What about, "The Queen Mum's Fanny"? - Ed.) Once you've done that, just follow our guide and Bob's your uncle.

2) Get yourself a cardboard cut-out of Justin Robertson.

3) You then need a warm-up DJ. By rule of law, he will come complete with spots, Fila trainers and a box of Leftfields. He is also always the mate of the younger brother of the promoter and is doing it for nish, cos it's, "A golden opportunity." He also by law, must play every one of cut-out Justin's top tunes.

4) You also need a Dean Thatcher Doggie Doo Darr, an essential balearic item for any club and post-club chill out session. Have hours of fun playing, "Pass the Doo Darr," "Name that Doo Darr." Who knows, someone might even write an article about it.

5) You then need the Boy's Own Guide to the Balearic Network DJ's Set ...

a) Start your set with an atmospheric, moody and always far too long intro.

b) Then start building up the set with, "chunky," "chugging," and "chinkly" choons.

c) Then chuck in a couple of records that you've stolen from Big Tony, now that you're playing American House.

d) It's starting to go barmy, fuck the garage, start to bang it. Who needs lyrics when you've got a cross fader.

e) It's the end of the night and time for that crap end of night hands in the air sing-a-long-a-faded-popstar-tune, that only the DJ's old enough to remember. Easy eh! See you in Scunthorpe for the Mr. Bojangles reunion party.

Boy's Own Parties 1991

Boy's Own Parties 1991

Whatever's Next?

We've seen it all now, haven't we? Baseball boots and paisley shirts, Kickers and purple tracksuit bottoms, Armani and Reporter, Chipie and Chevignon, John Richmond, Katharine Hamnett, sex and stockings, Vivienne Westwood, platforms, Versace and Yamamoto. Whatever your tipple, the clubbing world has seen the lot. The list could go on forever, but it won't because it's actually very boring. Or is it? The old, "It doesn't matter what you wear as long as you're comfortable," ditty keeps cropping up year after year, haunting the corridors of style. As far as I'm concerned though, this totally over-used and worn-out statement is a complete load of balls and usually uttered by those with either : A) No dress sense OR B) No money. Before you all start pretending that you feel sorry for them, don't bother, because the chances are that if they look like shit, they are shit. Now, the funny thing about all this, is that those who come into this strange and interesting category (ie. "Shit dressers") are usually BOYS. With the recent explosion of sexiness hitting the darker recesses of the underground, skirts have gotten shorter and shorter, (nay, have disappeared altogether) and girls attire has been shed off garment by garment, until nothing or little is left to the imagination.

Alas, has the same happened to the boys? I think not. "Why not," all the girlies cry? Wouldn't it be so super to see all those delicious bodies so rife amongst the male clubbers prancing about in a pair of Calvin Klein sporties? Well, let's admit it. Not really. Even though it may be almost impossible for the boys to look sexier, they could make a bit of an effort, couldn't they? I mean, imagine the situation reversed and the boys got all clobbered up and the girls stood around the bar in ripped jeans and record company T-shirts. What a horrible thought. To be fair to the poor sods there are a few who make an effort to dress up, although very few manage to look OK. Many try too hard, and end up wearing things like "Destroy" T-shirts, Gucci loafers, Michiko or combat gear. Those who refuse to try and look good at all, will wear any of the above two or more together.

The rather poor quality of the dress sense is set off even more as a rule by the rather battered state of the wearer. The more horrible the clothes are, the more drugs he's taking. Oh yes, it all makes sense now, they'd rather spend money on looking bad than looking good. It fits into the great scheme of clubbing that there's no point in wearing good clothes if you're just going to go out and get off your head and have a mad one. Fair enough, I suppose, you do get reasonably dirty on a night out on the razz, though not a proper excuse really, as if you bothered to make the effort a bit, you may look twenty times less disgusing at six o' clock in the morning. There's no point in trying to make excuses, we all know you'd rather spend your money on drugs. Dirty jeans that hang around your bum or combat gear? A polite hint from a subjective onlooker, to help you on your way - both looks leave a lot to be desired, your friends are probably too embarrassed to tell you that you look like SHITE.

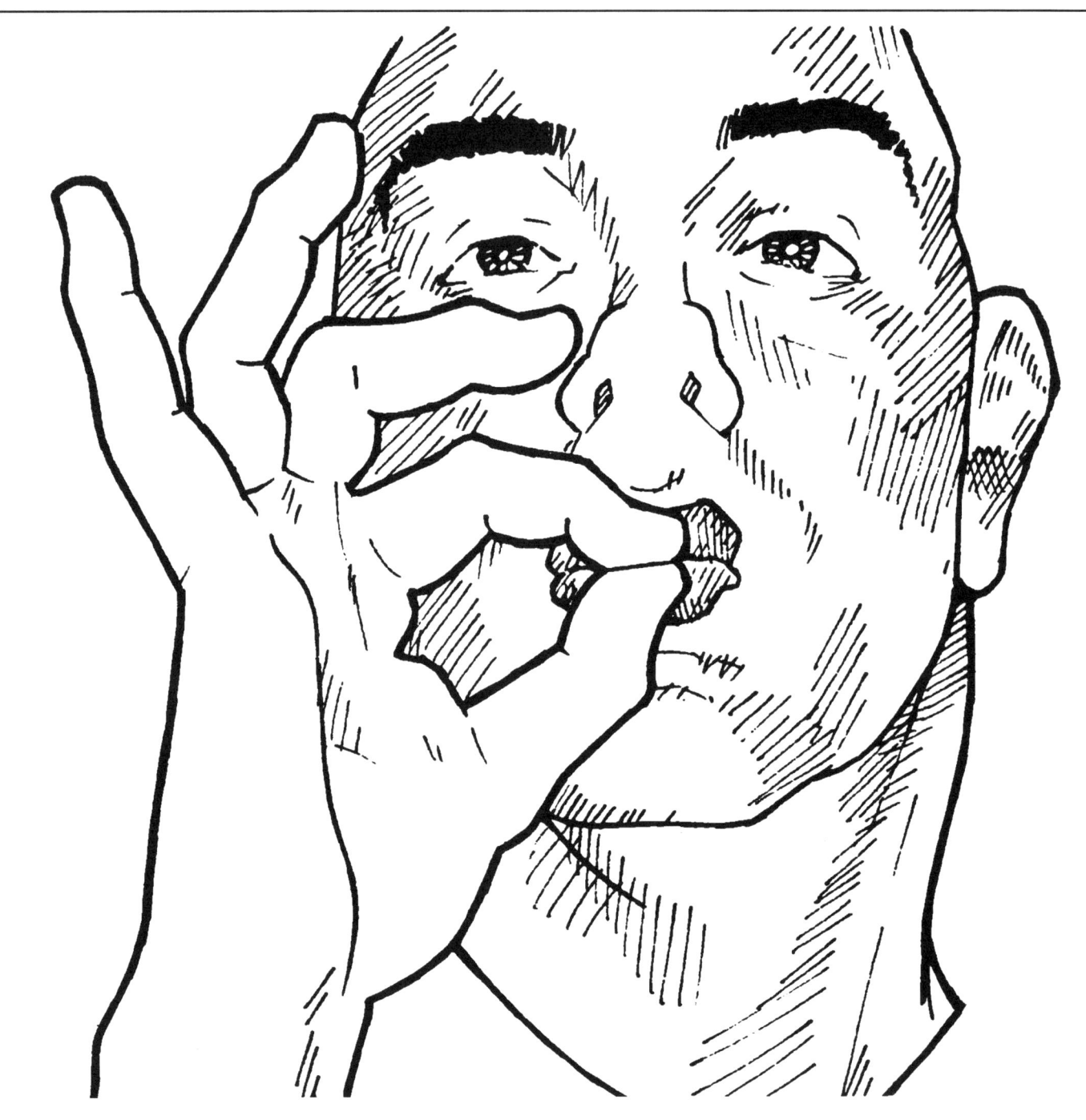

Perfecto Records

GARY CLAIL
ROWETTA
JIMI POLO
CARL COX
LOST
ROBERT OWENS

Danny Baker - The Millwall Wanker

Danny Baker has cracked it. Wedged up TV chiefs are beating down his door to host game shows, Jonathan Ross picks him as his writer, and he has just won the New York Radio Festival Award (it says 'ere) for his hysterical Greater London Radio Show.

But why is a man - with a face like a sackful of spanners (If he was a building he'd be condemned) and with the dress sense of Worzel Gummidge - quite simply the funniest man in broadcasting ? (No contest!).

The answer is, he is the same off screen as on screen. He is one of us. That is his gift to the world! He is the only showbiz face I have met who doesn't change for the camera (and I've met them all kid!). In short, he is the same, funny, warm hearted, larger than life, fast thinking, quick lipped boyo you see on the screen. Ladies and Gentlemen, I give you Danny Baker.

Q. **A brief life history.**
A. I'm a PR's wet dream. I was born in Deptford and still live in Deptford, despite living twenty six years in Bermondsey. Left school at fourteen, went to West Greenwich Comprehensive. Worked in a record shop for a while in South Molton Street. This is early '72 and '73, and Elton John and people like that had their accounts there - Paul McCartney and The Stones. People like Elton John used to come in the shop and spend up to £400 a week, and I had to walk maybe five feet to the till and if you've got £400 in your pocket... people don't want a receipt, they just walk out and I was earning up to £1000 a week this way and the shop went skint, surprise, surprise. Out of work for two years. I was a toy boy in Fulham for a while because it was all faggots in South Molton Street and they used to bring all their rich women in the shop and I was passed around.

Met Mark Perry, who I was at school with. He did the first issue of "Sniffing Glue," and the girl I was going out with, who lived two doors along, she really liked it and thought I should get involved. "Sniffing Glue" became a very big deal. Loads of TV companies were talking to us, one of which was LWT. We gave the magazine up after twelve issues.

I went to meet Tony Parsons, who I had met in the punk days at the NME and he said, "We need a receptionist, why don't you do it?" I learnt to type, was very good at English and started writing about disco stuff which I was hearing in the pubs - Bee Gees and The Gibson Brothers. I got a big following and the singles column. Then LWT rang me up to do a dog of a series called 20th Century Box and I got paid £100, which is what I light the fire with in the mornings nowadays to tell the truth, but at the time, it was a big deal, and got me the break for The Six 'O Clock Show and the radio show. Big time. Now I'm an old person's young person.

Q. **The most important thing in your life?**
A. Wendy and my kids, Laurel and Hardy and Millwall F. C. and I thank God that I'm intelligent, bright and sharp. I know loads of people who ain't and can watch something that is hysterically funny and can't see it. The people who made it know it is and I know it is. Like they say in the Arab countries, "My light has not been dimmed.

Q. **How do you see your career going?**
A. I'm resigned to the fact that I'm a success. I'm going to be a success and earn a fucking lot of money and it's great (chuckles).

Q. **How long do you think it will be before you are a tax exile?**
A. What's the time now? 2 pm? Let's say 2.45 pm.

Q. **Who's influenced you most in life?**
A. Lenny Bruce, even though I don't particularly like his stuff anymore because I've got older. At first, he made me think, "Voices of dissent - far out. Punk rock, change the government," and that was when I was about twelve. Plus, a whole bunch of comedians : Ken Dodd, Will Hay, Billy Bennett and it goes on and on and on. I'm a comedy bore. There's very little comedy I don't like. I'm annoyed when I watch TV because I know I can write that stuff with my eyes shut, but I'm a lazy bastard.

Q. **Three things you would take on a desert island?**
A. All of my video tapes and records. S. J. Perelman's "The Most Of," and Woody Allen's "Without Feathers," plus a 5-a-side goal and ball.

Q. **Why do you think people go to football?**
A. They go mainly to watch the football, funnily enough. It's like saying, why would anyone want to go and see Millwall v Notts County in the third division, but you do. If you're walking across a park on a Sunday morning and there's some local football, you have to stand and watch for five minutes and if you see a bit of needle in one match, two geezers squaring up, you say, "Oh, I'll watch this one for a minute." It's like a fight on the street, you stop and watch it and it's not that you go to football for the fights, but it's that kind of grotesque thing. I have never been involved in football hooliganism but my close mates have and you get these articulate nice geezers, pussycats even, and when they go to football they go fucking potty. A mate of mine, who's a lovely bloke and works in the Post Office, witty, the family and the whole bit, was at the Millwall v Portsmouth game. He was so far ahead of the Millwall bunch running after Portsmouth, he got hit on the head by a lump of concrete thrown by the Millwall mob - he's a crackpot.

Yes, there are a lot of monosyllabic goons, but at the same time there are intelligent, articultate guys who, for whatever reason, get in trouble at football. It's honour or all that old bullshit.

It's warm and witty on them terraces. When you talk about racism, when Fashanu was playing for Millwall against Gillingham, he nearly knocked a geezer right over the stand and when the fellow came back and had a go at him, someone shouted, "Fucking do him Fash" and another geezer shouted out, "Move in next door to him Fash." Hilarious. Inside a football ground all bets are off.

I can understand football hooliganism. It's that blood in your veins - you can't understand what football is about until you have that feeling. At Millwall you get little mobs coming down looking for trouble but when I see the Millwall mob go in and it's all off, I find myself standing there going, "Go on Millwall."

I've got into more rows than anyone else at LWT, including Saint and Greavsie, when I say inside a football ground, all chants are fair enough... It's got nothing to do with black or white, if a geezer has got a harelip, you pick on that harelip, if he's got ginger hair, you pick on that - anything to put him off his game. You've either got that feeling in your bones and you know what football is about or you don't.

Football is really personal to me. It's a terrible streak in me. When I'm out on the streets filming, being a cheerful colourful cockney and someone shouts out "You Millwall Wanker," I can't laugh at that at all.

There's two things I don't joke about, Millwall and Laurel and Hardy. Both are sacred.

Q. **Who makes you laugh the most?**
A. There's only been one or two people who have made me laugh so much that I've had to say shut up, "I'm going to die through laughing," and the main one was my brother who died a few years ago. He was only twenty nine and he was a docker, Michael, and I've got three or four mates who to them swearing is a work of art. They can really wrap their tongues around swear words. I've got mates who make me crease up and die - they are that hysterical. When I've got time, there's nothing I like better than being in a pub with mates who talk a load of nonsense.

Q. **Most embarrassing moment?**
A. I did a radio 'phone-in on LBC and no cunt rang up and the man was interviewing me for forty five minutes and nobody was ringing up - not even my dad or family rang up. It was the most humiliating thing I have ever done and I was crying with laughter because nobody wanted to ask me a question.

Q. **Best advice to a mate.**
A. Be wary of your peers, because so many blokes our age are frankly suspect.

With Condiments

Blue Source announce the imminent release
of their very own peculiarly spicey condiment

Lord Trumpingtons
"Massive Gust" Pickled Onions

"They're better today than they were the day before yesterday!"
see local deli's and press for details

We were asked by the Boy's Own chaps to provide some biting political comment, steering well clear of inane drug references and music babble. So, after much deliberation we bring you :

Politicians : A bunch of drug crazed maniacs, or what?

In 1973, acid philosopher Timothy Leary calculated that by 1998 two thirds of the members of the US House of Representatives will have been, thirty years before, fans of Bob Dylan and The Beatles. Two thirds will have sung, "Give Peace A Chance," and smoked pot. These adolescent imprints will, he claims, be permanently hard-wired to their hormones.

Following this logic, we assert that by 2020, a similar proportion of UK members of Parliament may have been, thirty years previously, fans of T99 and Bizarre Inc.. Two thirds will have tried ecstacy and stood shirtless on speaker stacks screaming, "I Can't Take The Power." These adolescent imprints may be permanently hard-wired to their hormones, with a resultant effect on their Parliamentary behaviour. So, what future changes might we expect in the 2020 Parliament of the future?

Will the Speaker's cry of "Order! Order!" be replaced by some ragga on the Woolsack encouraging the Rt. Hon. Gentlemen to, "Make some fucking noise," (dread wig optional)? Will the MP veterans of the Astoria and Busby's prefer to hang off the public balcony, whilst the Milk Bar contingent sit it out on the benches? Will live televising of proceedings in the House cease, with each sitting simply being, "recorded for future broadcast"? Will the notion of a divided House become redundant, as the loved-up Members ignore the three line Whip in favour of the three man hug? Will the standard of debate suffer, with the great tradition of oratory in this mother of all Parliaments being replaced by the shambolic ramblings of the elected morning after casualties? (Can't see the 2020 politician losing off too many rounds of deadly statistical ammo during Question Time - he'll be too busy remembering which party he belongs to, after guinea pigging all those experimental New Yorkers back in '91).

Obviously, you may well have noticed that scenes in the Commons already resemble your average Raindance bash, with hysterical scenes of shouting, screaming and arm waving lunacy, so no real change there. All that's currently missing is an abundance of sweating, twitching, dribbling and incoherent speech - unless of course, Roy Hattersley is at the Despatch Box. Plus, don't forget that the most barmy of Parliamentary longhairs, Michael Heseltine, was waving the Mace above his head long before anyone thought of taking an egg whisk to Venus. The reality is that the Commons has always enjoyed certain similarities with the club scene. This most famous of Central London venues granted itself Britain's first all night licence way before it allowed anyone else to have one : the Commons bar stays open whenever the House is in session, even during those overnight sittings, and has done practically since Magna Carta. Now, that's what we call parliamentary privilege.

SMILE!

WEDNESDAYS

CINECITTA DISCOTECA

74 Welbeck Street · London W1

10pm - 3am · £5

The Fine Art Of Lording It Up

Perhaps a small insight or definition might be appropriate before I launch into this one. "Lording it up," what can it possibly mean? Well, we are all "Artistes" of this game I'm afraid to say. Some obviously greater than others. Some anonymously and of course some quite famously. To quote a prominant well spoken member of the Boy's Own staff "We'll all be out lording it up when DSK goes top 40!" (It all went Pete - Ed.) If I were to say this was a pastime conducted primarily by the working classes would you perhaps have an inkling of an idea?

>   Def!
>   "Lording it up" : When one finds oneself in the kind
>   of situation whereby one has to check ones socks
>   before putting them on for those embarrassing thin
>   patches around one's heel and big toe!

Vague, but nevertheless quite accurate. Whether it be a fine restaurant, a day at the races, a trip to Henley or even a top night out at the Ministry of Sound (Ooh-er we must have missed that one - Ed.), it requires a certain etiquette most of us are relatively unfamiliar with. A slight alteration of character, a different frame of mind!

An act of lording would almost certainly be reported very differently to how it was actually executed. "So there I was staring at the wine list and the only words I recognised were house, red or white, thinking to myself ... well, it all tastes the bleedin' same anyhow, so I plumped for a Mouton Cadet 1985 'cos it wasn't the cheapest and I remembered seeing it on the Galloping Gourmet once!" Ring any bells?

We might all knock the upper end of our class hierarchy, but we certainly all love a taste of the lifestyle that comes with it. Should we just accept this, or put forward the propostion that this is a totally hypocritical pastime? (As hypocritical perhaps as a socialist celebrating the demise of Mrs. Thatcher with a glass of champagne. Think about it, everything she stood for can be epitomised by a glass of bubbly can't it?)

Should we however punish offenders too seriously? It is after all a bit of an artistry. It can be performed in one of two ways ... correctly and incorrectly, there's no happy medium, you've either got it or you ain't. I personally know several experts, we probably all do, and it's the experts we should be looking out for because these people really do take themselves seriously. Extremely subtle, to the extent that half the time they won't even realize that they are actually lording it up. These people really are the masters of this craft. Mistakes are indeed very rare. For example, mispronounciation of a bottle of wine, using the incorrect "eating iron" to tuck into a sorbet in between courses, putting a tub of mushroom a la greque in the Waitrose shopping basket, knowing full well it's served fresh on the deli counter, or even replying,"Well, in the middle really," to their tailor when asked which side they dress. If you were to engage eye

Venus
Club Gang No. 9

contact with the offender at this point you would almost certainly witness gross embarrassment and a hasty departure.

I'm not here to speak malicously about these people and I should emphasize that to witness a good lorder in full swing is a truly enlightening experience. They are after all behaving in a manner which is somewhat gratifying in a strange sort of way. Being able to carry it off both professionally and confidently should at the very least be applauded. Of course, there are those who do in fact totally miss the point, I mean, it's taken two years for a certain club owner to realize that the only benefit of mingling with his sweaty punters sporting a Gaultier suit is a discount at Sketchleys for being such a regular customer. Such strange parcels are without doubt a most annoying breed and for their own benefit should be informed that waving fifty pound notes around at the bar does not constitute to a lordly act. You see this rather intricate art cannot be convincingly executed if you are in fact quite contented with one's present lifestyle and status. This is a game to be played by achievers only.

In summary, is this vocation a hypocritical one or not? Well, I certainly have my own opinions , but it's obviously far more important for the individual to decide for themselves. You can either dismiss the last two minutes it's taken you to read this as total shite or hopefully feel somewhat more educated in the art of lording. Well, that's it for now and I believe it's your round ... She'll 'ave a Becks and mine's a bloody mary with a twist of lemon and a dash of worcester sauce please!

Five Things You Badly Wanted When It Was That Time Again, And The Five Things You Always End Up With ...

1) A top cuddle from a Helen Storey clad nubile naughty.
2) A frosted glass of the finest Molson.
3) The DJ to play Ten City's, "Love will find a way."
4) Your brand spanking new Joe Casely-Hayford shirt to remain looking as good as you feel.
5) You wishing the night will never end.

You End Up With ...

1) A cuddle from Plug or Lofty.
2) A mouthful of Charlie Chester's snakebite.
3) The warm-up DJ on a Leftfield overdose.
4) Your shirt soaked in sweat, feeling as sad as you look.
5) You wishing you were in bed, pass the nightnurse !!!

Boy's Own Parties 1991

Good Vibrations

After being given a vibrator for my 21st birthday, I can honestly say masturbation has taken on a new dimension. Needless to say, no respectable female should, in my opinion, be without one, or at least not deny herself the experience. It was given to me by a friend, whose outlook on sex is broader than the Pacific Ocean and more open than her legs will ever be, though no doubt she is working on it. Thus, I knew the vibrator had the sexual seal of approval. As an extra added bonus, my friend gave me a "handy tip,"

"A splash of baby oil, and aim for the flamingoes knee cap."

Now, I'm a little sceptical and dare I say it, naive about mechanical machinery that is designed to reach the parts that Heinekin certainly never could or ever will reach for that matter, so you can only imagine my delight ... (After setting the mood, a little candle light, a little music - "Initiation," by Gabriell Roth, a must for first time users - getting nice and snuggled under the duvet, an application of intoxicating coconut oil onto my hands, and following advice, an application onto the controversial objet d'art).

Having had no previous experience in such matters I decided to explore cautiously. I found the vibration alone to be powerfully calming as it loosened up my rather expectant body. Once over the embarrassment of actually having gone this far, the rest came naturally and I floated off into the first uninterrupted orgasm I've had for some years.

One thing that I feel it's important to stress at this point, is the female's and possibly the male's collective, most common image of a vibrator. A rather long, flesh coloured plastic willy with the human characteristics of the real thing, yet totally detached from all the emotions and feelings that go with it. Which is why, one can be forgiven for finding the whole concept rather low on passion, and the possibility of getting to know a vibrator, a real turn off. My thoughts exactly! Why try to recreate the tried and tested apparatus? After all, it seems a touch naff toying with the idea of a plastic replica.

However, technology it seems, has for once hit the right spot and to back up my play on words, touched on a nerve that is close to all our hearts, male species not excluded. The design is not trying to fool you into thinking you're going the rounds with something organic. It doesn't even resemble a willy. In fact, it looks more like ammunition for an army supply bazooka gun, though I regrettably add, scaled down a touch, and I think even the space age men of tomorrow will have a job trying to perfect it. It is simply a tool for the sole deliverance of uninterrupted stimulation that few men are capable of giving. That's not to say I rate machine over man, purely the observation that there's often more than you and your partner between the sheets. Don't forget the male ego that needs to know every five minutes whether you're closer to the all impending orgasm,

wholesale enquiries 071-6131070

which let's face it girls, is one way to kiss that special moment good-bye and quite possibly the man as well.

My thoughts are now unquestionably encouraging, as I ponder over the as yet untried situations that one could find oneself in with one's new best friend. I feel rather like a sinner who has seen the light, or in my case, seen the light on sinning, though I dare say a man of the cloth would have a word or two to say on my comparison. As a newly converted believer who wants to spread the word and share the buzz, and mark my words, I know what it's like to be a sexually repressed female dealing with all the frustrations of modern day living, I write one last line on the subject, and I quote,

"Be frugal with it, or you might just numb your bit!"

New DJ Duo's For '92

A quick look at the new movers and shakers on the DJ front about to hit your ears ...

1) *DJ Handbrake Turn and Busby Matt* - Oxford's finest says, " I like garage now, you know, sort of SL2 with vocals."
2) *MC Rape and DJ Pillage* - East London's people's choice, "Straight outta Essex."
3) *DJ "Big Oop North" and Roscoe* - "Big Oop North" says, "I only play small clubs now and that will be a monkey please." (Roscoe was unavailable at the time of press).
4) *MC Dead On Arrival and his mate Trevor* - "I'm bang into garage, but without the vocals, those American birds get on my wick." Nine out of ten Trevors, when asked preferred Leftfield.
5) *Diesel and his mate Todd Terry* - "Bring back Sprocket and dump the moody yank," we say.

Disco Revival Pressure (Part 2)

The Trammps	Where Were You When The Lights Went Out?
Arnie's Love	Date With The Rain
Village People	Fire Island
Curtis Mayfield	No Goodbye's
Linda Clifford	Runaway Love
The Carstairs	It Really Hurts Me Girl
Double Exposure	My Love Is Free
Benny Troy	I Wanna Give You Tomorrow
Diana Ross	Love's Hangover (Special Disco Re-Edit)
Visual	The Music's Got Me

Letters To The Chaps

Dear Chaps,
What's all this about frogs (Boys Own - Summer Edition) then? It's alright for Steve Mayes to ruminate about the dietary ups and downs of his frogs, but the question us punters are asking is are these frogs those mad little blighters with the hallucinogenic skin raved about in National Enquirer, Sunday gossips, etc.? If so, how does he keep his gob off them, and when are they going to be sent a-hopping around clubland so we can all have a lick? This all reminds me of a pal of mine who a few years ago reckoned he got sold one of the said amphibs when seriously chemisted down this place called City of Angels. Imagine his dismay, when on giving the little fucker a "lolly gobble choc bomb" stylee, it miraculously turned into a sixteen stone Roy Hudd lookalike "prince" who ejected him from the premises with the minimum of fuss. My advice chaps is JUST SAY NO TO FROGS.

Ta-ra.
Philly Douglas.
London.

Dear Boy's Own,
I feel compelled to write and express a social comment/moan - as an avid female reader of your tres classy fanzine.
Girls' moan of the month is this : There has been a lot of press coverage recently (I. D. etc. etc.) concerning the myth of the so-called "New Man" and how the real up and coming man of the '90's can cook a half-decent spag. bog., whilst dishing out large doses of T. L. C., but more the Boy's Own "type" geezer, who does, well you know, a bit of duckin' n divin', knobbin' n skivin'...

Well, I would certainly never knock the long awaited and much deserved rise of the Boy's Own clan, but I do cringe at the media promotion that to be a geezer you've got to be a rude cunt to 80% of people who cross your path, an all right mate, right on geezer to which all the little laddies will doubtless aspire and the girls swoon. So this 'type' is the New Age man of the '90's is it? Jesus wept, I hope not, call me old-fashioned, but what a horrible thought. If we're to believe the hype, then it looks like us girls will just have to get used to leery Northern bastard abuse, lolling eyes and incoherent grunts and dribbling. Geezer? "Gitzer" more like.
Yeah, OK, I'm sure that there are a few girls out there who get a kick out of putting on their purple nylon nighties, getting slagged off for serving up soggy chips, getting knocked around a bit for nagging when the football's on telly, and generally being treated like a lump of shit, but obviously that's by no means the norm. We don't want pouncy Tarquin posh facker excuses for men either - (God, there's no pleasing us women is there boys?) - but a little more respect and recognition beyond "Cor, she's got a nice pair of jugs," wouldn't go amiss - 'cos aside from anything else (and apart from the fact that this type of humour is vaguely amusing the first time it's spouted) - it's quite simply boring - with a capital 'B'.
I realise that this so-called 'New' Man of the '90's is a probable kickback to the 'Next' Man of the '80's, but looking at the state of the majority of them and listening to the standard shitfaced, "I'm a clever bastard" drivel, is more like a throwback, to Early Iron Age Man of around 2000 B. C.
And whilst I'm nagging, I might as well throw in that although the title "Boy's Own," infers to just that, and I'm sure that the initial idea behind

the venture was "Hey, we don't want to make any money out of this - up the proletariat and all that" (and why not?) but considering you have a large female readership owing to that fact that we are more than happy to part with a quid and hang onto your every word (almost) and we read our Geezer/Gitzer boyfriend's mags on the bog, how about adapting to your market a little more and giving us members of the fairer sex more of a voice rather than just the typing to do, as after all, variety is the spice of life is it not? And yes, I have had a good shafting recently thanks, and have of course discussed all this with my therapist.

Yours Very Truly
A Girl.
X.X.X.

Dear A Girl,
If you contact us, you're on the editorial firm straight away and as for the bit we've edited, we agree with you 100%! - Ed.

Dear Boy's Own,
After last issue's rare adventure into the female dark-half, in the guise of a reasoned account of the nocturnal capers inside a girls' bogs, I decided that it was high time you males were invited to share in some other mysteries of our little world.
Let's face it, we girlies have been dealt a pretty shitty hand over the past couple of years. We have been forced to dwell in the hinter-land of the media hype about all things male, the changing face of '90's man and other untold tales of eternal laddishness.
The time has come for us to fight back, regain pole position and glory in the limelight, kick against the pricks so to speak (ooh sounds painful!) Those thirty-something stalwarts of the so-called "style press" have been trying to force feed us their image of the perfect man for far too long. We're not passive receivers devoid of grey matter ... we know what kind of men we want, thank you very much. (The problem is that they don't exist).
They tried to kid us into thinking that real men ate quiche, looked good in white and wore crystal pendants, but as far as I'm concerned any man whose idea of fun is chanting mantras and smoking joss sticks, (even if they are cannabis flavour), can fuck right off.
This healthy option was new Age Man, clean cut, ozone friendly and with more empathy with his female partner than ever before experienced in the western world. Don't get me wrong, I'm not opposed to the idea of new men, I mean we all know how good a new man in your life makes you feel, right? But, I think that this year's revamped and updated version, the New Lad, is far more comfortable to have around. New ladity was personified for us in the unfathomable forms of Terry Christian, Mark Webster and Robert Elms (talk about blowing your own

Yorkshire's top new elite balearic network club.

EAST WEST RECORDS PRESENT
THE POPULAR GRAMOPHONE RECORDING

UNDERGROUND DANCE MUSIC

UDM

VOL. 1

SIX SUPREMELY MELODIC RECORDINGS IN THE HOUSE STYLE
FROM NEW YORK, NEW JERSEY, CHICAGO AND MIAMI

FEATURING THE TALENTS OF PAL JOEY, ROGER SANCHEZ
AND KERRI CHANDLER

AND ON CASSETTE AND CD ONLY, RUDUOLPHO'S 'TOUCH ME'
BIG WITH T. HUMPHRIES, ESQ IN 1989

horn). A far more exemplory bunch in my opinion would be our very own and much idolised pop heroes, yes, those cheeky chappies over at Boy's Own Mansions.

So what makes them more acceptable?

What are their redeeming qualities? To find out just look around you next time you're on the dance floor in mid wobble, the clubs are full of 'em. Never before has there been such an abundance of narcissistic manhood so readily available.

New Lads are fun loving creatures whose aim in life is to love, have a giggle and retain an element of childish charm. They like to party all night, drink loadsa lager, smoke tabs and neck as many drugs as they can possibly get their mitts on ... all in the pursuit of that elusive "top night." Habitually they can be found on the terraces at Stamford Road of a Saturday afternoon, playing big lads back slapping games and shouting abuse at the poor lame footy players. Sunday, the day after the night before, is then spent in the haze of a cerebral breakdown, either crashed out in bed or cranking it up at Colnbrook's infamous lunch time gathering. Far more exciting and attractive than ambient love-in's and carrot munching sessions.

So while our men have been undergoing this overdue make over, what chameleonesque happenings have been occuring in the girls camp? Have we not adapted to the change, in fact were we not the very reason for it?

Enter stage left, the new prototype females of the '90's, the New Girlies. No longer resigned to nights stuck at home twiddling our thumbs we're out there doing it just as hard and as mad as you lads and having a darn fine time too.

We don't need to spend every waking moment star gazing into the baby blues of the man of our dreams. Nights out with the lads don't bother us any more, we'd rather be out with the girls anyway. Saturday's at the footy give us time to go shopping and persue our own desires, we are confident and capable of having a good time even when there are no men around. New Girlies are out there promoting, DJ'ing and living it up despite everything.

Long gone are the figure disguising shifts of last summer, gone is the flower power virgin and the snub faced angelic smile - just as New Lads have recaptured their sartorial slickness, New Girlies have been sent lycra from heaven and have rediscovered how to be sexy.

On the prowl and on the dance floor, it's not just you lads that are managing to cop a free grope. Learn to recognise that wanton smile and next time you feel a stray hand around your tackle ... enjoy. The '90's female knows what she wants and how to get it, so don't ever underestimate her.

Unfortunatly nature deals us a cruel blow in that one day we are destined to become women (something to do with babies I think), whilst men are free to be boys for time eternal. The important thing is that we're all here to have fun and share in the buzz we've created. Men, women, boys, girls, who cares ... we all know what makes the world rock so stay young and stay happy.

Don't ever change.
Janeen.
Battersea. London.

Please send all letters, comments, moans, to The Editorial Team, Boy's Own Mansions, Unit 2, 249-251 Kensal Road, London. W10.

ART
OCCASSIONS OF JOY
VILLA STEFANO
SATS 92

Boy's Own Parties 1991

Do They Mean Us?

It's a funny old game, this clubbing mularky. One month everything's a right laugh, Italian screamers, hands in the air, big brown ones and dancing on tables, then the DJ goes all New Jersey and people stop smiling and it takes twenty minutes to get into the toilets. It's the same with the spoken word, one second everything's, "Bang on," then it all goes "Jeckyle," on you. It's enough to make you want to stay in.

Boy's Own, now give you an easy guide to regional club speak, what they say and what they really mean. The words of the bod outside the Limelight, "Shweet geez, you shorted for Bumbles?" says it all. What would that mean to some Luv Dupped character in Manchester or one of the Vic's Synex Possie, or to that matter, even one of the Flying lot? Anyway, read on, it might help you if you get stranded on a foreign dancefloor somewhere.

They mean : "I say, that was a rather splendid night out.
They say :
Flying : "Eye, eye, saveloy, you still up for it or what?"
Luv Dup : "Ooh, Justin's just played Bruce Hornsby. Gis a cuddle. Top one. Sorted."
Vicks Synex Possie (Oop North) : "Snog me bird Sasha."

They mean : "I say, that's a rather attractive lady over there."
They say :
Flying : "Eye, eye, shepherd's pie, you like chicken?"
Luv Dup : "Any chance of a slow dance, Justin's playing ABBA?"
Vicks Synex Possie (Shellys-Stoke) : "Snog me now Sasha."

They mean : "I say, that DJ's playing some rather splendid tunes.
They say :
Flying : "Eye, eye, Dean's fell over, Ali you're on my son."
Luv Dup : "Got any fucking vocals Justin?" (Obviously a Boy's Own intruder on the firm).
Vicks Synex Possie : (Can't think of any more barmy northener jokes - Ed.)

Fashion crazy victim of the Vics generation.

So there it is, regional differences, but, "Are you taking the fucking piss?" still sounds and means the same to us, whoever says it.

BOYS OWN SPRING EDITION

Editor: Fleur (Token Female & Typist)
Contributors:Dean O'Connor, Chris Sullivan, Paul Wellings, Roberta, Philipa Gant,
Camilla Deakin, Dave Hill, Farley 'n' Weaterall.
Photos & Styling: Richard Varden & Dionne.
To Contact: Boys Own Mansions, Unit 2, Portobello Business Centre,
249-251 Kensal Road, London W10.
Tel: 081-968 8459

Thanks & respects to:
Norman Jay & Son for the top cover, Mr & Mrs Stacey for the Youthful Mickey (above),
Butler 'n' Gina, Sir Les of Luv-Dup and his faithful Squire Maizeworth,
Sparks, Rocka 'n' Haisman, Steve "Pop Larkin" Lee, Pricey 'n' Timna, 2-Tab-Fab,
Ali, Fran 'n' Fiona, Clive, Lofty, Max, Peteski, Danny 'n' Jenni, Phil 'n' Fiona,
Charlie 'n' Karen, Stripey 'n' Linda, 2 Kevs up the M.1., Justin, Greg 'n' Ross,
Ginger, Mick 'n'; Ashley, Plug (Urban Legend), Chinny, Rod 'n' Wayne,
Sprock & Diesal (he's in the mix), Steve and the better days gang,
Little Lee, Plus all the girls on the firm and everyone who's still got the spirit.
Printed by Chip (Inc.)

CAUTION

'92

COUTURE
TOUR

MICHIKO LONDON KOSHINO – 70 NEAL ST. LONDON WC2 – 071 497 0165